Scandal and Democracy

Mary E. McCoy

Scandal and Democracy
Media Politics in Indonesia

SOUTHEAST ASIA PROGRAM PUBLICATIONS
an imprint of
Cornell University Press
Ithaca and London

First published 2019 by Cornell University Press

Library of Congress Cataloging-in-Publication Data

Names: McCoy, Mary E., 1968– author.
Title: Scandal and democracy : media politics in Indonesia / Mary E. McCoy.
Description: Ithaca : Southeast Asia Program Publications, an imprint of
    Cornell University Press, 2019. | Includes bibliographical references and index.
Identifiers: LCCN 2018029443 (print) | LCCN 2018032259 (ebook) |
    ISBN 9781501731051 (pdf) | ISBN 9781501731068 (epub/mobi) |
    ISBN 9781501731037 (cloth) | ISBN 9781501731044 (pbk.)
Subjects: LCSH: Mass media—Political aspects—Indonesia. | Press and politics—
    Indonesia. | Press—Indonesia—Influence. | Democratization—Indonesia. |
    Political corruption—Indonesia. | Indonesia—Politics and government—1998–
Classification: LCC P95.82.I5 (ebook) | LCC P95.82.I5 M43 2019 (print) |
    DDC 302.2309598—dc23
LC record available at https://lccn.loc.gov/2018029443

To my mother, Kathryn E. Pixley,
who raised me with a love of reading and writing
and to my father, Edward E. Pixley,
who taught me to venture into the unknown

CONTENTS

ACKNOWLEDGMENTS

The warmth and generosity of all of those who helped me in my research and writing continually amazed me, and I apologize to anyone I fail to mention here. In particular, I would like to thank my advisers at Northwestern University—Jim Ettema, Tom Goodnight, Jim Schwoch, and Jeff Winters—for their encouragement, suggestions, and careful readings of different drafts of this project. As the work continued, friends and colleagues—Gwen Walker, Erin Cantos, Denise Lamb, Duncan McCargo, Susan Zaeske, Rob Asen, Marty Medhurst, and Karen Rebholtz—gave helpful comments on my revised drafts. I am especially indebted to Eunsook Jung, who supported the project at critical moments and aided in the visual conceptualization of my argument, and Charlotte Frascona, who helped me think through various challenges at each stage.

I owe special thanks to all who gave me their time and provided insights in interviews and other conversations throughout my year of fieldwork in Jakarta and Manila. For sharing their files and allowing me an inside perspective on the workings of their organizations, I am grateful to Heru Hendratmoko, Lukas Luwarso, Ezki Suyanto, and Achmad Taufik of Aliansi Jurnalis Independen (AJI); the staff of Ramako-FM; Haris Jauhari and Despen Ompusunggu of Ikatan Jurnalis Televisi Indonesia (IJTI); S. Leo Batubara, Asep Sunara Martadiredja, and H. M. Purnowo of Serikat Penerbit Suratkabar (SPS); Ignatius Haryanto and Rusdi Marpaung (Ucok) of Lembaga Studi Pers & Pembangunan (LSPP); Lin Neumann of the Committee to Protect Journalists (CPJ); Andreas Harsono of Institut Studi Arus Informasi (ISAI); Budiman S. Hartoyo of Persatuan Wartawan Indonesia Reformasi (PWI-Reformasi); Kukuh Sanyoto of Masyarakat Pers dan Penyiaran Indonesia (MPPI); Hinca Pandjaitan of the Media Law Center; Ade Armando of the University of Indonesia; Magdalena Daluas of TVRI; Irawati Pratigno of AC Nielsen; Ilham Bintang of Persatuan Wartawan Indonesia (PWI); Syamsul Ma'arif of Tentara Nasional Indonesia (TNI); and the members of the Jakarta Media Center.

For their hospitality and insights while I was in Jakarta, many thanks to Alwi Dahlan, Aristides Katoppo, Atmakusumah Astraatmadja, Bambang Harymurti, Chusnul Mar'iyah, Daniel Dhakidae, Dede Oetomo, Djafar Assegaff, Eka Sitorus, Gunarso Kusumodiningrat, Ishadi S.K., Joesoef Isak, John McBeth, K. Basrie, Kathleen Reen, Marsillam Simanjuntak, Miriam Nainggolan, M.S. Zulkarnaen, Parni Hadi, Riza Primadi, Rosihan Anwar, Sumita Tobing, Trimoelja Soerjadi, Wimar Witoelar, Xanana Gusmão, and Yuli Ismartono. Thanks also to Teri Caraway, Beth Drexler, and Bronwyn Curran for their valuable friendship during our year of living through the turmoil and revelry of post-Suharto Indonesia. In Manila, I also benefited greatly from the counsel of Sheila Coronel, Melinda Quintos de Jesus, and Helen Mendoza.

Much love and gratitude to Jakarta friends Delfina Yuniara, Teguh Dewabrata, and Dameria Nainggolan, who taught me so much and helped me in more ways than I can begin to name here. Warm thanks also to my Jakarta research assistants, Sora, Eva, Hera, Sylvia, Yuli, Fenty, Yuni, Rully, and Joy, for all their work clipping, filing, and transcribing.

As the project moved toward publication at Cornell University Press, I received two invaluable reports from anonymous reviewers that served as my roadmap to revisions. In this process, Sarah E. M. Grossman proved an ideal editor, both providing encouragement and pressing me toward completion. When the book went into production, Karen Hwa, senior production editor at the press, and the book's copy editor, Florence Grant, were both assiduous and thoughtful.

Finally, and most importantly, I owe an enormous debt to my parents, Kathryn and Edward Pixley; my husband, Alfred McCoy; my in-laws, Margarita Piel McCoy, Margarita Candace Ground, and Marcella Pixley; and my brother, Stephen Pixley, for being the audience that gave my writing meaning, and to my children, Meg and Cyrus, for coming into my life in the middle of this project and bringing me happiness on even the hardest days.

NOTE ON SPELLING AND PERSONAL NAMES

Names in this book, with certain exceptions, are spelled using the post-1972 system (Ejaan yang Disempurnakan). Exceptions include those that appear in quotations from other sources and names of authors in the notes who use the old spelling. With the new system, the name of Indonesia's first president, for example, is spelled "Sukarno" instead of "Soekarno," "Soesanto Pudjomartono" becomes "Susanto Pujomartono," and "Akbar Tandjung" becomes "Akbar Tanjung." Also, as Western news sources frequently point out, many Indonesians, such as the former president Suharto, go by only one name. These cases are indicated in brackets [one name] in the first reference to the person.

For Indonesians with multiple names, there is no standard practice for shortened references. Instead, use of the first, middle, or last part of their full names, or a nickname, varies by individual. For example, the former minister of information, Muhammad Yunus Yosfiah, is called "Pak [Mr.] Yunus," while the former director general of press and graphics, H. Dailami, is called "Pak Dailami," and the former head of *Kompas*, Jakob Oetama, is called "Pak Jakob." For the sake of simplicity, after the first reference to an individual by his or her full name, subsequent references use the last component of the person's name, which in the United States would be called the surname. For example, the Golkar leader Akbar Tanjung is commonly called "Akbar" or "Pak Akbar," but in this book I refer to him as "Tanjung" after the first reference. Notable exceptions include the former president Megawati Sukarnoputri, who is referred to in short references as "Megawati" or "President Megawati."

Scandal and Democracy

INTRODUCTION:
UNDERSTANDING
DEMOCRATIC CONSOLIDATION

> While democracy in the long run is the most stable form of government, in the short run, it is among the most fragile.
> —Madeleine Albright, speech delivered at the conference "Towards a Community of Democracies," Warsaw, June 26, 2000

In May 1998, as the Indonesian capital of Jakarta smoldered from days of rioting, arson, and gunfire, the aging autocrat President Suharto resigned after more than three decades in power. With the nation slipping toward bankruptcy and separatist revolts simmering in remote provinces, his vice president, Bacharuddin Jusuf (B. J.) Habibie, took office, named a new cabinet, and promised democratic reforms. Less than two weeks later, sixty supporters of the once-outlawed Alliance of Independent Journalists (Aliansi Jurnalis Independen, AJI) gathered to discuss preventing a return of authoritarian media controls, a defining issue not only for these journalists but for the entire reform movement.

In marked contrast to the secrecy once required to avoid police raids, organizers of this gathering invited television crews to film their proceedings, and a top official from the once-feared Ministry of Information served as a speaker. In another sign of a new era, when these journalists later marched from the ministry to the state-sponsored Indonesian Journalists Association, instead of arresting them, the police led the way.

While the mood of this forum reflected the euphoria sweeping the country, many were still wary. The editor of the English-language *Jakarta Post*, Susanto Pujomartono, posed a critical question: Had the movement for press freedom triumphed just because Suharto was no longer president? He reminded his audience of the dashed expectations of 1966, when General Suharto, after deposing his autocratic predecessor, had lavished special attention on the media before shifting to the repression that marked most of his tenure. The lesson, Pujomartono said, was that though Indonesia was once again entering a new era, the media could rely on neither laws nor the government's "pity" to safeguard their future. Journalists, moreover, were still haunted by the ghosts of long repression and deference to the fallen regime.[1]

The head of AJI, Lukas Luwarso, echoed these concerns, pointing out that news outlets in this heady climate were behaving just as they had three decades earlier, openly rebuking the outgoing regime. Yet history had shown the Indonesian press to be no sturdier as a pillar of democracy than a pile of wood tossing about in the ocean. Given its freedom, he said, changing metaphors, the press bellows abusively before silently bowing in the face of pressure. Citing yet another metaphor favored by the publisher Jakob Oetama, he compared the press to a crab who quickly retreats when pelted with stones.[2] At some point during their struggle for survival under Suharto, members of the press had lost their nerve and, in turn, had taught this fear to the Indonesian people—perpetuating, consciously or not, the power of the regime.[3]

Now, after so many years of accommodating New Order dictates, Luwarso said he was not surprised that many in both media and government feared that removing restraints would lead to chaos. This was natural, he said, just as it is natural for one who has been in the dark for a long time to be afraid of the light. But if the mentality of the nation's leaders did not change, and if the press itself did not demand comprehensive legal reforms, "this era animated by the spirit of reform will become an absurd repetition of the past."[4]

The views expressed in this forum offer a snapshot of the challenges the Indonesian media would face during the country's transition to democracy, revealing the burden of Indonesia's authoritarian past as well as the promise of its democratic future. As eyewitnesses to the nation's turbulent history, many of these journalists had already seen the overthrow of an earlier dictatorship give way to Suharto's thirty years of authoritarian rule, thus lending gravity to Luwarso's warning that the current spirit of reform could be "an absurd repetition of the past." Suharto's New Order had lasted two full generations by embedding itself in constitution, law, and bureaucracy, while inserting itself into the language, media, and mentality of ordinary citizens and educated elites, journalists included. The pervasiveness of authoritarian values within Indonesian society, moreover, meant that democratic reform would require not only regime change but also a transformation of the country's political culture—thus lending particular significance to the work of the media.

GLOBAL CONTEXT

Though their focus was Indonesia, these journalists were addressing the chief problem facing similar democratic transitions worldwide: an inherent tendency to revert to authoritarian rule. Over the past quarter century, as crowds have toppled dozens of dictatorial regimes from Manila to Berlin, from Warsaw to Cairo, we have learned a simple lesson: democratic uprisings are relatively easy, almost commonplace, but successful transitions to enduring democracies are difficult and rare.

The moment of regime change sparks tremendous hope among both participants and international observers who anticipate the emergence of a more open, democratic society. Yet once a dictator has fallen, the most difficult question remains: How will the newly democratizing nation avoid reversing course, reverting to authoritarian solutions for the daunting problems brought by the transition? In Eastern Europe, central Asia, and much of the Middle East, this question has gained increasing salience as one democratic transition after another has given way to renewed authoritarian rule. Indeed, the tendency toward reversal is evident in any environment where the conditions that enabled authoritarianism are still in place. In Indonesia's transition, such conditions included judicial corruption, electoral fraud, a politicized military, elite rent seeking, and executive machinations to retain power. Rather than fleeing into exile, moreover, Suharto ceded power to a handpicked successor and retired to his luxurious compound in Central Jakarta to enjoy his grandchildren, his pet tiger, and access to an estimated $40 billion in accrued assets.[5]

Though tainted by the regime's corruption, Suharto's political machine had not lost power. Instead, with his loyal protégé at the helm, Suharto's long-ruling Golkar party retained control of both the executive and the legislature, providing a ready path to reversal as the country struggled to launch democratic reforms. The roots of the New Order's authoritarianism, moreover, ran deep, and most of the mechanisms that had enabled the executive to concentrate political and economic power were still in place—mechanisms that for decades had restricted media freedom, checked opposing centers of power, and thereby blocked the circulation of leadership. In retrospect, the country's democratic transition was far more precarious than many realized.

Despite these inauspicious beginnings, Indonesia's democratization has persisted, twice passing Samuel Huntington's benchmark of two consecutive elections for assessing a transition's long-term viability.[6] After two fitful decades of change, Indonesia now offers some lessons, as the world's largest Muslim-majority nation, for more recent democratic transitions, notably the Arab Spring of 2011–13. While myriad forces can promote or impede democratization, Indonesia's experience indicates that a transition's consolidation or reversal depends, to a surprising extent, on the role of the media—a set of actors whose freedom is widely recognized as a defining attribute of modern democracies but whose centrality in checking reversal remains only partly understood.

ACTORS VERSUS FACTORS

Following the succession of transitions starting in the 1970s that Samuel Huntington terms democratization's "third wave," a vast literature has emerged addressing the question of why some democratic transitions succeed and others founder, why some lead to "democratic consolidation" while others either fail outright or settle into a state of pseudodemocracy that often masks an atavistic authoritarianism.[7] Within this literature, studies of transitions tend to focus on two broad themes: actors and factors.

Taking the latter approach, analysts such as Huntington and Robert Dahl have sought to explain the origins and outcomes of transitions with a series of factors of varying complexity, including global economic trends, levels of modernization, or geopolitical forces.[8] Without discounting their value, others, such as Juan Linz, have critiqued factor-based analyses as overly static, focusing on the "social, economic, and cultural correlates of stable regimes in a given moment of time, [rather] than on the dynamic processes of crisis, breakdown, and re-equilibration of existing regimes or the consolidation of new ones."[9] Such studies also tend toward an almost teleological portrayal of democratization as a phenomenon that, once in motion, will continue of its own accord unless blocked by hostile forces or unfavorable circumstances.

Those who focus on actors, by contrast, look at the interplay of political leaders and social sectors in a process that leads to either reversal or consolidation, depending on the resources and strategies these actors employ. In the aftermath of the Cold War, residual elements from authoritarian regimes, whether military or civilian, have been persistent sources of resistance to democratization. Similarly, in Indonesia after Suharto, reversal was not an abstraction but a process promoted by actors determined to avoid accounting for past derelictions and to preserve privileges, whether political office, government contracts, or protected markets. These actors formed a disparate alliance of regime cronies, incumbent officials, and military leaders who coalesced around the Golkar party, which had dominated parliament under Suharto and preserved much of its influence after his fall.

Within this democratization literature, the military, as the sole actor with the raw coercive power to lead a reversal, merits the close attention it has received. Indeed, in the latter half of the twentieth century, militaries in developing societies tended to be vehicles for the establishment of, or reversion to, authoritarianism. Yet when atavistic forces are so entrenched that the inevitable tendency is toward reversal, the primary concern is not who has the power to lead a return to authoritarian rule, but rather who has the means and motivation to resist. Those who do are often identified as reformists, democratic actors, or simply democrats. They might include journalists as well as students, intellectuals, nongovernmental organizations, opposition political parties, or even members of the military. Among these many actors, however, members of the news media are uniquely positioned to counter the forces of reversal and further democratic consolidation. Such was the case in Indonesia, although there the synergy between media actors and civil society has been, and likely will continue to be, the critical force in deciding democracy's future.

DEMOCRATIZATION AND THE MEDIA

From the earliest democratization scholarship, there has been general agreement that freedom of the press, or the media more broadly, is necessary to building a modern democracy, primarily through promoting government accountability and serving as a key vehicle in citizens' communication of political preferences. Much of this older literature, however, tends to treat such freedom in the binary terms of presence versus absence. In the 1990s, scholars began examining the media as a more dynamic force but generally focused on their role in regime change.[10]

While this book addresses the media's influence in Suharto's downfall, its emphasis is on the critical consolidation phase during democratization. In this second phase, the main concern is not the cessation of authoritarian rule but rather the reversibility of democratization and challenges in building democratic institutions.[11] Numerous scholars have examined the post-1999 wave of democratization. Many of these have focused on the conditions conducive to media support for democratization. Some have taken a primarily empirical approach, and others have been predominantly prescriptive, outlining what news outlets *should* do to strengthen democracy while critiquing media failings in specific political contexts.[12] By contrast, this volume examines what media outlets actually do, or are inherently inclined to do, that helps ward off reversal in practice.

THE NEWS MEDIA'S UNIQUE ROLE

In their diurnal responsibilities, members of the media differ little from other professionals. But the news outlets they serve stand apart from other sectors, in part because the services they provide are distinctive. In producing and disseminating news and commentary on public affairs, they are the only sector whose primary job is to observe, record, and analyze the actions of other players and so inform the public. Media actors in democracies may not cut deals and form coalitions to the same extent as others, but individually and collectively, intentionally and haphazardly, they shape the environment in which other actors make decisions and forge alliances, affecting in multiple ways the calculations of contending forces. Moreover, simply by reporting on key players and unfolding events, the media help impose transparency on both, alerting the public to developments affecting power relations and general welfare.

But as Indonesia's democratic transition illustrates, in shaping this decision-making environment, the media's most critical function may be their contribution to what the political theorist Adam Przeworski has described as the institutionaliza-tion of uncertainty—a process that serves as both a force for democratization and a critical deterrent to reversal.[13] In most societal contexts, the word "uncertainty" carries a host of negative connotations. In Indonesia, for decades Suharto's relentless campaign against suspected Communists created a climate of fearful uncertainty among ordinary people ever vulnerable to charges of subversion. Throughout the New Order, the regime itself faced what Andreas Schedler calls the "twin uncertainty" of authoritarian rule—the "institutional insecurity" all autocrats face in maintaining power and "informational uncertainty" exacerbated by the repression of civil liberties.[14] In Suharto's last years, uncertainty over who would succeed him hung like a cloud over much public discourse. Following Przeworski, my analysis treats uncertainty not as a general state or a type of absence but as a central element in ruled-based, yet open, democratic contestation that yields outcomes unknowable in advance.

At the start of democratization, myriad changes introduce far more uncertainty into the political arena than could have been tolerated under authoritarianism. The emancipation of the public sphere exposes everyone—reformers as well as the old guard—to new forms of criticism. The democratic process itself, for all its promises of fairness and inclusion, offers no guarantees that outcomes will satisfy all participants. In the face of democratization's heightened uncertainty, even those committed to reform in principle may lose the courage to allow democratic outcomes in practice. The challenge for reformers in any postauthoritarian society is managing the insecurity felt by those with the power to derail the transition without allowing reform itself to founder.

Przeworski addresses this problem by arguing that democratization should be understood as the institutionalization of continuous conflicts and, simultaneously, "the process of institutionalizing uncertainty" inherent in democratic contestation. He compares this uncertainty to the certainty that characterizes authoritarian rule, in which some groups (often the military) have the power to manipulate the resolution of conflicts to protect their interests. While those outside the ruling circle may face considerable uncertainty, he continues, those close to the regime "have a high degree of control . . . in the sense that they are not forced to accept undesirable outcomes." In a democracy, by contrast, "no group is able to intervene when outcomes of conflicts violate their self-perceived interests."[15] Democracy, in sum, is a form of governance that subjects all players to uncertainty.

Paradoxically, what lends stability to democracy's continuous churn of contesta-tion is that outcomes of individual contests are always, to some degree, indetermi-nate. "In a democracy," Przeworski explains, "no one can win for once and for all: even if successful at one time, victors immediately face the prospect of having to struggle in the future."[16] By the same logic, this indeterminacy also guarantees that no defeat is ever final and there will be a chance to play again.

Under authoritarianism, there is a strikingly symmetrical inversion of these principles. Indeed, authoritarianism is generally marked by an obsessive pursuit of security through predetermined outcomes—whether in elections, the distribution of government contracts, or court cases. Once established, authoritarian regimes survive by affording this freedom from uncertainty to collaborating elites. In addition, as long as a regime can control the outcomes of most contests, there is little reason to main-tain the mechanisms of indeterminacy that promise future open rounds. Only when an authoritarian grip weakens and a country's political situation is in flux does the need arise to build, or rebuild, a society that combines a critical component of uncertainty with the complementary promise of indeterminacy.

At the start of democratic transition, when electoral outcomes are no longer preordained, new players have a chance to compete. But fears that the first open contest might also be the last can trigger a frenzy of power grabbing that can lead right back to authoritarianism. Conversely, faith in the indeterminacy of current rounds—that is, assurance that there will always be another chance to compete—can stave off this inclination to reversal.

Even without a downward spiral of power grabbing, the fear that there will not be a chance to play again may seem to justify the impulse to cheat and weaken commitments to the norms of fair play. Cheating in the first round is likely to distort the electoral process in future rounds. By contrast, belief that there will be future open contests encourages players to focus not simply on winning but on guarding the process to improve their odds in the next round should they lose the first. In short, the promise of ongoing rounds gives players reason to invest in the integrity of the process—specifically, the practices and rules of the game that will maintain a level playing field for future contests. Through building this faith in indeterminacy and increasing investment in a fair process, the uncertainty of democratic contestation becomes institutionalized.

More broadly, the institutionalization of uncertainty is the process by which the unpredictability of democratic contests comes to be tolerated and eventually expected by a polity accustomed to outcomes decided in advance by political patronage or executive caprice. As Indonesia's experience demonstrates, a nation's media can play a critical role—first, as actors self-consciously promoting reforms, transparency, and democratic values (including the norms of fair play) and second, as vehicles for the display of uncertainty, that is, democracy's inherent unpredictability and the facts, opinions, and partisan battles that sustain it. These are the battles that play out in the secondary contests between elections: political, as well as economic and judicial.

When we apply Przeworski's concept to actual democratic transitions, the abstraction of uncertainty needs to be integrated into an unfolding political process. Viewed at the moment of authoritarianism's collapse, amid the tumult of mass demonstrations and fallen dictators, democratic change seems primarily a conjuncture of regime incapacity and mass mobilization. Yet viewed analytically, a political transition and the subsequent struggle to prevent authoritarian reversal require mechanisms to break up elite collusion and promote the free interplay of competing forces whose sum is uncertainty. By both providing information and, at times, promoting political scandal, the media engender division among competing elites, delegitimate collusive pacts, and inspire public mobilization that can maintain a process that moves forward, by fits and starts, toward democratic consolidation.

Not only does Przeworski's conceptual model effectively encompass Indonesia's two-decade struggle for democracy, it also illuminates key aspects of parallel processes that have roiled four continents since the end of the Cold War. Its application to the progression of specific democratic transitions produces a paradigm that places the media at the fulcrum of change. Most of the regime changes that mark democratization's "third wave" were pacted transitions that left large elements of the old authoritarian coalition in place.[17] Among such elements, members of the media, even those once allied with the old order, are potentially leading actors uniquely equipped to promote the transparency and competitive contestation central to democracy and thereby ward off authoritarian reversal.

MEDIA IN THE INSTITUTIONALIZATION OF UNCERTAINTY

In any transition, momentum for change produces broad expectations, including the belief that democratization will lead not just to fair elections but to more sweeping changes, from better governance to social equity. As a transition takes off, Silvio Waisbord notes, "High hopes are placed on the democratic press."[18] Observers have identified numerous ways in which the news media could—and should—promote democratization, including informing and educating the public, fostering cooperation and civic culture, acting as watchdogs, providing accessible forums for public debate, giving voice to the marginalized, fortifying democratic institutions, promoting reforms, easing conflict, and facilitating reconciliation.[19]

While recognizing the importance of these standards in evaluating media performance in furthering transitions, this book sets them aside to assess the media's role in a specific process, institutionalizing uncertainty, that checks reversal and promotes democratic consolidation. This seemingly narrow definition of democratization, moreover, has surprisingly broad application when examining the media.

At a basic level, Przeworski's frame allows us to see political opening itself from a new perspective, as a process in which the media shift from a subordinate role that reinforces the certainties of authoritarianism to a provocative, often contentious one that involves highlighting, even amplifying, the uncertainties of democratic contestation among rival individuals and groups. Ultimately, this interpretation also helps illuminate what makes democratization "self-enforcing" (and thereby consolidated), beyond favorable conditions and good intentions.[20]

To understand the critical role of the media in transitions, we need to combine consideration of this sector's inclination toward transparency, unique among the major political forces, with a narrative of media actors. The latter, whether publishers, producers, editors, or reporters, often take enormous personal risks to translate this inclination into concrete actions that together create and revitalize the free communication that is the oxygen of democracy, frustrate the rigging of contestation, and thereby counter reversion to authoritarianism.

Equally important, however, is a finding that seems at first glance counterintuitive: among the chief mechanisms for preventing reversal are precisely the elements of media coverage that tend to attract the most criticism in stable democracies, particularly focus on scandal, contest frames, and partisan conflict. The findings that emerge from this close study of Indonesia's two-decades-long democratic transition resonate with comparable cases in Asia, Africa, and Latin America discussed in the concluding chapter. While the combined dynamics at work in these countries are uncommon among the many nations emerging from the authoritarianism of the Cold War, it is in these few cases that democratization seems to be taking hold.

The chapters that follow probe Indonesia's ongoing democratic transition to tease out the dynamics that either drive or curb the media in imposing transparency and fostering the institutionalization of uncertainty, and to explore the complex motivations—both self-serving and civic-minded—that can make the media central to democratization's success. The analysis offers both an interrogation of Indonesia's transition, its progress and limitations, and a model for understanding similar democratic transitions worldwide.

Phases of Transition

In the aftermath of authoritarian rule, a nation's media—whether print, broadcast, or digital—can contribute to institutionalizing both uncertainty and indeterminacy in democratic contestation in ways that vary as a transition moves through different stages. For the purposes of this analysis, democratic transitions, Indonesia's included, can be broken roughly into three phases: (1) delegitimation and collapse of the ruling regime; (2) a trial period of institutional change when confidence develops in the rules, institutions, and indeterminacy of democratic contestation; and (3) a long-term process of consolidation pulled between the reversibility of democratization and the durability of democratic institutions. In Przeworski's model, democratization moves toward this end state of consolidation when political players, anticipating future contests, invest not only in winning individual rounds but also in ensuring fairness in the democratic process over the long term.[21]

Delegitimation and Collapse

As opposition forces organize in response to the excesses of authoritarian rule, they spark, in the first phase, a burgeoning of discontent that precedes protest, agitation, and action. The many possible channels for disseminating critiques and organizing for action include the samizdat circulation of documents, as in the Soviet bloc, and latter-day incarnations on social media, as in Egypt, or through the emergence of an independent media, as in the Philippines under the dictator Ferdinand Marcos. Regardless of medium, such communication can help precipitate a transformation, unsettling the staid predictability of the authoritarian status quo.

As Vicky Randall notes, when elements of the media, especially those considered "alternative," are able to foster a critical stance toward the regime, they help undermine its legitimacy.[22] When waning legitimacy destabilizes the coalitions that have sustained the ruling order, the bolder of mainstream media outlets may also begin airing dissenting views or revelations damaging to the regime. For some, this communication may also provide authorization or affirmation for action. At a minimum, whether through critical reporting or simply covering unfolding events, the media as a whole highlight, and often encourage, new contestation over the right to rule.

In Indonesia during this phase, discussed in chapter 3, all the major news outlets eventually reported the economic crisis and consequent protests that hit the country in 1997. Alternative channels, such as nascent computer networks, also disseminated revelations damaging to the regime and facilitated coordination among activists.[23] While the media's part in the regime's collapse was complex and sometimes contradictory, in the end, few outlets could avoid the crisis and demonstrations. Even coverage supportive of Suharto heightened awareness of new uncertainty emerging from changing power relations among elites. While this uncertainty was not yet the "ruled open-endedness" or "organized uncertainty" of Przeworski's model, the media were still highlighting, even normalizing, a departure from the predictability of an unchallenged regime.[24]

Trial Phase

In the second phase, political uncertainty tends to revolve around whether leaders will support fair and open elections. There is a danger that media outlets might be captured by actors with sectarian agendas, triggering a downward spiral into competing propaganda and fostering fears of once-and-for-all victories that will preclude future competition, thereby reducing faith in the indeterminacy of democratic contestation. But to the extent that the media, on balance, give voice to all competitors, they help maintain uncertainty over which group will prevail in the end—a state essential, in Przeworski's model, to democratization before and during the start of official campaigns.

During this trial phase, the media play a supplemental role in institutionalizing the uncertainty of democratic elections when imposing transparency on the electoral process, whether through a daily drumbeat of campaign reporting, critical coverage of decision-making, or investigations into electoral fraud. Such scrutiny discourages fraud but also maintains the focus on fairness that all players must sustain to prevent a return to the distorted outcomes of authoritarianism.

In Indonesia, the trial phase included the first post-Suharto elections of June 1999, when the country faced its most critical challenges in warding off reversion to fixed outcomes. Wary of setting off clashes and still inhibited by taboos against reporting on religion, race, ethnicity, or class, the majority of media, as described in chapters 4 to 6, avoided a slide into sectarian agendas, even during the violent interreligious conflict that erupted in the eastern islands. Moreover, in election coverage of the same period, a surprisingly wide range of opposition voices was able to gain media attention, an outcome that also helped level the playing field for competitive contestation.

Yet from rule writing through tabulation, the performance of Indonesia's media in imposing scrutiny on the parliamentary elections was decidedly mixed—at times aggressively promoting fairness and transparency, while at other times compromised by partisan biases and fears of inciting violence. In their compromises, the media responded to ruling-party machinations and opposition complacency in ways that, if we apply Przeworski's model, left the country poised for reversal via a return to rigged elections orchestrated by colluding elites. Surprisingly, however, this threatened reversal was later halted, in effect, by the same media's collective pursuit of a campaign finance scandal that finally broke the ruling party's grip on power, derailing its maneuvers to keep Suharto's protégé, B. J. Habibie, in the presidency.

DEMOCRATIC CONSOLIDATION

The media can play an equally critical role in the final consolidation phase. Following Przeworski, this phase involves (1) the normalization of regular, open-ended contestation that produces meaningful shifts in the balance of power, (2) strengthening faith that there will be future fair chances to compete, and (3) development of a political culture that resists a return to predetermined outcomes.

Reversals that block consolidation often begin not with the restoration of the old dictator but with the emergence of a pseudodemocratic regime with an indefinite lien on power—a trend extending from Alexander Lukashenko in Belarus to Abdel Fattah el-Sisi in Egypt, the Aliyevs of Azerbaijan, Nursultan Nazarbayev in Kazakhstan, Islam Karimov in Uzbekistan, and Hun Sen in Cambodia. A recurring dynamic in such reversal is the formation of an ad hoc coalition of old and new actors around a party and leader who together manipulate democratic forms for a protracted hold on power, producing collusive pacts and engineered outcomes in elections as well as in secondary contests for government contracts, favorable court rulings, and advantageous economic regulations. Competitive media can play a key role in disrupting collusive coalitions, even late in the transition, by imposing scrutiny on actors and providing a vehicle for actors to impose scrutiny on each other (whether out of civic duty, partisan maneuvering, or personal revenge).

In Indonesia's tempestuous transition, we can mark a major milestone in this phase with the election in October 1999 of a new president, Abdurrahman Wahid (Gus Dur), which denied the long-reigning Golkar party a continued lock on the executive. Though much of the media ignored the fraud that had compromised the parliamentary elections just three months earlier, relentless postelection coverage of a campaign finance scandal known as "Baligate" irreparably damaged Golkar's candidate, President Habibie, in the presidential race and for the first time in decades forced an incumbent president and his party to accept an unfavorable outcome. In retrospect, Baligate was the start of an era of politics by scandal in Indonesia that made the media a lead player in a volatile pattern of intraelite conflict and marked a turning point in the country's democratic transition.

The long-term change lay in the transformation of the public sphere, no longer controllable by any one party. Now freed from New Order restrictions, media exposés and political scandal began to play a central yet unpredictable role in mediating intraelite conflict, as warring factions used the media to maneuver against each other and news outlets weighed in independently. Most significantly, elite collusive pacts were now less viable, weakened by the use of scandal as a political weapon and ensuing cycles of revenge. During five critical years of this transition, 1999 to 2004, Indonesia saw a relentless cycle of elite attack and counterattack through a succession of media-driven scandals—Buloggate I, Buloggate II, Taperumgate, Bruneigate, and Banpresgate.

Through a process described in chapter 7, the carefully negotiated, ritual resolutions of the Suharto era were now breaking down, weakened by the politics of public revenge and the new transparency that the media were imposing upon events and elite rivalries. This factional infighting, played out in the media, was central to the ultimate endurance of democratization. By fostering intraelite conflict and making alliances ever more fluid and unpredictable, this new politics by scandal moved Indonesia away from authoritarian stasis and closer to the institutionalized uncertainty of democracy. Though advanced democracies may view such cycles as a degraded form of politics, in this postauthoritarian setting, they were critical in derailing the political collusion and electoral manipulation that threatened to end the country's democratic transition.

RECONSIDERING SCANDAL

Examining the intersection between the media and democratic uncertainty highlights the potential emergent role in democratization of tendencies for which news outlets are often faulted—namely, preoccupation with scandal, partisan conflict, and contest frames, particularly horse-race election coverage. Critics have condemned these tendencies for "hollowing out" democracy, fostering divisive politics rather than informed debate, and perhaps most insidiously, promoting apathy and cynicism.[25] Some disparage horse-race coverage for reducing election reporting to sports metaphors and strategy analysis, trivializing the political process while crowding out substantive issues and wider perspectives.[26] Others hold the media responsible for "undermining" democracy by failing to convey the significance of news stories within a larger context.[27]

The media's recurring fixation on scandal and partisan conflict, manifest in sensationalized reporting on personal peccadilloes and political vendetta, has inspired equally trenchant critiques. "'Gotcha' politics," Lanny Davis argues, is "about partisanship, not about uncovering genuine corruption." He adds, "It is about revenge and payback, not about due process and investigations in search of the truth." Ultimately, he concludes, "it is about personal and political destruction, not winning in the marketplace of ideas."[28] Studying the newly democratic Republic of Benin, Chris Allen has faulted the media for "indulging in cynicism, propagating rumors, or, at worst, simply fabricating scandal for payment," while failing to report more serious issues.[29] Veven Wardhana has dismissed scandal reporting in Indonesia as "exploitative infotainment."[30] Similarly, Howard Tumber and Silvio Waisbord argue that "democracies are inherently prone to be regularly shaken by scandals," but the media, particularly in mature democracies, are notorious for "short-lived attention" that "makes scandals prone to have a brief existence," inducing a "numb public opinion" and little real change.[31]

While such criticism is often warranted in both new and established democracies, horse-race coverage, partisan vendetta, and above all, scandal, can also play an important emergent function in democratic transitions. Indeed, there is some fragmentary yet compelling historical evidence from the past four centuries indicating that, in times of regime change, scandal over matters substantial or sordid can serve as a discursive lever for widening the public sphere, discrediting the old regime, and contributing to democratization. In his study of the Overby scandal that roiled the court of James I of Great Britain, Alastair Bellany argues that sensational accounts of murder by poison and sexual intrigue contributed to a changing "news culture" that culminated, through a complex causality, in the English revolution of the 1640s.[32] A century later in France, a succession of salacious courtroom dramas, exemplified by the "diamond necklace affair" that stigmatized Marie Antoinette, sparked public fascination. Print runs of up to ten thousand each for legal briefs "carried afar interest and scandal," exposing the corruptions of France's absolutist monarchy and hastening the French Revolution.[33]

In America's postrevolutionary decade of the 1790s, partisan scandal aided democratic consolidation as journalists led by Noah Webster, founder of New York's first daily newspaper, set aside civility to become "peddlers of scurrility." In this brawl, America's early press challenged the Federalists' dominance over government and public debate, ultimately helping to usher in the more democratic Jacksonian era.[34] Similarly, in Wilhelmine Germany, the Social Democratic Party resisted repression via exposés of financial scandals involving the kaiser's government, undermining the aristocratic order's legitimacy and contributing to the regime's collapse in 1918, thereby launching a decade of democratic governance.[35]

Examining more recent events, Chappell Lawson has found that media liberalization was the "primary cause of the devastating scandals that rocked Mexican politics" in the 1990s, delegitimating the ruling party and facilitating political change. Simultaneously, the scandals "signaled to elites that the rules of the political game were changing," thus making media coverage of once-forbidden topics a major force behind Mexico's successful democratic transition.[36] Similarly, Miklós Sükösd observes that news coverage of the Danubegate scandal "helped dislodge" Hungary's ex-Communist government.[37] While the role of Indonesia's media in Suharto's downfall in 1998 was mixed, scandalous revelations, particularly concerned with the president's staggering accumulation of wealth, severely damaged his legitimacy and hastened his fall.[38]

Framing issues in relation to ongoing contests may contribute little to solving problems or forming ideal policy. But understanding democratization involves examining transitional dynamics apart from the anticipation that the process will lead to good governance. Beyond opening political space and unsettling entrenched regimes, media focus on scandal, partisan battles, and even elections as horse races can also contribute to the second (trial) and third (consolidation) phases of postauthoritarian transition outlined above, in part by increasing the public's familiarity with and interest in one of the most essential components of democracy—recurring open-ended contests.[39]

In the trial phase, particularly in societies accustomed to the suppression of participation, fostering interest in political contests serves at least two functions: habituation to key democratic norms and education for the exercise of vigilance. As Larry Diamond argues, building support for democracy, including the elusive development of "trust," takes place largely through successful experience with democracy.[40] Gaining such experience involves deepening familiarity with democratic elections. But as Benedict Anderson notes, "the representative mechanism [elections] is a rare and moveable feast," and the "generation of the impersonal [collective] will is . . . better sought in the diurnal regularities of the imagining life."[41] Media exposure is one of those diurnal regularities; consuming a daily barrage of news filtered through contest frames is, quite possibly, a more penetrating form of experience with democracy than even the most faithful participation in more episodic elections.

At a minimum, representations of politics as a series of ongoing contests can reinforce the values, such as commitment to fair play and intolerance of fixed outcomes, that we associate with other open contests (e.g., sports and legal disputes)—leading to the second function of contest frames: educating people for vigilance, specifically in monitoring the way the democratic game is played. Reporting on scandals, even at the expense of more substantive coverage, can help normalize the imposition of transparency as an expected part of media performance and establish openness as an expected component of democracy.

SECONDARY CONTESTS

In the third phase of consolidation, the role of scandal and partisan attack goes beyond the electoral process to highlight the centrality of the infinite series of smaller contests played out between elections, from factional scuffles to bruising battles of revenge that often wield a decisive impact on elections themselves. It is in the responses of different actors to these smaller contests that consolidation often moves forward or falters.

In any transition, media coverage that publicizes these smaller contests, though often sensationalist, can further consolidation in several ways. It can alter the balance of power among likely contenders in future elections, precipitating possible turnover in leadership while helping acclimate a citizenry to democracy's inherent unpredictability. Though revelations ideally come from journalists or others acting out of nonpartisan civic responsibility, scandal motivated by revenge or partisanship can help sustain flux in the balance of power. In either case, the media help normalize the unpredictability of politics in a democratic system where reputation and public opinion, more than patronage or electoral manipulation, decide the fate of political careers.

Admittedly, scandals can erupt from false accusations or other misinformation often exacerbated by partisan motivations. They may be particularly dangerous in the fragile early days of a democratic transition. In Egypt after the Arab Spring of 2011, contending forces responded to biased voices by trying to silence oppositional media.[42] A key difference in Indonesia's transition, detailed in chapter 4, was the commitment by journalists' associations to establish professional standards, averting crackdowns and quelling anger at critical coverage.

The potential for backlash against unwelcome aspects of media freedom returns us to Przeworski's element of indeterminacy, that is, the promise that there will be future opportunities to compete. Using his model, I argue that democratic consolidation requires that contenders develop faith in this indeterminacy not only of elections but also of the smaller, intervening contests that play out in the court of public opinion—faith that a media nightmare for one faction one week could just as easily be followed by a triumph the next. More broadly, confidence in the indeterminacy of media-influenced shifts in the balance of power can mitigate fears of the unpredictable effects of a free media. The alternative to contest- and scandal-oriented media, moreover, is not necessarily a better-informed citizenry. It may instead be a depoliticized, disenfranchised public that simply watches politicians act—perhaps with decorum but also, as many an authoritarian regime has shown, with little transparency and even less accountability. Another alternative could be the devolution of a nation's public sphere into praetorianism, a development that, at least in China, appears to be compatible with continued authoritarianism.[43]

In its own transition, Indonesia's experience indicates that the media are critical in institutionalizing the uncertainty of democratic contestation not in spite of their preoccupation with horse-race coverage, conflict, and scandal, but in many ways because of it, particularly in breaking up collusion and the concentration of power. Within the country's newly constituted public sphere, the right to report freely on stories of scandal and partisan conflict that influence the secondary contests between elections transformed the print and electronic media into a parallel arena of electoral politics. From 1999 to 2004, as recounted in chapters 6 and 7, candidates rose and fell and rose again in often spectacular dramas played out on a public stage. The inability of individual players or parties to control these battles constituted a significant departure from the past.

Over the following decade, 2004 to 2014, intraelite contestation produced a continuing cycle of revenge via revelation that served to constrain the forces of authoritarian reversal. During this period under the presidency of Susilo Bambang Yudhoyono, discussed in chapter 8, a succession of megascandals showed the ability of the media, in collaboration with civil society forces, to challenge the ruling party, block elite collusion, and facilitate yet another change of government. In the 2014 presidential election, a full fifteen years after Suharto's fall, the forces of reversal coalesced around his son-in-law and regime enforcer, Lieutenant General (Ret.) Prabowo Subianto, in an explicit antidemocracy campaign, playing upon nostalgia for the New Order in a desperate, determined effort to defeat a populist candidate. Through an alliance of media and civil society activists, the opposition blocked this bid for authoritarian reversal and elected the country's first nonelite president, illustrating the paramount importance of such synergies between media and public in maintaining momentum toward democratic consolidation.

In sum, when reconsidering media practices often viewed as degrading to democracy and exploring their role in checking democratization's reversal, Indonesia's recent history is rich in lessons for pragmatic reformers and insights for academic analysts. Perhaps most critically, examining the media in Indonesia's transition reveals its central role in maintaining the uncertainty of democracy's ongoing contests, thereby promoting the critical elements of accountability, competition, transparency, and above all, circulation of leadership.

CHAPTER ONE

ORIGINS OF MEDIA CONTROLS

There is no power holder who dares to use his power if there is not a people excessively afraid of that power.
—Ignas Kleden, "The Fear of Fighting Fear"

In 1945, sixty-eight of Indonesia's political leaders met in Jakarta to draft a constitution casting off three centuries of Dutch colonial rule and drawing the archipelago's seventeen thousand islands and seventy million inhabitants into a unified nation.[1] Amid contentious debates threatening to divide the delegates over the choice between secular and Islamic principles, Sukarno [one name], a spellbinding speaker who later became Indonesia's first president, rose to address the assembly.

Meticulously attired in a white colonial suit and black Muslim cap, Sukarno presented a vision bridging the growing rift, offering "a unifying philosophical foundation" they could all accept. "First and foremost," he asked, with words to defuse demands for an Islamic state, "are we seeking to establish a nation . . . [that is called] Free Indonesia, but in reality is only for elevating one person, for giving power to one wealthy group, for giving power [only] to the aristocracy? Is this our intention?" Answering this question, he said, "It is clear it is not! . . . We seek to establish a nation of 'all for all.' Not for one person, not for one . . . ethnic group or group that is wealthy—but 'all for all.'"[2]

In an early condemnation of partisan politics, Sukarno warned that this new nation should not espouse Western notions of freedom: "If we create freedom . . . based on philosophies as promoted by American and European nations . . . be assured that our hearts will be filled with conflict." He offered instead a vision centered on indigenous decision-making with Islamic roots, explaining that "the crucial requirement for the strength of the Indonesian state is mutual deliberation [*musyawarah*]." It is this, he said, "that gives life, namely political-economic democracy that can bring about social justice!"[3]

Embedded in these impassioned statements was not only a unifying rejection of Western democratic precepts but also the espousal of a distinctively Indonesian form of democracy aspiring to a consensual model of governance. In little more than a decade, however, these same constitutional principles would help facilitate a shift from a functioning democracy—with free speech, open elections, and contentious parliamentary debate—to an authoritarian state headed by just two powerful leaders, President Sukarno and his successor, Suharto, for over forty years.

When authoritarian rule began to unravel in Indonesia during the 1997 economic crisis, President Suharto quickly became the target of the country's burgeoning democratic opposition. Once seen as a welcome change from the unstable and increasingly dictatorial rule of his predecessor, Suharto was now, after thirty-two years in power, the personification of the corruption and authoritarianism that marked his own regime.

But even as the prodemocracy movement railed against him, reformers realized that a true break with the past would require not only his removal but also the more daunting task of dismantling his entrenched New Order regime. Further complicating the challenge, the authoritarian controls that defined the New Order were not a simple manifestation of one ruler's managerial style. Their roots, institutional and ideological, reached back to the origins of the Indonesian republic and were part of a complex structure that had evolved from Dutch rule through the Sukarno era into Suharto's New Order. Fully assembled by the late 1980s, this structure rested on a foundation of both colonial law and Indonesian political theory inspired by a corporatist, or "integralist," vision of the relationship between the state and society. It formed an institutional base through multiple bureaucracies overseeing a maze of regulations, licensing, and tightening controls over ownership.

For reformers, the system underlying Indonesia's authoritarianism was thus elaborate and deeply rooted, requiring bureaucratic change as well as transformation of a larger political culture. Exploring this layered historical legacy, dating back to the country's first constitutional debates, reveals the weight of the past that confronted the media during the democratic transition over forty years later.

ORIGINS OF AUTHORITARIAN CONTROLS

The ideological foundations of these corporatist political principles can be traced to counter-Enlightenment concepts first articulated by German philosophers in the early nineteenth century. Their embrace by Dutch colonial scholars of the early twentieth century, in turn, strongly influenced the thinking of the Indonesian nationalists who framed the country's 1945 constitution.[4]

On the eve of independence, the sense among Indonesia's young leaders emerging from centuries of colonial rule was that Western liberalism and its accompanying materialism tended to produce greed and exploitation, and they sought an alternative model for their new nation. Their democracy would be based not on an adversarial process, but on governance through consensus and cooperation.

During Indonesia's constitutional debates, Raden Supomo, a former colonial judge, laid out a frame for this form of governance, calling it "integralism" and invoking the philosophies of Benedict de Spinoza and Georg Wilhelm Friedrich Hegel.[5] As scholars of this period have noted, Supomo's integralism was a form of corporatism—a statist ideology casting society and government as an integrated whole, whether a living organism or a vast family governed by a father figure who embodies the spirit of the people and therefore can divine their greater interests.[6] In Indonesia, the ideology would incorporate all citizens on the principle of jus soli (right of the soil) and cast the national community as both a body bounded by geography and a vast, harmonious family (a construction dubbed *kekeluargaan*, or "family-ism").[7]

Most importantly, in Supomo's words, an integralist state is one "that is united with the whole of the people, transcending all groups in all sectors."[8] Such a state does not stand outside the people but *is* the people, led by a head of state who is also one with the people and therefore attuned to their aspirations. In short, unlike Western democracies, filled with discord and self-interest, Supomo's vision was of a unitary state governed through consensual deliberation free of political conflict. Offering evidence that Indonesia could establish such a democracy, fellow framer Muhammad Yamin invoked a golden era of village-centered collectivism traced back to the Majapahit era. Sukarno's model of decision-making—inclusive mutual consultation (*musyawarah*) leading to a consensus (*mufakat*) articulated by a wise leader—was central to this imagined past.[9]

Three days later, in a riveting address to the assembly, Sukarno made his own contribution to Indonesian political theory with his formulation of the Pancasila, a doctrine that would become the defining principle of the Indonesian state. Its five "pillars" were (1) belief in one supreme God, (2) justice and civility among peoples, (3) the unity of Indonesia, (4) democracy through deliberation and consensus among representatives, and (5) social justice for all.[10] With deliberations deadlocked, Sukarno's Pancasila appealed to all factions, encompassing and subordinating their competing visions of the state. The word "integralism" never entered the constitution, and the five pillars did not necessarily preordain the rise of any particular political system. But over time the Pancasila doctrine came to be seen, in the words of Adam Schwarz, as "synonymous with and justification for an integralist view of the state"—ultimately serving as the ideological foundation of Suharto's authoritarian order.[11]

How did Sukarno's diffuse doctrine, seemingly compatible with a working democracy, later justify integralist views and facilitate authoritarianism? And how did it legitimate the accretion of controls that stunted the development of a democratic media? The answer lies partly in the third pillar's focus on "unity," a term easily invoked to justify suppression of dissent. But the regime also reinterpreted Pancasila's fourth pillar to further the concentration of power by focusing overwhelmingly on consensus. While the pillar itself seems to promise an inclusive and egalitarian form of democracy—mandating mutual deliberation to reach unanimous consensus—in Suharto's Pancasila democracy, the ideal of *musyawarah untuk mufakat* was replaced in practice by a premium on closure, with consensus redefined as acquiescence rather than agreement.

Articles within the 1945 constitution also stipulated that decisions be made through consensus-oriented mutual deliberation—more specifically, through consultation between the head of state, envisioned in these debates as a "just king" (Ratu Adil), and members of a quasilegislative body representing all sectors of society. Significantly, the framers named this supreme body the People's Consultative Assembly (Majelis Permusyawaratan Rakyat, MPR), underlining its advisory character in ways that predicted the limited role it would later play.

The more proximate reason that this plenary parliament and one of its two chambers, the People's Representative Council (Dewan Perwakilan Rakyat, DPR), became rubber stamps for executive policy rather than constituting an independent legislature is that the 1945 constitution lacked provisions for the separation of powers. It instead stipulated that different branches of the national government would share responsibilities and engage in mutual support and consultation, miming the imagined cooperation of Indonesia's village councils. In practice, this fluid sharing of functions, particularly through provisions empowering the president to legislate, led to unilateral decision-making and executive concentration of power.

Though Supomo's vision, emphasizing consensus and repudiation of individual rights, had strong proponents in the assembly, several framers expressed concern over its potential to justify the abuse of power. Notably, the future vice president Mohammad Hatta, backed by Muhammad Yamin, fought for provisions protecting civil rights, particularly freedom of speech. But both Sukarno and Supomo argued that such individual protections would go against *kekeluargaan* and lead to conflict sparked by greed and self-interest. Hatta countered that without free speech, "the shape of the nation may become . . . one we cannot agree with." Hatta supported a state of corporatist leadership (*negara pengurus*) but argued such power must be checked by "an article [ensuring] that every citizen will not be afraid to express an opinion . . . [and guaranteeing] the right to assemble, to convene, to write."[12]

Supomo and Sukarno ultimately did concede to Article 28, which appeared to protect free speech through a statement that the freedom "to express thoughts orally and in writing and so forth shall be determined by legislation." Yet by granting government the power to determine the boundaries of free speech without delineating such boundaries, Article 28 effectively affirmed the opposite: to comply with the imperatives of the constitution, the state *will* make laws that regulate speech, potentially circumscribing it. Ironically, through this apparent concession to individual rights, the framers created a constitutional clause formalizing the state's authority to abridge rights, including freedom of speech, and thereby limit society's ability to check the abuse of power.

GUIDED DEMOCRACY AND A GUIDED PRESS

Following four years of armed struggle against the Dutch, Indonesia's revolutionaries won formal independence in 1949. They ratified the original 1945 constitution but soon replaced it with two interim documents that created a more autonomous parliament and stronger protections for civil rights, including freedom of speech. In 1954, leaders of the new republic demonstrated further commitment to press freedom by nullifying a regulation identified with Dutch repression called the Persbreidel Ordonnantie, or the Press Muzzling Ordinance, that allowed the government to ban publications viewed as threats to public order.[13] With this nullification and the more liberal interim charters, Indonesia enjoyed a decade of parliamentary democracy under its first president, Sukarno, marked by competitive multiparty elections and a print press that was, by most accounts, outspoken and critical of the government.

Yet the new government also retained several other laws giving the state broad discretion to punish speech. By force of legal continuity, the sections of the criminal code known as the lèse majesté articles that had protected Dutch colonials from disrespect survived independence to outlaw any speech that might offend the new republic's president, vice president, or other officials.[14] Another Dutch legacy, the *haatzai artikelen*, or "hate-sowing articles," criminalized spreading animosity in society or contempt toward the government and remained part of Indonesia's legal code for the next half century.[15]

Thus even in this democratic era, we see the foundations for the later suppression of speech under Suharto. Tolerance among the nation's first leaders for Jakarta's vociferous print press was also surprisingly brief. By 1953, the Ministry of Information was threatening to sanction any media outlet giving a "false picture" of the nation's affairs. Soon after, the attorney general ordered the media to refrain from any reporting on government matters that might be inflammatory or highlight disagreements.[16] In 1956, the army's chief of staff issued a new, more draconian regulation to prohibit virtually all speech critical, degrading, or suspicious of public officials. Borrowing almost verbatim from the Dutch *haatzai artikelen*, the new regulation also outlawed writings that could give rise to "expressions of antagonism, hatred, or contempt" among or toward societal groups, or that contained information able to produce a public sensation.[17] Although protests soon forced the government to revoke this regulation, within a year, the imposition of martial law to suppress revolts in the outer islands allowed even more severe strictures on news outlets. That same year,

Sukarno declared an official state of emergency as he stepped up the campaign against these secessionist movements, leaving news outlets with little recourse.[18] Protections for the media were overridden by government imperatives, and further reforms that might have eradicated the Dutch legacy were repeatedly preempted by fears over the perceived fragility of the new republic.

In 1959, as political divisions deepened and negotiations over a permanent constitution became deadlocked, Sukarno dissolved the constitutional assembly and declared Indonesia's democracy a failure. He then discarded the provisional constitution of 1950 and reinstated the 1945 charter, removing checks on executive authority, and transferred patronage power from political parties to the president.

This constitutional crisis marked the beginning of Sukarno's "Guided Democracy" that was, as Schwarz observed, "a return to a system of personal rule more reminiscent of Javanese feudalism than the chaotic democratic experiment of the 1950s."[19] For the first time, the 1945 constitution became a living document for realizing Sukarno and Supomo's original corporatist vision.[20] Consistent with this ideology, Sukarno originally conceived Guided Democracy as a government in which the opposition would "disappear." There would still be "differences of opinion" in government, but they "will bring us to progress" because "deliberation, musyawarah, will go hand in hand with the family principle."[21] But when legislators refused to pass his budget in 1960, Sukarno replaced them with an appointed parliament, a body beholden to him that preserved the veneer of decision-making by mutual consultation.[22]

Guided Democracy also meant a guided press. The new regime was nominally committed to media freedom but imposed restrictions aimed at upholding the public interest, the nation's character, and respect for one God. New regulations from the military added to these restraints. Publishing bans became regular occurrences as regulations multiplied, each enumerating in greater detail not only restrictions but also the media's responsibilities as an "instrument of national struggle."[23]

In addition to regulations and decrees, the Sukarno administration introduced licensing to control the media, the signature mechanism of the later Suharto period. In 1958, the regional military command began using licensing in Jakarta to eliminate publications that were considered sensational or dangerous to morality. One historian emphasized the significance of this development by noting that even the Dutch had never used this form of media control.[24] A 1963 presidential decree then elevated licensing to national policy.[25]

Sukarno also established the agencies that Suharto would later use to discipline the media, including the Ministry of Information and the National Press Council, charged with controlling financial subsidies and monitoring publications for dissidence. Finally, government interference in the internal affairs of the Association of Indonesian Journalists (Persatuan Wartawan Indonesia, PWI), also began long before Suharto took power, making the organization a key means of drawing the media under state control and banishing independent journalists from the profession.[26]

The Sukarno era also left a memory, carefully cultivated by Suharto's New Order, of democracy as a failed experiment—a form of government ill-suited to Indonesian society. The initial weakness of Indonesia's political institutions, compounded by confusion over what kind of state it should be, exacerbated the instability of the republic's first years. Benedict Anderson has characterized the political environment of the 1950s as "a kind of round-the-clock politics in which mass organizations competed with each other at every conceivable . . . level without there being any real resolution."[27] Similarly, Robert Cribb and Colin Brown describe political parties as sliding "between fluid, self-serving factionalism and rigid ideological polarisation."[28] Even after the 1955 election, widely regarded as free and fair, faith in the parliamentary system was faltering. As the economy deteriorated, public tolerance for the unpredictability of the democratic process declined.[29]

The extent of liberal democracy's "failure" in Indonesia during the 1950s is still a matter of debate.[30] Whether elites abandoned democracy because it had failed or it failed because elites saw their interests better served by authoritarianism, Sukarno and then Suharto cultivated the impression that liberal democracy had been a disaster—in part to preempt calls for its return and in part to justify suppression of democratic rights, including freedom of speech.[31]

RISE OF THE NEW ORDER

In tandem with growing repression, Indonesia's economy fell into disarray under Sukarno. The country reeled from soaring inflation, and food shortages were imminent; international tensions increased as the president nationalized foreign firms, rejected US aid, and provoked a confrontation with Malaysia. Concurrently, the Communist movement, now more closely allied with Sukarno, pushed hard for land reform, raising tensions with Muslims and the military, and pressured artists and journalists to adhere to the guidelines of its People's Cultural Institute. Strained by these conflicts, President Sukarno's political coalition became increasingly untenable. In a final bid for stability in 1963, parliament elected him president for life.[32]

In 1965, an alleged Communist coup and a military countercoup set in motion events that effectively stripped Sukarno of power and allowed the little-known General Suharto to seize control and launch his New Order. Suharto's subsequent crackdown on what he called a "counterrevolutionary movement" set off a brutal, army-led purge of suspected Communists that left up to a million dead. "In terms of numbers killed," the CIA reported, "the anti-PKI [Indonesian Communist Party] massacres in Indonesia rank as one of the worst mass murders of the twentieth century."[33]

Thus, Suharto's regime rose to power on a wave of terror that left an indelible mark on the nation's consciousness, creating a formidable legacy for future democracy advocates to overcome. Promotion of regime propaganda by surviving media and the absence of public debate on the killings deepened their impact. As the regime held public trials of suspected Communists, Suharto asserted his version of events, arguing that liberal democracy—with its contentious pluralism, partisan press, and confrontational politics—had produced the deep divisions responsible for the 1965–66 massacre. With this portrayal shaping the country's collective memory, Suharto recast the bloody military-led campaign that brought him to power as a spontaneous eruption of mass violence.[34] This reconstruction reinforced a larger, two-pronged point: Indonesia's short period of democracy had led to the societal disintegration of the 1960s, and strict political controls, including restrictions on speech, were necessary to prevent the recurrence of violence.

EARLY POLITICAL JOURNALISM

President Suharto began his reign in the spirit of reform, liberating the print press from controls imposed by his predecessor. Over the next decade, however, he would employ and expand Sukarno's entire arsenal. The resulting apparatus restricted media outlets through a web of laws and regulations. Increasing control over ownership, corporatist norms, and the carrot of a protected market all cultivated a culture of compliance.

In the regime's early days, despite ongoing bloodshed in the name of restoring order and the relentless pursuit of suspected members of the Indonesian Communist Party (Partai Komunis Indonesia, PKI), there was relief among many journalists and intellectuals at being liberated from Sukarno's Guided Democracy. There was, moreover, optimism over new reforms. Although one of Suharto's first acts was to shut down forty-six newspapers associated with the PKI, many previously banned publications were revived, including Mochtar Lubis's *Indonesia Raya*.[35]

In late 1966, the new parliament passed the long-awaited Basic Press Law, containing twenty-one sections covering nearly every aspect of media functions, from journalists' duties to the composition of the National Press Council. The law protected news outlets from outright bans and promised abolition of the notorious press license system once the transition to the New Order was complete.[36] As David Hill notes, during Suharto's first years, "those newspapers which had supported [the regime's] emergence . . . enjoyed opportunities for often robust debate."[37] One cabinet minister compared this period to 1968's Prague Spring.[38]

In the new regime's early years, Jakarta's surviving newspapers were instrumental in imposing transparency on the government—particularly its management of the government oil monopoly, Pertamina. Scandal, fed by leaks, was the primary mechanism. What was arguably the most famous scandal broke in November 1969, when *Indonesia Raya* published a scathing critique of Pertamina's management.[39] The article featured a photograph of the company's director, the Suharto crony Ibnu Sutowo, next to his new Rolls Royce and accused his organization of "waste, inefficiency, and all kinds of irregularities and unjustifiable expenditures."[40] It backed these charges with leaked data documenting nepotism and payoffs as well as the purchase of assets at far above market value.[41]

The controversy that followed saw the beginnings of the logic that would stigmatize political journalism and legitimate the proliferation of media controls. Disregarding the value of investigative reporting in helping avert economic disaster, the regime and several newspapers accused *Indonesia Raya* of adopting a "crusading" style of journalism and began treating it as a threat. After raising suspicions about the paper's motives, the regime began to condemn such journalism as fostering what editor and scholar Daniel Dhakidae calls "the politics of negation."[42]

Despite its unwelcome reception, *Indonesia Raya*'s exposé prompted the government to appoint a special investigative group, the Commission of Four. The commission's findings were damning, confirming the paper's allegations and uncovering tax evasion so egregious that it nearly drove the state into bankruptcy. The 1970 leak of this official report by another major daily, *Sinar Harapan*, kept public attention focused on Pertamina, forcing enactment of a 1971 law increasing the company's payments to the state.[43]

This controversy demonstrated the media's vital role as an early warning system for economic mismanagement. As the government scrambled to cover Pertamina's payments and save it from a bankruptcy likely to bring down the New Order, each revelation was a reminder of the costs of the failed oversight of this most valuable state enterprise. But the revelations also showed scandal's potential to weaken the regime's legitimacy.[44] Even after vowing to clean up the corruption, President Suharto condemned the media's reporting as "excessively mean" and "confusing [to] the society."[45]

Sinar Harapan's leak added insult to injury by usurping the president's authority to present the commission's report in his own way. Lacking any legal basis for sanctions, Suharto pressured the PWI to do what the courts could not—"discipline" the paper for leaking a "state secret."[46] However, the conditions that would eventually make the PWI the "long arm" of the regime were not yet in place.

Little came of this pressure on the PWI. Yet Suharto continued where Sukarno had left off in subordinating other sectors to the presidency. Rather than stifling political activity through raw coercion, he co-opted competing centers of power and reconfigured government institutions, including the parliament. In 1967, he claimed the right to appoint one-third of the full parliament, or MPR, responsible for choosing the president, and more than one-fifth of its lower house, the DPR. Explains Schwarz, "[T]he idea was to restructure the political system in such a way that it could no longer compete with the executive office for power."[47]

The new configuration allowed the regime to engineer elections to insulate itself from political challenge. Testing the system's efficacy, the country held its first post-Sukarno elections in 1971. The new government party, Golkar, won a crushing 63 percent of the vote after the regime rigged the process, requiring all civil servants to vote for Golkar, giving village and district leaders vote quotas, and promising development funding to pro-Golkar districts.[48] New official "rules of conduct," which came to be known as the "Twelve Commandments," advantaged the ruling party further with severe restrictions on public speech during the campaign, barring candidates and the media from criticizing the state ideology, the constitution, and anyone in government. Any speech that might provoke religious, ethnic, or racial antagonisms and glorify either Sukarno's Old Order or the Communist party was also strictly forbidden.[49]

In the election's aftermath, the regime concentrated power further by dissolving all opposition parties to create two new, substantially weaker ones that were barred from representing specific social sectors, thereby reducing representation of the country's extraordinary diversity to just three political parties. While Suharto claimed that he was preventing a return to the divisive politics of the past, the system produced the pliant parliament he sought and turned elections into vehicles for the affirmation of his agenda. "With one and only one road already mapped out," he reasoned, "why should we then have nine different cars?"[50]

Yet civil society remained unsubdued, leaving Suharto's system incomplete. In 1973, *Sinar Harapan* leaked another government report. This time, Suharto found a legal basis to suspend the paper's license, charging it with "contempt of Parliament."[51] But he refrained from banning the paper outright because, notes Dhakidae, civil society, through both the media and university students, could still unite to check executive power.[52]

THE MALARI INCIDENT

The events that ultimately reversed this power relationship began in 1974 with demonstrations culminating in what became known as the Malari incident. During the months leading to these protests, students, intellectuals, and military factions had been growing restive over continued corruption, particularly among senior army officers, certain ethnic Chinese entrepreneurs, and Suharto's wife, Ibu Tien. At the same time, the government was courting foreign investors, especially the Japanese, with incentives to establish capital-intensive factories that were putting indigenous companies out of business, provoking angry protests from displaced workers and sympathetic students. During a visit by the Japanese prime minister, Kakuei Tanaka, in January 1974, thousands of students protested the rising cost of living, corruption, predatory foreign investment, and cronyism. Called the "Disaster of 15 January," or "Malari," the demonstrations became riots that destroyed hundreds of buildings and left at least eleven people dead.[53]

The regime's subsequent repression began a step-by-step depoliticization of civil society, largely through measures that closed off or co-opted the available channels for criticism. Early in his honeymoon period, Suharto had moved preemptively, resurrecting the Sukarno-era Anti-Subversion Law that defined subversion as any "action [that] could distort, undermine or deviate from the ideology of Pancasila or the Broad Outlines of State Policy, or otherwise destroy or undermine the power or the authority of the lawful government or the machinery of the State, or disseminate feelings of hostility or arouse hostility, disturbances or anxiety among the population."[54] Such broad strictures effectively criminalized all critical reporting and most public debate. Following Malari, the regime dismissed officials accused of inciting the students and filed criminal charges against hundreds of civilians.

Suharto also punished the print press by closing twelve news publications, including *Indonesia Raya*.[55] While several newspapers had been critical of corruption and government policy, their gravest transgression in the Malari incident was exposing intraelite divisions. Suharto responded by preventing such divisions from reaching the public in the future.[56] With the 1974 media crackdown, John Bresnan notes, the country lost "a valuable source of information that helped the government to track the outcomes of its policies and articulated and projected elite opinion during a period in which no other institutions were doing so."[57]

In 1975, Suharto continued to depoliticize society while further weakening opposition parties by introducing a "floating mass" policy restricting subregional party activity and limiting the rural population's role in politics to just voting. The logic, Cribb and Brown explain, was to protect people from becoming "distracted from the tasks of national development . . . so that they would be fully responsive to government instruction and advice."[58] A.S. Hikam adds that the policy also aimed to "protect the people from political manipulation by competing parties" and a return to Sukarno-era divisiveness.[59]

By requiring permits for gatherings of over five people, the regime made political rallies outside state control virtually impossible. The government further restricted political parties by limiting issues they could raise and appointing an electoral commission to review campaign materials. Finally, parties had to submit candidate lists to the commission for approval.[60]

Even before this forced depoliticization, elements of the media felt that responsibility for representing citizens had shifted to them. As the daily *Harian Kami* put it, "[W]hat is expected from the press is to function as a 'parliament outside the parliament.'"[61] Dhakidae takes this further, explaining that print press efforts to expose state corruption in Suharto's first years "represented a last ditch defence of the society in a self-imposed task of redefining the interest of a nation in the absence of political parties."[62] In other words, as the legislature lost its ability to check the executive and opposition parties lost the ability to compete fairly in elections, the media became the last institutional vehicle of political contestation.

For four years following Malari, surviving news outlets, though more cautious, managed to retain a critical perspective through favorable coverage of protests by students who were angered by economic mismanagement and fraud in Suharto's reelection in 1977. Student criticism of the president and his family became "the daily menu" of many newspapers.[63] Though the regime was now shielded from serious electoral competition, the print press, giving voice to the students, could still challenge this claim to uncontested power.

In January 1978, however, student protests culminated in a new crackdown when the government's internal security agency, Kopkamtib, disbanded all student councils and ordered temporary closure of seven campus newspapers and seven Jakarta dailies. The interim minister of information, Sudharmono [one name], justified the newspaper closures, explaining that coverage supporting the students threatened to shatter the nation's stability. The military then occupied universities and arrested more than two hundred undergraduates. To depoliticize the students for good, the Ministry of Education introduced a policy called the Normalization of Campus Life, which severely restricted their rights to engage in political activity and placed all campus publications under official control.[64]

To depoliticize the media permanently, Kopkamtib told anxious editors awaiting word on when they could resume publication that they should "just continue to pray." During the crackdown's third week, the agency summoned chief editors individually to participate in what Dhakidae calls "a ritual submission to annihilate any remaining pride by forcing them to wait for a turn."[65] Their submission was cemented with signatures on a pledge that they would (1) take responsibility for protecting national stability and reducing social tensions; (2) protect the authority of the government, avoiding insults aimed at national leaders or their families; (3) declare their readiness to carry out introspection, self-correction, and internal reform; and (4) avoid quoting blacklisted individuals.[66]

The chastened papers fulfilled the mandate of point three by declaring their willingness, in the spirit of Pancasila, to engage in internal reform through editorials that demonstrated humility and contrition. *Kompas* told the government, "We need more time to learn to walk again."[67] Although all papers escaped permanent closure, the ritual submission, Dakhidae writes, did equal, if not greater, damage to the survivors, leaving permanent scars. The most debilitating outcome, he continues, was accepting that their future survival depended on Suharto's whim. These two journalistic showdowns of the 1970s, he concludes, "ended an era of Indonesian political journalism."[68]

LEGITIMATING MEDIA CONTROLS

As he maneuvered to depoliticize society, Suharto was building a comprehensive apparatus for media control that included both formal administration and ideological justification. He constructed a nexus of ministries and regulations that rewarded compliance and punished defiance while reinventing Indonesia's past, reviving principles from the 1945 constitutional debates that valorized cooperation, and invoking the post-1965 slaughters to stigmatize any form of dissent.

The decade after Malari saw the steady accretion of media controls, greatly narrowing the scope of acceptable public discourse. The four-point pledge signed by chief editors in 1978 prohibited criticism of national leaders or their families. The acronym MISS SARA, set out in formal guidelines that same year, specified other areas the media should avoid: anything seditious, insinuating, sensational, or speculative, or that might provoke ethnic, religious, racial, or intergroup (class) tensions.

The peak of re-regulation was the overhaul of the 1966 Basic Press Law in 1982. Like the earlier legislation it modified, this revision contained several clauses promoting freedom of the press. Article 4 guaranteed that the national press would not be subject to censorship or other forms of "muzzling," and Article 8 stated that publications did not need a license (Surat Izin Terbit, SIT) to publish. Article 5 identified freedom of the press as a basic human right. However, the law contained multiple provisions contradicting these three articles while leaving in place the Dutch lèse majesté and "hate-sowing" articles prohibiting speech that might insult the president or provoke contempt toward the government.[69]

The most controversial provision was Article 13, requiring that all publications obtain a Press Publication Enterprise Permit (Surat Izin Usaha Penerbitan Pers, SIUPP). The regime declared that this requirement was distinct from the Sukarno-era SIT and therefore not in conflict with Article 8. Yet the SIUPP was more effective as a control mechanism than the content-oriented SIT it replaced, because of the rewards it offered cooperative publications and potential sanctions for noncooperation.

According to the minister of information, General Ali Murtopo, a primary function of the new SIUPP was to allow the government to block "irresponsible elements" from entering the media market, including "adventurers in press publications that can hamper the growth of a healthy national press."[70] Restricting the number of publications, the argument went, would prevent the entry of too many players into an ostensibly limited market, thereby safeguarding the viability of smaller papers and magazines already struggling to survive. This advantaged existing publications of all sizes by shielding them from new competition, thereby turning the licenses into a lucrative rent, benefiting their owners and reducing incentives to oppose licensing. Nevertheless, there was little security in owning a SIUPP. If the government wanted to silence a publication, the same reasoning that protected its market position could also be used to revoke its SIUPP. By reward and potential sanction, the licensing system created a corrupt bargain that would induce media collaboration for the next two decades.

INCULCATION OF SELF-CENSORSHIP

With these mechanisms in place, 1980s news outlets faced constant threats of bans, while individual journalists and editors could be fired or thrown in jail for reports that caused offense. Yet New Order media control was noteworthy not for its reliance on physical threats or legal penalties but for its effective imposition of self-censorship, a phenomenon Ashadi Siregar described as "almost a disease from which no one is immune."[71] Schwarz attributes this success to the regime's emphasis on preventative rather than punitive measures in policing the political arena.[72] While Malari's most visible repercussion was the closure of twelve publications, the National Press Council's action three years later was more significant in fostering habitual self-censorship.[73] The council also determined that journalists were to cultivate "positive interaction" among the press, state, and society.[74]

Yasuo Hanazaki argues that to survive under the New Order, "publishers and editors were forced to accept the positive interaction concept."[75] Yet, as in any system of control, legitimacy was key to maintaining long-term compliance. In Indonesia's state propaganda, the concept of positive interaction acquired a level of legitimacy among public and media far higher than it might have had with external policing alone. Though dismantling regulatory controls was a priority for media reformers before and after Suharto's fall, the legitimacy of the positive-interaction doctrine would be the more critical legacy to overcome in establishing a new political culture.

This legitimacy had several sources. Sukarno's rule had left a memory of a paralyzed government, lacking the mechanisms to resolve conflicts among parties sharply divided along ideological lines. Suharto's reconstruction of the 1965–66 military-led massacre as a spontaneous eruption of civil war, virtually unchallenged throughout his reign, fostered widespread belief that the country's harmony was fragile and Indonesians were inherently prone to volatility.[76]

Against this background, the New Order agenda to depoliticize the media and broader civil society, to reject the "politics as commander" (*politik sebagai panglima*) mentality of the previous era, held a certain appeal. Evidence of this attitude among news outlets can be seen as early as 1969 in the response to *Indonesia Raya*'s investigative reporting. *Kompas* called this journalism an anti-corruption "crusade," while an armed forces publication, *Angkatan Bersenjata*, accused *Indonesia Raya* of harming the national interest by aiding foreign oil companies in their plot to "destroy" Pertamina. *Kompas*, joined by another large daily, *Pedoman*, also began questioning Mochtar Lubis's motives, sparking a debate over the proper place of the press in politics.[77]

Following the 1978 four-point pledge, statements by *Kompas*'s chief editor, Jakob Oetama, reveal a deeper internalization. "While the Western press prioritized the oversight [function]," in Indonesia, he said, "the 'partnership' between the press and government needs to be supported." Demonstrating his belief in a cultural foundation for such positive interaction, he continued: "The relationship that ties together the press and the government under Indonesian democracy in this era is not submission . . . [nor] opposition, but agreeable discussion, often called 'partnership' . . . based on the spirit of gotong-royong [mutual help], and consensus-oriented deliberation, and kekeluargaan that constitute Indonesia's public character."[78] Over time, this rhetoric of partnership, positive interaction, family-ism, and consensus gave self-censorship increasing legitimacy, while "politics" came to be considered "dirty."[79]

Abetting the legitimacy of government restrictions and self-policing was the regime's construction of the news media as "free but responsible—where freedom includes the right not to publish."[80] This phrase reduced the cognitive dissonance between the constitution's guarantees for press freedom and the Basic Press Law on the one hand, and the tight constraints the news media faced on the other. It also legitimated self-censorship. Within the model of freedom with responsibility, news outlets could nominally use their own judgment, and the Suharto regime cited the absence of a priori censorship as evidence of media freedom. But consequences for wrong decisions could be severe, and daily judgment calls relied on uncertain assessments of appropriateness, making the question of boundaries almost unanswerable. Such uncertainty, combined with arbitrary enforcement of perceived violations, produced a conservatism approaching paranoia among news outlets and a "climate of fear" that became far more stultifying than overt government censorship would have been.[81]

Appropriation of Pancasila

Perhaps the most effective means for giving self-censorship legitimacy, however, was the regime's revival of integralism and its appropriation of the Pancasila ideology to serve a corporatist agenda. The legitimacy of the "positive interaction" doctrine, for example, formalized in the National Press Council's 1974 guidelines, drew on integralist norms articulated by the information minister, Mashuri [one name], during a speech at the University of Indonesia. The press could not, he insisted, behave as if it were separate from society or the state, nor could it contribute to the alienation of other parts of society from the whole, since all belonged to "one great family that [is] supposed to think positively, to live harmoniously, and thus to interact positively"—a logic that made positive interaction itself a subset of integralism.[82] Showing acceptance of this logic within the media community, the publisher Oetama's statements above affirmed the importance of consensus and *kekeluargaan* in determining the proper relationship of the news media to the state.[83]

Another 1985 law on mass organizations required political parties, nongovernmental organizations, and other social groups to register their members with the government and declare Pancasila as their sole ideological foundation.[84] To reinforce this commitment, the government also established a Pancasila indoctrination program for all soldiers, civil servants, students, and professionals.[85]

Through these trends, the meaning and function of Pancasila changed, as Cribb and Brown put it, from a "vague, cover-all slogan whose chief message was that no ideology was to be permitted to dominate Indonesia" to a corporatist ideology with an underlying emphasis on harmony among all societal sectors.[86] In practical terms, this emphasis denied the value of airing differences of opinion or subjecting policy to public debate.

Common parlance reinforced this cultural conditioning as Pancasila metamorphosed to impose corporatist norms on nearly all institutional relationships, redefining whatever noun it modified. "Pancasila democracy" turned the ideal of deliberative democracy into consensus-by-fiat that silenced competing views. "Pancasila industrial relations" envisioned employers in a paternalistic, rather than antagonistic, relationship with workers, making strikes inappropriate for defending labor's interests.[87] A "Pancasila press," in turn, would promote harmony and unity through positive reporting on the nation's leaders, military operations, and government policy.

TRANSFORMATION OF LANGUAGE

The language of public discourse came to reflect the increasingly repressive environment in other ways, most notably through the use of indirect phrasing to soften any reporting that might suggest criticism of the regime. As one editor explained, "We played with words. We didn't call it poverty—it was 'pre-prosperity.' You didn't say corruption. It was 'high-cost economy.' If a minister was caught misusing funds, it wasn't corruption—it was a 'procedural error.'" Prisons became "socialization institutions," while disaster coverage might call a famine a "disturbance in food provision."[88] Reports of soldiers committing human rights abuses blamed "oknum," or "rogue individuals," exonerating those in command.[89]

The passive voice also removed agency, denying readers sufficient information to assign responsibility. Supporting the opacity, acronyms began to overwhelm the simplicity and accessibility of Bahasa Indonesia. Following the news required mastery of a bewildering array of abbreviations often left undefined—FSPSI, SIPPT, SD IMBAS, SBKRI, PTTUN, PPW-LIPI—making information accessible only to those familiar with the current code.[90] English words, in turn, added another layer of obfuscation for anyone outside the educated elite.

More broadly, Hill describes the New Order press's linguistic style as a "cautious, measured, some would say cringing, way with words."[91] Indonesians and foreigners alike derided the media, particularly *Kompas*, the conservative daily that became the country's "paper of record," for this often tortuous language. Yet the primary source of proliferating euphemisms and labyrinthine prose was not journalists but the offi-cials they routinely quoted through a practice called "recording journalism" (*jurnal-isme rekaman*).[92] Todung Mulya Lubis describes this as "a kind of politics of avoidance [that] emerged as a calculated news policy." When the media felt "obliged to publish certain news, it attempt[ed] to rely more on interviews with those . . . regarded as experts, rather than writing about the event directly."[93] Such experts were overwhelm-ingly public officials.

As late as 1995, a survey by the Institute for the Studies on Free Flow of Informa-tion (Institut Studi Arus Informasi, ISAI) of routine coverage from five leading dailies indicated that 20 to 30 percent of front-page stories consisted of "recording journalism": articles composed from a patchwork of official quotes.[94] In coverage of a crisis or particu-larly sensitive matters, such reporting could rise to well over 50 percent. For two weeks following the 1991 army massacre of 271 civilians in Dili, East Timor, *Kompas* filled its front pages almost entirely with official quotes, even in articles unrelated to the mas-sacre.[95] Euphemism and the passive voice also pervaded these official statements, pro-ducing ever more recondite stories that obscured both the event and its investigation.[96]

Following the news thus required audiences to develop special skills of interpretation—the art of reading between the lines, or "reading between the lies," as Aristides Katoppo put it in what became a standard quip.[97] A 1998 history of the PWI noted that readers had to sort out three versions of "truth" in daily reporting: the "press version," the "government version," and the "real version."[98]

Jalaluddin Rakhmat has argued that such euphemism and linguistic sleight-of-hand reflected a deep insecurity among New Order leaders who came to rely on "impression management" to avoid not only public criticism but also honest self-appraisal and responsibility for problems.[99] But the media played along, exhibiting what Katoppo once called "the wisdom of cowardice."[100] While this "New Order-speak" may have originated in government circles, the mass media served as the critical vehicle for its dissemination and normalization.

Some saw this period's media as almost a sentient organism, engaged in advance-and-retreat tactics that avoided sustained criticism but delivered short blows on unre-lated issues in different articles or even publications—a combination called "sniper journalism."[101] If people read between the lines, they might notice that a newspaper apparently supportive of the regime was often critical.

Yet even practices of resistance were problematic, creating habits that may have inspired opposition among critical readers but arguably also reinforced New Order assumptions about the proper role of the media, such as the belief that any critical reporting should be in the form of "constructive criticism."[102] Hill describes the most common method that the media used to fault the government as "criticism by praise," explaining that "headlines never focus on negatives; articles bury barbs in the final paragraphs. Criticisms are rarely written in the active voice, and a circumlocutory passive form of speech disguises disapproval."[103] Similarly, *Indonesia Raya*'s founder, Mochtar Lubis, once described New Order newspapers as relying on "very subtle allu-sions to avoid hurting anyone's feelings, having to be like a snake, circling round and round without ever striking the target."[104]

While this image of cautious subversion challenges the picture of the mass media as, in Hill's words, "the most important area of maintenance and reproduction of the New Order's legitimation," such "guerilla" resistance might have boosted the New Order's power by reinforcing fears of directly challenging the regime.[105] The circling snake may seem lethal but never strikes.

PROFESSIONAL CO-OPTATION

A final legacy of New Order media controls was the government's co-optation of the country's only legal journalists' association, the PWI, transforming it from an organization that represented journalists vis-à-vis the state to one that controlled them on the state's behalf. After serving Sukarno, the association switched allegiance in 1966 and began advancing the New Order's political agenda, first by purging members connected to the PKI. In his study of the association, Togi Simanjuntak argues that this purge marked the beginning of Suharto's "taming" of the journalistic profession. From the PWI's declaration of support for the new regime at its first post-Sukarno congress, he suggests, "one could already see that all activities of professional journalists would be made to conform to the decisions of the Information Ministry." At the same time as this physical integration, "the very thought patterns of many Indonesian journalists . . . would be controlled or absorbed into the New Order's political discourse."[106]

The PWI maintained some independence in the early days of New Order rule, rejecting the continuation of Sukarno's press licensing system as an unconstitutional violation of freedom of the press.[107] More dramatically, when the Ministry of Information required all journalists to become members of the PWI in 1969, the association's Jakarta office head, Harmoko [one name]—later a top member of the Golkar ruling party who became minister of information—strongly opposed it, arguing that nothing in the PWI's charter gave it the right to "create journalists."[108] Divisions among the PWI's leadership, however, soon undermined its capacity to resist such measures, and the association declared its support for the 1969 decree.[109]

Starting in 1975, the Ministry of Information institutionalized the PWI's monopoly over the representation of journalists through a series of decisions that made it the sole legally recognized association, or *wadah tunggal*, for journalists in Indonesia.[110] Simanjuntak explains that the concept of *wadah tunggal*, that there should be only one association to represent journalists, was justified on "the pretext of raising the image and quality of the press."[111] In practice, however, incorporating the PWI into the state effectively consolidated the latter's power over print publications.

The ban on alternative associations, in conjunction with required membership, gave the PWI, and thus the state, considerable power over the media. Applications for publishing licenses required approval from government agencies, such as the Ministry of Information, as well as the PWI and the Association of Newspaper Publishers, a parallel sectoral organization. Moreover, license applications required would-be publishers to list their entire editorial staff, any of whom could be rejected by the PWI. License holders were not allowed to make changes to their staff without advance approval from the association. Finally, "for the rank-and-file journalist," reports Hill, "a PWI membership card [was] theoretically essential, and rejection by (or . . . expulsion from) the Association, for whatever reason, [was] likely to close the door formally on a press career."[112]

The full co-optation of the association, however, occurred through its integration into first the state bureaucracy and then the regime's de facto ruling party, Golkar. Ironically, a key player in this process was the former journalist and future information minister Harmoko, who had been the most vocal opponent of the 1969 decree making PWI membership mandatory. While rising to head the association's central office, Harmoko was also climbing within Golkar. A former PWI vice-treasurer, Atmakusumah Astraatmadja, has argued that these political connections altered

Harmoko's perspective and led the association to become increasingly politicized, or "Golkarized," under his leadership.[113]

In 1993, Harmoko became the party's chairperson in parliament; he also served as minister of information from 1983 to 1998. In moving to the ministry, he gave up the PWI leadership but maintained influence in choosing its officers as well as the members of the National Press Council. Through such machinations, Simanjuntak argues, the PWI came to constitute "the long arm of Golkar."[114]

At first glance, the PWI's story is its absorption into the state apparatus and the larger system that embodied integralism—with four theoretically separate institutions (the Ministry of Information, the National Press Council, Golkar, and the PWI) incorporated in an interlocking matrix of controls under Golkar. At another level, the story illuminates the inner workings of a licensing system that gave all stakeholders, from publishers to working journalists, a rentier status. Unlike the externalized controls of state-run media, Suharto's use of licensing to "create journalists" in privately owned media encouraged them, along with their employers, to buy into a corrupt bargain that limited competition for staff positions by establishing a rent for those lucky enough to gain employment. Government control through licensing over these nominally independent journalists incentivized what were essentially collusive media that strengthened the Suharto regime. More critically over the long term, it also normalized—among journalists and owners—the practice of colluding with the powerful, particularly the ruling party. Combined with the increasing crony ownership of media, this normalization would create a legacy more enduring than the media's bureaucratic incorporation into the formal state apparatus.[115]

Consequences

The consequences of Suharto's gradual "taming" of the media were myriad. The co-optation or elimination of competing centers of power helped Suharto insulate himself from the uncertainties of political contestation. The media outlets that stayed in business cooperated, exchanging their editorial independence for market protection and survival, enabling his regime's escalating corruption and human rights abuses.

With media and parliament tightly managed by the mid-1980s, Suharto amassed one of the world's largest fortunes, which *Forbes* magazine estimated in his last months in power at between $10 and $40 billion, making him the third wealthiest person in the world.[116] Though Suharto began this accumulation during his first years of office, much of the plunder came during the last decade of the New Order, through what was, in retrospect, fairly obvious manipulation of executive powers that might have been checked by a critical media.

The Suharto empire grew, in part, through commissions the family collected as middlemen between the state and those wishing to do business in Indonesia. After Suharto's fall, the Ministry of Mines and Energy identified 159 companies engaged in contracts with the state oil and gas company, Pertamina, that had links to his inner circle.[117] In other lucrative deals, government offices arranged for Suharto's children to purchase shares of state-owned companies at below-market value, which the children then sold for windfall profits.[118]

Finally, presidential decrees allowed Suharto's children and cronies to siphon millions in "loans" from state reserves, such as the Ministry of Forestry and Plantations's

Reforestation Fund. Among other ventures, they financed the 1997 Southeast Asian Games and a multimillion-dollar loan to a pulp paper company controlled by Suharto's golfing partner and former minister of industry, Mohamad "Bob" Hasan.[119] Such decrees also created the monopolies and tariff protections that generated wide profit margins for even the most poorly run of the Suharto empire's companies.[120] A report from the Indonesian Transparency Society released five months after Suharto's fall identified seventy-nine presidential decrees between 1993 and 1998 that directly benefited the business interests of Suharto's family or cronies.[121] Although Suharto was able to bypass parliamentary oversight in issuing most of these decrees, they still entered the public record—almost without mention in the media.

In Suharto's last eighteen months, the costs of spreading corruption and a silenced media would become painfully apparent as the economy collapsed during the 1997 Asian financial crisis, plunging the nation into massive unemployment and widespread hunger. The 1974 and 1978 crackdowns that had muzzled the print press and the country's university students also encouraged the subjugation of broader civil society. These events moved Indonesia into a decade marked by stifled public debate, deepening corruption, and an increasingly quiescent media, subdued further by *Sinar Harapan*'s closure in 1986 and the ban of another publication, *Prioritas*, in 1987. Without critical reporting as a check on the regime's excesses, the following decade saw deepening structural corruption and a steep increase in Suharto's use of the state to enrich his entourage, particularly his children, whose business empires soon penetrated nearly every sector of the economy.

The foundations of control and corruption that came to define the New Order were in place long before Suharto took power. Reviving the ideology of integralism, Suharto augmented these controls by transforming the media into an embedded element of state power, making journalists complicit in his regime's legitimating discourse and inculcating a reflexive self-censorship that helped insulate the regime from political challenge.

Consequently, when the Asian financial crisis hit Indonesia in 1997, the regime's organizing principle was not fair and open competition rewarding the best business plans with government contracts or the best candidates with public office. Rather, it was a system of institutionalized collusion providing the regime and its favorites with the certainties of rigged political, legal, and economic contestation. Cronies enjoyed no-bid contracts and the extraordinary profits afforded by protected markets. Wealthy or well-connected parties in lawsuits enjoyed the assurance of favorable verdicts. Candidates won office not through the uncertainty of free elections but through outcomes engineered by the ruling party's political machine. These overlapping and interwoven elements of patronage politics, shielded from the scrutiny that might have checked them, left the Indonesian economy vulnerable to the shock of market discipline from the financial crisis.

The elaborate media controls developed under the Old and New Orders, from 1959 to 1998, weighed heavily on Indonesia's postauthoritarian media. Reformers, cohering as a community by the mid-1990s, therefore faced two main tasks. The first—challenging regulatory controls—involved a binary opposition between compliance and resistance that would, over time, lead to legal reforms. As later chapters show, the second, even more complex, task was transforming the media's underlying political culture, tainted by collusion, legitimated by ideology, perpetuated through self-censorship, and privileging consensus over accountability.

CHAPTER TWO

DELEGITIMATING AUTHORITARIANISM

We know that when conversation, or the lack of it, becomes a function of total power, words become victims of sacrifice. They may sound free or untied, like sacrificial horses in ancient India, but actually they are guarded and sent roaming to mark out new borders of colonization. And at the end they are slaughtered like any other victim to appease the gods controlling the terror.
—Goenawan Mohamad, "A Kind of Silence," closing remarks at "Pramoedya Unbound," Asia Society, Jakarta, April 22, 1999

On June 27, 1994, some three hundred demonstrators arrived at the National Monument in downtown Jakarta, demanding the Indonesian information minister's resignation and the end of print press licensing. The square was full of riot troops dressed in T-shirts bearing the words "Operasi Bersih" (Operation Cleanup). When the demonstrators reached the Ministry of Information, troops suddenly attacked with riot sticks—bloodying heads, breaking bones, and beating people senseless. As the protestors fled, the troops followed, randomly pummeling those within reach.[1] In this twenty-eighth year of Indonesia's "Pancasila democracy," protestors were calling for neither a religious revolution nor sweeping change but, very specifically, freedom of speech—a demand that would become a defining issue for the reform movement that ultimately ousted President Suharto.

In studying democratic transitions, an initial problem lies in identifying, in retrospect, their genesis in developments often unfolding years before a regime's actual fall. Understanding the media's role in democratization requires first examining precursors of change. In Indonesia, well before the economic crisis and mass demonstrations that forced Suharto from power in May 1998, numerous events took place that would influence the character of the country's later transition. Among these, the sudden ban of three newsweeklies in 1994 was a transformative event for the media and the country that both anticipated Suharto's eventual fall and shaped the agenda of the prodemocracy movement.

THE ERA OF "OPENING"

By the late 1980s, after a quarter century of deepening authoritarianism, the Suharto regime had absorbed nearly all competing centers of power into a corporatist apparatus and had transformed the national ideology, Pancasila, into a tool for stifling dissent. Ongoing newspaper bans—notably the closure of the country's last independent daily, *Sinar Harapan*, in 1986—left a print media paralyzed by self-censorship and onerous regulation.

However, in 1987, Suharto approved a program of economic opening to attract foreign investment, bringing unanticipated consequences as this liberalization slowly extended into the media. When he reversed course with new press bans in 1994, this political trend ended abruptly. Reverberations from this brief liberalization, particularly within the media, would play a crucial, though often invisible, role in eroding acceptance of authoritarian rule and ultimately setting a specific course for the country's democratic transition.

In this same period, a deeper critique of Suharto's use of integralism to legitimate his authoritarian rule began moving from the private to the public sphere, culminating in a major confrontation with the regime. During the decade before Suharto's fall, this critique, progressively widening the scope of dissent, emerged in four significant arenas of public discourse: discussions in intellectual circles, new trends in the print press, political talk shows in the broadcast media, and an unprecedented public trial in the legal arena. Each manifestation posed a significant challenge to the regime's legitimating rhetoric and functioned at a deeper level, disrupting the placid exterior of New Order Indonesia by unsettling its imposed certainties and collusive pacts.

The first level of critique had roots in private conversations among intellectuals who began interrogating the political order, particularly the regime's authoritarian ideology. By the early 1990s, several newsweeklies with an urban middle-class readership were challenging the regime more directly through investigative reporting, critical interviews, and provocative commentary. Broadcast "infotainment" programs, including political talk shows, also emerged to stretch the bounds of permissible discourse, challenging the New Order's integralist norms of public conversation.

As demand rose for more varied media fare, democratic space opened and criticism of the regime grew more overt. Seeking to check these changes, Suharto cracked down on three of the boldest publications, effectively reversing liberalization in the print press. While the bans intensified a climate of fear in surviving newsrooms, they also inspired defiance when two publication owners refused the chance to reopen under conditions set by the regime.[2] Owners, editors, and journalists then used another byproduct of political opening, a new court that allowed challenges to government decisions, to pursue a landmark lawsuit against the minister of information. The unprecedented public trials that followed fractured the manufactured consensus of the New Order, prompting an implicit repudiation of print press licensing by two courts. In a surprising break from the past, Suharto failed to engineer a predetermined outcome, thereby unleashing an uncontrolled narrative and inspiring a resistance movement that would outlive the regime.

INTERROGATING INTEGRALISM

One of the earliest challenges to the regime's ideological underpinnings emerged among academics. By the 1980s, despite multiple press bans and policies to depoliticize universities, critiques of the New Order were percolating in intellectual circles. Their influence was narrow but significant, not fanning public dissent but slowly discrediting the regime's justifications for its system of control.

This discourse took particularly salient form in an academic thesis by Marsillam Simanjuntak, a medical doctor and former student activist. Submitted to the University of Indonesia Faculty of Law in 1989, the thesis probed the corporatist foundations of integralism, the statist ideology first articulated by Supomo during the 1945 constitutional debates. Simanjuntak observed that from the mid-1970s, integralism had enjoyed a state-sponsored renaissance under Suharto but refuted its legitimacy as a founding doctrine, noting that the term did not appear in the 1945 constitution. The framers, he argued, in rejecting monarchy and hereditary rule, had also rejected key integralist assumptions, particularly the principle that sovereignty belonged to the state and not the people. Given this historical reality, he asked why integralism had regained status as a founding philosophy under Suharto.[3]

The question was rhetorical and necessarily academic. But with the New Order at the peak of its authoritarian power, Simanjuntak's thesis posed a profoundly subversive challenge. Primarily, it questioned the foundations of the doctrine legitimating New Order controls. In teasing out integralism's Hegelian antecedents, Simanjuntak produced a trenchant critique of its antidemocratic tenets and normative authority, warning that Suharto's adherence to Supomo's original vision would "carry serious consequences" for democracy and the people's sovereignty by fostering "totalitarianism and authoritarianism."[4] Perhaps most damningly, Simanjuntak noted both Supomo's and Sukarno's 1945 laudatory references to the Third Reich and imperial Japan as models for emulation, documenting fascist principles' influence on integralism's conception.

Though the treatise gained only limited circulation, intellectuals took up its tenets as they started engaging the constitutional questions it raised in open debate. In 1989, the year Simanjuntak submitted his thesis, the news media, most notably the magazines *Forum Keadilan* and *Majalah Persahi*, began airing these critical views. In November, the daily *Kompas* convened a three-day seminar on the critique, giving Simanjuntak the opportunity to attack regime-sponsored academics who had given integralism constitutional legitimacy. In August 1990, *Forum Keadilan* followed up with a twenty-one-page spread highly critical of the ideology, quoting numerous public intellectuals. Among these was Goenawan Mohamad, editor in chief of the news magazine *Tempo*. Mohamad shared the growing skepticism over Supomo's understanding of Indonesia's history, casting doubt on the latter's assertions of immutable cultural foundations for integralist governance.[5] A month later, *Tempo* gave Simanjuntak another platform to attack the regime's repression of rights and enjoin the people to "clobber" any government attempt to "block, hamper, or impede the channels of free expression."[6]

Seizing the momentum, some forty prominent public figures, including Simanjuntak and Abdurrahman Wahid, the leader of the Muslim association Nahdlatul Ulama, united around this emerging critique and convened the new Democratic Forum in 1991. The regime responded by breaking up their meetings with force, rejecting, as Robert Hefner put it, the need "for a pro-democracy organization in a country that had already achieved a 'Pancasila Democracy.'"[7] Officials then intensified Pancasila indoctrination programs, inserting integralist doctrine in textbooks for Pancasila and Citizenship Education and expunging references to human rights from tertiary school curricula.[8]

SIDELINES: SUBTLE SUBVERSION

Despite this crackdown on debate over the nature (and future) of Indonesian democracy, the media continued pushing the boundaries of political opening, and critiques of integralism took diverse forms. One was Mohamad's widely read weekly column in *Tempo*, Catatan Pinggir (Sidelines), which challenged, albeit obliquely, the regime's integralist rhetoric through content and through its distinctive discursive form.

At several points, resonances between Simanjuntak's treatise and the ideas in Sidelines are clear, particularly in discussions of the New Order's denigration of individual rights. In a column boldly titled "Human Rights," for example, Mohamad quotes Sukarno's announcement during the constitutional convention of 1945: "We are drawing up the Constitution with the sovereignty of the people (rakyat), and not the sovereignty of the individual (individu)." Mohamad then asks, "Why the people and not the individual?" and presents Sukarno's explanation: it is "the rights of liberty of man-as-individual 'that [have made] the countries of Europe and America full of conflict, unrest, class struggle and war.'" But Mohamad rejects this logic, asserting that "Sukarno was surely mistaken"—an implicit critique of President Suharto's similar denunciations of individual rights.[9]

In a different column, "Family," Mohamad's defense of individual rights is prefaced by a deconstruction of the family metaphor Suharto used to popularize integralist doctrine. The discussion concludes, "the country is never a family, and a head of state can never be like a real father to the citizens."[10] Similarly, in "Monsters," Mohamad describes his epiphany "that not everyone agrees with Professor Supomo, who . . . described the 'state' as like a wise father to its children, the 'people.' After all," he continues, "hasn't the experience of the young Republic shown that the 'father' can act wrongfully toward the children?"[11]

Published in February 1992, "Han Sui," a column about three children whose father was tortured and killed, opens by asking: "Where do rights come from?" Echoing Enlightenment theories of natural law, Mohamad speculates: "From God, one opinion would say. . . . [Rights] have existed since our existence began and therefore cannot be taken away." His commentary becomes more poignant as he recounts the children's story. The voice of the oldest, Han Sui, haunts him, making him "always ask," when thinking of rights, "why it was that Han Sui seemed to have no right to make an issue of the death of his father—and why I felt that I had no right to tell it." He reflects on debates over rights that have inspired statements like that by the American Association of Anthropology: "What are held to be human rights in one society may be regarded as anti-social by another people." At a philosophical level, he acknowledges, "'West' is indeed 'West' and 'East' is 'East.' How complicated." Yet for Han Sui's father, and others suffering a similar fate, "the matter is not abstract: they have been tortured."[12]

"Han Sui" ventures an implicit critique of the "Asian values" discourse popularized in the 1990s by neighboring autocrats Lee Kuan Yew of Singapore and Mahatir Mohamad of Malaysia to justify authoritarianism throughout Southeast Asia. Other Sidelines columns focus more narrowly on "Indonesian values" and Suharto's promotion of a distinctive "Indonesian democracy" to legitimate suppressing rights. Recalling Sukarno's command "Indonesia, choose your own genuine democracy!" that prefigured Suharto's call for a "Pancasila democracy," Mohamad predicts "the twentieth century will probably end in disillusionment. . . . [T]his original democracy," he explains, "with its distinctive style—this better alternative that we have hoped for—is extremely difficult to find."[13]

Other pieces can be read as defenses of Western democracy. In "Management of Conflict," for example, Mohamad again addresses fears that liberal democracy breeds conflict—a phobia, he says, shared by all totalitarian regimes that view conflict as "the rider on the horse of the apocalypse, bearing chaos." Indonesians are "afraid of conflict," he explains, "because conflict, in our situation of never-ending poverty, brings with it risk, and risk is not something that we can take." Indonesians learn from childhood to avoid behavior that might inflame conflict. Consequently, they "tend to react to conflict with a lack of self-confidence." Democracy, by contrast, is reassuring because it admits "conflict as an integral part of us, even when we are all within one fishpond." Democracy is not the source of conflict; democracy is, rather, "the management of conflict."[14]

In these and other ways, the Sidelines columns repeatedly challenged the regime's disparagement of the West and individual rights. Yet a defining element of Mohamad's style is not consistency nor conviction but a certain ambivalence. He is being cautious, often critiquing the regime indirectly and evading the immediate threat of censorship. But he is also employing a distinctive genre of writing he identifies as the "essay" that presented its own challenge to Suharto's use of integralism to maintain control over public discourse.

Mohamad does not describe the essay genre as specifically subversive, but identifies elements that seem to run counter to integralist norms. The genre's "use of language and allegories," for example, "disturbs journalistic linearity" and stands "against the acronym-studded columns of bureaucratese" pervading New Order public discourse.[15] Quoting Theodor Adorno, Mohamad says that the essay "starts not with Adam and Eve but with what it wants to talk about . . . and stops when it feels finished rather than when there is nothing more to say." Its substance, in a sense, *is* its form—a form with "the quality of someone in an abstracted mood aimlessly sauntering on the sidewalk." He concludes, "Precisely because it is largely an insubstantial undertaking," the essay is "polemical," and thereby "stands against [the government's] mania for result and regularity." It offers a means to "circumvent [authoritarianism's] utilitarian demand for predictability."[16]

Taking Mohamad's analysis further, part of the Suharto regime's "mania for result and regularity" was its demand for continual renewal of consensus, for resolution and elimination of doubt or lingering queries. As Jennifer Lindsay notes, Sidelines ignores this requisite, rarely delivering a sense of resolution, much less consensus. What these columns offer instead is the opposite—not conflict, nor even disagreement, but simply questions. "Are human rights the same as Coca-Cola?" Mohamad asks in 1977.[17] Later he asks, is the state—"as Hegel said—the defender of the common good?" and "What does the individual mean to society, in fact?"[18]

Such questioning alone was potentially subversive in a culture where, as Yusuf Bilyarta Mangunwijaya (Romo Mangun) says, asking questions had become taboo.[19] Yet the ambiguity in Sidelines also presented a deeper challenge to the regime. One can imagine the New Order's culture of consensus as spherical, enveloping public discourse within an orb in which conflicting views and unresolved questions were smoothed over—"phased out," in Suharto's words.[20] Tellingly, the Indonesian word for "unanimous" is, in fact, *bulat*, meaning "round" or "spherical."

The perplexities of Sidelines resisted absorption into this self-contained public sphere, suspended instead in tacit opposition to demands for order and certainty. The columns' meandering propositions, the questions they raise but do not answer, became, in a sense, like threads hanging loose from an otherwise smooth surface of consensus and resolution. If one were to tug at these threads, Mohamad suggests, the regime's very legitimacy might begin to unravel. "A slight tear in the cloth," he notes, "quickly can be seen as a gaping hole."[21]

Apart from the specific ideas the columns carried, their essay form, marked by wandering ruminations and resistance to resolution, posed its own challenge to the Suharto regime, or at least its authoritarian certainties. More broadly, the columns began questioning New Order controls on public discourse justified by both integral-ist rhetoric and the regime's construction of the nation as inherently unstable.

INTERVIEW TALK SHOWS

A related trend was developing in broadcasting during this period, as commer-cialized television popularized a different array of news and entertainment genres. Imported primarily from the West, the programs expanded the range of fare avail-able to viewers and the boundaries of shared culture. Several also posed potentially subversive challenges, through both form and content, to the Suharto regime's inte-gralist discursive norms and their legitimating logic. Foremost among these was the political talk show, pioneered on television by Wimar Witoelar's *Perspektif*, which, like Sidelines, attempted to cultivate the critical thought stigmatized under authoritarian-ism.[22] In the rise of the talk show, we see again the intentional use of a generic form to perform political resistance. But we also see a genre taking on a life of its own, as *Per-spektif* inspired imitators—shows that risked regime backlash but, bolstered by their profitability, continued multiplying long after *Perspektif*'s cancelation, even, in some cases, contrary to the pro-regime biases of the broadcasters airing them.

Prior to commercialization, the state-controlled network, Televisi Republik Indo-nesia (TVRI), had been the sole provider of television fare, functioning primarily, in the words of Philip Kitley, as a site for manufacturing "consensus and convergence through corporatist structures and policies."[23] In its promotional literature, Kitley notes, the network emphasized "the spirit of unity" and rejected "sensationalism and exploitation of violent, destructive or negative incidents." Consequently, state news under Suharto, as under many authoritarian regimes, became little more than cover-age of ribbon-cutting ceremonies marking the inauguration of various development projects, delivered by anchors sitting woodenly against a monochromatic backdrop.[24] More broadly, Kitley explains, news programs became rituals for the promotion of an idealized order, a veritable "container for human action," supportive of the regime.[25]

In the late 1980s, TVRI's monopoly ended as citizens gained access to foreign television through cross-border satellite transmissions. The foreign fare, Kitley notes, troubled Suharto early on for its potential to undermine New Order values. Children's animated films were seen to reflect Western values by downplaying the collective, assigning higher value to "aspects of individualism." Commercials, designed specifi-cally to "*differentiate* between individuals and groups," worked against the integralist imperative to merge all individual identity into a cohesive collective identity. Finally, increasingly popular Western soap operas were problematic both in form and content. With their ceaseless churn of conflicts and family infighting, the shows presented portraits of domestic interaction radically divergent from state-promoted images of the harmonious family. Their recurrent cliffhangers, holding audiences through com-mercials and from one episode to the next, deferred the expected narrative closure of state-sponsored dramas and instead normalized conflict without end.[26]

Suharto, wary of commercial television from the beginning, banned its entry into Indonesia for most of his reign.[27] But with parabolic antennas multiplying on roof-tops, blocking access to foreign programming proved increasingly difficult, politically and logistically. The regime first tried, with little success, to counter the influence of these shows by producing competing, ideologically acceptable versions on Indonesian television—notably the TVRI-produced serial drama, *Keluarga Rahmat* (*The Rahmat Family*).[28]

Another way to compete with foreign television, favored by Suharto's children and cronies anxious to expand their business empires, was to launch domestic commercial stations producing their own Indonesian versions of foreign shows. Yielding to pressure, Suharto began granting commercial television licenses in 1987, first to his oldest son, who launched RCTI (Rajawali Citra Televisi Indonesia), and then to his oldest daughter, his foster brother, and two close business associates.[29] The expectation was that the new stations, as loyal members of the national "family," would promote Indonesian values and regime interests.[30] Most critically, the government-run TVRI would retain its monopoly on news, which would be rebroadcast by the private stations throughout the day.

In practice, however, the private stations responded to commercial imperatives and soon became a Trojan horse in the New Order's control over the public sphere. Concerned less with state mythologies than with financial profits, they found ways around regulations barring their own news production. RCTI began airing "soft news," or "information" shows that gradually expanded coverage to include segments on crime, "everyday issues," and sometimes more controversial matters, such as slum clearances and the business exploits of Suharto's youngest son.[31]

These quasi-news shows, paralleling similar trends in radio, not only pushed the boundaries of allowable content but also took risks in introducing unscripted interviews to commercial television.[32] Then in 1993, with stations seeking ways to increase their audiences, Witoelar went further by convincing producers at SCTV to launch a full-length interview talk show, *Perspektif*, modeled on CNN's *Larry King Live*.[33]

Witoelar imagined that even though it aired on a regime-connected station, such a show could be liberating in breaking through the fear and obfuscation he saw paralyzing the public sphere.[34] Of the era's many possible approaches to the talk show, Larry King's staid, nonconfrontational format of one-on-one conversation may have seemed the least threatening to Suharto's New Order. Nonetheless, King's show possessed the key elements of the talk show genre that represented, in Indonesia's authoritarian context, real change to a television landscape heretofore marked by highly controlled, predictable, monologic, and often didactic speech.

Despite King's apparent "ordinariness," Witoelar later argued, his genius— being "curious" rather than contentious—lay precisely in delivering the authentic and unplanned.[35] In contrast to many US talk shows that were staged to frame brief moments of unscripted spontaneity, King required his celebrity guests to drop the safety net of prepared questions and risk a full half hour of genuine conversation.[36] Following this model, Witoelar described the unedited spontaneity of his own show as its greatest strength. "I emphasize to each guest," he explained, "that *Perspektif* discussions do not use lists of questions of any sort. Conversations are allowed to take their own course."[37] Guests on *Perspektif* were generally public figures, and discussions tended to hew closely to each person's particular realm of expertise. Regardless of topic, the ultimate goal was to lead guests just outside their comfort zones, generating unrehearsed "emotions and thought" and thereby producing the dynamic required to transform talking heads into dialogue.[38]

In his book on *Perspektif*, Witoelar expands on the importance of genuine dialogue in holding audience attention, pointing out that "conversation cannot just be two people taking turns."[39] The latter merely grants guests a platform for holding forth—an example of what Edwin Jurriëns calls TVRI's "monologism disguised as dialogism."[40] In Witoelar's words, such conversation is "boring." For the speaker, "it is no problem, but s/he does not know the TV sets in people's homes are all being shut off." What viewers really seek, Witoelar argues, are unscripted conversations. These conversations can be about anything—the key is that people think for themselves when they feel they are "part of the conversation," that "there is something still unresolved to be discussed."[41]

Perspektif delivered open-endedness, spontaneity, and ventures into the taboo, creating the commercially profitable tensions missing from government-produced talk shows. Finally, the show added one more element that violated the regime's preference for resolution and closure. Like the foreign soap operas that proved so popular with Indonesians, Witoelar's show kept audiences tuned in through commercials by using conversational cliff-hangers—breaks at dramatic moments in an unfolding dialogue.

A 1995 *Perspektif* interview with author Seno Gumira Ajidarma, "Expression through the Short Story," exemplifies these elements.[42] What begins as a discussion of literature, focusing on an intriguing, if grotesque, short story by Ajidarma, veers into perhaps the most sensitive political terrain of the Suharto era—Indonesia's military pacification of East Timor, the site of an ongoing struggle for independence. This topic alone pushed at the boundaries of acceptable speech, creating the kind of tension that made the talk show format alluring, if not addictive. The conversation that followed, however, committed a deeper transgression by raising questions about freedom and its proper limits and then leaving them unanswered, dangling in suspension for audiences to contemplate on their own.

Witoelar begins by providing viewers with a summary of Ajidarma's short story, "Telinga" ("Ear"), about a beautiful girl who gets a package from her boyfriend, who is at war, and finds a severed ear "with blood still on it." Presently, "she receives another ear, then several, more and more," and begins "stringing them up in her house, blood still dripping." Ajidarma confirms that these ears belong to people who have heard something forbidden, presumably from "spies." Witoelar then asks, "OK, but why do more and more [ears] come—because more and more people are having their ears cut off? More and more people hear news that's not allowed to be heard?" Perhaps, Witoelar speculates, as "more and more people want to rebel . . . the eyes must be cut out, or simply the whole head [until] eventually his girlfriend is sent a head." He ends by asking: "OK, what does all this mean?"[43]

Until this point, the interview concerns a story about a soldier, a girlfriend, and severed body parts. The story's implicit suggestion that soldiers of any nationality are committing actual atrocities is a risky topic of conversation. But an Indonesian audience would be in suspense, wondering whether Ajidarma will admit to criticizing Indonesia's military. Defying this anticipation, Ajidarma neither confirms nor denies, but instead ventures into even more dangerous territory: "Yeah, it's like this. As far as the concrete idea, why an ear, that is because of a news story published by [the magazine] *Jakarta-Jakarta* sometime around 1992 that shocked me. At that time, the governor of East Timor . . . Mário Carascalão, received guests who were going to file a complaint. The article wrote that when four youth entered, two of these did not have ears. Cut off . . . These two lines hooked, stuck [*nyantel*] directly into my head."[44]

Through this conversational twist, an invisible political line has been crossed. Ajidarma has broached the taboo subject of East Timor and implied that the military is censoring information or committing atrocities—or both. Yet in keeping with the conventions of the show, Ajidarma still avoids any direct challenge to the Suharto regime. For viewers asking whether he wrote the story to condemn either the military or government censorship, his answer is simply that he was inspired by the oddity of the situation. "So there are people who like to cut off ears, what does this mean?" the writer asks. "What's the point? [Do they] think people whose ears are cut off like it?" He ends by saying: "I was amused by this, amused by sadism, by cruelty. And so this story." Witoelar responds: "So, humor then."[45]

As Witoelar closes with the simple word, "humor," sidestepping the author's political agenda, the viewer is left with unanswered questions about ears and blood. Are soldiers committing atrocities? Is information being censored? What is it the government does not want the East Timorese, or other Indonesians, to hear?

At this juncture, the interview is producing an effect similar to that created by Goenawan Mohamad in his *Tempo* essays, raising serious questions but leaving them unanswered. But then Witoelar goes further. With these disturbing implications still in the air, the discussion takes a new turn as he asks Ajidarma about freedom of speech—another subject that would have been particularly touchy at that time. "We are already free," Ajidarma says in a surprising reply, and therefore "do not have to ask for freedom." In this simple statement he takes the conversation in a philosophical but fundamentally subversive direction, casting freedom as a natural right, not something to be sought in increments from a controlling government. He is challenging the Suharto regime's preferred understanding of freedom as conditional, a privilege to be granted or revoked. He then raises the stakes even higher by saying, "We earn our freedom as far as we struggle for it"—words that could almost be a call to arms.[46]

Just when the conversation seems headed toward a controversial debate over "asking" versus "struggling," Witoelar suddenly, cheerfully, pauses for commercials, promising to pick up the same point after the break. Arguably a more natural breaking point would have been just after his concluding statement on Ajidarma's severed ear story: "So, humor, then." As in other interviews, however, Witoelar pauses in the middle of an intensifying discussion, a choice that no doubt served SCTV's economic imperative to hold the audience through the commercials. But then he never returns to the original subject, and therefore never finishes the conversation.

Why? Fear of government ire is plausible, but insufficient, given the temerity of the entire interview. Witoelar has offered another explanation for such decisions. In his memoir *Stealing Clarity from Confusion*, he says he would consciously steer his interviews away from conclusion so as "not to claim the guest/host was smarter than the viewer." Rather than delivering answers, he sought to encourage viewers to think for themselves. "Otherwise," he explains, the show "would become indoctrinating."[47] As with Mohamad's column Sidelines, the unanswered questions became threads left dangling in the country's public discourse rather than tied neatly back into the state's ordered construction of social reality.

OPENING'S CLOSURE

While political opening in the early 1990s helped transform public conversation from scripted to unpredictable, the regime's tolerance for this transformation was short-lived. In September 1995, upon learning Witoelar's next guest on *Perspektif* would be Mochtar Lubis, the publisher of the banned newspaper *Indonesia Raya*, government officials forced SCTV to cancel the entire program. A key factor was the topic of the offending interview: a crackdown on the print press that had begun the previous June with the government's unexpected decision to ban three popular news-weeklies, *Tempo*, *Editor*, and a tabloid named *DëTIK*.

The context for these bans was both political opening and an intraelite power struggle spilling into the media. After four years of relaxed controls, news outlets overall had become increasingly aggressive in reporting and commentary. But the boldest were exposing intraelite conflict and publishing exposés based on leaks from this same elite. The youngest of the three banned publications, the weekly tabloid *DëTIK*, had made its name through interviews with critics from within the military, revealing growing resentment over Suharto's promotion of civilians to posts traditionally reserved for generals. Just before the bans, *DëTIK* had published a leak that implicated the president's family in the Bapindo banking scandal.[48]

With this confrontational reporting driving *DëTIK*'s rapid growth, *Tempo* and *Editor* also became increasingly aggressive in their coverage of elite conflict.[49] All three began vying for interviews with political insiders critical of the government. They also reported on cover-ups protecting the regime, presidential succession, and the major loan scandals of the early 1990s. The relative freedom they had to report such stories was an encouraging sign that the government was serious in its political opening.

In the spring of 1994, however, a controversy developed between a Suharto favorite, the minister of research and technology, B. J. Habibie, and the finance minister, Mar'ie Muhammad, over Habibie's purchase of thirty-nine former East German warships. The transaction had sparked heated protest from Germany's parliament over concerns that Indonesia would use the ships for human rights abuses in outlying provinces. In Jakarta, Muhammad repeatedly rejected Habibie's requisitions for expensive renovations, which required millions of dollars above the purchase price.[50]

Significantly, as Duncan McCargo notes, news of this conflict emerged not from investigative reporting, but from infighting among the political elite.[51] *Tempo* broke the story, but by June, most of the national media had followed. Reflecting the regime's rising displeasure, the information minister, Harmoko, summoned the editors of the Jakarta press to accuse them of denigrating the nation's ideological principles and prohibit any further reporting on the warship purchase.[52] Yet media attention to the ministerial infighting continued.

On June 9, Suharto delivered a sharp reprimand during a speech opening the harbor for the new fleet. In an indirect reference to the media, he stated angrily that those "who half-understand the issue, then declare their opinions, have . . . pitted parties against each other . . . to the point of threatening [the nation's] stability." He concluded, "If they cannot be warned, we will have to take steps."[53] Following this speech, rumors began circulating that the government would act on this threat. Angered by *Tempo*'s report, Habibie prepared to file a million-dollar libel lawsuit.[54] But before he could follow through, on June 21, the Ministry of Information passed a decree revoking *Tempo*'s SIUPP, along with the permits of *Editor* and *DëTIK*.[55]

The ministry claimed to be shutting down *Editor* and *DëTIK* for technical violations. *DëTIK*, it said, had become a political tabloid, publishing general news with a license for crime reporting. But there was no clear explanation for *Tempo*'s closure.[56] When pushed, Harmoko stated that *Tempo*'s reporting had the potential to ignite ethnic, religious, racial, or intergroup conflict, citing three articles and a political cartoon published years earlier.[57]

The announcement sparked immediate protest. Journalists, students, artists, and members of the wider public joined employees of the banned weeklies in unprecedented demonstrations. One observer described a thousand people, "ignoring their own safety," protesting peacefully for days in "the biggest demonstrations held in Jakarta during the last ten years." Similar protests took place in other cities, while "hundreds of non-governmental organizations, alternative youth and students' organizations, [and] labor unions, along with domestic and foreign intellectuals" issued written declarations protesting the bans.[58]

Leading intellectuals, such as academic Ashadi Siregar and artist Emha Ainun Najib, were among the most outspoken. Siregar proposed caustically to one group of protesters, "If we're not allowed to report honest news, then let's just consume lies."[59] Demonstrators carried placards condemning the bans and Harmoko's role. After several failed attempts to meet with Harmoko, one group sent 150 balloons to Allah to highlight the absurdity of their inability to communicate with their government.[60] At a time when people were routinely arrested for such criticism, letters expressing disapproval of the government's actions poured into media outlets, while intellectuals submitted unsolicited articles condemning the bans.[61] Several advocacy organizations sent faxes directly to President Suharto, the vice president, the attorney general, and the armed forces commander, arguing that the bans would instill a sense of powerlessness among members of the media, hampering their ability to inform the public.[62] In a bold televised statement, attorney Todung Mulya Lubis called the bans "a naked violation of the law."[63]

"HISTORY HAD BEGUN TO CHANGE"

Objections to the crackdown on *Perspektif* were equally impassioned and equally ineffectual in influencing the regime.[64] At first, surviving outlets spoke out. The daily *Media Indonesia*, in an unusually frank editorial, stated, "A climate like this is truly unhealthy. The press must not be paralyzed by constant fear." The editorial warned further that the Ministry of Information should not take for granted its power to revoke licenses as a weapon for winning conflicts with the media. Abuse of this authority, it declared, "is too expensive for democracy and openness."[65] In an editorial for the magazine *Panji Masyarakat*, Arbi Sanit praised the print press as a channel for conveying the public's "aspirations" and cautioned that the bans would prove dangerous in a country where demands for greater democracy had grown "increasingly loud and clear."[66] On the streets, demonstrators from other media outlets held up banners saying, "Next Will Come Our Turn to be Banned."[67]

In the week following the bans, protests around the country received wide coverage. But by the next week, the media stopped this reporting after the Ministry of Information warned editors to "cease blowing up the issue." Such coverage, the ministry explained, was making people "confused."[68] These warnings were effective, and observers reported a climate of fear developing in the nation's newsrooms. Surviving outlets ultimately redoubled self-censorship, prompting one journalist to compare the industry to an "ostrich."[69]

But in a surprising break from the past, the bans' victims—publishers, employees, street hawkers, even subscribers—fought back, staging protests, filing lawsuits, launching an independent journalists' association, and inspiring new opposition to the regime. In attempting to reassert control, the regime inadvertently set the stage for further confrontation in the courts, on the streets, and inside university campuses.

Although this pressure was insufficient to reverse the government's decision, commentators believed that the heated response by fellow media and public alike marked a significant change from past resignation. *Tempo*'s editor in chief, Goenawan

Mohamad, noted that past bans had led media outlets to lie low until the confrontation passed, afraid of becoming the next target. Some survivors would even applaud the government's decision, happy to have fewer competitors. Then, "isolated and undefended," the banned publications would proceed to the Ministry of Information—the same ministry that had shut them down—and beg for a new license, fear driving them to pay large bribes to facilitate this process. Their licenses restored, the banned publications would start up again, "as if their feet were not bound and their mouths not gagged." Each time, Mohamad concluded, "amnesia follows, even forgives," allowing "the arbitrariness of what happened [to escape] the loathing that might prevent it from occurring again."[70]

This time, Mohamad said, the bans led to neither silence nor the usual "amnesia, trembling, and indifference." Instead, protests emerged across Indonesia, marked by a new determination that made the government nervous. Observing continued defiance in the face of violent crackdowns, Mohamad concluded that anger over the bans had become "public property." History, he said, "had begun to change."[71]

"Democracy Is Dead"

Exploring the sources of this anger and determination illustrates the extent to which history had begun to change. A key element was profound disappointment. The 1994 media closures hit when expectations for the future were running high in Indonesia amid economic growth, political stability, and foreign investment. Despite its brevity, Suharto's new policy of "openness" had made a tangible impact and generated widespread hope that this political trend would continue.

Dashed expectations in any situation can be a powerful impetus to action. In Indonesia, belief that the country was developing into a first-world democracy, able to compete in a global economy, was accompanied by tense anticipation that Suharto, already in his early seventies, might allow a peaceful transition to a new administration in the next election.

Alarm over the regime's backtracking gave the bans significance beyond concerns over displaced workers and lost investments. Foreign observers expressed disbelief and warned of diminished investor confidence and damage to Indonesia's reputation abroad.[72] The most anguished statements, however, came from Indonesians who flooded media offices with calls and letters expressing everything from bewilderment to outrage. One fax read, "I am disturbed, sad and sick at heart. Opening and democracy are already gone in this beloved Republic." In an emotional speech before demonstrators, writer Umar Kayam asked, "If we still have bans, where is democracy?" As if answering this rhetorical question, a banner held by demonstrators read, "Democracy is dead."[73]

The bans also hit as a new middle class was emerging, anxious for opportunities in a climate of economic growth and political openness. Poised precariously between the wealthy, well-connected elite and the country's vast underclass, the middle sectors of society depended on the level playing field and legal protections provided by the rule of law. *Tempo* itself had become symbolic of the middle class's rising status as the country developed into a modern nation. Historian Onghokham (Ong Hok Ham) argued that the public's reaction represented "an important test . . . which validates the role, function and mere existence of the middle class in Indonesia," since this class "needs information, [and] will never develop in a totalitarian system."[74] That class, reported Arief Budiman, included "intellectuals, students and other fighters for democracy [who] took to the streets."[75] In sum, one of the most important breaks from the past was the public's reaction: viewing the bans as an attack not only on the publications but on the entire middle class that threatened to derail the country's political and economic advances.

Another factor inspiring the new determination was the surprising response of the banned publications' owners and personnel, particularly from *Tempo* and *DëTIK*. Only five days after the ministry's decree, starting the cynical pattern that Mohamad describes, regime cronies prepared to turn the closures into market opportunity.[76] The regime's restriction on the number of publishing permits, to about 264 in 1991, made media ownership a lucrative rent for privileged members of this de facto publishing "cartel," including *Tempo*. Consequently, new investments in the publishing industry required acquisition of an existing license.[77]

Seizing the chance to gain access to this protected market, Habibie was planning to not only sue *Tempo* but also require that it replace its editors and shareholders before resuming publication.[78] According to several sources, he told *Tempo* representatives to approach one of Suharto's closest friends, timber tycoon Mohamad "Bob" Hasan, to discuss a business relationship.[79] The information minister, Harmoko, moreover, was reportedly soliciting cash bribes and company shares for granting new print press licenses, while Suharto's son-in-law, Prabowo Subianto, was also maneuvering to control *Tempo*.[80]

A few weeks after the bans, the government offered *Tempo*, *DëTIK*, and *Editor* the opportunity to obtain new licenses, conditional upon replacing management and shareholders.[81] In effect, the newsweeklies faced the same political and practical choices that had confronted all print media since 1978. To stay in business was to compromise. To resist would allow their publications to "die" and be replaced by others that were crony controlled.[82]

Each journal responded differently to the dilemma. Few among *Editor*'s staff joined the protests staged by *DëTIK* and *Tempo* employees, some expressing irritation at being grouped with the others in the crackdown.[83] Recognizing the closures as a market opportunity, *Editor*'s representatives accepted the government's conditions for a new SIUPP. By January 1995, *Editor* resumed publishing under the new name *Tiras* with start-up capital from the minister of manpower, Abdul Latief—increasing regime ownership of media.[84] By contrast, *Tempo* and *DëTIK* sent delegations to meet with legislators and members of the National Commission on Human Rights (Komnasham) to demand, unsuccessfully, restoration of their licenses.[85] In the following weeks, *Tempo*'s parent company, PT Grafiti Pers, dispatched representatives to negotiate a new license, and the magazine's board of directors talked with outside investors.[86]

Ultimately, however, *Tempo* and *DëTIK* refused to replace their editors or shareholders. Nor did they sign any statements promising to circumscribe future reporting to obtain new licenses. *DëTIK*'s largest shareholder, Surya Paloh, who suffered an earlier ban in 1987, said he was "tired of building up papers only to have them banned or beaten around."[87] Mohamad, noting that *Tempo* employees had held a majority of shares since its inception, refused to allow his magazine to be taken over by new investors and bridled at pressure to replace senior staff. "Personally," he commented, "rather than give in to such pressure, it would be better if *Tempo* were not revived."[88]

After these decisions, *Tempo*'s largest investor negotiated with regime crony, Bob Hasan, to launch a new publication called *Gatra*, and thirty-five of *Tempo*'s journalists joined the staff.[89] An even larger group, however, rejected this opportunity. They worked instead with Mohamad to start a new magazine, but were ultimately denied a license.[90] Similarly, Eros Djarot and his *DëTIK* staff launched a parallel publication using an existing license, but immediately lost it when the Association of Indonesian Journalists (PWI) withdrew its approval.[91]

THE FOUNDING OF AJI

Reacting to the regime's apparent success in crushing independent journalism through this maneuvering, many of the country's leading journalists broke precedent in another way, joining forces to take a principled, potentially dangerous stand for media freedom. A key factor prompting this development was the response of the PWI—the country's sole journalists' association. Rather than defend the journalists it claimed to represent, the association stated that it "could understand" the government's actions.

A book on the bans explained that it was this final betrayal by the PWI that gave birth to the new professional association, the Alliance of Independent Journalists (AJI).[92] While few, if any, had expected the PWI to condemn the Ministry of Information outright, its response seemed excessively deferential. On July 5, 1994, a delegation claiming to represent the country's journalists delivered a letter of protest bearing 357 signatures to the PWI's leadership.[93] In early August, the group launched a campaign called Aksi Tagih Janji (Action to Demand Fulfillment of a Promise) to hold the PWI to account.[94] Finally, on August 7, more than eighty journalists and *Tempo* columnists met outside Jakarta in Sirnagalih to plan a course of action for continued opposition to the bans.[95]

The meeting produced a statement, later called the Sirnagalih Declaration, that condemned "all forms of interference . . . which limited freedom to express opinion[s] and the rights of citizens to obtain information." It further rejected the *wadah tunggal* "concept of a sole authorized professional association for journalists."[96] This last clause, backed by the founding of AJI, was an attack on the PWI's right to be that association. But it also challenged the New Order's entire system of corporatist control through sectoral representation.

The new association "promised to be more in solidarity towards colleagues that face bans." It rejected the paternalistic attitude of owners claiming to have a greater responsibility to protect their employees' jobs than to protest crackdowns.[97] Their real responsibility, AJI argued, was to take a tougher stance against the bans.

While AJI's official membership would remain small under Suharto, journalists now had a professional association with no compromising links to the government.[98] AJI also began publishing an underground newsletter—*Independen*—that soon claimed ninety members of parliament as regular subscribers.[99] In the news vacuum left by the closure of *Tempo*, *DëTIK*, and *Editor*, *Independen* developed a loyal following for covering sensitive issues, such as the sizable media interests held by the information minister, Harmoko, and his relatives.[100]

Within a year, however, police raided AJI's offices, seizing its computers, files, fax machine, money, and correspondence. On March 17, 1995, plainclothes intelligence officers arrested three members for violating Article 19(1) of the Basic Press Law, which prohibited the use of the media for private interests, and criminal statutes outlawing defamation of the president, the spread of hatred against the government, and instigation of animosity among the public.[101]

A criminal court sentenced the three AJI members to long jail terms, and the attorney general banned *Independen*. The PWI then aided this government crackdown by attempting to ostracize all those associated with AJI—evicting thirteen journalists who had signed the Sirnagalih Declaration from its Jakarta branch and creating a blacklist of those associated with the three banned publications. Within a few days, the PWI's Jakarta branch summoned editors from eight publications deemed "critical" to demand that they fire the thirteen journalists it had just expelled.[102] As this pressure forced AJI members from their jobs, a new slang word, *mengAJIkan* (to AJI-fy), gained currency as a term for blacklisting someone for defending freedom of the press.[103]

LANDMARK LAWSUIT

Under these pressures, support for AJI moved deeper underground. Simultaneously, however, the movement began fighting on another front: in open confrontation with the regime through the courts. The challenge began in September 1994, when Goenawan Mohamad and forty-three *Tempo* journalists used a new state court, the Pengadilan Tata Usaha Negara (PTUN), to sue the minister of information for damages from the arbitrary revocation of their license.[104] A few weeks later, more than a thousand media employees, newsagents, and subscribers filed their own class-action suits at the Central Jakarta District Court, calling for judicial review of the 1984 licensing decree on the grounds that it conflicted with the Basic Press Law. The first suit was lodged by more than thirty nonjournalist employees of *Tempo*, joined by several newsagents and street hawkers, demanding compensation for two years' lost income.[105] The second group consisted of nearly one thousand former subscribers and 121 journalists who had worked for the closed publications. The subscribers complained that the bans had robbed them of "the right to obtain objective, quality information," and the journalists argued that they had lost their ability "to fully pursue their function as agents of social control (over government), as is demanded by the Basic Press Law."[106] In addition to their call for judicial review of the 1984 licensing decree, this group also demanded nullification of the 1994 decree revoking the licenses of *Tempo*, *Editor*, and *DëTIK*.

The Central Jakarta District Court refused to hear any cases, but the PTUN—a court created specifically to allow citizens to challenge government decisions—accepted the *Tempo* journalists' suit. News outlets barred from reporting on street protests now moved to cover this developing story. As public attention shifted to the suit, the case became a "national obsession."[107]

The *Tempo* journalists protested lost income and arbitrary decision-making that ended their jobs without due process. But they also claimed damages from less tangible losses, including their constitutional right to freedom of expression, "the opportunity to enrich the life of a nation," and loss of a forum "to disseminate objective information, channel the public's aspirations, and [impose] constructive social control."[108]

Plaintiffs were further emboldened by the moral imperative of their cause. In a collection of essays explaining the decision to sue, Ahmad Taufik, one of the AJI members later sentenced to three years in prison, explained, "Maybe because my hopes were wrong, anger in me burst forth like a tidal wave. . . . Banning is the murder of press creativity, the revocation of information choice needed by the public."[109] Although several expressed an almost quixotic faith in the courts, many plaintiffs insisted that winning was not what mattered, with larger principles at stake. Most wanted merely to demonstrate that the government could no longer "make decisions as they please, without going through legal channels."[110] One editor joined the suit to oppose the "desecration of human rights" represented by the bans.[111] Others spoke of a desire to gain moral strength, regardless of the outcome. The hunger for this strength, a photographer said, must overcome the fear of losing one's livelihood.[112] Editor Ivan Haris admitted that he was also "afraid of being beaten by soldiers, and worse, then being arrested and tortured." Yet, like others, he felt an obligation to future generations, asking, "What will my children say if I stay quiet?"[113]

Over Harmoko's strenuous objections, the PTUN launched eight months of deliberations. Until the final hour, the *Tempo* plaintiffs' expectations were low. The day before the decision, Mohamad learned from a court insider that the judges planned to rule in the minister's favor.[114]But on May 3, 1995, the chief justice, Benjamin Mangkoedilaga, announced that Harmoko had acted in an unlawful and "authoritarian" manner by revoking *Tempo*'s license.[115] The verdict, which nullified the revocation, was based on the finding that canceling the license did amount to banning the magazine, something expressly forbidden in the Basic Press Law. The court ruled further that Harmoko had not followed due process, escalating suddenly from a first to a final warning.[116]

The plaintiffs were nearly as shocked by the victory as they had been by the bans; their disbelief was redoubled by the stipulation that the minister must cover their court costs. Skeptical of "the independence of Indonesia's judicial institutions," Mohamad and the other plaintiffs were slow to grasp that the judges were ruling in *Tempo*'s favor. "For almost an hour we listened," he said, and "only then [did we understand]. . . . I shook hands and had my hand shaken, hugged and was hugged by our lawyers, countless friends, including those who sobbed openly, or tried to hold back tears."[117]

The ruling prompted loud cheering and applause, with Mohamad praising Chief Justice Mangkoedilaga and his colleagues, reminding supporters, "what has to be celebrated is not the victory of [the plaintiffs], but rather the courage of the three judges."[118] He also cautioned their ruling would become "an empty victory unless we can make use of it. . . . If the press shows a small portion of courage, it will take up this issue. Now is the time to do it."[119]

While none of the surviving media outlets answered Mohamad's call to push for abolishing the 1984 decree, most gave prominent coverage to the PTUN's ruling.[120] More cause for celebration came when the plaintiffs, facing an appeal by Harmoko, won another surprising victory before the next-highest court, the Pengadilan Tinggi Tata Usaha Negara Jakarta. But on June 13, 1996, the Supreme Court overturned both lower court rulings, finding that the information minister's cancelation of *Tempo*'s license did not conflict with the Basic Press Law.[121] The high court not only nullified the PTUN's landmark ruling, it also left news outlets in a weaker legal position than before, leading Mohamad to declare: "Today is [the day] the Supreme Court legalized repression of the press."[122]

The ruling denied the plaintiffs the opportunity to appeal. Despite the historic nature of the two-year battle, *Tempo*'s license revocation was final. While the magazine's demise inspired emotional eulogies proclaiming its irreplaceability, in the end, the country adjusted, and the new, crony-owned *Gatra* had little trouble filling its predecessor's slot at newsstands.

To eradicate the memory of *Tempo*'s lower court victories, the regime pressured the media to stop covering the subject, barring SCTV from airing an interview with the PTUN's now-famous chief justice.[123] Other intimidation followed. Armed with Article 510 of the criminal code, stipulating that groups of more than five people must obtain a permit for a public gathering, police began raiding seminars, religious events, lawyer-client conferences, and even a poetry reading.[124] Surveillance cameras and undercover officers kept track of who was attending potentially subversive events. In one instance, police jailed a pregnant woman simply for speaking up about a police assault on another woman at an earlier rally.[125] Intelligence officers also arrested a British schoolteacher for attending a discussion on the bans, subjected her to a harsh three-day interrogation, and eventually deported her. "Although I didn't utter a word during the meeting," she said, "my attendance seemed . . . sufficient evidence that I was a 'subversive.'"[126]

Challenging "Unity and Stability"

With this heightened repression, anger over the bans faded from public view, challenging the proposition that history had begun to change. Yet there were several indications that the new "determination" Mohamad described did not fade but grew stronger, at least among a subset of journalists.[127] One was ongoing defiance despite repercussions. The renegade journalists' association, AJI, continued its activities even after the government outlawed *Independen* and sent three members to prison for involvement in its publication. Among these activities was the unrepentant launch of *Suara Independen*, which, like its predecessor, was unlicensed and critical of the government. Former *Tempo* staff also revived an old magazine, *D&R* (*Detektif & Romantika*), owned by *Tempo*'s parent company, and turned it into a critical political weekly.

Other journalists started producing unlicensed opposition publications on the internet, while email-based news networks kept activists informed and in contact.[128] Mohamad directed his attention to new projects, including establishing the election watchdog the Independent Election Monitoring Committee, which arguably posed a greater threat to Suharto than the suppressed magazine, *Tempo*. Finally, *Tempo* itself stubbornly persevered online through *Tempo Interaktif*, which was not only more openly critical of the regime than its print version but also an important information source for its audience of students and other activists.

Wimar Witoelar exercised similar defiance. With its cancelation, *Perspektif* was effectively banned as a television show. But it gained new life elsewhere as outraged fans convinced Witoelar to take it on the road, hosting live shows in cities across the archipelago. Witoelar also syndicated a radio talk show, *Perspektif Baru*, carried by stations nationwide, and published in more than two dozen regional newspapers. Producers were pressured to stop broadcasting the new program, demonstrating Suharto's continued control.

More significantly, *Perspektif*'s influence continued to expand through imitation as similar talk shows on radio and television survived and new ones were launched, gaining in number and popularity even on stations owned by Suharto's family.[129] When the regime forced stations to pull interviews or even, as with *Perspektif*, cancel entire programs, these decisions simply blocked one broadcast or ended a single show.[130] They could not reduce the appeal of the format or effectively discourage other producers from launching similar shows. In effect, profit repeatedly trumped fear.

With continued resistance, a new rhetoric of opposition emerged, tying together a growing activist movement committed to long-term change. The lawsuit itself set in motion an educational process within the media and among the public by widening knowledge of the law and its manipulation by Suharto, inspiring discussions of the bans' legal basis. For example, the plaintiffs' charges of arbitrariness called attention to the government's ability to circumvent due process, sparking criticism that the regime had bypassed the courts and disregarded the National Press Council. All these accusations discredited New Order claims to have developed Indonesia into a *negara hukum*, or "country based on the rule of law."

The government's unity rhetoric began generating an increasingly articulate counterdiscourse that subverted the integralist "Pancasila jargon" used against free speech.[131] One commentator asked, "In a country of Pancasila democracy, why is speaking the truth outlawed?"[132] Others challenged the claim that bridling the media was necessary to national stability, and some charged the government with undermining the very stability it claimed to protect.[133]

Though cautious, these statements resonated with the unspoken hypothesis developing among elites that the bans signaled the beginning of the New Order's decline. Some anticipated that a stifled media would allow increased corruption, which in turn would weaken the government.[134] Taking a broad view, historian Onghokham warned that the closures would discourage investment and thus damage economic development, an important pillar of Suharto's legitimacy.[135] The most explicit prediction of the regime's decline, however, came from columnist Julia Suryakusuma, who warned, "Fear generates fear. The need to revitalize fear through bannings and beatings indicates that the powers that be are beginning to fear their own shadows. In the end, the bannings are a tacit recognition of the power of the word, and a tacit admission of the fragility of power, in an era of succession in Indonesia."[136]

In hindsight, it is tempting to view Suharto's fall in 1998 as the realization of such predictions. However, if we examine the interval between the Supreme Court ruling against *Tempo* and Suharto's resignation two years later, any causal links between the media bans and the regime's downfall seem tenuous. After the Asian financial crisis undermined Suharto's legitimacy, the triumph of the *reformasi* movement might seem a logical consequence of the country's growing rejection of New Order repression and the regime's own internal decay. The 1994 bans did contribute to both, sparking new opposition to authoritarian controls and accelerating this decay after the media lost virtually all ability to impose accountability on public officials. "Suharto lost power in May 1998 partly as a result of his failure to listen to criticism and his intolerance of dissenting voices," argues Duncan McCargo. "The policy of 'killing the messenger' seen in the 1994 bannings marked the beginning of the end for Suharto and the New Order."[137]

Growing access to foreign broadcasts and the privatization of television also helped undermine the regime's system of control. The new genres of this period, from soap operas to political talk shows, contradicted the New Order's integralist vision by challenging its immersion of individuals into a collective national body, its celebration of the family as a harmonious microcosm of the nation, and its assertion of consensus as the aim of all public conversation. These challenges helped unravel the regime's tidy integration of individual, family, and nation.

On the other hand, Suharto had already survived three decades of rising corruption, low transparency, and periodic surges in opposition. During Asia's financial boom before 1997, even with high levels of graft, wealth in Indonesia increased and the middle class grew, reinforcing the regime's legitimacy. Its success over three decades in absorbing independent civil institutions also left would-be reformers with few channels for protest. While frustration among Indonesia's media-oriented middle class did explain, in part, the unprecedented public protest against the closures of

Tempo, *DëTIK*, and *Editor*, this sector was still neither big enough nor rich enough to launch a serious challenge to Suharto's New Order.

Nor is it clear that, before the crisis, the middle class had sufficient will to try. As late as August 1996, after a regime crackdown on demonstrations in support of opposition leader Megawati Sukarnoputri, Goenawan Mohamad was still pessimistic over whether any group in Indonesia was willing, much less able, to sustain a reform movement. He felt the middle class was too enamored with the country's new, rampant materialism to become the base of such a movement.[138] It took an economic crisis a year and a half later to jolt a dormant, scattered opposition into action. As Vince Boudreau argues, it was the fiscal crisis, specifically the 1997 currency devaluations, that "produced what no opposition had so far achieved: coordinated and multisectoral grievances across Indonesia."[139]

Nevertheless, the regime's bans sparked a movement focused on media freedom and independence that would significantly influence an emerging anti-Suharto opposition and, in turn, the character of the transition that followed. The bans forged a new solidarity between the shuttered publications and the public they had served. Mobilization continued through the fledgling AJI, whose members defied the government prohibition of alternative professional associations and continued to influence the reform process after Suharto's fall. Equally important, *Tempo*'s lawsuit opened government policy to unprecedented legal scrutiny that posed a new challenge to one pillar of the regime's legitimacy—its claim to the rule of law. The two court rulings for the plaintiffs, in turn, were a surprising break from the predetermined outcomes characteristic of the country's judicial process. Though the regime ultimately won the case in the Supreme Court, the lower court verdicts were, in effect, the most public defiance of the fixed contests of authoritarianism in decades. These verdicts also foreshadowed protests against the engineering of the 1997 national elections and the subsequent demonstrations that pushed Suharto from power.

Perhaps the most significant unexpected development, however, was the refusal of *Tempo* and *DëTIK* to accept the government's terms for reopening, eschewing the corrupt bargain of engineered contestation in yet another arena—the country's protected media market.

These decisions, moreover, established an important precedent in the press community as *Tempo* and *DëTIK* owners gave up a share of that market to lay bare the unspoken reality of media ownership: survival, with its lucrative rewards, required collusion. Democratization, by contrast, would require independence. *Tempo* and *DëTIK*, along with the members of AJI who risked blacklisting and prison, set a standard for both owners and journalists, eroding the rationalizations that had made capitulation in the name of survival acceptable.

The legal dramas that followed also shook the regime and subjected its media controls to unprecedented scrutiny. Over time, the lawsuits gave a nascent democratic opposition the opportunity to develop both a reform agenda and a coherent critique of the regime's use and abuse of the law. The sustained resistance of the new activists mobilized by the 1994 bans also influenced later events, helping normalize and even legitimate dissent. Even before Suharto stepped down, it was already unfashionable to be anti-*reformasi*. By the time Suharto's successor, B. J. Habibie, began arresting demonstrators in late 1998, serving time in jail had become a badge of honor, making this new repression unsustainable. Moreover, groups fighting for media reform allied with other activist networks, including student supporters of opposition figures. Significantly, when students began the demonstrations that evolved into a broad-based reform movement, they regularly communicated with and sought advice from activist elements in the media.[140] When the demonstrators finally forced Suharto from office, freedom of speech was one of their chief demands.

While we can only speculate on how a reform movement might have progressed without the galvanizing effect of the 1994 bans, the protests and lawsuits they inspired became important forums for articulating both a platform of opposition to the New Order and a critique of the regime's system for controlling information. Although there is no clear causal connection between this public outcry and Suharto's eventual resignation, the anger had a transformative effect in the emergence of a new consciousness among Indonesians who later formed the backbone of the *reformasi* movement.

In the process, the bans helped pave the way for democratic reform to become the dominant agenda of those seeking change after the Asian financial crisis hit. This new core of activists was dedicated to freedom of expression and fair contestation, positioned to influence the direction the country took as it weathered the collapse of the New Order.

CHAPTER THREE

SUHARTO'S FALL

Because we are silenced
and you never shut up . . .

Because we are threatened
and you impose your will by force . . .
therefore we say NO to you.

Because we are not allowed to choose
and you can do what you like . . .

Because we wear only sandals
and you use your rifles freely . . .

Because we have to be polite
and you have the prisons . . .
therefore NO and NO to you.

Because we are like a flowing river
and you are a stone without a heart
the water will wear away the stone.
—W. S. Rendra, "Water Will Wear Away the Stone,"
  delivered at Trisakti University, in response to
  the shooting of four students on May 12, 1998

With the ban of newsweeklies *Tempo, Editor,* and *DëTIK* in June 1994, Indonesia's brief political opening came to an abrupt close, and constraints on civil society tightened. The country had begun to change, but there was little evidence in the public sphere. Throughout his reign, President Suharto's legitimacy had rested on providing order, stability, and economic development. As long as he appeared to deliver on these grounds, opposition forces had difficulty questioning his authority. But in 1997, the Asian economic crisis hit Indonesia with devastating force, undermining his regime's claim to all three accomplishments and creating an opportunity for a student-led reform movement to challenge his continued rule.

This chapter tells the story of this challenge and Suharto's subsequent fall from power. But it also looks critically at the complex and often contradictory nature of the media's relationship to the student movement. Complicating its reciprocal nature was a division between mainstream outlets, which remained cautious to the end, relying upon the sacrifices of student demonstrators to win them greater freedom of expression, and more critical publications forced underground by the bans, such as *Tempo,* whose martyrdom and continued resistance set a standard for students as well as fellow journalists. This dissident movement, led by media activists, further influenced students via collaboration with nongovernmental organizations that themselves recruited from campuses.[1] By branching out into new terrain, such as poll watching, the movement also made fair elections a primary focus for students and other reform leaders. Through these relationships, both freedom of expression and transparent electoral contests became key objectives for the emerging *reformasi* movement—clear priorities that carried over into the postauthoritarian period and had a significant impact on the trajectory of the transition.

Movement Before the Movement

In the early 1990s, national debate over the media's proper role in a specifically Indonesian democracy regained prominence; it was then silenced in the crackdown following the 1994 bans. With the approach of the 1997 parliamentary elections, repression escalated to include raids on public gatherings, particularly those related to election monitoring, human rights, and the opposition leader and daughter of President Sukarno, Megawati Sukarnoputri.[2] A pro-Megawati speech at one demonstration, for example, brought a member of parliament nine months in prison for "insulting the President, armed forces and other public institutions."[3] Such prosecutions were also noteworthy for reviving the draconian antisubversion law banning "any activity which directly or indirectly can influence state policy and its implementation."[4]

In this climate, the most visible mediators of public discourse—the news outlets that had survived the bans—became cautious to the point of a painful self-censorship. Following the bans, *Tempo*'s editor in chief, Goenawan Mohamad, had foreseen a process of "forgetting"—that is, widespread acceptance of a corrupt bargain that would "make the victims lose their will to say 'no' to the injustice" of the government's actions. "High wages, job security, opportunities to advance—along with fear—can indeed mesmerize," he said, "until the victims themselves lose their perspective as victims, until what's fair and unfair get mixed up in their heads, until they themselves become irritated at being reminded of how important self-worth, solidarity and freedom are for humanity."[5] Indeed, the bans quashed the critical reporting fostered by the regime's earlier opening, and much of the media continued on as if nothing had changed.

But beneath this surface of compliance, journalistic resistance continued in ways both symbolic and concrete to shape future events. In concrete terms, such dissent enlarged the activist community who first articulated the civil rights discourse that would be critical to the later transition. The defiant stance of this community had symbolic import that valorized individual sacrifice and risk-taking in the name of a greater cause—freedom of speech—and elevated that cause to become a defining issue of the emerging, student-led *reformasi* movement.

Much of this valorization came through ascent of a rhetoric of political martyrdom introduced by victims of the media bans and later picked up by students and mainstream media. First voiced in street protests, this discourse grew in reach and force during *Tempo*'s protracted legal battle to reverse revocation of its license. Ultimately, through language and symbolic action, *Tempo*'s advocates transformed an impersonal institution, a suppressed newsweekly, into a still-warm body that represented the hope of greater democracy.[6] In effect, they transmuted a banned magazine into a national martyr.

With ritual and rhetoric, the press community mourned *Tempo* as an anthropomorphized icon of media freedom. The journalist Ahmad Taufik, for example, called the ban "murder" and convened funeral rites for the newly embodied victim, using the Islamic prayer Salat al-Janazah in a public ceremony.[7] Media activists, students, and artists also incorporated rituals of mourning into protest activities, such as carrying funeral biers in marches and flying flags at half-mast.[8] Finally, activists wrote essays that were tantamount to eulogies, mourning the passing of the magazine as if it were a martyred leader.[9]

Daniel Dhakidae, a writer for *Kompas*, injected perhaps the most vivid language of martyrdom into this discourse, calling the bans an "execution . . . a felony, the murder of the right to speak, murder of the right to do business." He condemned the regime's methods for seducing owners of banned publications "to sell their souls for new permits."[10] Students urged the owners not to capitulate, and *DëTIK*'s and *Tempo*'s refusal to compromise won them widespread recognition as heroes, inspiring songs and poems, notably "The Ballad of Unchecked Arrogance" by Y. Soesilo—a somewhat sardonic but ultimately upbeat tribute to *Tempo*.[11]

More broadly, a discourse of courage and principle evolved out of the court battles and prison sentences that protesters now faced. Young journalists in particular were suddenly prepared to sacrifice their careers in order to, as Goenawan Mohamad put it, "say 'no' to kissing the ass of Satan." Students, a significant share of *Tempo*'s readership, embraced this discourse, summarized in the magazine's manifesto *Why We are Filing Suit*: "Freedom indeed carries expensive risks, but the choice is not negotiable."[12]

While casting *Tempo* as a murdered martyr was a key discursive element in the resistance, more concrete was the stubborn perseverance of the renegade journalists' association, AJI, in meeting, recruiting, and launching an underground press with its newsletter *Independen* and, after *Independen*'s ban, *Suara Independen*.[13] Internet providers made the online publication of *Suara Independen* and a half dozen other illicit news bulletins possible through email lists such as Apakabar, reaching thousands of readers and surprisingly difficult to censor. In mid-1996, police did arrest a university lecturer for printing and xeroxing an emailed report, and the military assigned intelligence agents "to search office by office, editor by editor" for the culpable internet-based journalists.[14] Nonetheless, this clandestine circulation continued, frustrating government intervention.

Former *Tempo* journalists also maintained resistance through above-ground publications.[15] Without awaiting official clearance, in March 1996, one group launched a web publication named *Tempo Interaktif*, whose first edition broached the sensitive subject of a privileged "national car" project run by Suharto's son.[16] Other *Tempo* alumni revived a defunct entertainment magazine, *Detektif & Romantika* (*D&R*), transforming it into a hard-edged news weekly. Journalists blacklisted for their AJI affiliation continued their careers by writing for *D&R* under pseudonyms. Although its chief editor once insisted that "we did not design the magazine to oppose the government," the initials *D&R* came to stand not for *Detektif & Romantika* but rather for *Demokrasi & Reformasi*—the catchwords of the anti-Suharto movement.[17] Living up to its opposition image, the magazine developed an increasingly adversarial stance yet escaped government censure for nearly its entire run before Suharto's fall.

Nongovernmental organizations—such as the Legal Aid Institute, the Indonesian Forum for the Environment, and the Institute for Policy Research and Advocacy—also maintained their activist campaigns through this period. Though their programs had clear political overtones, the state made few attempts to restrain them. One member of the Institute for Policy Research and Advocacy speculated that the regime's tolerance reflected their minimal impact beyond Jakarta's narrow political elite, amounting to little more than "turbulence in a glass" that kept middle- and upper-class activists occupied in harmless opposition activities.[18]

Simultaneously, the media's contribution to the reform movement was weakened by the regime's repression, which split their community in the wake of the bans. Above-ground, mainstream news outlets complied with Suharto's dictates, muting their criticism and miming the regime's rhetoric. In the expanding underground media, however, resistance deepened, spreading a spirit of defiance adopted by student demonstrators, and ultimately many mainstream journalists, just three years later.

These underground networks formed through efforts by Goenawan Mohamad to "channel money" from sympathetic funders and "spread the struggle," thereby generating projects that both employed blacklisted journalists and united them with other activists. Out of this convergence came the Institute for the Studies on Free Flow of Information in early 1995. Inside a few unassuming buildings behind a small café in South Jakarta grew a community, known as Komunitas Utan Kayu, that served as cover for the institute's operations. Mohamad set up an artists' gallery next to the café and eventually a small theater behind, all part of the "'subterfuge" that obscured this group's main activity: the digital dissemination of information blocked by the regime. In back rooms, from a server secured via encryption funded by the Asia Foundation, the Utan Kayu community distributed online newsletters, strengthening opposition networks at home and abroad.[19] Behind the café's modest facade there was, moreover, a latter-day salon that strengthened the intellectual core of the opposition movement. At the café's tables, journalists and activists met in clouds of clove cigarette smoke for conversation and debate.

From a realpolitik perspective, the underground news bulletins, D&R's provocative reporting, and even AJI's ongoing defiance arguably were just so much "turbulence in a glass" and would have remained so had it not been for the 1997 economic crisis. Yet apart from increasing the flow of information, these activities also strengthened inter-activist connections, knitting together a wider movement as media reformers collaborated with emerging nongovernmental organizations. Together, these groups supported presidential candidates to replace Suharto, organizing "free speech forums" specifically for the exercise of pro-opposition speech. They also served key rhetorical functions that kept the community united and focused, modeling continued resistance in the face of defeats and intimidation. Finally, though few in number and operating deep underground, these activists repeatedly performed the courage that others—journalists and nonjournalists alike—sought in themselves. "It's very symbolic just to say that we will never succumb," explained Goenawan Mohamad, adding, "Courage, like fear, is contagious."[20]

It is impossible to know how far such contagion in Indonesia would have spread without the 1997 economic crisis. It was decidedly slow in reaching the majority of media professionals, even on the eve of Suharto's fall. But there is little question that courage did sweep through the nation's universities in the mid-1990s as students took the lead in the reform movement. The economic crisis may have emboldened them, but their courage was also influenced by Tempo's earlier fight against the regime's media bans and the rhetoric of political martyrdom this struggle inspired.

CONSEQUENCES OF A STIFLED PRESS

For nearly four years, 1994 to 1997, a confluence of factors—fear of another crackdown, crony ownership of media outlets, and government control over the only legal journalists' association—stifled editorial criticism and discouraged reporting on the regime's excesses. Freed from oversight, the regime entered a period of virtually unrestrained and ultimately self-destructive economic plunder that culminated in the 1997 economic crisis. The bad debt and losses to the state facilitated by presidential decrees and media silence eventually led the country into financial collapse that drove Suharto from office and challenged earlier assumptions about the thinly disguised authoritarianism of "Pancasila democracy."

The oppressive climate after 1994 limited the media's ability to impose economic transparency, facilitating the acceleration of corruption. Unrestrained by press or parliament, Suharto used the state apparatus to enrich cronies and family, above all his children, whose business empires penetrated nearly every sector of the economy. In July 1997, *Forbes* magazine estimated Suharto's wealth at between $10 billion and $40 billion, making him the third-wealthiest person in the world after the sultan of Brunei, Hassanal Bolkiah, and King Fahd bin Abdulaziz Al Saud of Saudi Arabia.[21]

Most mechanisms enabling such accumulation were technically legal. Through presidential decrees, for example, Suharto forced companies to pay levies or donate to his "charitable" foundations and simultaneously allowed his children and cronies to siphon millions in loans out of state reserves. In one blatant instance, the Ministry of Forestry and Plantations made a multi-million-dollar loan to a pulp paper company controlled by Suharto's golfing partner and former minister of industry and trade, Bob Hasan.[22]

The president's decrees also created the monopolies and tariff protections that generated wide profit margins for even the most poorly run crony companies. Among the seventy-nine such decrees between 1993 and 1998, Decree No. 42 of 1996, for example, exempted a car company owned by Suharto's son from tax and duties on the Korean-made vehicles that it imported.[23] Though Suharto was able to bypass parliamentary oversight in issuing most of these decrees, they still entered the public record. Yet almost no mention of them appeared in the media.

As often occurs in a rent-seeking economy, these deals advantaged the president's entourage while disadvantaging the state and ordinary Indonesians. An audit by PricewaterhouseCoopers revealed that at the end of Suharto's reign, the state oil monopoly Pertamina alone had been losing billions of dollars per year to corruption and inefficiency.[24] A study by the World Bank found that at least 30 percent of Indonesia's development budget over the previous twenty years had evaporated through such deals.[25]

The Suharto empire also grew through commissions the family collected as middlemen between the state and virtually anyone who wished to do business in Indonesia. After Suharto's fall, the Ministry of Mines and Energy identified 159 companies that held contracts with Pertamina through links to Suharto's family or cronies.[26] In other lucrative deals, government offices arranged for Suharto's children to purchase shares of state-owned companies at below-market value, which the children then sold for windfall profits.[27]

The key vehicles that family and cronies used to accumulate and then launder their fortunes were the dozens of foundations, exempt from taxes and external review, that the regime had created over the years. Established to support charitable causes, such as mosque construction or school scholarships, these foundations controlled several billion dollars by the late 1990s. They grew through small deductions from the salaries of all civil servants beginning in the 1970s and "donations" from state banks or entrepreneurs seeking business opportunities. Larger foundations sometimes acted as banks offering low interest rates for state-sponsored projects. They also funneled money into political campaigns or private accounts as part of Suharto's patronage system and financed the purchase of controlling shares in hundreds of companies for regime insiders.[28] Again, there was virtually no media coverage of these activities.

The most flamboyant of the president's six children, Hutomo Mandala Putera, or "Tommy," owned majority shares in a golf course in Ascot, England; one-half of a share in a $4 million yacht in Darwin, Australia; and 60 percent of the Italian sports car company Lamborghini.[29] Domestically, Tommy owned controlling interests in several businesses, including an airline, the Humpuss conglomerate, and a company granted exclusive tax concessions to produce a "national car." The estimated $200 million of assets owned by Suharto's middle daughter, Siti "Titiek" Hediati Harijadi, included interests in a Burmese cement factory and a large railway company in Turkmenistan. Before his father fell from power, the estimated worth of Suharto's oldest son, Sigit Harjojudanto, was $450 million. By far the largest empires were those of Suharto's eldest daughter, Siti Hardiyanti Rukmana, or "Tutut," and his second son, Bambang Trihatmojo. Tutut's estimated worth in 1997, according to one source, was $2 billion—accrued largely from a vast conglomerate spanning petrochemicals, banking, and television. The estimated worth of Bambang was even greater—$3 billion in 1997—with a business consortium, Bimantara, holding over one hundred subsidiaries with interests including automobiles, oil, and telecommunications.[30]

An investigation by the Ministry of Forestry and Plantations found that Suharto's family and friends owned or controlled nine million hectares of rain forest, an area roughly the size of the main Indonesian island of Java.[31] Despite international coverage, Jakarta's above-ground news outlets managed a knowing avoidance of the spreading corruption, in effect becoming complicit in this ongoing concentration of power.

THE ASIAN ECONOMIC CRISIS

Between the 1994 bans and mid-1997, most news coverage of the Suharto regime steered away from criticism and practiced a local variant of "development journalism" that gave a sense of continuing growth. Although support for certain opposition leaders, particularly Megawati Sukarnoputri, grew in boldness, there was little coverage to suggest that a major political storm was brewing beyond vague concern over Suharto's failure to designate a successor.

Then, in July 1997, the Asian financial crisis, sparked by the crash of the Thai baht, prompted a run on Indonesia's currency, the rupiah. By January 1998, the rupiah had lost 70 percent of its value and per capita income had dropped from $1,000 to $400.[32] By mid-March, the banking system, riddled with bad loans, trembled on the brink of collapse, creating what one observer predicted would "go down [in history] as the worst financial crisis ever witnessed, certainly since biblical times."[33] As other growth indicators sank, inflation rose rapidly, at one point passing 200 percent.[34] With the economy's sharp plunge, nature itself seemed to rise in revolt as forest fires produced smog thick enough to crash planes and blacken skies all the way to Kuala Lumpur. Without warning, Indonesia suddenly faced its worst drought in fifty years.

The regime attempted to contain the crisis by prohibiting public debate over its cause or cure, blocking private television stations from broadcasting a November 1997 dialogue between the finance minister and parliament about plans to liquidate sixteen national banks. Though two stations had already advertised the event, the ministry insisted on its cancellation, claiming that a broadcast by stations other than the government-run TVRI would violate the 1997 Broadcasting Law. In the end, even TVRI did not air it, denying audiences any chance to watch this widely anticipated conversation on economic reform.[35]

The underground press, which by now included the online *Tempo Interaktif*, reported some of these public secrets as news, including detailed exposés of Suharto's hidden wealth by George Aditjondro, an activist exiled to Australia. His reports, with revelations in the international media heavily censored by the regime, were disseminated on the growing email lists, such as Apakabar, Pijar, and SiaR. Yet while this dissemination revealed much to a small online public, its function was still largely symbolic, demonstrating continued journalistic defiance.

THE STUDENT MOVEMENT

Despite efforts to suppress debate, by the end of 1997, rumblings of discontent grew into overt criticism of the government's performance, though only tangentially through the mainstream media.[36] As the rupiah continued its free fall, losing nearly 90 percent of value, and parliament's selection of the next president approached, criticism found voice in protests emerging across the country, defying government restrictions. Many were led by newly laid-off workers. But the rising number of student demonstrations was, in retrospect, the clearest sign of a dramatic shift in the country's political climate.

In Indonesia's comparatively brief history, university students had twice before played a pivotal role at moments of crisis, lending this upsurge of activism a powerful symbolism that helped protect demonstrators from outright repression. These protests also represented rising anger among middle- and upper-class Indonesians, whose children were forming the front lines. By spring of 1998, observers noted a new confidence on the streets as students realized that the government's fear of international attention was making officials cautious. Even students left relatively unscathed by the crisis, aware of the leverage their privilege afforded them, felt compelled to speak out on behalf of others.[37] Within the larger public, many Indonesians—from taxicab drivers to business leaders—viewed the students as defenders of the nation's interests. As one university president said, "Somebody has to represent public opinion." There were even rumors, corroborated by later events, that segments of the military were quietly backing the students as part of their behind-the-scenes efforts to force Suharto's resignation.[38]

As the plight of the poor worsened, idealism infected the *reformasi* movement, and students saw themselves as the voice of the *rakyat*, an emotive term for Indonesia's vast impoverished underclass. Indeed, early demonstrations were relatively conservative and centered on economic rather than explicitly political issues. Seth Mydans observed, "One telling sign posted on a bulletin board here suggests their priorities. 'Wanted,' it reads, 'Rice. Sugar. Cooking Oil. Democracy.'" A student leader explained, "We want change but we don't want to be involved in conflict."[39] Soon, however, conflict became unavoidable.

In February 1998, student leaders started disappearing. According to Allan Nairn, insiders acknowledged that the disappearances were part of a terror campaign by military intelligence units.[40] Others speculated that they were part of the military's carrot-and-stick approach to contain and co-opt the rising opposition—offering "dialogue" with select groups while curbing the movement's autonomy by kidnapping and torturing key leaders.[41]

This terror also involved intimidation through telecommunications, when the military began using cell-phone companies to monitor and occasionally interrupt private calls. One human rights lawyer reported a voice breaking into one of his conversations, saying, "I will kill you tonight."[42] Such threats became serious as evidence mounted that the military was operating death squads. A Jakarta hospital reported receiving 165 unidentified corpses over the next two months, most discovered along railroad tracks and marked with signs of torture.[43]

Whatever the intent of these operations, anger replaced fear as word of the kidnappings circulated. By contrast, Indonesia's thousand-member parliament continued full-throated support, reelecting Suharto on March 10 to his seventh term by a unanimous voice vote followed by thunderous applause and a standing ovation.[44] With news of this vote, protests grew bolder, and a new rhetoric of martyrdom gained force. One student who had been beaten unconscious in a demonstration stated, "We will continue the struggle, whatever the Government does, even if that means we die!"[45]

The Suharto regime responded with increased repression. In mid-March, military leaders went beyond requiring permits for gatherings by announcing a total ban on demonstrations.[46] This edict had little impact. By the end of the month, there were daily protests at universities nationwide. Students at one of the more radical campuses began burning Suharto in effigy, shouting, "Reform or death!"[47] The crackdown only led students to escalate demands.[48] The military responded by banning all electronic media from broadcasting the rallies.[49]

Even in this climate of growing protest, above-ground media remained cautious, still avoiding overt criticism. An exception was the provocative newsweekly *D&R*, which in March 1998, after two years of increasingly critical reporting, featured on its cover a caricature of Suharto as the King of Hearts with a caption reading, "The President in Crisis."[50] According to one editor, *D&R* staff ran the issue fully aware that the cartoon would lead to a ban. But, he added, there was already reason to believe the regime would fall before it could issue the order.[51]

Despite the media's general self-censorship, Suharto lashed out personally at journalists in April 1998, blaming negative coverage for the crisis. At the president's bidding, the information minister, Alwi Dahlan, warned the media about publishing news items that were unproportional, lacked proper perspective, and left the public "disinformed."[52]

By this time, however, free speech had become a wider cause taken up by students, who began wearing handkerchiefs as gags and covering their mouths with duct tape. At one rally, a demonstrator reinforced the symbolism of the tape over his mouth with a banner that read: "The price of honesty is [even] more expensive than the price of sembako [the nine basic necessities]."[53]

Anger intensified when kidnap survivors ignored threats from their abductors to keep quiet and appeared in public with chilling accounts of electric shock and water torture.[54] Their reappearance called attention to the many victims who still had not returned, adding a disturbing undertone to these rallies. The mainstream media shed some of its caution by devoting significant attention to the disappearances.[55] The movement then picked up more steam as students started coordinating between campuses, using computer networks as their primary communication to bypass bottlenecks and surveillance on more public channels.[56]

Trisakti and May Riots

Despite the growth of intercampus networks, nearly all student demonstrations were confined to campuses until May 1998. Then on May 4, the government raised the price of fuel by 71 percent, sparking public protests across the country punctuated by several days of riots in Medan that left six dead.[57] The unrest had begun to spread beyond the universities.

Five days later, President Suharto left for a week-long visit to Egypt. While he was away, the moment many feared finally arrived. On May 12, 1998, in broad daylight, military snipers fired on a student demonstration at the elite Trisakti University in downtown Jakarta, killing four. The next day, journalists at RCTI, which was owned by Suharto's son, insisted on airing a "full account" of the event, including a spontaneous eulogy by the station's weatherman, Kukuh Sanyoto. Though their act occurred very close to Suharto's fall, Sanyoto later noted that a mood of rebellion at the station had been brewing for many weeks, if not months.[58] The shooting, he explained, "pushed the Indonesian media deeper into the activist mood of the times."[59] The progression that led to the RCTI staff's defiance, however, reflected the reciprocal influence of the movement on the media and the media on the movement.

News of the shootings sent shockwaves through Jakarta. Despite the growing tension between demonstrators and government, the realization that soldiers, the "people's army," had actually killed unarmed students—particularly at a school attended by children of top military and civilian officials—stunned many Indonesians. The fallen students became heroes, and thousands marched behind the weeping relatives who carried their bodies to a Jakarta cemetery. At one of the graves, a student explained her disbelief: "The army should never have shot them. This is not a war. We don't have any weapons. We have only our voices."[60]

Jakarta erupted in violence. On May 13, residents reacting to television images of "police firing indiscriminately at students" poured into the streets in protest.[61] Elsewhere, less identifiable mobs formed, pulling down lampposts, setting fire to motor vehicles, and smashing storefront windows, looting as they went. Security forces in other areas fired tear gas and rubber bullets into crowds and shut down major highways. These actions prompted eight foreign governments to urge the Indonesian military to end the crackdown and instead quell the riots with democratic reforms.[62] Washington sent a military delegation to "warn their Indonesian counterparts in blunt terms that the country could face collapse without restraint by the armed forces."[63]

Despite this pressure, the rampage continued. From his vantage point on a high-rise rooftop, one correspondent reported that the city "looked like a vast inferno," while "huge columns of smoke rose in every direction, with new fires erupting every few minutes. Police helicopters circled, while down on the streets, ambulances weaved their way through crowds of people chanting and clapping at each intersection."[64] In just two days, hundreds of buildings were burned and over a thousand people died.

To the outside world, it appeared as though Indonesians had spun out of control. Much of the violence hit Chinese Indonesians, as roving groups—assumed to be enraged rioters—looted and burned businesses and homes, leaving many victims inside to die in the flames. Later reports revealed that packs of young men also raped and mutilated an estimated 150 women and girls of Chinese descent.[65]

Western coverage portrayed these events as expression of deep resentments against ethnic Chinese for the wealth and privilege they had enjoyed under Suharto.[66]

The *New York Times*, for example, reported that mobs sought to vent their rage against Suharto, but "the Chinese [became] the hapless proxies for an unpopular president."[67]

Later investigations, however, including one by a government fact-finding team, revealed that much of the violence against Chinese-Indonesians had been orchestrated by military provocateurs as part of an elite power struggle. The reports cited eyewitness accounts of trucks discharging well-built young men with military crew cuts, dressed in student-like clothing. These groups would arrive at shopping areas, throw out burning tires, shout antigovernment slogans, and then invite people to join a looting frenzy in the neighborhood's shops and malls. The instigators would then disappear, leaving behind burning buildings, some with hundreds trapped inside.[68]

Other indications of military involvement included reports that some of the surviving rape victims had noticed military uniforms inside their rapists' vehicles. But the most compelling evidence was the sheer scale, sophistication, and systematic character of the destruction. As Wimar Witoelar noted, a "pile of evidence" showed that "people of the military of course did start it," including "a geographic analysis [showing] 60 riots within a period of one hour moving in a certain direction across town." He added, "students could not move with such military precision and set a five-story building on fire in half an hour. I know. It takes them three hours to light a bonfire."[69] With similar logic, Ariel Heryanto argued, "No racial or ethnic groups in Indonesia, no matter how agitated, could possibly inflict a systematic violence in which 1198 lives . . . were lost, 150 females were raped, 40 shopping malls and 4,000 shops were burned down and thousands of vehicles and houses were set afire simultaneously in 27 areas in a capital city . . . in less than 50 hours."[70]

ELITE RIVALRIES

As the violence continued, the stock market crashed and the country's currency plunged another 16 percent. Aware of the extraordinary powers parliament had granted Suharto just three months earlier, many worried, when he cut short his trip to Egypt, that the aging president might impose martial law.[71] Instead, he returned home to a barrage of criticism and calls for his resignation.

Perhaps the most dramatic defection was that of the MPR Speaker, Harmoko, who stated on May 18, "For the unity of the nation, the President should wisely take the decision to resign."[72] Known as a die-hard loyalist, Harmoko still suffered notoriety for banning *Tempo*, *DëTIK*, and *Editor* as information minister in 1994. During the heaviest rioting, a mob stormed one of his houses and burned it down—an event that may have influenced his shifting loyalties.[73] Whatever his motivations, Harmoko's change of heart marked a turning point. The following day, he announced that leaders of all parliament factions would meet to ask Suharto to step down. The president's hand-picked legislature had turned against him.

In response to this stunning announcement, the commander of the armed forces, General Wiranto [one name], declared that Harmoko's statement "had no legal basis" and insisted that Suharto "still has duties and obligations to perform." Wiranto accused the students of starting the riots and warned them not to hold protests planned for later that week.[74]

But rumors were also spreading of a military split between Wiranto and Lieutenant General Prabowo Subianto—Suharto's son-in-law, commander of the Army Strategic Reserve and leader of the elite Kopassus rangers. Earlier in the crisis, Wiranto had made overtures to the students, assuring them that the military supported reform. By contrast, Prabowo commanded the troops that had shot the Trisakti students. Rumors were rife that if Prabowo replaced Wiranto, there would be a Tiananmen Square–style crackdown on the students.[75]

Within hours of Wiranto's warning, the country witnessed a turn of events few could have imagined. On May 19, thousands of students, escorted by soldiers, poured through the gates of the parliamentary compound in downtown Jakarta and occupied the main buildings. Legislators found themselves unable to leave. One observer described "extraordinary, dream-like scenes" of thousands of angry students holding sit-ins, waving protest banners, and dancing to rude anti-Suharto songs in a place that normally functioned as "a political temple used to worship Mr. Suharto."[76] At the end of the day, however, the students left peacefully, riding buses presumably provided by the military.[77]

During one tense moment, Kopassus soldiers loyal to Prabowo drove into the compound, looking uncomfortable as students hugged them and handed out roses.[78] Despite their submission to these embraces, the Kopassus visit appeared to be a show of force in the power struggle between Prabowo and Wiranto. Regular soldiers on guard around parliament, for example, were wearing bullet-proof vests. Since the students were not carrying guns, observed one journalist, "the vests suggest that some general may [be] worr[ied] about an assault by rival army units."[79]

That evening, Prabowo led military leaders to announce on television that they had ordered troops to "defend the nation" against protesters.[80] Throughout this broadcast, scrolling text warned viewers not to join the next day's nationwide rallies commemorating Indonesia's independence movement. The opposition leader Amien Rais also appeared, urging people to stay home. Significantly, Wiranto was not present, though he issued a separate warning against more demonstrations, suggesting an end to his tolerance of the student occupation. Finally, President Suharto himself delivered a televised address, promising he would hold a new election and would not run.[81]

JAKARTA LOSES FEAR

These broadcasts had little effect. The next day, May 20, Jakarta residents swarmed into the streets by the tens of thousands to demand Suharto's resignation. For many, participation stemmed from a belief that the army was bluffing with its wire barricades and tanks. Some hypothesized, however, that this boldness could lead to a crackdown because the army might find that mere threats no longer meant control. "In other places in Asia," Nicholas Kristof added, "soldiers have often showed a measure of camaraderie with students shortly before shooting them." Kristof nevertheless concluded, "Almost by the hour, the fear of Mr. Suharto and his generals has been draining away in Indonesia. . . . The bottom line is that for the first time in decades the Indonesian government seems more afraid of the people than they are of it."[82]

Back at parliament, students, now numbering nearly fifteen thousand, again flooded through the gates. Reporters allowed in to cover this unprecedented event described the students as having the run of the buildings, turning the place into what one called "an Indonesian version of Fort Lauderdale, Fla. during spring break."[83] One side of a building became a "Democracy Wall" covered with *reformasi* posters and slogans. The students also took turns at the podium of the main chamber doing comic impersonations of national leaders, including Wiranto and Harmoko. Outside the buildings, the atmosphere was even more raucous. According to one report, students "pranced atop the broad green roof and carried a coffin through the grounds, chanting, 'Suharto is dead!'"[84]

As the students swept through the legislature's hallways, the economy collapsed further and Jakarta faced a serious food shortage. Lawyers and business leaders joined the demonstrations. The same parliament that had voted unanimously in March to give Suharto a seventh term now announced they would reverse this decision.[85] Foreign leaders also began pressuring the president to concede power. While American officials argued that they did not have as much influence over Suharto as they had had over the Philippine president Ferdinand Marcos in 1986, they made quiet plans to offer the general safe passage into exile. The International Monetary Fund then suspended payments from the $43 billion bailout package recently established to help Indonesia through the crisis.[86]

On this second day of their occupation, the students, rather than leave the grounds at sundown, camped out for the night while various factions attempted to broker a resolution to the standoff. The situation was precarious. Several Western officials believed it likely that the military would take over, repeating the scenario that had brought Suharto to power thirty-two years earlier.[87]

In the official version of the events that followed, Wiranto spent the night persuading Suharto that resigning would be preferable to facing impeachment proceedings, and pledged to defend him and his family. Suharto finally gave up. On May 21, in a short televised ceremony, he handed over power to his vice president and protégé, B. J. Habibie. While conceding his effective expulsion from office, he insisted throughout his resignation speech on a corporatist conception of society with himself as Bapak, or "father"—head of a still-embodied nation. Dropping the convention within Malay languages that uses the passive voice to efface ego, Suharto invoked the first person singular no fewer than eight times in just twelve sentences. That same day, eleven members of his cabinet resigned.[88]

STUDENTS AND THE MEDIA

For the mainstream media, the events culminating in Suharto's resignation were a wake-up call, rousing them from their complacency, rupturing their privileged relationship with the regime, and forcing them into an unaccustomed activism. When the Asian economic crisis hit, the country's news media had largely avoided negative coverage. Even when students' growing boldness began to create opportunities for critical commentary, most outlets remained cautious. Yet, as editor Endy Bayuni noted, in the end, the demonstrations simply grew too large to ignore. Once a few outlets began covering them, there was no turning back.[89]

It was not the media, therefore, but students and workers, through their own protests, who first exploited the political opening created by the economic crisis, using it to break the long taboo against criticizing the president. More significantly, through determined defiance of the government's ban on demonstrations, the students began normalizing public dissent and gave members of the media their own opening.[90] In the reinforcing dynamic of the political firestorm that emerged among protesters, the media, and dissident elites, news coverage became an accelerant by providing demonstrators a wider audience for their criticisms. In short, as Bayuni put it, "The [student] movement broke the barrier against freedom of expression, and with it came freedom of the press."[91]

With the onset of the economic crisis in 1997, the legitimacy of Suharto's New Order began to crumble, creating an opening for the emerging *reformasi* movement that eventually felled the regime. As Edward Aspinall argues, however, this nascent opposition lacked organization and offered "no credible democratic alternative" to the collapsing regime, making it difficult to explain how the subsequent democratic transition gained footing and proved resilient against forces of reversal. The students who led the movement, for their part, had developed only a nebulous critique of the regime and presented a relatively slender agenda for a post-Suharto transition.[92]

While many elements are relevant to understanding the transition's trajectory, the 1994 newsweekly bans and the media reform movement they set in motion were key. The bans blocked news outlets from imposing transparency, thereby leaving the country vulnerable to the shock of the Asian economic crisis that undermined Suharto's legitimacy.[93] Protests they sparked unleashed new defiance, knitting budding activist groups into multiplying alliances and producing a political synergy that was mediated and inspired by dissident journalism. Through these alliances, the new movement, while breaking ground for the eventual *reformasi* revolution, served as an organizational webbing that held a loose community of media activists, nongovernmental organizations, and political oppositionists in resistance to a regime that tried to isolate and close down all such activities. During the seemingly quiescent years from 1994 to 1997, moreover, the students who led the anti-Suharto charge were also influenced by the drama of the bans. One of their widely shared priorities was the unshackling of public speech—in the media, on the streets, and within college campuses.[94]

As they advance to new phases, movements, which are by nature ephemeral, can be both principled and pragmatic in maintaining coherence and commitment. By articulating a critique and a common agenda for change, the dissident journalists' movement in Indonesia created a community with a shared commitment to abstract principles and concrete policy reforms—above all, freedom of speech. In a period when demands were essentially negative, expressing opposition to the regime, repressive laws, and a politicized military, one of the few positive programs for change that could guide reform in the postauthoritarian era was a broad faith in transparency, fairness, and freedom of speech as correctives for the many problems blamed on the Suharto regime. Though the student-led *reformasi* movement was inherently short-lived, a commitment to institutionalizing freedom of speech and effecting electoral reform endured long after Suharto's fall, making both goals defining issues of the transition.

CHAPTER FOUR

REFORMASI

Press freedom is a line in the sand.
— Bambang Harymurti, editor in chief of *Tempo*,
"Media: Pressing for Their Freedom"

On May 21, 1998, facing rising public anger and international pressure, President Suharto resigned and ceded power to his vice president, B. J. Habibie. Even as Indonesia reeled from riots and arson that left over 1,200 dead, euphoria quickly spread. With the start of this transition, known as *reformasi*, for much of the country—from the upper classes to the unemployed—everything suddenly seemed possible. Labor unions and nongovernmental organizations could organize openly. The hundreds of political prisoners jailed under the New Order had new hope of freedom. Public denunciations of corruption, collusion, and nepotism signaled new resolve to curb these practices that were undermining both good governance and economic progress. With this resolve came hopes for economic recovery and new opportunities. For those denied due process under Suharto, his removal offered possible legal redress. Even those living in provinces torn by separatism had cause for optimism as the curtain of silence shrouding the regime's human rights violations began to lift.

The open climate also emboldened people to test the government's new tolerance for critical speech in myriad settings, but most visibly in the news and entertainment media. Correspondingly, among the many reforms needed after three decades of authoritarianism, freedom of speech was an immediate focus for *reformasi* leaders and supporters, who feared a sudden reversal of this liberalization and other gains.

At the start of any democratic transition, reformers must confront forces favoring reversal, whether simple inertia or reactionary resistance. In its first year, Indonesia's democratization was beset by conservative opposition in multiple forms. Initial exuberance overcame much of this pressure for reversal, and in the rush to get on the right side of history, even Suharto's former allies were declaring themselves "pro-*reformasi*."

Among the broader coalition that had backed the New Order, however, members of the once-tethered media, now freed from authoritarian controls and bolstered by an expanding civil society, were among the only institutional actors to resist democratization's reversal over both the short and long term. This inclination, though uneven across outlets, was evident throughout the transition's first year in two distinct forms: mobilization in the press community to defend and institutionalize new freedoms; and the exercise of these freedoms to expand the boundaries of permissible speech, impose transparency on the reform process, and further the contestation necessary to the democratic circulation of power.

Initial Challenges

With Suharto's fall, the challenge for the entire *reformasi* movement, including media reformers, was to carry their agenda beyond this initial victory. Despite the installation of a new president, it was difficult to know where the transition would lead. Initially, there was considerable cause for cynicism. Unlike other ousted dictators faced with a choice of death or flight, Suharto placed his cronies in the cabinet, picked a loyal successor, and retired to his luxurious compound in Central Jakarta. As Jeffrey Winters noted, with Habibie's inauguration, Indonesia's *reformasi* movement "both peaked and collapsed on the same day"—removing Suharto, but resigned to a successor regime that was "a continuation of the same government."[1] In the same vein, Todung Mulya Lubis declared the Habibie administration "the New Order minus Suharto."[2]

At numerous points throughout this first year, the nation's stability also appeared at risk, creating ample pretext for reimposing authoritarianism. The most immediate challenge came from the economic crisis that had undermined Suharto's legitimacy but did not end with his resignation. Instead, circumstances for millions of Indonesians continued to deteriorate, creating conditions ripe for unrest.[3] "In hardly more than a year," reported the *Los Angeles Times*, a nation that had been "a star performer" among Southeast Asia's economies now found that "a generation of growth [had] simply been wiped away."[4] By mid-1998, the crisis had forced more than twenty million people out of work, with millions more likely to follow by year's end.[5] By September, inflation approached 80 percent, a twenty-three-year high, while seventeen million families faced "dire food shortages" and workers were losing jobs, by one estimate, at a rate of fifteen thousand per day.[6]

Economic desperation converged with the government's weakened social controls, producing 1,714 demonstrations and 69 "riots" in the first four months of the new era.[7] In rural Indonesia, *Forbes* magazine reported, "hungry Indonesians have taken to raiding food warehouses, shrimp farms and paddy fields."[8] On Java, roving gangs plundered coffee plantations while another group hauled fifteen thousand chickens away from a farm. Elsewhere, people were ripping up Chinese graves to steal jewelry from the corpses and, in some cases, the teak coffins. Farmers in one town "chased a group of golfers off the ninth green with hoes and axes and began planting vegetables."[9] Loekman Soetrisno reported, "After two months, the rural reform movement mysteriously stopped and plundering began. For the urban poor and village landless, *reformasi* means plundering. This could destroy all that has been achieved."[10]

The country's leadership also posed problems during the transition. Habibie faced challenges overwhelming for even the most dedicated proponents of reform. But the administration's commitment to meaningful change seemed tenuous, a reality underscored by early moves to punish critics and reassert control over public speech.[11]

Compounding this dubious turnover in leadership, the new era left all the old institutions firmly in place. Particularly relevant to media reform, the notorious Ministry of Information retained jurisdiction over the mass media. While the public mood restricted officials' actions, the ministry retained all its mechanisms for media control, including the restrictive SIUPP licensing system that, as one editorial suggested, still hung like "the sword of Damocles" over editors' heads.[12]

Nevertheless, by the time Jakarta cleared away the broken glass and skeletons of burned-out cars, the country's political landscape had been altered substantially by the events of the previous months. The regime that had ruled unchallenged for three decades had crumbled, and leadership no longer revolved around the dictates of one man but instead had to accommodate a multitude of competing factions, all claiming to be pro-*reformasi*. The same parliament that had voted unanimously in March to grant Suharto a seventh term had discovered, in the general's last weeks, the courage to act as an independent branch of government. Even the once infallible "father of development" appeared chastened, offering in his resignation speech a remarkable apology for all his "mistakes."[13] His successor, President Habibie, promised to repeal repressive laws, allow opposition parties, hold new elections, and—in keeping with *reformasi* rhetoric—rid the country of corruption, collusion, and nepotism.[14]

Indonesia was also transformed by the sudden expansion in political participation. Student protests had forced open the public sphere to a degree not seen for decades, and by the time the students allowed soldiers to escort them from parliament grounds, their boldness had infected most of the country. In the following weeks, a figurative dam burst as people of all backgrounds openly participated in political conversations. Most visibly, the media moved quickly to exploit the postauthoritarian climate, casting off layers of taboo to publish ever more sensational stories on everything from financial corruption to the plight of political prisoners.

Aware of the fragility of this political moment, representatives of print and broadcast media moved immediately to secure legal protections for their new freedom and overhaul the New Order's apparatus of regulatory controls. After organizing underground for nearly four years, media reformers were prepared to articulate a clear agenda. Within a week of Suharto's fall, a group of journalists, editors, and newspaper owners staged a protest before the Ministry of Information, ready to confront Habibie's new minister of information, Lieutenant-General Muhammad Yunus Yosfiah, with demands for three major reforms: abolishing the press licensing system; allowing journalists to form their own associations free from mandatory membership in the government-sponsored Indonesian Journalists' Association (PWI); and permitting blacklisted reporters to write under their own names.[15]

Yosfiah was a controversial figure whose military affiliation alone justified wariness from the delegates. He also had led security in Balibo, East Timor, during Indonesia's 1975 invasion, when five Australian journalists were killed in what was later determined to be a military-sanctioned assassination, earning Yosfiah the nickname "Butcher of Balibo."[16] Yet on this day in 1998, he invited the delegation into the Ministry of Information and responded affirmatively to nearly everything they said.

Yosfiah's positive response may have reflected deference to the Habibie administration's professed support for free speech, but he later articulated deeper personal beliefs. While he had been studying at the US Army Command and General Staff College in Fort Leavenworth in the 1980s, a course on US First Amendment law convinced him of the importance of a free news media in developing Indonesia into an advanced society. In his first year as information minister, he repeatedly paraphrased Thomas Jefferson's famous statement, "[W]ere it left to me to decide whether we should have a government without newspapers or newspapers without a government, I should not hesitate a moment to prefer the latter."[17]

Yosfiah acted on this conviction by abolishing the notorious 1984 decree that had empowered the government to revoke a publication's business license at will. In its place, he issued a new decree on June 5, 1998, barring license revocation except via a court of law. The decree also eliminated the state's onerous requirements for obtaining a publishing license; what had taken years, connections, and costly fees was now reduced to filling out a form.[18] Another new regulation allowed multiple journalists' associations, freeing the press from the *wadah tunggal* system that had given so much power to the PWI.[19] Finally, new rules on broadcasting reduced the number of government news bulletins that radio stations had to relay from thirteen to three a day and freed radio and television broadcasters to produce their own hard news.[20]

Many felt these measures did not go far enough. Leo Batubara from the Association of Newspaper Publishers complained of the media's continued susceptibility to executive manipulation, particularly via the courts.[21] Legal expert Robinson Hamonangan Siregar argued that, despite the reforms, media were just as constrained as they had been under Suharto because the notorious "hate-sowing articles" of the criminal code remained in effect. Siregar also took issue with the government's continued right to "freeze" press licenses.[22]

Like most media representatives, the reformist Alliance of Independent Journalists (AJI) welcomed the changes, but also characterized the ministry's efforts as "half-hearted," offering three main criticisms: First, despite reforms, the continuation of the SIUPP system left the government with too much power over the print press. Second, though journalists could now choose any affiliation, the stipulation that they must belong to at least one journalists' association violated their freedom of association and organization. And third, though less onerous, the requirement that broadcasters must still relay government-produced news "constituted a violation of the principles of media freedom and pluralism."[23]

IMPACT OF THE FIRST REFORMS

Even these limited reforms, however, had an immediate impact. Within five months, the Ministry of Information had issued 333 new publishing licenses, more than doubling the total allocated during Suharto's entire reign. By the end of 1999, the number of new licenses reached well over a thousand—transforming coverage, as shown in the appendixes below. Opposition political parties ran at least four of the tabloids, flouting decades of New Order–cultivated antipathy toward partisan journalism.[24] On the streets, newsstands were soon overflowing with low-budget tabloids and glossy newsmagazines, and hawkers struggled to display long armfuls for customers in passing cars. The arresting headlines and graphics in these curbside arrays promised the reporting on corruption and elite conflicts that now typified media fare.[25]

Established publications accustomed to burying controversy deep within articles now splashed provocative quotes from shunned opposition figures, including labor activist Muchtar Pakpahan and East Timor rebel leader Xanana Gusmão, across front pages. Even more dramatic was the frenzy triggered by reports on the once untouchable subject of Suharto's wealth, as the print media scrambled to top one another in revelations about the family's vast accumulation of property and possessions. Callers on talk radio vented outrage at unfolding details. Street hawkers added to the spectacle by selling xeroxed lists of Suharto family assets accompanied by matching mug shots.

The media also began airing exposés on the abuses of power that had built the Suharto family empire. The *Jakarta Post* reported that at least 120 businesses holding contracts with the state oil company, Pertamina, were owned by Suharto's children or friends. The paper further revealed that city council members were now imposing $1.86 million in fines for building permit violations on a Suharto family hotel, and police were reviewing contracts for processing driver's licenses controlled by

Suharto's daughter. *Bisnis Indonesia* reported on the cancellation of four contracts for port services held by Suharto's son.[26]

Even on television, still controlled by Suharto's children and cronies, little was off-limits. After Habibie's speech promising new elections, a televised panel featured an opposition candidate delivering a stinging critique inconceivable under Suharto.[27] Producers on TPI (Televisi Pendidikan Indonesia), owned by Suharto's daughter, began airing exposés, including one on the pacification of the province of Aceh showing graphic footage of military atrocities.[28]

Publications and radio programs shut down under Suharto now resurfaced in new forms. *Tempo* magazine, "consigned to the glorious dustbin of history" just two years earlier, resumed publication in August 1998.[29] The banned weekly tabloid *DëTIK* also started up again as *DëTAK* and quickly reestablished itself as a leader in both circulation and temerity. Canceled broadcast programs resurfaced in forms far bolder than the originals. At the vanguard of what one announcer dubbed "reformasi radio," Safari-FM launched the radical call-in show *Wacana Jakarta* (*Jakarta Discourse*) featuring Ahmad Taufik, one of the AJI activists jailed in 1994, as a host. Safari-FM's program director, Nor Pud Binarto, launched the show believing in radio's revolutionary potential and its power to defend the media's new freedoms. Binarto's earlier cutting-edge show, *Jakarta Round-Up*, had been canceled after guest Goenawan Mohamad condemned the government for banning his magazine *Tempo*.[30] Now *Wacana Jakarta* regularly went much further, covering everything from the army's role in politics to ethnic and religious conflicts.

Uncensored debate also became a staple of television programming. Talk shows resembling CNN's *Crossfire* multiplied, and several earned higher ratings than even the most popular *sinetron* soap operas.[31] Wimar Witoelar, whose show *Perspektif* had been canceled in 1995, launched two new television talk shows, *Selayang Pandang* and the more controversial *Dialog Aktual* on rival station Indosiar. *Pro dan Kontra* on TPI facilitated combative one-on-one debates.[32] One of the most innovative shows, TPI's *Dialog Partai Partai*, featured unscripted debates between politicians before a live studio audience of outspoken university students.

With the end of mandatory membership in government-sponsored professional organizations, more than twenty new media associations formed within a year. Some claimed to represent the interests of all media workers, while others focused on groups such as photographers and television journalists. In 1999, several also joined the Southeast Asian Press Alliance, a coalition of journalist organizations from countries throughout the region that was created to "demonstrate that press freedom is a universal value."[33]

EARLY THREATS

President Habibie, the center of the controversy that precipitated the 1994 press bans, expressed pride in his administration's liberalizing role. When the media featured student calls for his resignation, he appeared committed to freedom of speech, at one point thanking the students for their contribution to reform. Speaking before a language conference, he urged government officials to reform their use of Bahasa Indonesia, the national language, to promote more transparent governance.[34]

These words, however, followed moves to circumscribe the media's new freedom. In July 1998, only a month after his information minister had relaxed business licensing, Habibie proposed that journalists be required to obtain renewable professional licenses. Proponents argued that such a mechanism was needed to enforce industry standards. The Ministry of Trade and Industry then tried to garner support for the idea by linking it to a proposal to abolish Suharto's 15 percent tax on newsprint. The plan sparked a storm of protest from both the wider press community and officials in the president's own Supreme Advisory Council and never became policy.[35]

Jakarta's burgeoning civil society also played a critical role in resisting new controls on public speech. On July 24, 1998, soon after the licensing controversy, the new government issued an emergency decree (No. 2/1998) requiring written police authorization forty-eight hours in advance for gatherings of more than fifty people and banning all protests at night or "in the vicinity of the Presidential Palace, military installations, places of worship, hospitals, airfields, ports and railway stations."[36] Heated opposition forced the Habibie government to revoke this decree.[37]

Responses to a subsequent attempt at suppression further indicated a changing power equation between civil society and government. In September, Habibie took offense at speeches made at a conference, "Dialogue for Democracy," that had been held in August. For the first time since taking office, the new president ordered legal action against his critics, summoning the actress and playwright Ratna Sarumpaet to appear before the police for insulting the president and "organizing a conference without a permit." Ironically, Sarumpaet had been one of the last prosecuted for a speech violation by the Suharto regime, imprisoned for organizing the "People's Congress," which opposed his March 1998 reelection. This time, Sarumpaet ignored the summons, explaining, "I figured if they really wanted to talk, they could come to me."[38]

In these same weeks, tensions over public speech rose as students returned to the streets, protesting the upcoming parliamentary session that would establish the legal framework for the 1999 elections. In early October, angry that these decisions would be made by Suharto's handpicked legislature, over a thousand students forced their way through security cordons onto parliament grounds, repeating their dramatic siege of May. In other cities, tens of thousands joined concurrent rallies, refusing to accept the session's legitimacy. In response, the armed forces commander, General Wiranto, began pressuring students to end their rallies, and Habibie supporters disseminated pamphlets calling the movement "Communist-inspired."[39]

LINES IN THE SAND

In the face of mounting tension, most news outlets set aside caution and tested the limits of government tolerance—a task critical to maintaining democracy over the long term. As Jean Goodwin has argued, what we think of as "freedom of speech" has little to do with the vast majority of public expression. At issue instead are boundaries dividing acceptable speech from that which threatens or offends.[40] Or as *Tempo*'s Bambang Harymurti later said, "Press freedom is a line in the sand."[41]

In Indonesia, pushing such boundaries—in effect, crossing lines to expand the range of acceptable speech—served the transition by helping secure the media's right to impose accountability on leaders and their decision-making. If journalists in a democracy do not stretch boundaries consistently, such rights become an abstract principle rather than actual practice. If space for such reporting is not actively asserted and maintained, the state will gradually narrow the boundaries of permissible speech, citing national security or privacy or the dignity of the president and others in office.

There is a difference, however, between the noncontroversial coverage that fills most of a daily newspaper or newscast and reporting that aggressively pushes the limits of tolerance, potentially striking at the core of power. The latter is particularly important for its ability to provoke confrontations with the state, prompting officials to draw one of those lines in the sand. In Indonesia, such confrontations were necessary to construct a legal framework defining speech that deserves legal protection from state agencies, enabling news outlets to predict, with some degree of certainty, the consequences of airing provocative content. Over the long term, such certainty could empower the media to defend territory already gained and rights already asserted.

News exposing malfeasance or incompetence and forcing political figures onto the defensive further increased transparency and accountability during Indonesia's democratic transition. In addition, stories that produced "scandal" helped shake up the political process, shift the balance of power, and inject new uncertainty into electoral and other contests—all of which helped counteract trends toward stagnation and reversal.

Some news outlets pushed harder than others in pursuing such coverage, testing the boundaries of their new freedom with full-blown exposés, almost daring officials to react. Significantly, *Tempo*'s inaugural post-ban cover story revealed military involvement in the rapes of ethnic Chinese women during the May 1998 riots, arguably the most sensitive controversy of the day.[42] *DëTAK* was equally aggressive. In November 1998, a point of maximum tension between the military and students, *DëTAK* published a hard-hitting exposé on military involvement in a mysterious murder spree by killers dressed like Japanese ninjas throughout East Java.[43]

The serial murders had already fueled widespread speculation about possible conspiracies. Military and police officials claimed that descendants of the Indonesian Communist Party cadres killed in 1965–66 were exacting revenge for the participation in that purge of the Muslim organization, Nahdlatul Ulama (NU). NU representatives insisted that the killings were part of a scheme to pit the largest Muslim associations against each other, weakening their base before the national elections.[44] Significantly, one spate of killings coincided with NU's efforts to form a new political party headed by its leader, Abdurrahman Wahid, who accused President Habibie's cabinet of involvement.[45] Others speculated that elements of the armed forces were engineering the attacks to justify the military's continued role in politics.[46]

The Indonesian media reported such accusations, and a few outlets highlighted evidence of military involvement, though this was largely circumstantial.[47] In its November exposé, however, *DëTAK* went further. At the heart of its detailed report was an eyewitness description by a deserter from a military-connected camp training agents provocateurs, including the ninja murderers, to create political instability. Significantly, the report linked the operations to Kopassus, an elite unit once commanded by Suharto's son-in-law, damaging the military's credibility as defender of public order. *DëTAK* also traced control over these units to Jalan Cendana, the Suharto clan's street in central Jakarta, reporting that the "Cendana" family was using these campaigns to divert attention from *reformasi* initiatives, including the investigation of Suharto's wealth.[48]

The exposé also connected the East Java murders and May's military orchestration of anti-Chinese violence reported by *Tempo*, citing the deserter's claims that Kopassus soldiers were dispatched "to set fire to stores" to incite violence, and that each recruit was given resources to enlist the aid of five to ten civilian rioters. Confirming earlier, more speculative reports in other publications, the deserter stated that the ninja murders aimed to disrupt the congress in Bali being held by the opposition Indonesian Democratic Party of Struggle (Partai Demokrasi Indonesia Perjuangan, PDIP).[49]

Although the Suharto clan's suspected role in the ninja murders had been the subject of countless rumors, *DëTAK's* insider testimony on the operations of the Kopassus deserters, a group the military denied even existed, was indeed news.[50] Not only did the exposé confirm earlier reports on these deserters and detail the infrastructure of their training camps and command. It also revealed the Suharto family's continued capacity for psychological warfare and political destabilization.

The timing of the *DëTAK* report was significant, hitting the streets just before the November parliamentary session, when barbed wire barricades began reappearing in Jakarta and students prepared to square off against security forces. The report strengthened their case in protesting the military's continued hold on dedicated parliamentary seats; it also justified efforts to contain the young men of the Pam Swakarsa (Voluntary Security Units), who were being bussed in and armed with spears and sharp sticks ostensibly to help with security, but who became a force for inciting violence.[51] Simultaneously, a joint fact-finding team, composed of members of the government and nongovernmental organizations, released a report implicating the military in the destruction and sexual violence against ethnic Chinese during the May 1998 riots, affirming *Tempo's* earlier findings.[52]

The impact of these reports on the transition is difficult to measure. But the most serious threats to democratization in the first year included high-level efforts to foment intergroup conflict. Violence fueled by the military was used to justify states of emergency and suspension of civil liberties in specific regions, such as Maluku following the outbreak of interreligious violence in 1999.[53] News coverage reinforcing the impression of a breakdown in order legitimated such measures. Conversely, reports on military instigation of violence justified restraint in authorizing a military crackdown to restore order.

These reports also tested government tolerance for the media's new freedom by challenging the military's privileged position. Yet they did not prompt a backlash. This nonresponse seemed to affirm acceptance by officials, including the military, of the media's critical stance. Alternatively, it demonstrated only a suspension of authoritarian controls. In either case, the lack of repercussions may have emboldened colleagues, while the reports' success created a market incentive for rival publications to push the boundaries of free speech even further.

BLACK FRIDAY

At the time of the *DëTAK* report's release, journalists met a different kind of backlash in covering a scheduled November special session of parliament. Initial planning for the session provoked vehement student opposition to the slate of Suharto-era legislators who would, by default, set the rules for the democratic transition. As the government forged ahead, demonstrators again flooded the streets outside parliament chanting, in solidarity with journalists, "Banning is banned!" News outlets once again provided prominent coverage.[54]

The media's use of their new freedom manifest in this coverage, whether intentionally or inadvertently, helped defend the transition from reversal in three important ways: magnifying objections to legislative biases in setting the rules for the transition; asserting the media's right to report civil unrest; and sustaining pressure on legislators to concede to several student demands critical for the transition, particularly a decree guaranteeing the right to free speech.[55]

A key incentive for the heavy coverage was, of course, increased audience share, and not all reporting supported the students' agenda. Television stations, as the next chapter will describe, were still owned by Suharto's circle and favored the military and the ruling party, Golkar, over the students.

Regardless of motivation or partisan bias, both print and broadcast media imposed unprecedented scrutiny on the legislative process. All five private TV stations, once barred from airing parliamentary discussions on the economy, were now broadcasting breaking updates on the session's controversial proceedings. ANteve even showed a satiric montage of legislators dozing off and chatting on their cell phones during the session.[56] Throughout, Jakarta's radio stations broadcast blow-by-blow accounts, interspersed with live interviews, bringing the highly charged atmosphere of the streets right into listeners' homes and cars.[57] The volatility they presented made government tolerance of this coverage even more remarkable, particularly since television and radio were broadcasting demands to expel the military from politics and dissolve the current parliament.

In the end, this tolerance was limited. With memories of images showing brutality toward students in May still vivid, security forces were hostile to journalists carrying cameras. The day before the November session, soldiers assaulted five journalists covering an altercation with students on a central Jakarta boulevard. On the session's second day, police and soldiers turned on three photojournalists filming a clash outside a downtown university campus, kicking one reporter and clubbing another as he tried to flee, damaging their cameras and sending all three to the hospital.[58]

The reaction of the media was significant for its solidarity. General Wiranto apologized to the photojournalists when he visited them in the hospital and later vowed to punish the soldiers responsible. This response failed to mollify media representatives, who were particularly angry that soldiers had started the assaults after reporters showed their press cards. "It is hard to escape the impression that ABRI [Angkatan Bersenjata Republik Indonesia, Armed Forces of the Republic of Indonesia] has no clear desire to control its violent character," read a statement from AJI. "The word 'sorry' is very easily said, much as ABRI sees little difficulty in opening fire on or clouting unarmed citizens peacefully protesting."[59] Over two hundred journalists staged a mass protest on the parliament's front steps, using their access to this sanctum to get the government's attention. They also filmed the gathering to ensure the public would see it on the evening news.[60]

As the session proceeded, reports only grew bolder, as images of soldiers in full riot gear brandishing weapons filled television and print media. Then, as legislators were voting for the last resolutions on Friday, November 13, soldiers fired into the crowds, killing three protestors and injuring hundreds more. Later that night, troops fired on the students again, fatally wounding another three.[61]

The print press responded by filling the next morning's front pages with graphic photographs and large headlines, some dripping with blood. As citizens marched down otherwise empty streets to honor the fallen students, Jakarta was again filled with an eerie mix of anger and sadness. Even the popular daily *Pos Kota*—owned by Golkar leader and former information minister, Harmoko—condemned the crackdown with sensational coverage that drew crowds of readers to newsstands.

In a televised statement, President Habibie extended condolences to the victims' families but also spoke of attempts by "various societal groups" to use the students to advance their agendas in clear violation of "the law and the constitution." Their actions, he said, were a form of treason that "aimed to topple a legitimate government" and "threatened the unity and integrity" of the nation.[62]

Military commentators likewise mixed statements of regret with suggestions that the students were pawns of darker forces. Television news anchors on both TVRI and the private stations reinforced this hostile interpretation with leading questions about student alliances with certain suspicious groups. But the print media, including the conservative *Kompas*, challenged this interpretation as an attempt, in Wimar Witoelar's words, "to divert attention away from the true issues to be investigated—the use of live ammunition and extremely harsh handling of unarmed student demonstrations."[63]

The crackdown showed that freedom of expression at the street level remained illusory, a "right" that students had enjoyed only at the pleasure of ruling elites. But news coverage during the November session also demonstrated significant gains. Television coverage, as noted above, ultimately undercut the students' objections to a biased legislative process that could derail the democratic transition. But these stations also established a precedent in reporting on proceedings of the full parliament (MPR), providing the public with access that, a year later, would include live coverage of another special session showing legislators attacking a sitting president. Equally important, the nation's print and broadcast journalists showed unprecedented unity in protesting military assaults on reporters. Finally, the combination of escalating protests and media coverage pressured legislators to concede to numerous student demands important to the transition, including a formal decree guaranteeing freedom of expression.[64]

"Dancing on a Rotten Stage"

Despite these milestones, media reformers feared that the window for institutionalizing recent gains could close at any moment.[65] In a troubling reminder of how quickly *reformasi* trends could end, the vanguard talk show of *"reformasi* radio," *Wacana Jakarta*, whose slogan was "we say what we want," unexpectedly went off the air with little explanation. The show's staff, which included AJI activist Ahmad Taufik and radio personality Sri Megawati Kurniadi, were suddenly unemployed. Simultaneously, some of the bolder print media outlets, *DëTAK, Merdeka, D&R*, and *Tajuk*, found themselves confronting lawsuits over their investigative reports—a reminder of how little legal protection journalists actually had.[66]

One of the more articulate statements on the problem of legal protection came from AJI leader Heru Hendratmoko, who expressed reservations about the ongoing "euphoria over democracy" infecting the country. "It is as if the press were dancing on a rotten stage," he said. "There is no guarantee [we] can enjoy [our current] freedom forever. Because . . . all the products of press law are very weak." Though acknowledging the government's repeal of the ministerial decree allowing arbitrary revocation of media licenses, he cited new threats from the public, who "often [do] not use their right of reply as the first mechanism to solve a problem."[67]

The heart of the matter, Hendratmoko explained, lay in the media's lack of fundamental legal rights. He explained, "I imagine we could be like the U.S. [where the press is protected by] the First Amendment, but in Indonesia we are blocked by our constitution that [guarantees only] freedom of association, assembly and expression of one's opinion, as regulated by law. . . . There lies the problem. Because, it could be [that] a law is made specifically to curtail freedom of the press, as was done by the New Order."[68] Consequently, Hendratmoko and other reformers turned to overhauling the country's convoluted media laws through the Indonesian Press Society, a consortium dedicated specifically to such reform and comprising representatives from several professional associations.[69]

After the November session, reformers and sympathetic legislators felt renewed urgency to institutionalize the media's new freedoms before pressure for reversal could build. The promise of national elections in 1999 only added to the urgency by producing uncertainty, reformers reasoned, that could prompt the Habibie government to reinstate media controls to guarantee victory. The administration's draft of a new bill, in fact, contained numerous articles empowering it to regain control over the media. The Indonesian Press Society therefore stepped up efforts to perfect its own draft press law quickly, while fashioning separate bills for broadcasting and film. The good news was that legal reform advocates, bolstered by international prodemocracy programs and sympathetic parliamentarians, now wielded considerable influence over the policy agenda for their industry.

THE SMOKING TAPE

By late 1998, the campaign to legalize media freedoms was gaining momentum. Most critically, the information minister, Muhammad Yunus Yosfiah, continued to defend the industry's liberalization, even debating critics on live television about the media's role.[70] Yet there still had been no test of the media's legal rights in a direct conflict with the president.

Then, in February 1999, the news magazine *Panji Masyarakat* published a report embarrassing the Habibie administration, prompting the president to threaten a lawsuit and launch an investigation of the magazine's sources. The report damaged the standing of the ruling party, Golkar, in the run-up to the June elections, forcing the party to confront the prospect of losing to a challenger after decades of assured landslides. Considered among news outlets as a "test case" of both media freedom and journalistic solidarity, the confrontation that followed was the first time that news outlets were seen behaving collectively as an independent fourth estate instead of the rent-seeking and generally self-serving businesses they had become under Suharto.[71] Through the politics it unleashed, the unity it produced, and the principles it highlighted, the case became the most important media controversy in the transition's first critical year.

The case began in January 1999, when a number of Jakarta's news outlets acquired a cassette containing a wiretapped telephone conversation between two voices that sounded like those of the attorney general, Andi Muhammad Ghalib, and President Habibie discussing the government's investigation of Suharto's fortune.[72] In this exchange, allegedly a day after Suharto had visited the attorney general in November 1998, the speakers pondered how long Ghalib should question the former president about his assets to avoid the impression that the government's inquiry was a sham. In one revealing quote, the voice attributed to Ghalib explained that he had interviewed Suharto for three hours because "if [it] had been only two hours, then later people [would say], oh, this is just another charade."[73]

The exchange revealed a careful plot to fool the public, or at least an inside joke at the public's expense. After Habibie asked how Suharto's case was going, the attorney general replied that summoning the ex-president had mollified the public, transforming its anger into "pity."[74] Ghalib also updated the president on investigations of oil tycoon Arifin Panigoro, one of the regime's staunchest critics, and another businessman, possibly Sofyan Wanandi. Commentators interpreted the update as confirmation that these investigations had been ploys to divert attention from Suharto's case.[75]

The taped dialogue was, essentially, a "smoking gun" that belied the Habibie regime's professed dedication to justice and reform. Of the many outlets aware of its circulation, only a small tabloid, *Berita Keadilan*, had already reported the tape's existence, receiving almost no notice.[76] But on February 18, *Panji Masyarakat* released a cover story detailing its full contents.[77]

The *Panji* version sold out almost as soon as it hit the streets. By the next day, xeroxed copies of the report were selling at major intersections for nearly the price of the entire magazine. Originals were going for six times the cover price. *Panji* then printed three times its normal production and still ran short.[78] For the next few weeks, it became Indonesia's must-buy newsmagazine, selling out quickly in Jakarta and other major cities.[79] The rest of the media, in turn, pumped out endless follow-up stories on the case covering nearly every possible angle, from speculation on who was behind the wiretap and comparisons with the US Watergate scandal to detailed diagrams of the technical aspects of wiretapping.

Ghalib responded by denying that he had ever had such a conversation. Habibie effectively contradicted his attorney general by ordering a police investigation to find out who had tapped his phone, thereby acknowledging the tape's probable authenticity. Officials also began "hunting for" charges—as a *Panji* lawyer put it—that could be filed against the magazine.[80]

The day after the report's release, police appeared at *Panji*'s office and escorted its acting chief editor, Uni Zulfiani Lubis, to their headquarters, where they interrogated her for nearly five hours. The legal basis for the summons was a pre-Independence law passed in 1946 that barred the "dissemination of untruthful information."[81] However, the purpose of the interrogation, Lubis later explained, was not to attack *Panji*'s reporting per se, but to induce her to name the tape's source. "From the first," she said, "Habibie didn't deny [it] was his voice. But he wanted General Wiranto to find out who did [the wiretap]." Her interviewers told her that if she revealed *Panji*'s source, "they would find the guy" who had tapped the phones and leave her alone.[82]

Lubis said that the interrogation was intense, but she knew that the police and the government were wary of pushing the situation too far. The officers who came to pick her up "said they had already prepared [a] letter [declaring] me a suspect. But they didn't use it," possibly fearing public backlash.[83] Lubis remained only a "witness" in the investigation, and not a very helpful one.

The police widened their net and, reprising the devastating press crackdown of 1978, summoned fourteen chief editors from other news outlets that had either broadcast the recorded conversation or published its transcript.[84] The goal, as with Lubis, was to compel these outlets to disclose their sources.[85] Those summoned underwent individual questioning because "the police were hoping one would give in."[86]

The response from these editors was very different from the media leadership's response to similar summonses in 1978. The day after Lubis's interrogation, she received a call from *Tempo* saying that someone from the police was spreading word that she had already cracked and named her source. But a well-known attorney was present during the questioning and, with him backing her account, *Tempo* told her that they had not believed the rumor. Realizing the dilemma these police tactics could create for the other editors summoned, Lubis warned them, "Don't go alone. Because if you go alone, there is no witness who can testify that you didn't [give up your source]." After her warning, "no chief editor . . . [went] to the police offices alone." And no one revealed the tape's source.[87]

Two weeks later, Roy Suryo from Gadjah Mada University used voice spectrum analysis to determine the tape's authenticity. He first compared the voice on the tape to one of Habibie's televised speeches, and then compared it to a tape of the comedian Butet Kartaredjasa impersonating Habibie. The match between the tape and Habibie's televised speech was very close, Suryo told the media, much closer than the match between the voice on the tape and Kartaredjasa's impersonation.[88]

Shortly after announcing these findings, Suryo was summoned by Indonesia's notorious military intelligence agency, Badan Intelijen Negara (BIA). He agreed to meet, but not without some trepidation, he later explained, as he was fully aware of the agency's involvement in the disappearance of political activists under Suharto.[89] He alerted members of the media and, armed with his cell phone, traveled from Yogyakarta to BIA's headquarters. A few hours later, he called to explain that after driving him around for a while, his interrogators had treated him to lunch and were now his good friends. Journalists who had stood by, ready to publicize any mistreatment of Suryo, concluded that BIA, at least, did not intend to harass either *Panji Masyarakat* or Suryo to protect Habibie.[90] Suryo spent the rest of the afternoon relating his story on a popular radio talk show.[91]

PRESS COMMUNITY RESPONSE AND CRITIQUE

The enormous publicity that *Panji* enjoyed after the report showed competitors how profitable such a high-risk story could be. Other outlets not only felt obliged to storify *Panji*'s exclusive but also appeared to jump in eagerly, devoting serial coverage to the case. The scandal dominated radio and television for several days and generated heavy print coverage for another two weeks: On February 20, for example, the newspaper *Merdeka* carried eleven articles, an editorial, and a political cartoon on the case. Nearly every report, in print or over the air, gave a de facto plug to *Panji* by naming the magazine as the outlet that had first published the tape's transcript.

The continued coverage indicated that the story had also become a boon for these other outlets, a lure for expanding their own audiences. *Panji* claimed a spike in circulation following the report and enjoyed a 27 percent increase in advertising between February and April.[92] It also raised its cover price from Rp7,800 to Rp8,500.

Amid this media blitz, however, journalists from other publications were privately critical. M.S. Zulkarnaen from *D&R* dismissed the wiretap report as "gossip" and "sensationalism." He claimed that *D&R* had also known about the tape but "on principle" decided not to report it. As a news magazine, he added, "We cannot exploit gossip . . . we have to know the truth."[93] Budiman S. Hartoyo, a senior editor for *D&R* blacklisted under Suharto, took a somewhat different position. In publishing the tape's transcript, he said, *Panji* had exhibited "unusual political courage," particularly since other media had access to the same information. On the other hand, what *Panji* had done was not investigative reporting, which involves "digging and digging." Instead, he argued, the report was "a kind of lucky break" for the magazine.[94]

Ezki Suyanto, from *DëTAK*, argued that *Panji* was more opportunistic than brave. Her critique was at two levels, assessing the report's value for both journalism and political reform. She said that *DëTAK* had learned of the cassette weeks earlier and that she had heard it at the office of the legal aid organization LBH. During an editorial meeting, she said, *DëTAK*'s staff had debated whether to report it. They decided not to, primarily because they could not confirm the tape's authenticity. Habibie's spokeswoman, Dewi Fortuna Anwar, had avoided meeting with *DëTAK* to hear the tape, and Ghalib had denied, without listening to it, that the other voice was his.[95]

Panji had no more luck than *DëTAK* in getting on-the-record verification for either voice, but found a way around the legal and ethical challenges this presented, stating only that the voices "resembled" (*mirip*) Habibie's and Ghalib's and reporting not that the conversation on the tape proved anything, but simply that it was circulating.[96] In her critique of *Panji*, *DëTAK*'s Suyanto did not dispute that her own paper might have published the tape's contents if its editors had found a journalistically sound way to do it. But they decided that it was "not [a] legitimate" news story because it was "only a conversation" about a situation that was "already apparent from the way [the government] was investigating Suharto." She further explained that "without data," the tape "doesn't prove anything. It's not evidence." Therefore, "from a legal perspective, it can't be used."[97]

Even more problematic, Suyanto argued, the ambiguities of *Panji*'s reporting had diverted the public's focus from the Suharto investigation to *Panji*'s alleged transgressions. Airing the conversation, moreover, served almost no purpose in advancing political reform. The report's transformation of a public secret into a media scandal was "just sensationalism" that amounted to "wasting time" for more important endeavors.[98]

As Suyanto predicted, attention did shift from the Suharto investigation to a hunt for the mastermind behind the wiretap.[99] But the ground shifted again when the police summons of Uni Lubis and the other chief editors provoked a response of defensive solidarity. Whatever private reservations they might have had about *Panji*'s reporting, publicly the press community united in defense of journalists' right to do what *Panji* had done. The consensus was that *Panji* had neither violated journalistic ethics nor broken the law, and the government should cease interrogations.[100] Even the historically progovernment PWI announced readiness to provide legal and logistical support to defend *Panji* should the magazine face a lawsuit, stating that "[w]hat was published by the magazine was in the public interest" and "the product of successful investigati[ve] reporting."[101]

Perhaps most critically, one editor after another cited the newly created Journalistic Code of Ethics as the basis for not cooperating with the investigation. In doing so, they united around both a collective assertion of their rights and a mutual commitment to specific journalistic responsibilities. The controversy bound together journalists, editors, and owners in professing mutual commitment to a shared ethical code.

The controversy also led the press community to affirm their responsibility to the Indonesian public's "right to know" and to claim their own right to protect sources (*hak tolak*)—both of which at this point enjoyed only limited legal status. The *hak tolak* had been codified in the nation's Basic Press Law, as amended in 1982.[102] A closer look at the 1982 amendment reveals that, had the wiretap case gone to trial, the invocation of either "national security" or "public order" could have rendered this right moot.[103] Similarly, the public right to know had a tenuous legal foundation. The recently passed MPR Decree No. 17 stated that "each person has the right to seek, obtain, possess, store, process, and convey information using all available channels."[104] But as long as the government could invoke a security issue, neither the *hak tolak* nor the public's right to know offered real protection.

The minister of justice was already threatening to use state security laws against those responsible for the wiretap, any of which could have been invoked against outlets airing the tape.[105] President Habibie also accused *Panji* of violating his "human rights" by invading his privacy, declaring this breech an "intellectual criminal act that cannot be tolerated." What if, he asked, cabinet discussions or other important telephone conversations were also being tapped? "What if [conversations between] wives speaking with husbands about their families are then tapped?"[106]

Rebutting both the national security and privacy charges, *Panji*'s defenders noted that the magazine had published the wiretapped conversation after the tape had been circulating for months and its contents were no longer a "secret" of any kind.[107] *Panji*'s attorney, Adnan Buyung Nasution, also challenged the national security claim at its foundation, arguing that Indonesia could not leave it to those in power to decide "arbitrarily" what was a state secret "lest all crime, dishonesty, corruption, collusion and nepotism, everything that harms the public, is covered up on the grounds of [being] a state secret."[108] In a forum on the case, AJI members determined that no "national secret" had been revealed, nor had anyone's privacy been violated. The issues in the tapped conversation were public, not private. But as one member pointed out, public figures in Indonesia were not yet considered "public property," and an Indonesian public figure's right to privacy was more protected than that of ordinary citizens.[109]

IMPACT OF THE WIRETAP SCANDAL

This debate was a reminder that, eight months after Suharto's fall, there was still no clear statutory basis in Indonesian law for distinguishing speech that was simply inconvenient for those in power from speech that constituted either a threat to national security or an invasion of privacy. Nor was there a body of case law offering applicable standards for resolving such issues. Had the wiretap case gone to trial, as many advocated, this situation might have changed.[110] But it never reached the courts, leaving the legal arena a potential minefield for journalists reporting controversial information. The wiretap's revelations also did little to advance the reform movement's agenda of seeing Suharto stand trial.

Nevertheless, the *Panji Masyarakat* report and its aftermath furthered the democratic transition in multiple ways. The debate over the case transformed a passing political crisis into an enduring legal principle. Five months after the scandal had pitted the public's right to know against the government's invocation of national security, reformers achieved passage of the 1999 Press Law, supplanting the New Order's Basic Press Law that had been used by the information minister, Harmoko, to close down *Tempo*, *DëTIK*, and *Editor* in 1994.

The new law did not directly address the question of privacy, and the *hak tolak* was still readily overridden by the invocation of national security or public order. Despite these limitations, the law marked a clear break with the past, inspired in part by the wiretap controversy, by explicitly recognizing the public's right to know, a principle absent from previous legislation. Significantly, this right is a central theme of the new law, which not only enshrines the principle, but cites it four times. The wiretap case thus provided an opportunity to form a consensus leading to legal protection for the right to know against the invocation of national security and public order, the cornerstones of the New Order's media controls.

At an industry level, the case's de facto resolution in *Panji*'s favor also confirmed that, in the context of political transition, the conversion of private rumor into public scandal produced commercial success, collegial solidarity, and political protection. Attorney General Ghalib's reputation suffered a serious blow, magnified by later revelations by Indonesia Corruption Watch that he had accepted Rp9.2 billion ($1 million) in bribes from business tycoons under investigation by his office.[111] In June, Ghalib was suspended from his post after the media aired this latest scandal. *Panji Masyarakat*, by contrast, survived to become one of the country's leading news magazines.

In its first year, Indonesia's transition faced multiple threats to its long-term viability. The media, supported by an expanding civil society, were central in resisting reversal at every stage. This resistance took two primary forms: the exercise of new freedoms to widen the bounds of allowable speech and inject needed uncertainty into political contestation, and the mobilization of members of the media to defend these new freedoms.

Responding to the rapid liberalization following Suharto's fall, the media were aggressive in asserting newly won autonomy and widening the scope of permissible public discourse. Over a thousand new players obtained publishing licenses, and print and broadcast media rushed to outdo each other with sensational headlines on corruption and elite conflicts. Established media players, apprehensive about the influx of newcomers, extended a cautious welcome. But rather than lobbying for a return to the protected market ensured by the New Order's restrictive licensing, veteran journalists, publishers, and editors convened workshops to increase professionalism and shield the industry as a whole from the reimposition of government controls.

Wary of the ephemeral nature of this climate, media reformers also collaborated to secure institutional protections for their new freedom. Sixteen months into the transition, they won passage of the 1999 Press Law. This new legislation, described by Janet Steele as "arguably the crown jewel of Reformasi," offered twenty-one articles that fulfilled nearly every demand of media activists.[112] Broadcast representatives worked to pass the similar 1997 Broadcasting Law, which opened their industry to over one hundred television stations (from six under Suharto) and 2,600 radio stations by 2010.[113]

Key to understanding the media's role in democratization, however, is not the extent of liberalization, nor even legal guarantees for new freedoms, but what the media do with these freedoms. In Indonesia, the exercise of freedom served multiple functions, but the most consequential advanced democratization by expanding the boundaries of permissible speech and, critically, provoking confrontations with the state.

In any society seeking to maintain freedom of expression, such pressure is vital in normalizing speech that is threatening to those in power. Without it, freedom itself becomes an abstraction. In democratic transitions, boundaries must be actively tested and stretched because the state will naturally push them back, often a precursor to reconstituted authoritarian rule.

Boundary testing that provokes confrontations with the state, however, can advance a transition beyond expanding de facto limits of tolerance to de jure protections more critical in establishing a legal framework that can permanently protect journalists. After decades of insufficient protection from the constitution's vague guarantee of "freedom of expression" in Article 28, such clarity was particularly important as reformers set out to codify specific rights and responsibilities, such as the right to protect sources and the obligation to serve the public's right to know.

Tempo and *DëTAK* produced some of the most forceful reports pushing the limits of government tolerance, especially *Tempo*'s October 1998 cover story on military involvement in the rapes of ethnic Chinese women and *DëTAK*'s November 1998 investigation revealing high-level orchestration of the "ninja" murder spree in East Java.[114] In presenting carefully researched findings, *Tempo* and *DëTAK* pulled no punches, almost daring officials, particularly military leaders, to react. Both publications recast a troubling narrative of past events, presenting evidence that seemingly spontaneous violence that had marred the democratic transition was elite-directed and designed to make Indonesia seem a cauldron of interethnic conflict requiring a return to authoritarian rule. Together, *Tempo* and *DëTAK* helped prevent reversal by discrediting the military's claims to be a defender of order and casting suspicion on attempts to use intergroup violence to slow reforms.

Despite the element of provocation in both reports and the disturbing implications of their revelations, neither produced an open confrontation with the state. Therefore, while both publications helped broaden the range of permissible speech beyond what had been conceivable under Suharto, the reports did little to institutionalize these widened boundaries, and neither report triggered government backlash or became a major scandal. In short, these hard-hitting investigative reports momentarily expanded the de facto bounds of permissible speech, but in the absence of any confrontation, did not formalize these gains or force accountability on state actors.

Just a few months later, *Panji Masyarakat* released its wiretap report, which accomplished what *Tempo* and *DëTAK* had not, sparking a serious scandal that soon became a confrontation between the government and the print press community. Although the case never reached the courts, it produced new clarity in the battle for media reform, strengthening support among fellow journalists and sympathetic legislators for formal recognition of specific rights, later codified in the 1999 Press Law.

The *Panji* case did not impose legal accountability on actors, but it did impose political accountability. The controversy exposed the new regime's continuity with the old, revealing Habibie's collusion with his attorney general to protect the deposed dictator and dispelling his image as a reformer, which had given legitimacy to his plans for a second term. It also inspired other media outlets to pursue related revelations and question Habibie's fitness as a leader right when Golkar was floating potential presidential candidates for the next election, with Habibie at the top of the list.[115] In sum, the furor threw the ruling party off balance and put Habibie, its best hope for retaining power, on the defensive.

Critics of *Panji* were correct that the wiretap story was neither investigative journalism nor even news. But its impact showed the importance of political scandal, even without the investigative reporting valued by media professionals and observers.[116] Scandal commands sustained public attention by raising rather than answering questions, creating narrative tension, and inviting nonproprietary follow-up coverage by competing media outlets that can produce new revelations, multiplying the impact of the original story.

Though little more than a transcript, the *Panji* report produced a series of reactions that extended the life of the original story and amplified damage to the legitimacy of Habibie's continuation of the Suharto regime. At a delicate moment in Indonesia's democratic transition, scandal served a function of central importance by breaking up collusive pacts suddenly made visible by the exposure of Habibie's telephone conversations. Media-driven scandal thus checked a recurring inclination in democratic transitions toward restoration of the old order by eroding the residual power of the superseded regime.

Following the *Panji* report, Habibie suffered open speculation that he was too damaged to win the next election.[117] With such speculation, the scandal advanced the critical transformation described by Adam Przeworski: the normalization of contests with uncertain outcomes.[118] By their nature, scandals tend to heighten political uncertainty. The wiretap controversy, by reducing the inevitability of a second Habibie term, added a new element of unpredictability to the electoral process. After nearly thirty years in power, Indonesia's ruling party suddenly confronted the possibility that new leadership might take control. The wiretap revelation thus became a key test of Indonesia's progress toward democratization, generating unfamiliar uncertainty through this upset in the balance of power just as the country was preparing for the historic elections of June 1999.

The confrontation that the story provoked with the state served one final purpose: binding the press community together in defense of the public's "right to know." In the unity that Jakarta's media showed in resisting government intimidation through summonses and interrogation, we see the media collectively asserting their right to protect the confidentiality of sources and defend a public right to information. But as chapter 5 will show, even as media reformers worked to pass the 1999 Press Law that established a firm legal foundation for this right, the majority of news outlets would fail the next critical challenge: providing the public, in June 1999, with uncompromised coverage of the nation's first free parliamentary elections in four decades.

CHAPTER FIVE

MEDIA IN RETREAT

It's not the voting that's democracy; it's the counting.
—Tom Stoppard, *Jumpers*

Two weeks after Indonesia's first free elections in forty-four years, in a Jakarta ballroom once packed with hundreds of reporters, a lone journalist rose to ask a question. In the euphoria immediately after millions had cast their ballots, both domestic election officials and international observers had crowded this same space to proclaim the elections "free and fair." But now, after the observers had returned home, this last reporter from the *Jakarta Post* asked, "At what point does the mounting evidence of fraud invalidate the elections?"[1]

In Indonesia's dramatic first year of transition, the culminating event was this June 1999 election of a new parliament that would select the next president, making its integrity critical to the nation's future. As Indonesians registered to vote, expectations were high that these elections would produce a fresh start under a new slate of leaders. The earliest returns showed Megawati's Indonesian Democratic Party of Struggle (PDIP), leading the incumbent, Golkar, encouraging a surge of optimism. But during the subsequent six-week count, Golkar's position steadily improved until it became clear that the ruling party, although losing the popular vote, would dominate parliament and, through coalition-building, likely retain the presidency. Through systematic manipulation, the country's first "free and fair" elections in over four decades saw the old guard reconsolidate power and produce an electoral outcome more artfully engineered than any under Suharto. Indonesia's June 1999 elections and their aftermath revealed a reality facing democratic transitions worldwide—an inherent inclination toward reversal.

With election monitors and international observers lulled by peaceful voting and the opposition's unprecedented lead, those best positioned to expose Golkar's manipulation were the domestic media. Yet in this critical test of a newly empowered fourth estate, most news outlets failed, downplaying signs of fraud and emphasizing the acceptability of the outcome over the integrity of the process, bringing Indonesia close to an effective reversal of the country's transition.

Preceding, and underlying, the drama of these elections were two legislative sessions, one public and contested and the other closed and consensual, that would greatly influence the future character of electoral contestation. Events unfolded in three stages, beginning when the Habibie administration commissioned a group of academics to draft new laws governing the transition and then convened a special parliamentary session in November 1998 to ratify their rules. During that session, reformers mobilized to eliminate the most formidable cog in the old guard's ruling machinery—the bloc of seventy-five appointive military seats (15 percent of the DPR) that reliably voted with Golkar. Activist students and their supporters seemed most fearful of the long-term consequences of compromise on this issue. After mass demonstrations and violent repression, a negotiated resolution reduced but did not eliminate military representation. Parliament, led by Golkar, then spurned calls from student demonstrators for a reform body and asserted its prerogative to finalize these laws, including the new election rules.

Starting in January 1999, the new rules that parliament passed included recondite regulations that advantaged Golkar, allowing the party to set the terms for a referendum on its own rule. Facing little publicity, legislators debated on less dramatic but ultimately critical procedural issues whose closed-door resolution would facilitate Golkar's subsequent systematic electoral manipulation. In sum, through sustained bargaining, key institutional actors—the ruling party, the military, and some minor party politicians—drafted a new electoral structure that reduced some endemic inequities of the past but overall let current stakeholders protect their positions. Finally, in June 1999, rules controlling the parliamentary elections allowed the Golkar machine to implement a counterintuitive strategy of "winning by losing" that positioned it to retain the presidency.

In furthering democratization, a key challenge for the media, as well as other actors, was to normalize and then institutionalize fair, open-ended, and inclusive contestation. At each stage, the media's performance was decidedly mixed—at times aggressively insistent on promoting fairness and transparency, while at others self-consciously compromised in the name of stability. In making these compromises, particularly during the long vote count of June and July, members of the media responded to the ruling party's machinations and the complicity of other actors in ways constituting a critical departure from democratization.

A broader challenge that Indonesia faced, common to pacted transitions, was the need to rely on members of the ruling coalition to preside over reforms that could reduce their power or remove them from office entirely. Thus, the first question for reformers, and the media covering their demands, was not whether the Habibie administration would attempt electoral reform, but whether current power holders owing their positions to the patronage-based electoral process could be trusted to eliminate biases serving their interests.

Indonesia's transition was at its most tenuous during this tumultuous period of electoral reform. While chapter 4 describes the ways in which members of the media confronted threats to their own safety and freedom, what follows is an examination of their contribution to democratization itself in covering the rule writing and the elections' implementation. During this structural change, from the earliest rule writing in September 1998 through the end of the ballot count in July 1999, the country oscillated between progress and reversal, ending safely, albeit tentatively, on a path to continued reform. The oscillation reflected an inherent inclination toward reversal during democratic transitions and showed that, in the absence of aggressive media scrutiny and corresponding public pressure, there were few restraints on this inclination.

REPORTING THE RULE WRITING

Indonesia's democratic transition began in late summer 1998, when the Habibie administration commissioned a group of political scientists, Team Seven, to draft new bills replacing the New Order's political laws. By shifting power away from the executive and liberalizing the party system, the drafts offered limited structural changes to reduce the incumbency advantages enjoyed by Golkar.[2] This early stage of rule writing generated little criticism, and media coverage was largely stenographic. Nevertheless, this coverage imposed transparency, and some accountability, on efforts to address past imbalances.

More critical reporting began in October when conflicts emerged over the bills submitted to the DPR. Main points of contention included the number of legislative seats reserved for the military, which Team Seven's bill set at fifty-five, and the use of a district system of representation, replacing the previous proportional system.[3] Other unresolved questions included what percentage of seats each party must win to qualify for the next election cycle and whether civil servants should be active in political parties.[4]

On television and in print, coverage of this stage mirrored debates among legislators fairly closely, focusing on the few issues preoccupying insiders. Complicating the media's role, however, was pressure to cover those outside the process, some of whom rejected the existing parameters altogether. Most visibly, thousands of students rallied outside parliament to protest the upcoming legislative session that would cement the current leaders' claim to power and their right to determine the rules governing the transition.

As the special session approached, actors fell into roughly two camps, labeled "insiders" versus "outsiders."[5] The outsiders were pushing for major reform, led by students but supported by civil society groups, some retired military, and (with fluctuating enthusiasm) opposition politicians. The group of insiders resisting such reform consisted of regime allies, military stakeholders, and much of the incumbent parliament, all coalescing within the ruling Golkar party.[6] Members of the media could be found across this spectrum, but all outlets faced pressure to "cover both sides," a mantra repeated frequently in this period. Relative to the more independent print press, television stations, all owned by either the government or Suharto's family and cronies, were more sympathetic toward the Habibie regime, the military, and their supporters.

In reporting student efforts to stop the session that would cede this control to the old guard, media coverage, on balance, neither condemned nor endorsed the students' objectives. As the parliamentary session drew closer, however, tensions in Jakarta grew, and the impending showdown put news outlets in an increasingly difficult position.

The protests, inspired by belief that the current government was illegitimate, presented two major predicaments for news outlets. The first involved negotiating the physical risks in covering events on the ground. With tanks rolling through Jakarta's streets and military-recruited civilians (Pam Swakarsa) attacking students, reporting on the demonstrations meant covering confrontations between protesters and security forces and facing the possibility of direct assaults by soldiers and police.[7]

The second predicament was more complex. Covering the protests meant covering the questions they raised: Was the session legitimate, and would the transition be compromised irredeemably if current legislators decided the rules for new elections? Much of the student movement objected to the incumbents' involvement. At this early stage, even strictly factual reporting on the students tended to validate their agenda—including demands that Habibie resign, parliament be dissolved, and genuine reformers with no vested interests take over. The students were pushing for conditions more conducive to effective democratic reform, aiming to inhibit, rather than facilitate, incumbent manipulation of the process. A supportive media might have demonstrated equal passion through editorials challenging the parliament's legitimacy or spotlighting student leaders' demands for a new interim government. Avoiding such coverage risked endorsing a biased process.

Yet encouraging the students' idealism also carried risks, notably that of sanctioning an extraconstitutional resolution to their impasse with the state. The students' preferred way forward was to establish a "reform council" to replace serving legislators.[8] As the session approached, however, a very different extraconstitutional outcome seemed more likely. By November, Jakarta again looked like a city under martial law. Wire barricades reappeared, and soldiers returned to posts along the main roads. Thousands of Pam Swakarsa—young men bussed in by the military and armed with knives and sharpened sticks—stood ready to confront student demonstrators, signaling that the military had no intention of letting students force their demands.[9]

As tensions grew with the approach of the special parliamentary session, so did the possibility that the standoff between students and state would end in an extrasystemic transfer of power, with a coup more likely than a people's presidium. As the session started, journalists found themselves covering a situation similar to that of the previous May, which had ended in a takeover of parliament and a change of regime. This time, however, there was little support beyond student circles for repeating this earlier triumph. The media's challenge, once crackdowns on demonstrations began, was finding a way to support both the students and the parliamentary session they were opposing.

MEDIA TIGHTROPE

In the end, most news outlets supported the students as the nation's conscience while dismissing their demand for an impartial process as impractical.[10] This stance was grounded in a logic that became prevalent in the following months, as concern for survival of the process increasingly trumped concern for its fairness.

The first defining moment in this balancing act was the media's response to a declaration by four reform leaders on the session's first day, November 10. When the session opened with none of the country's main opposition leaders present, a student coalition representing over sixty Jakarta-area campuses made a last-ditch attempt to redirect events. After hours of negotiation, the group convinced the four leaders—Megawati Sukarnoputri, Amien Rais, Abdurrahman Wahid, and the sultan of Yogyakarta, Sri Sultan Hamengkubuwono X—to meet at Wahid's house in Ciganjur, South Jakarta. Students hoped to persuade them to establish a long-sought reform council, though all four were reluctant participants in this student-led convocation. Instead of supporting a transitional government, the "Ciganjur Four" issued a declaration listing moderate demands, including a shorter gap between the general and presidential elections and a six-year phase-out of the military's presence in parliament.[11]

The declaration, the Ciganjur Agreement, fell far short of students' expectations. But its timely appearance at the session's start gave news outlets a middle road, allowing them to critique the session without supporting the students' call for an extraconstitutional transfer of power. Neither ignoring the declaration and affirming the status quo, nor treating it as a betrayal of the students' demand for reform, most media showcased the Ciganjur Agreement as a monumental event—a tangible advance in the reform movement's agenda.

This coverage did not challenge the parliamentary session's legitimacy but did intensify pressure on legislators to meet reformers' more modest demands. Significantly, the session's final decrees reflected all but one of the recommendations. The students, nevertheless, were disappointed. They continued to reject the session and escalate protests, still pressuring the Ciganjur Four to proclaim themselves the nation's interim leaders.

COVERING THE CRACKDOWN

Despite the Ciganjur Agreement, the media's dilemma continued. Arising from the decision to support both the students and the session they rejected, this predicament was compounded by growing security brutality against students and journalists. As events unfolded, media coverage of the standoff between students and the military went through four distinct shifts in interpretation.

Leading up to the session, print and broadcast coverage cast students as a moral force performing their historic role as the nation's conscience. After the session began, however, coverage of the students' standoff with security forces began to shift, particularly on television. Commentary and visuals combined to portray the students as unreasonably pushing the military into a corner. In this view, the problem was not that the country was already facing a crisis because current leaders were biased, but that students were creating a crisis by forcing their demands.

In the first shift, television newscasters began describing the military and police as public servants doing their jobs while falling victim, along with the students, to growing violence. Sympathy for security forces first emerged on the television station RCTI, partly owned by Suharto's oldest son, and on the government-run TVRI. It was clearest in the November 11 reports on the military assaults on students and three photojournalists described in chapter 4. SCTV and ANteve led their evening newscasts with the assaults, interviewing victims who gave gripping descriptions of soldiers beating students like "animals" and battering journalists with riot sticks before smashing their cameras. But RCTI and TVRI coverage was cursory, stating only that journalists "had been struck" before reporting at length on the soldiers' injuries.[12]

By November 12, sympathy for security forces increasingly dominated all television stations, marking the second shift, and was most obvious in coverage of a sit-in protesting the assaults on journalists the previous day. On SCTV, the Antara state news agency's Parni Hadi called for sympathy "yes, for the journalist and student victims, but also for [the military]."[13] On RCTI, Desi Anwar, sister of presidential spokeswoman Dewi Fortuna Anwar, encouraged Hadi to repeat this plea for broader sympathy but then pressed him, using leading questions, to shift blame for security force violence onto the journalists themselves. Through a convoluted exchange, Anwar led Hadi to the desired, exculpatory conclusion that the shooting "was indeed a pure accident." Anwar then pushed this interpretation of events further, asserting that the military was "cornered" both by the MPR fight over their parliamentary seats and "by public pressure from the military's negative image."[14]

That evening, three student protesters died in clashes with security. The next day, November 13, newscasts were a jumble of breaking reports on developments inside and outside parliament, marking the third shift in the narrative. By midafternoon, tens of thousands of people had poured into Jakarta streets to join the students pushing their way toward parliament. Inside the main building, the five commissions worked to finalize the twelve decrees that would set the government's agenda for the rest of Habibie's term.

The commissions were deciding several contentious issues, and resolutions included limited victories for reformers. The decision to name Suharto in a decree on corruption, though short of ordering an investigation into his wealth, still represented a clear win over conservatives on a key issue.[15] Likewise, a decree mandating "gradual" elimination of the military's appointive seats constituted a concession to the Ciganjur signatories, who had proposed a six-year phaseout.[16] Yet the compromises did little to appease student demonstrators, particularly those demanding the military's immediate removal from parliament.

As pressure built, rumors began circulating that unnamed parties planned to use the students to unseat Habibie and install a military junta, making the students unwitting puppets in an extraconstitutional maneuver.[17] That afternoon, security forces fired into the crowds, killing three more students and injuring dozens.

Six months earlier, the shootings of four students at Trisakti University had so shocked the nation that even reporting by the television stations owned by Suharto's kin and cronies began to turn against his regime.[18] Now the same stations, though conveying condolences over the latest casualties, persevered in supporting both the students and the current regime, using variations of the dominant message celebrating students' sacrifice while casting them as victims of larger forces. In one iteration, students were represented as well-meaning but overwhelmed by "brutal" stone-throwing crowds and "uncontrollable masses" who provoked the crackdowns that claimed student lives.[19] In the darkest iteration, a shadowy third party was said to be manipulating the students and the masses in an effort, as President Habibie said, to "topple a legitimate government."[20]

This coverage was not uniform. While TVRI and RCTI were fairly consistent in sympathizing with security forces and parliamentarians, Indosiar, SCTV and ANteve aired more critical content favoring the protesters' perspective.[21] On November 13, ANteve aired arguably the most damning portrayal of the assembly—a video montage showing legislators dozing off and chatting on their cellphones inside parliament while decrees were being passed and students were dying outside.[22] Yet even these stations reported that security forces had been "forced to fire shots" to disperse thousands of unruly students.[23] By evening, all stations used the dual theme of a military cornered by students and growing crowds who were, in turn, being exploited by some third party.

Constructing the students as victims of larger forces undercut their leadership in rejecting the session and their status as the voice of the reform movement. Newscasts further damaged students' credibility through a fourth and final shift in the narrative: the claim that parliament was in fact heeding their demands, which made the session and its resolutions "legitimate."[24] A key voice affirming these points, ironically, was Amien Rais—one of the Ciganjur Four, but also reliably pliant in concurring with television interviewers, particularly those from RCTI and TVRI. On the session's bloodiest day, TVRI announced that Rais had declared that the session's results reflected the people's aspirations, then warned students that attempts to repeat the events of the previous May would likely lead to a military takeover, "to the collapse of everything we have been building."[25]

That same night, RCTI cohosts Adolf Kusuma and Desi Anwar elicited more commentary from Rais in which he discredited the ongoing demonstrations, prompting him first to describe a "mass hysteria that . . . produces a dissatisfaction, a feeling of disappointment, . . . maybe also a mass sadness now . . . exploding here in the capitol."[26] When Kusuma remarked that "earlier provocation actually coming from the people" might have compelled the military to take "a repressive attitude," Rais noted that blame also lay with the military-recruited civilian militia and their "organizers," but ended by criticizing the students. "I think people like this don't have . . . sympathy towards the military," he said. "[The armed forces] also are children of this nation," and if they suddenly lost all their seats, "they would . . . be angry because they would feel humiliated [literally, "knocked down"]."[27] Viewers were left with a message validating indignation at the students' persistence, particularly their demand for the elimination of military seats.[28]

Opinions of the other Ciganjur Four were noticeably absent from these interviews, as were those of the students, who received little airtime to defend their continued mobilization.[29] In one of the few opportunities students had, their logic became clearer. Responding to an SCTV reporter's claim that the demand for elimination of military seats from parliament "has already been accommodated in an MPR decree," a student countered, "In reality, [the military's] presence as a percentage of parliament just increased from 7.5% to 7.68%."[30] This, along with other reasons for rejecting the session's outcome, was left out of other television commentary. Instead, voice after voice declared the special session's results legitimate, leaving viewers with little understanding of why protests continued.[31]

Finally, in a broadcast carried by all stations, MPR Speaker Harmoko issued a formal announcement on the session's final results, including Decree No. 14, which stipulated only a "gradual" reduction in military seats.[32] By the session's close, the MPR had passed a total of twelve decrees establishing the agenda for the transition, including rules for the next election.

Two hours later, TVRI reported that three more students had died, concluding, "The demonstration that caused the casualties . . . is still in progress."[33] Inside news-rooms, staff were reacting to events on the streets whose implications were far larger than the violence they were reporting. In May, the Trisakti shootings had triggered protests, and the ensuing military-engineered violence that claimed over 1,200 lives had destroyed what remained of Suharto's legitimacy. Six months later, the country again confronted news that the military had fired on university students, putting the government's legitimacy in question.

The next day, November 14, signs of public anger were apparent throughout Jakarta as thousands marched in solidarity with the students and thousands more lined the streets to watch. Newspapers displayed graphic images of the previous night's violence capped by bold headlines dripping with blood. Throughout the day, news outlets were barraged with phone calls, emails, and faxes from people expressing outrage over the student deaths. One of the smaller private television stations, Indosiar, aired statements by public figures Sri Bintang Pamungkas and Amien Rais (in marked contrast to his tone the previous day) calling on General Wiranto to resign.[34]

Elsewhere on television, however, a different picture emerged. President Habibie appeared on all stations to reinforce the now-dominant message: third parties were manipulating the people. "There are movements and actions," he explained, "being carried out by . . . groups that plainly are working to violate the law and the constitution by mobilizing the masses to force their will in an effort to undermine . . . the special session's results." These results, he emphasized, "have . . . been decided democratically and constitutionally." TVRI followed with similar statements from other officials.[35] In contrast to print media reports on the dozens of groups demanding that Wiranto and Habibie resign, the station claimed, based solely on statements from the Indonesian Moslem Forum, there was widespread support for the session's results.[36]

The military, for its part, faced little scrutiny over its efforts to discredit the students who had mobilized to remove them from parliament. There was remarkably little criticism of its insertion of Pam Swakarsa into the crowds, a move arguably destined to incite violence, or of its use of snipers and live bullets. As the body count mounted, the recurring message instead was that security forces were "cornered" by demonstrators, "forcing" them to shoot. This message went virtually unquestioned despite, as Wimar Witoelar noted, evidence "that numerous options came and went to stop the shooting or . . . prolong a bloodless standoff by using retreat points predetermined by riot control planning."[37]

None of the stations pursued this critique of military leaders. Instead, the dominant image as the session ended was of Jakarta teetering on the brink of anarchy and soldiers working patiently to establish calm. Significantly, in a final bid to end the demonstrations, the military deployed the marines, a telegenic force in fuchsia berets, who deftly befriended student protesters, producing visuals of amity and acceptance used in coverage by all stations.

Reinforcing what now appeared to be a media consensus, TVRI's 7:00 p.m. news reported that while thousands of citizens sympathized with the students' "moral movement," "uncontrolled mobs" were engaging in burning and looting. A group of public figures, including Amien Rais, the report continued, had held a press conference to urge all sides to restrain themselves to prevent more deaths. The head of the president's think tank, the Indonesian Association of Muslim Intellectuals, appeared again, urging "all sides, including the mass media, to reassure the public because the session's results have been agreed on and accepted by President Habibie."[38] After replaying General Abdul Haris Nasution's earlier warning against "unconstitutional actions," TVRI closed with a picture of order restored, functionally closing the media narrative and ending the crisis. "[T]housands of students, intermingling with masses" now sat quietly listening to orations outside parliament.[39] The orderly dispersal of the crowds after this broadcast signaled the end of the students' demonstrations—and their last unified campaign to challenge incumbent control over the transition.

Only twenty-four hours after the violence of November 13, it was clear that Habibie, his party, and military supporters had defeated the student-led bid to shift control over the transition to nonincumbents. The media, primarily television, assisted the regime in this development, in part by disregarding the demonstrators' main contention—that letting the incumbent parliament write the rules for the country's next elections was inherently unsound. With limited exceptions, coverage affirmed the legitimacy of current leaders' command over the transition, reminding audiences of the danger that rejecting their leadership would pose to national stability.[40]

Despite this outcome, the Habibie administration remained critical of TV coverage and, reprising Suharto's standard tactic, moved to facilitate a government-led buyout of SCTV and Indosiar.[41] One official stated that the SCTV takeover would "be carried out to restore [the station's] health." But SCTV insiders asserted that the move was punishment for critical reporting on clashes between students and security forces. A press release reported pressure on the station "to change its news director as a penance for 'mistakes' committed . . . through its news reporting policy."[42] If this charge was correct, the regime was seeking to skew the democratic process further in its favor by ensuring positive coverage for the president in the lead-up to the coming elections.

FINAL NEGOTIATIONS

With the issue of who would decide the transition's framework resolved, attention turned to final negotiations over three political bills on elections, parties, and the legislature scheduled for passage in January 1999. The bills raised a question for both the media and the public: Would the new rules level the playing field or simply perpetuate the distortions of the past?

As the majority party in parliament, Golkar dominated the new eighty-seven-member committee charged with drafting these bills and pressed for an electoral system that would advantage its political machine. In negotiating, the party confronted two main challengers: independent local leaders who could win by name recognition and minority parties that could aggregate votes at the provincial or national level. By contrast, opposition parties wanted to maximize their minority status and held mixed opinions on local politics.

The most contentious issues, however, were the allocation of unelected seats for the military and the activity of civil servants in political parties, given their access to the state bureaucracy.[43] A final question was whether to retain proportional representation or switch to a district system in which voters would choose not from a slate of political parties but from among individual candidates.

The media, by following these three battles, bolstered opposition efforts to ensure a fairer process. Since civil servants overwhelmingly belonged to Golkar—a legacy of mandatory membership under Suharto—barring them from campaigning would limit the ruling party's unfair access to state resources. Similarly, reducing the number of military appointees, whose interests and votes coincided with Golkar's, would curb the party's advantages in the legislature. Finally, concern for fairness emerged in debates over whether to use a district or proportional system of representation. Under the latter, voters choose from a list of parties rather than candidates, and parties receive seats proportional to votes won at the provincial level. Party leaders then select individuals to fill the seats. A district system, advocates argued, would let voters choose among party candidates in the country's more than three hundred districts and special municipalities, increasing the accountability of representatives to their constituents. But opponents worried that such a system might foster regional separatism, and incumbent legislators, who generally lacked connections to the areas they represented, feared competing against local personalities.[44]

For multiple reasons, the drafting committee voted overwhelmingly to retain the proportional representation that advantaged incumbents, particularly Golkar. But they could not agree on whether to count votes at the provincial level (Level I), allowing minority parties to preserve votes otherwise lost, or at the regency level (Level II), as Golkar representatives advocated. If votes were counted at Level II, a party could easily win a first-past-the-post victory in a regency or township without winning the majority of local votes. Anticipating the 1999 elections, an opposition party representative estimated that Golkar could win more than half the vote using a Level II system, versus no more than 20 percent if votes were counted at Level I.[45]

Though these battles would affect how opposition parties would fare against Golkar's nationwide machine, the arcane details received little media attention. Nevertheless, pressure from other parties forced compromises. The drafting committee agreed to use a Level I system, and Habibie decreed that civil servants must take leave to support a political party.[46]

These concessions suggest that this relatively democratic legislative process—allowing open debate and giving voting power to all parties—had worked, reducing the media burden of critical analysis. But journalists failed to scrutinize other aspects of the new rules that would impact both the parliamentary and presidential elections, including the disproportional allocation of seats favoring Golkar's outer island strongholds.[47]

Nor was there significant coverage of biases favoring Golkar in appointing nonelective provincial representatives (Utusan Daerah) and sectoral group representatives (Utusan Golongan), although these two hundred appointive seats, plus the thirty-eight appointive military seats, would make up a third of the new seven-hundred-member MPR that would select the president in October. These biases would sow bitter controversies later, but as the January 28 deadline for the bills' approval approached, the media's dominant concern was whether they would be rejected and the elections canceled. This concern for the survival of the process over its integrity would emerge repeatedly in the months to come.

After the three bills passed, numerous print outlets focused briefly on Golkar engagement in "money politics" to influence members of the General Election Commission (Komisi Pemilihan Umum, KPU).[48] As June 7 approached, however, such concerns were sidelined by stories anticipating violence and fears that the elections might not go forward at all.[49] In the following weeks, continued emphasis on possible violence prevented scrutiny of the systematic electoral manipulation that would posi-tion Golkar to retain its control over government.

COVERING THE COUNT

On June 7, 1999, after much speculation that Indonesia's first free elections in forty-four years might collapse in violence, over 87 percent of the country's 128 million eligi-ble voters cast ballots.[50] In this landmark contest, overseen by the new KPU, forty-eight parties competed for parliamentary seats. When voting ended without major incident and early returns showed the popular opposition party PDIP in the lead, relief among local and international observers was palpable. The former US president Jimmy Carter called the elections a "festival of democracy" and declared the voting "fair and peaceful." Carter added a cautionary note, saying he had "never seen so complicated a process to choose a president," but the characterization "free and fair" circulated around the globe, virtually closing the books on the story for the international press.[51]

Within Indonesia, however, euphoria soon faded, and the situation grew murky. There was little question that voting had been peaceful and, according to initial reports, conducted fairly in all but two provinces, Aceh and East Timor.[52] PDIP's early lead, unimaginable in past elections, encouraged optimism that Indonesia was launched securely on a path to political change. But its strong showing distracted attention from Golkar's manipulation of the process which, though more sophisticated, was as extensive—and successful—as in past elections.

The manipulation took place both through ordinary fraud and a strategy that one could call "winning by losing." Unlike the simple majority needed to win a direct election for president, Indonesia's indirect selection by parliamentary delegates provided multiple points for maneuvering that eluded most observers. Instead of blatant cheating to steal the elections, Golkar could adopt a more subtle strategy of limited fraud—in the voting and the count—to give its parliamentary delegation a less conspicuous second place and then build coalitions with smaller parties to elect its candidate from the floor of parliament.

Complaints over "ordinary fraud"—primarily poll violations—began coming in as soon as the polls closed on June 7. Only three days later, the Independent Election Monitoring Committee had already received reports of 19,504 violations from their observations at 79,000 of the country's 250,000 polling centers.[53]

Most violations involved Golkar, with the most serious in provinces where the party had fared best, particularly on Sulawesi, the president's home island. In South Sulawesi, after Golkar took two-thirds of the vote, twenty-eight rival parties united to demand a recount, accusing the ruling party of handing out cash bribes.[54] In two regencies, thirty-five parties rejected the results wholesale, citing serious Golkar infractions.[55] By June 29, the Independent Election Monitoring Committee had con-firmed over 9,800 violations in this province alone.[56]

Controversy was greater in North Sulawesi, where Golkar won over half the vote. In mid-June, one observer wrote, "the entire province . . . decided in a tense meeting . . . to hold the entire election over again thanks to Golkar's violations."[57] Significantly, among the forty-eight parties contesting these elections, Golkar won a landslide 57 percent, gaining the party four of the province's seven DPR seats. In Central Sulawesi, another site of myriad violations, Golkar won a crushing 70 percent of the national vote and half of the regional legislative seats.[58]

The Golkar machine was equally strong in the remote eastern islands. In East Timor, where the party also took an early lead, election workers in three districts found ballot boxes opened before they began counting. In another regency with only 30,028 registered voters, workers reported receiving 160,000 ballots. Similarly, reports from West Nusa Tenggara implicated government officials, assumed to be Golkar members, in vote-tampering schemes.[59]

Before the election, there were numerous signs of embezzlement, providing clues to much of the election fraud's funding. In May 1999, evidence surfaced that nearly half of the Rp17.9 trillion ($256 million) that the World Bank had provided for Indonesia's Social Safety Net program had been "misappropriated." Election monitoring groups reported that some of this money had gone to Golkar campaigning in the outer islands.[60] The same month, observers had estimated that Golkar's campaign would spend at least one billion rupiah ($116,000) per electoral district—nearly $35 million nationwide.[61] Despite clear indications that much of the money was obtained illegitimately, few questioned how party officials could accumulate such vast sums during an economic crisis.

Media Dilemmas

Before and after the vote, the media devoted little space to these reports. Their dilemma was now that reporting fraud risked discrediting the electoral process and derailing the transition; remaining silent risked undermining the transition less perceptibly by allowing the perpetuation of engineered outcomes.

Biases in media ownership also discouraged critical coverage, particularly within television stations owned by Suharto supporters, where staff complained of strong pressure to favor Golkar. Yet as the nation began the long process of ballot counting, the historic nature of these events imposed caution on everyone involved, particularly news outlets. For the first time in decades, Golkar was not heading to another landslide victory. Early returns showed the once-entrenched ruling party trailing PDIP by double digits, suggesting that even if Golkar was subverting the process to stay in power, the strategy was failing.[62]

This outcome, regardless of fraud, seemed synonymous with democratization's triumph, making irregularities appear inconsequential. For the first time but not the last, a desirable outcome was equated with the advancement of democratization. Yet Golkar was not failing in its bid to retain power. There was another, less visible dimension to the story ignored by all but a few journalists—the party's implementation of the second-place strategy of "winning by losing."

As international observers declared the elections free and fair, two little-noticed trends signaled Golkar's implementation of such a strategy. Advantages that the party had secured in the earlier rule writing grew more apparent—specifically, those allocating more seats per registered voter to outer island provinces (one per 172,750 voters) where Golkar support was stronger than to opposition bailiwicks on Java and Bali (one per 203,917 voters).[63]

After the vote, returns from the outer provinces were coming in far more slowly than from Java and Bali—an apparent use of the machine strategy of withholding votes until the minimum number necessary for victory becomes clear.[64] By June 10, with just 16 percent of votes tallied nationwide, Megawati's PDIP was winning 44 percent of votes cast for the five largest parties in the six most populous provinces on Java and Bali, building a wide lead over Golkar's 12 percent (see table 1). By contrast, in five outer-island provinces—three on Sulawesi—Golkar was winning an average of 45 percent to PDIP's 32 percent.[65]

Golkar's lopsided showing in these five provinces was not necessarily remarkable, given the party's strength and overall organization. More noteworthy was the significantly faster rate of early returns from PDIP strongholds compared to those from remote provinces where Golkar was leading. In its stronghold Yogyakarta, PDIP held a substantial 23 percent lead over Golkar on June 10, with 32 percent of total votes counted. That same day, in the Golkar-dominated South Sulawesi, whose twenty-four seats were weighted heavily, at 176,000 voters each, returns were trickling in with only 6 percent tallied. Significantly, though South Sulawesi was Habibie's home province, Golkar and PDIP were in a dead heat, with 19 percent each.[66] Four days later, when excitement over PDIP's early showing had faded, South Sulawesi's unlikely neck-and-neck race of June 10 had disappeared, leaving Golkar with an overwhelming 75 percent of the vote versus only 10 percent for PDIP.[67]

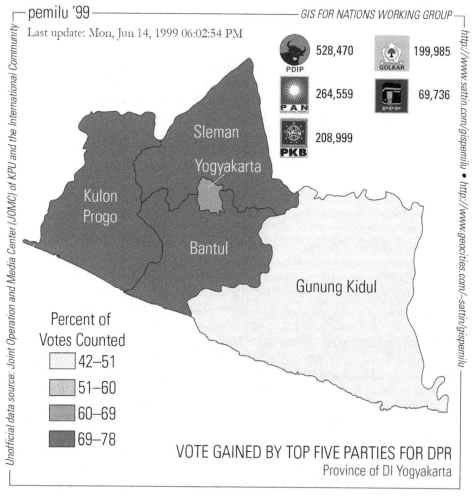

Maps and tables downloaded at the KPU's media headquarters in Jakarta on the seventh day of the count, June 14, 1999, showed a telling pattern indicating that the Golkar machine was withholding votes to allow a late-hour inflation of the party's returns. In the opposition district of Yogyakarta, where the insurgent PDIP had won 42 percent of the total, the numbers were pouring in, rising fast from a range of 42–78 percent tallied at 6:02 p.m. (map on left) to an overall 78.64 percent by 7:30 p.m. (table 2). By contrast, in South Sulawesi (map on right), where the ruling Golkar party was winning 75 percent of the total, by 11:25 p.m. on June 14, only 31 percent of the votes had been reported.

VOTE GAINED BY TOP FIVE PARTIES FOR DPR
Province of Sulawesi Selatan

Mamuju

Luwu

Majene Polewali Mamasa

Tana Toraja

Palopo

Enrekang

Pinrang

Sidenreng Rappang

Pare-Pare

Wajo

Soppeng

Barru

Bone

Pangkajene Kepulauan

Ujung Padang

Maros

Sinjai

Gowa

Takalar

Bulukumba

Bantaeng

Jeneponto

GOLKAR — 765,070

PDIP — 101,027

PPP — 93,805

PAN — 43,878

15,816

Percent of
Votes Counted

0–17

17–34

34–51

51–68

Last update: Mon, Jun 14, 1999 06:02:54 PM

Table 1. Indices of electoral fraud, Indonesian elections, June 10, 1999.
Votes counted: 16%.

Province	Golkar (% of votes for top 5 parties)	Golkar votes	PDIP (% of votes for top 5 parties)	PDIP votes	Votes reported (%)	Number of seats	Registered voters/ seat
INNER ISLANDS							
Bali	8	9,192	88	100,081	18	9	226,685
Jakarta*	12	93,463	41	322,333	18	18	281,792
C. Java	16	201,853	47	603,555	12	60	312,010
E. Java	14	372,548	40	1,050,108	20	68	320,759
W. Java	7	11,321	9	14,970	25	82	308,945
Yogyakarta	17	85,000	40	204,830	32	6	321,567
OUTER ISLANDS							
Aceh	15	7,816	8	4,186	6	12	123,858
E. Kalimantan	31	63,184	39	80,006	25	7	190,763
Lampung	24	51,905	52	114,462	12	15	245,087
E. Nusa Tenggara	52	53,328	41	42,050	6	13	153,984
N. Sulawesi	50	59,268	32	37,648	11	7	248,346
S. Sulawesi	19	13,883	19	13,747	6	24	176,234
S. E. Sulawesi	69	61,337	17	14,920	11	5	180,166
E. Timor	34	15,032	53	23,291	12	4	105,024

* Includes overseas ballots.

Source: Joint Operations Media Center, Aryaduta Hotel, Jakarta, June 10, 1999.

On June 14, with 58 percent of votes counted nationwide, the pattern of slower returns from pro-Golkar regions became apparent (see table 2 and maps). In Bali and the whole of Java (East, West, and Central), over two-thirds of votes were already tallied, and PDIP's lead had reached 50 percent. Yet in the eight provinces where Golkar had a double-digit lead, only two-fifths of returns had come in. There was a clear correspondence between provinces with heavily weighted seats, a wide Golkar majority, and a slow rate of return—a situation indicative of manipulation through an electoral machine.

This discrepancy in return rates was the first indication that the Golkar machine might be holding back votes from provinces where the party was strong and there were more seats per registered voter—the formula Golkar had fought for earlier.[68] The second, little-noticed trend aiding Golkar was the slow but steady erosion of PDIP's lead, also facilitated by the sluggish pace of outer island returns. While Golkar had

Table 2. Indices of electoral fraud, Indonesian elections, June 14, 1999.
Votes counted: 58%.

Province (report time)	Golkar (% of votes for top 5 parties)	Golkar votes	PDIP (% of votes for top 5 parties)	PDIP votes	Votes reported (%)	Number of seats	Registered voters/ seat
INNER ISLANDS							
Bali (2:46 p.m.)	11	202,613	84	1,523,048	97	9	226,685
Jakarta (11:06 p.m.)*	12	297,800	43	1,020,130	60	18	281,792
C. Java (9:42 p.m.)	15	1,514,821	52	4,958,759	63	60	312,010
E. Java (9:44 p.m.)	14	1,436,047	39	3,929,818	52	68	320,759
W. Java (9:23 p.m.)	31	2,998,999	38	4,040,994	52	82	308,945
Yogyakarta (7:30 p.m.)	16	199,985	42	528,470	79	6	321,567
OUTER ISLANDS							
Aceh (7:36 p.m.)	19	54,333	15	43,612	25	12	123,858
Bengkulu (11:25 p.m.)	36	129,262	39	138,769	62	4	202,016
Irian Jaya (7:18 p.m.)	51	89,169	39	68, 225	22	13	77,066
Jambi (11:16 p.m.)	40	118,100	34	98,194	27	6	228,785
C. Kalimantan (11:16 p.m.)	31	127,235	41	169,702	50	6	166,235
E. Kalimantan (9:37 p.m.)	32	189,755	40	228,199	54	7	190,763
S. Kalimantan (10:01 p.m.)	26	154,999	30	176,298	48	11	158,647
W. Kalimantan (9:33 p.m.)	34	104,769	35	107,631	20	9	230,506
Lampung (9:36 p.m.)	25	329,504	53	711,321	48	15	245,087
Maluku (9:01 p.m.)	34	79,696	39	93,626	29	6	170,955
E. Nusa Tenggara (7:27 p.m.)	23	268,779	23	269,499	35	13	153,984
W. Nusa Tenggara (6:29 p.m.)	56	378,085	21	140,110	49	9	231,363
Riau (9:18 p.m.)	35	345,246	32	312,149	50	10	254,358
C. Sulawesi (8:07 p.m.)	64	254,689	18	72,438	41	5	240,558

(continued)

Table 2 (*continued*)

Province (report time)	Golkar (% of votes for top 5 parties)	Golkar votes	PDIP (% of votes for top 5 parties)	PDIP votes	Votes reported (%)	Number of seats	Registered voters/ seat
N. Sulawesi (11:17 p.m.)	57	294,413	26	132,238	56	7	248,346
S. Sulawesi (9:09 p.m.)	75	765,070	10	101,026	31	24	176,234
S. E. Sulawesi (9:16 p.m.)	77	240,576	12	37,262	43	5	180,166
N. Sumatra (11:06 p.m.)	2	49,696	50	1,018,586	43	24	242,969
S. Sumatra (9:38 p.m.)	26	511,612	47	919,200	60	15	271,434
W. Sumatra (11:22 p.m.)	28	278,081	13	126,732	53	14	168,886
E. Timor (2:01 p.m.)	47	58,238	44	54,826	39	4	105,024

* Includes overseas ballots.

Source: Joint Operations Media Center, Aryaduta Hotel, Jakarta, 11:25 p.m., June 14, 1999.

won up to two-thirds of the popular vote in past elections, such margins were no longer credible. Given support for PDIP, even engineering a more modest win would have risked rejection from the opposition, delegitimating the entire election.[69] However, by allowing PDIP a wide margin in the first volatile days after the voting and then closing this lead over time, Golkar avoided provoking a backlash against its eventual strong showing.[70]

Although observers paid little attention and opposition parties appeared unaware or complacent, Golkar remained confident, a position that, in retrospect, was a harbinger of a predetermined outcome. Three weeks in, the party chair, Akbar Tanjung, boasted that Golkar would narrow the gap with the front-running PDIP to just thirty-five seats, allowing it to form a coalition government.[71]

Tanjung's prediction was eerily precise. In the near-final results released in mid-July, Golkar had closed the gap with PDIP to thirty-four seats. Significantly, Golkar's strongest showing was in the eastern islands, where the party won an average of 36 percent of provincial seats compared to only 17 percent on Java and Bali.[72] Tanjung also predicted that PDIP would have trouble convincing Muslim parties to support a woman, Megawati, for the presidency, allowing Golkar to build coalitions with the three largest Islamic parties and gain another 105 seats.[73] He further speculated that by asking General Wiranto to be Habibie's running mate when the presidential slates came before parliament, Golkar could ensure the votes of the MPR's thirty-eight armed forces delegates in the final ballot.[74]

By mid-July, Indonesian observers began to see the prescience of Tanjung's remarks. On the basis of a penultimate count, the *Jakarta Post* projected that Golkar would win 120 seats, with roughly two-thirds from the outer islands. PDIP would secure 154 seats, with well over half from Java and Bali. The three putatively sexist Muslim parties had won 125 votes, giving a possible Golkar-Muslim coalition a total of 245 votes—a clear majority among parliament's 462 elective seats.[75] Combining this majority with Golkar's influence over the remaining 200 appointive seats, with or without the military's 38 votes the ruling party was in a strong position to retain the executive in the October selection of the president by the plenary 700-member parliament (MPR).[76]

MINIMIZING THE FRAUD

Although these observations are not definitive, this pattern should have raised questions for working journalists downloading up-to-the-minute tallies from computers at the election's media headquarters in the Aryaduta Hotel. Yet in the following weeks, the dozens of local and foreign reporters crowded four-deep to print out these tallies failed to report the pattern.[77] Instead, coverage cited the KPU's explanation that the slow count was the result of "technical problems," such as assiduous reporting procedures and "poor transportation," and relied heavily on statements from foreign election monitors, who consistently dismissed the violations as insignificant.[78]

While news outlets publicly adopted a reassuring stance, Indonesian reporters privately indicated concern over discrepancies in the pace of the returns. Two days after the ballot, SCTV's news director, Riza Primadi, noted that it seemed suspicious that counts from opposition strongholds in Bali and Java were coming in quickly while tallies from the outer islands were trickling in.[79] Later, however, he dismissed his observation, citing the KPU explanation that poor transport and communications had caused the slower returns.[80] But this justification failed to explain why fraud allegations from the outer islands were also far more numerous and serious than those reported from Java and Bali, or why four of the outer island provinces experiencing the slowest returns were in Sulawesi, a well-developed island with relatively strong communications and transportation.

Primadi, with other members of the media, appeared reluctant to focus on distortions. Journalists found themselves in a difficult position. In conversations at the Aryaduta Hotel during the count, some explained their caution. Reporters from four regional Indonesian papers were among the most nervous, stating that "it was best not to look into evidence of cheating." They added they "had a sense" such investigations were not what their editors wanted, and appeared relieved that little was expected of them on this subject.[81]

During lunch with a Jakarta-based television crew two days after the vote, another journalist from SCTV, Raymond Kaya, was more candid, admitting he and others thought that the violations were possibly serious. But, he explained, they were wary of television's power to incite the public and preferred to downplay the cheating to avoid sparking riots among opposition supporters that could invalidate the entire election.[82]

Until the end of the count, "technical problems" explained the slow returns from outlying areas in commentary that relied on the KPU.[83] As the count dragged on, media attention waned. Over a month before the final tally, the Aryaduta ballroom, once crowded with journalists, had emptied out. At a last press conference, a lone journalist from the *Jakarta Post* finally asked KPU delegates, "At what point does the mounting evidence of fraud invalidate the elections?" The commission answered evasively, leaving the question hanging. Whatever the official reply might have been, there were no other news outlets present to report it.[84]

EXPLAINING THE COVERAGE

In the KPU's final tally, released in late July, PDIP won the elections with 33.74 percent of the popular vote, a surprising plurality in a forty-eight-party contest, causing jubilation among supporters and a general sense among observers that the elections were a success. In what seemed a reversal of fortunes, Golkar received 22.44 percent.[85] Yet while conceding to PDIP, Golkar had successfully secured a solid position to form a government through coalition building.

Golkar's subtle subversion of the electoral process to reach this end, aided by a disproportionate allocation of seats favoring the outer islands during the rule writing, went virtually unreported. Most coverage, both Indonesian and foreign, reiterated the message that the elections had been free and fair and the ruling party's infractions were neither serious nor systematic enough to be significant.

There were exceptions to this reassurance, particularly among the Jakarta-based newsweeklies, whose election coverage included several investigative reports.[86] The most hard-hitting was an exposé published in the June 21–27 issue of *Tempo*, accusing Arnold Baramuli, chair of President Habibie's Supreme Advisory Council and Golkar party boss, of practicing "money politics" in North Sulawesi to swing the election in Golkar's favor.[87] The next week, *Tempo* published a ten-page investigation on electoral fraud nationwide.[88] The two reports cited evidence that Baramuli had funneled Golkar funds to religious organizations in North Sulawesi to influence the vote, and further implicated his company, Poleko, in two separate scandals.[89]

Though damning, these reports attracted almost no follow-up and failed to garner attention that might have checked the cheating.[90] More media focus on irregularities might have induced the KPU to intervene in the outer-island provinces where Golkar was getting its strongest majorities. Had the KPU declined, public pressure might have forced the issue, imposing greater accountability on the commissioners. Without this pressure, they were free to turn a blind eye.

Also missing from most reporting was the relentless horse-race coverage all but inescapable in Western elections. Such coverage, though easily criticized for its reductive tendencies, would nonetheless have drawn attention—through daily or hourly coverage—to the shrinking gap between the top parties toward the end of the race. In Indonesia's first post-Suharto elections, discussion of the closing gap was minimal, and even the major opposition parties appeared to accept Golkar's gains with equanimity.[91]

How can we account for this seeming complacency? Fundamentally, there was relief that the elections had gone forward with almost no violence. Pragmatically, there was also a general understanding that Indonesia lacked the resources and the political will to invalidate the results and oversee a second vote. Though the elections were compromised, a consensus formed that the level of fraud was acceptable. Finally, as later reports revealed, the major opposition parties, numerous religious organizations, and much of the media were being bribed for their discretion with funds from the swelling coffers of the state rice monopoly, Badan Urusan Logistik (the State Logistics Agency), known as Bulog.[92]

The one opposition leader who took a stand, Abdurrahman Wahid, did not get far. A few days after the June 7 vote, the Singapore-based *Straits Times* reported that Wahid had met secretly with the army chief, Wiranto, on the eve of the elections to accuse the military of interfering in the balloting. The report said that soldiers "had insisted on accompanying the ballot boxes to their tally centres at various districts in and out of Java," violating election rules banning both "military and civilian bureaucracy" from any involvement. Wahid then argued that because "Special Forces (Kopassus) soldiers were 'meddling' in the vote-counting process" on Golkar's behalf, the ruling party needed to be removed from power and an emergency government established.[93]

In the following weeks, Habibie's government made it clear that it would not tolerate such challenges, particularly by people contesting election results on the streets. After the foreign press and most international monitors had departed, those who remained noticed the reappearance in Jakarta of the barbed-wire barricades, army tanks, and anti-riot troops that had all but disappeared after the November 1998 parliamentary session.[94]

Daily protests began outside the KPU, at first met with only light security. But on July 2, a group of students, joined by the People's Democratic Party, squared off against dozens of riot police outside the KPU's complex. Mobilizing to prevent rigging of the country's elections, they demanded that Golkar "be disqualified for . . . cheating by rigging the vote count and using its . . . cash reserves to buy votes in the outlying provinces."[95] In response, police began firing into the crowd and beat protesters back from the building with rattan riot sticks.[96]

As the count dragged into July, cynicism over the delays rose, along with unease among PDIP supporters who had, like much of the media, equated a win of the popular vote with an eventual Megawati presidency. Even Desi Anwar (RCTI news anchor and sister of Habibie's spokeswoman Dewi Fortuna Anwar) admitted, "It is fortunate that . . . Indonesians are getting used to dashed hopes and unfulfilled promises," since "with every delay," the democratic process was further "usurped by Machiavellian political intrigues."[97]

When the KPU announced the final results after six weeks, over half the election's forty-eight parties refused to sign off on the final tally, citing 120,000 "unresolved violations," while much of the media treated the complaints as politicking by small parties disgruntled by their failure to win seats.[98]

The KPU responded by handing the election results to President Habibie, who issued a decree validating the final outcome, and thus the allocation of seats among parties. On August 9, Indonesia's poll supervisory committee, Panwaslu, seconded the president's decision, stating that the decree "should be considered as a collective validation that the election was relatively free and fair."[99] In effect, Habibie's decree ended the popular phase of the elections and shifted focus to parliament, where delegates would elect the next president.

Adding to Golkar's advantages in the maneuvering that followed, there was another MPR block likely to be weighted in the party's favor—the two hundred appointive representatives with seats in the seven-hundred-member body that would elect the president. These would consist of 135 Utusan Daerah, or provincial representatives, and 65 Utusan Golongan, or delegates from interest groups representing "non-political" sectors of society, such as women's organizations, "youth and students," civil servants, and various religious blocs. Theoretically, the Utusan Daerah and Utusan Golongan blocs would "comprise personalities . . . not involved in political parties, i.e., neither a member on the board of parties nor a party candidate in the general elections."[100] In practice, the two groups were far from nonpartisan.

Two months after the election, officials still had no clear criteria for choosing the two hundred representatives, much less a formula to ensure their neutrality. Election commissioners were considering two alternatives for deciding the 135 provincial representatives, and both favored Golkar.[101] By August, it became clear that the process for selecting the sixty-five sectoral members was strongly weighted toward the ruling party.[102]

As the media remained quiet on these critical issues, the only protest came from a group of some two hundred student demonstrators who rallied on August 9 outside the KPU headquarters over the selection of sectoral representatives, slaughtering a white goat with the initials "KPU" painted on its side. The students demanded that the commission dissolve the "Team of Fifteen" selecting the sixty-five interest-group delegates, charging that it lacked independence and that members were abusing their authority to serve partisan interests.[103]

Press in Parliament?

Ironically, even as news outlets downplayed electoral manipulation, leaders of the twenty journalists' associations were fighting to protect their industry's new independence. Among the sixty-five interest-group seats in the MPR, the KPU was planning to reserve at least one for "the press." As Golkar maneuvered to increase seats for its loyalists, the Indonesian Journalists' Association (PWI) put forth their Jakarta branch head, Tarman Azzam, a Golkar supporter who had helped blacklist members of the Alliance of Independent Journalists (AJI) after the 1994 bans.[104]

In response, AJI head Lukas Luwarso expressed hope that his organization would also win one of the sectoral MPR seats. But when AJI convened a meeting with four other journalists' associations, all present concluded that they should oppose the appointment of any member of the media to parliament.[105] Somewhat unexpectedly, the group that articulated the winning argument against media representation was the Indonesian Television Journalists Association, whose head, Haris Jauhari, was a lead contender for one of the sectoral posts.[106] Jauhari argued that MPR membership would compromise the standards of professionalism that his association espoused.[107] How could the media report objectively on the MPR if they became part of the MPR?[108] Other attendees agreed that the media should not be represented in the legislative body that decided the next president.[109]

In an effort to block a seat for the pro-Golkar PWI, Jauhari, host of the talk show *Partai-Partai*, invited the main actors to discuss the issue before a live audience.[110] By the end of a spirited debate, opponents of media representation made it clear that such participation in government would compromise media independence. Two days later, the television journalists' association and AJI invited all twenty new journalists' associations to a meeting that ended in unanimous opposition to any media representation in the MPR.[111] The next day, August 11, their leaders appeared before television cameras to present their rejection of media representation to the chair of the KPU. "[Since] journalists are required to always guard [their] independence," the statement said, "with involvement in the MPR it is feared that journalists will become caught up in politicking that could undermine their independence."[112]

A week later, KPU members favoring media representation fought to appoint a PWI delegate to what was now the only sectoral seat for the media. "Fortunately," noted Jauhari, "at a critical moment," journalists covering the meeting decided to intervene. Shifting roles from observers to participants, they drew up a petition protesting the seat's award to the PWI, circulated it among reporters present, and interrupted the meeting to deliver it.[113] After this development, the commission finally voted to eliminate the media seat from the Utusan Golongan.

The associations' success had significance beyond its partisan context. They could claim victory in blocking Golkar from installing a supporter in parliament since securing an MPR post for the PWI, an instrument of Suharto's control, would have cost the media professional distance and restored the PWI's position as the official representative of all journalists. More broadly, the battle united the jumble of new journalists' associations around a common goal clearly articulated in their statement to the KPU: "The journalistic profession constitutes a fourth power ('fourth estate') that is expected . . . to perform the function of control over the other three powers: executive, judicial, legislative."[114]

"Today, whether history takes note or not," Jauhari said, "we have launched an effort of no small significance to work together . . . to situate the press in its proper place, that is, free from the three [branches of government]." Whether the media's sectoral seat would be granted to another Golkar supporter was also irrelevant. "What matters," Jauhari argued, "is that we have advanced one more step in our efforts to position the media as the fourth estate in our democratic nation."[115]

This victory bore little relationship to actual reporting practices that, by default, had helped skew the parliamentary elections toward Golkar. But it did draw a clear dividing line between the news media and the state, which would become critical in the final phase of the 1999 elections—the selection of the next president.

On the eve of Indonesia's first democratic elections in over forty years, many saw Suharto's successor, B. J. Habibie, as a weak, transitional figure, and his party, Golkar, as a discredited, fading force. Yet together they came remarkably close to retaining the presidency and perpetuating Golkar's lock on power. As the electoral process moved into selection of the president, the ruling party enjoyed advantages in the appointive bloc, strengths in coalition building, and pluralities in the outer islands.[116] By the final ratification of the count on July 28, Golkar—though trailing the top opposition party, PDIP, in the popular vote by double digits—seemed poised for its seventh presidential win. With little violence or visible fraud, the party had manipulated the parliamentary elections, widely hailed as "free and fair," to produce an outcome as carefully engineered as any under the New Order.

Throughout this period, Indonesia's media bore witness to an extraordinarily contentious process—from the incumbent parliament's debates over the transition rules to their implementation in the June 1999 ballot. During the long count that followed, the media, influenced by factors ranging from owner biases and the seeming complacency of opposition leaders to fears of invalidating the elections and thereby sparking riots, downplayed reports of irregularities that were indicators of systematic fraud.[117]

In the realm of electoral politics at least, Indonesia, with its newly freed media, appeared to be back where it had started, tacitly accepting a rigged process in the name of stability and compromise. This caution aided Golkar's manipulation, threatening the gains of a year of democratic reform, including progress in institutionalizing the uncertain outcomes inherent in fair and open contestation. After a year of electoral reform and, at times, reckless experimentation with their new freedom, the

Indonesian media succumbed to pressure to ignore the cheating to save the elections, and in doing so, failed to guard the integrity of the electoral process.

Yet as the following chapter shows, the country was not right back where it had started, largely because the media had, in fact, undergone a fundamental change. From the rule writing through the count, outward manifestations of this transformation remained largely superficial, filling the public sphere with bluster, sensationalism, and some critical debate but effectively ignoring the fraud that compromised the country's first post–New Order elections, tilting the transition toward reversal. In the next stage, however, the run-up to the October selection of the president, the power of Indonesia's newly liberated media to block this same reversal became clear with a campaign finance scandal that jolted them into action, setting off a competitive frenzy among news outlets, each vying to break the next development. The revelation and counterrevelation that followed would pitch Indonesia into a maelstrom of factional infighting and partisan warfare that, surprisingly, made continued democratization possible.

CHAPTER SIX

BALIGATE AND ALL THE GATES

Everybody's for democracy in principle. It's only in practice that the thing gives rise to stiff objections.

—Meg Greenfield, "The People's Revenge"

At the close of Indonesia's first post-Suharto elections in July 1999, the top opposition party, PDIP, had won the popular vote, beating the ruling Golkar party by double digits and leaving its supporters confident of capturing the presidency. Over the next few weeks, however, the position of PDIP and its presidential candidate, Megawati Sukarnoputri, only grew weaker as Golkar and its allies outmaneuvered them on every front. "Now, as her political rivals dance rings around her, building coalitions in rooms heavy with the stale smoke of kretek cigarettes," wrote journalist David Jenkins, "Megawati may be in danger of losing the presidency, the greatest prize in Indonesian politics." Newspaper executive Sabam Siagam warned, "We could end up with the party that has managed to win the largest number of seats in the house finding itself outside the system. If that happens," he added, "I don't know what democracy is about. Never mind that there will be riots outside. It will mean that the largest party in the system is marginalised—not speaker of the house, not chairman of the MPR, not president."[1]

As observers noted these ironies for the transition, the government prepared for anticipated riots, deploying tens of thousands of soldiers to contain demonstrations and pushing a state security bill through parliament to give the executive emergency powers to ban protests and seize control of the country's communications.[2] At this point in Indonesia, there was a palpable threat of authoritarian reversal manifest in the massing of troops, passage of a bill that authorized repression, and continued electoral maneuvering to block the rotation of power.

Apparently designed to ensure, if not impose, public acceptance of a second Habibie presidency, these developments posed a serious challenge to Indonesia's transition at several levels. Returning to Adam Przeworski's conceptual framework, they constituted a clear setback in the institutionalization of the uncertainty of open-ended contestation central to democratization.[3] Indonesia was confronting the possible emergence of at least two conditions, or "perverse elements," that the theorist Samuel Valenzuela identifies as incompatible with or subversive to democratization: the existence of tutelary powers and the absence of "meaningful turnover in leadership via elections." As Chileans had done in their country's earlier transition, Indonesians faced maneuvering by the departing regime to "establish the institutional and organizational basis" for the possible exercise of "military tutelarity over the democratic process."[4] Fear of military intervention gave the regime's incumbents leverage in advancing their own interests. Furthermore, the looming prospect of Golkar's continued control over both the legislature and executive threatened to reverse the progress toward democratization promised by the opposition's victory in the June elections. There were clear signs that Indonesia could be heading the way of Chile and other nations where democratic transition had stalled.

Complicating this incipient reversal, however, a campaign finance scandal broke, striking mortal blows to President Habibie's candidacy and throwing his party's deal making into disarray. While this scandal, dubbed "Baligate," did not force Golkar to give up any seats won with fraudulent funds, its impact was profound. The same news media that had been so cautious in reporting fraud during the elections in June and July seized upon these new revelations, splashing them across front pages and evening newscasts for weeks. In the months leading to parliament's selection of the president on October 20—the final phase of the 1999 elections—it was the media's sustained attention to the scandal, and protests mobilized in response, that returned the uncertainty of open-ended contestation to Indonesia's electoral process and facilitated a meaningful circulation of leadership.[5]

More broadly, if Golkar's successful engineering of the 1999 legislative elections examined in chapter 5 demonstrates democratization's inherent inclination toward reversal, the convergence of a media-driven electoral scandal and Habibie's final bid to retain the presidency illustrates the central role that a competitive media, combined with civil society, can play in blocking this same reversal. Moreover, close examination of Baligate offers insight into the phenomenon of political scandal itself, helping to explain why some stories surface only to disappear, while others escalate to produce political change.

Baligate

A month after *Tempo*'s close-grained investigative report on Golkar's systematic campaign fraud in Sulawesi faded with little impact, a similar story of electoral corruption snowballed into a full-blown scandal reconfiguring the country's political landscape.[6] The story began in late July 1999 with an unexpected disclosure at a bank-restructuring seminar in Jakarta's Millennium Hotel. During this otherwise sedate event, a financial analyst named Pradjoto [one name] exposed a dubious transaction between the private Bank Bali and a finance company with ties to Golkar. That same day, the former underground email list SiaR broke the story to its limited readership.[7] The following day, *Kompas* reported it in its English edition.[8] By August 3, it was headlined by most of the major news outlets (print and broadcast) and even the government-run news agency, Antara.[9] The story and subsequent revelations rocked the nation, capturing media and public attention to an extent not seen since Suharto's fall.

In a political environment where, as the *Straits Times* observed, "one scandal a week [was] the new yardstick," the Bank Bali story dwarfed everything to date, overshadowing nearly all other issues for weeks.[10] "Even if all the country's top young models appear naked on the front pages of local newspapers tomorrow," commented the *Jakarta Post*, "they couldn't top the latest bank scandal to have hit this country."[11]

The scandal had its origin in the banking collapse triggered by the 1997 Asian financial crisis. As part of a $130 million bailout, Indonesia's bank restructuring agency (Badan Penyehatan Perbankan Nasional, BPPN) had taken control of the privately held Bank Bali. More than a year later, in the middle of the night, an unknown source dropped a package of documents on Pradjoto's doorstep. In response to a question during the July seminar about holdups in foreign investment, this banking law expert shared the documents' revelation that Bank Bali had paid the Golkar-connected firm Era Giat Prima (EGP) a whopping fee of nearly $80 million to facilitate payment from BPPN of $120 million as compensation for defaulted loans.[12]

These negotiations were curious from the start since a blanket government guarantee already covered Bank Bali's claims to BPPN's rescue funds, obviating the need for any third-party involvement.[13] More surprising still was the size of the debt-collection fee, which amounted to 60 percent of the loans recovered. Pradjoto said the amount sounded so "crazy" that at first he did not believe the transaction could have happened. He discarded the documents left at his door, forcing the anonymous whistle-blower to leave another copy a few days later.[14]

MEDIA COVERAGE AND POLITICAL INTERESTS

Instead of downplaying the story, news outlets pounced on it, plunging headfirst into the factional warfare it brought to the surface. Almost immediately, observers drew parallels with the United States' Watergate scandal that brought down Richard Nixon's presidency. As with Watergate, the suspense that built with each new revelation stemmed from the question, How high did responsibility reach? The scandal quickly implicated increasingly prominent figures. Its rapid escalation, fed by leaks and political infighting, would both reinvigorate the Jakarta media and effectively check the reversal of the country's democratization threatened by the corrupt bargains and media reticence of the transition's first year.

After the initial burst of media coverage of Pradjoto's revelation, Baligate expanded as news outlets reported increasingly dramatic allegations. Among the most sensational came from a report that the head of EGP, the company that received the $80 million fee, was Golkar's deputy treasurer, Setya Novanto. This revelation prompted allegations that the money had ended up in the coffers of a special "Habibie Success Team" created to assure the president's victory in the 1999 elections.[15]

Further leaks sustained the scandal's momentum, spurred in part by the release of new information by sources. When mounting pressure prompted the police to name nearly a dozen suspects, officials shared only the initials of those named, heightening suspense by shifting focus to the media, who now scrambled to guess the full identities.[16] On August 8, Golkar's treasurer, Fadel Muhammad, told SCTV that "provisional evidence in the case showed suspect practices."[17] Then, on August 12, Marzuki Darusman, Golkar's deputy chair, called a press conference at which he offered no new information but directed the media to ignore red herrings and find the real perpetrators.[18] This seemingly deliberate blow to fellow Golkar members set off a new flurry of speculation.[19]

On August 15, the magazine *Gamma* published the transcript of a leaked phone exchange between Novanto, a central figure in corruption scandals for years to come, and the Golkar leader Arnold Baramuli, who coached Novanto on how to speak to the media about the high fee EGP had charged Bank Bali.[20] Unlike reaction to *Panji Masyarakat*'s similar report in February of a phone exchange between President Habibie and Attorney General Ghalib, the focus of both media and government remained on the wiretap's revelations rather than shifting to *Gamma*'s ethics, reflecting support for the public's "right to know" guaranteed in the pending 1999 Press Law.[21] The scandal widened further to implicate officials at BPPN, including the agency's deputy chair, Pande Lubis.[22]

At each stage, as headlines promised new revelations, editorials expressed outrage. "There is nothing more obscene than people stealing large sums of money from people who are in dire poverty," said the *Jakarta Post*, "[which] is what the story of the Rp546 billion heist at Bank Bali essentially boils down to."[23] The country's paper of record, *Kompas*, breaking from its usual muted style, warned parliamentary investigators that "disastrous indications with negative effects to the rupiah" would result if they failed to find "an open and total solution."[24]

The broadcast media turned Pradjoto—who had first exposed the dubious EGP fee—into a minor celebrity. Pradjoto embraced the spotlight and continued giving speeches and interviews even after Habibie supporters staged hostile rallies outside his house and threatened "to shoot his infant daughter in the head."[25]

As Pradjoto faded from view, further leaks and counterleaks reflected a widening rift inside Golkar between two factions that the media dubbed "Black Golkar" (Habibie's supporters) and "White Golkar" (his opponents).[26] Most sensational was a rumor circulated by the Habibie camp that the original whistle-blower, the "Deep Throat" who had dropped the critical documents on Pradjoto's doorstep in July was, in fact, Golkar's deputy chair Marzuki Darusman.[27]

Partisan warfare also escalated as rival factions began buying television airtime to further competing agendas. Talk show host Wimar Witoelar described this strategy as part of a growing use of such shows as "political weapons." When TVRI denied airtime to a group wishing to debate the Bank Bali scandal, the group bought a slot on the private station SCTV. The discussion also addressed the military's bloody rampage following East Timor's independence referendum. "The joke was," Witoelar recounted, "that when Suharto moved up to be the chairman of the board, he assigned the violence division to Wiranto and the corruption division to Habibie. And this was elaborated on in the panel discussion."[28]

In mid-August, the Habibie government, under pressure from the International Monetary Fund (IMF), hired PricewaterhouseCoopers (PwC) to conduct an audit of the institutions implicated in the scandal. On September 6, PwC stated that it had found "numerous indicators of fraud" in the transaction between Bank Bali and EGP.[29] On September 9, parliament opened hearings on the Bank Bali case. Imposing unprecedented transparency on legislative proceedings, two private television stations gained access and broadcast the entire proceedings live, gavel to gavel.

Though the members of the parliamentary commission were generally ill prepared, the case produced Indonesia's first televised hearings of an investigation into official malfeasance. Recalling his time as a student in the United States in the 1970s, Witoelar said the impact of this coverage for Indonesians "was exactly like watching the congressional hearings or Senate investigation of Watergate." He described audiences as "glued to their TV sets for hours and some people are remembering all the names [of Watergate defendants] like Gordon Liddy. . . . And we had Setya Novanto, Baramuli, Tanri Abeng." The result was that people became "so involved . . . that when the public discussion actually came to the parliament, the public pressure [was] very significant."[30]

The novelty of front-row access to televised parliamentary deliberations attracted audiences. In contrast to the silencing of the parliament that had elected Suharto to a seventh term, the microphones in front of legislators this time were switched on, broadcasting their voices—and opinions—to the entire country. MPR members, moreover, were acutely aware that their sessions were airing live nationwide, prompting some delegates to remind colleagues repeatedly of their public responsibility.[31]

The media's role expanded again when PDIP leaked a private journal detailing meetings between Bank Bali's president, Rudy Ramli, and members of Habibie's "inner circle" and between party boss Baramuli and a former director of Bank Bali.[32] Amid his denunciations of Ramli as a "liar" and a "drug addict," the DPR parliamentary investigating team summoned Baramuli for questioning, insisting that he was "clearly" involved.[33] Journalists and observers packed into the gallery, cheering and applauding, while parliamentarians grilled Ramli for four hours, all of which was watched by audiences across the archipelago.

When Ramli began naming top Golkar leaders on national television, pressure for resolution appeared to have reached an unstoppable momentum. But then the prosecution began to stall. When members of the DPR demanded access to key sections of the PwC audit—most critically, a "flow of funds" report—the state audit body refused, arguing that the report revealed personal bank account information and its release would violate bank secrecy laws.[34] On September 20, the *Jakarta Post* described those investigating the case as "impotent and incapable in pushing through the investigation to its conclusion." One legislator said, "I have a feeling, a political one, that this commission will never succeed."[35]

The danger for the transition in this stalemate was twofold. It postponed the reckoning Habibie would face once implicated directly in Baligate, the likely culmination of continued investigation. Indeed, in the final days before the parliamentary balloting, Habibie reportedly was "trying to move the investigation from the politicized parliament to the more pliable courts, which are likely to delay hearings until after the elections."[36] In turn, this end run risked an extraelectoral outcome if protesters flooded the streets prompting military repression, even martial law. That same week, opposition leaders threatened such demonstrations to break the deadlock while international donors froze further aid disbursements, hoping to force "full and prompt disclosure" of the PwC report.[37]

During these events, a synergy developed between the media and international donors, particularly in the print press through editorials calling the stalled investigation a government "cover-up."[38] Rather than rail against foreign interference, the papers used the freeze on international aid to argue for a quick resolution. In an interview with the *Jakarta Post*, economist Tony A. Prasetyantono warned that the donors "are not playing around" and that cancellation of aid "would make the wheels of the economy stop."[39]

Kompas took a similar tack, stating in an uncharacteristically blunt editorial, "It has become clear that facts have been covered." The paper then warned of the dangers that a cover-up posed to investment, twice emphasizing the importance of pursuing an immediate resolution "regardless [of] personalities" involved.[40]

During the standoff, on September 23, media reformers secured the passage of a new law protecting press freedom and the public's "right to know."[41] Yet even as supporters hailed this victory, countermaneuvers to keep Habibie's damaged candidacy alive continued to threaten a reversal of democratization that might have reduced these legislative reforms to irrelevance.

THE MILITARY'S CAMPAIGN

At this juncture, the military reappeared as a dominant player. With thirty-eight seats in the parliament and numerous ways to influence Indonesia's political elite, military leaders, when they took a clear position, could have a decisive political impact. Aware of this reality, Habibie's team courted General Wiranto, commander of the newly renamed Indonesian National Army (Tentara Nasional Indonesia, TNI), to stand as their vice-presidential candidate.[42] As the presidential race moved to the floor of parliament, the critical question became, Would the military again back Golkar, as they had in the last six elections, or would they allow a transfer of power to a new party?

After the humiliating referendum in East Timor that ended the military's quarter-century occupation, President Habibie had numerous enemies in army circles. PDIP's presidential candidate, Megawati, by contrast, had a solid core of support among the generals. Even in his own party, Habibie was seen increasingly as a sinking ship.[43] Yet rather than working to ensure an alternative outcome that might be acceptable to the 78 percent of Indonesians who did not vote for Golkar, military leaders prepared to quell the protests that would likely follow a Habibie victory. In short, TNI appeared to be getting ready for the incumbent, Habibie, rather than the opposition leader, Megawati, to win, bracing to defend an outcome that much of the public was likely to view as illegitimate.

In a development potentially even more threatening to the transition, several sources indicated that some within TNI were preparing to take control of the executive themselves—either indirectly, with General Wiranto as president, or directly, via a state of emergency. Most significantly, in the final days of the incumbent parliament's term, before newly elected legislators could take office, military leaders and Golkar allies began pushing for the passage of a new security bill, the polar opposite of the liberal 1999 Press Law.[44]

The State Security Bill, originating in the Ministry of Defense, would have granted TNI broad emergency powers to assume the duties of civilian government, ban public protests, impose curfews, conduct investigations and raids, seize private property, and take control of the country's communications. As opposition built, critics, including students who again filled the streets, declared it more draconian than the recently revoked Anti-Subversion Law.[45]

During these weeks of lobbying, TNI was working the system from two directions. If Habibie won with Wiranto as his running mate and the country accepted this outcome, TNI would have the vice presidency. If Habibie won and the public did not accept him, the unrest would provide an opportunity to take power more directly. Either way, a Habibie win with the new security law in place would greatly strengthen the military's position.

TNI faced pressure to get the bill passed quickly before more independent legislators could take office. A corresponding sense of urgency grew among opponents who feared that the military would try to provoke violence to justify the bill's passage and then use it to cancel the next session of parliament.[46]

The prospect of military control over communications gave members of the media particular cause to fight the bill's passage. Intentionally or coincidentally, news coverage and sharpening editorials greatly amplified public opposition as the measure made its way through the legislative process. When protesters finally took to the streets, legislators responded, adding a requirement that the president seek legislative approval before declaring a state of emergency.

This concession was substantial, showing the continued power of public protest to shape the transition. Nevertheless, critics doubted that legislators would have either the will or the ability to prevent such a declaration, and observers predicted that the bill would pass easily.[47] In a last-ditch effort, members of the media assumed a more activist role. On September 18, as journalists joined the swelling demonstrations, their editors organized a strategy meeting, pressing party leaders to take a formal stand against the bill. In a move indicative of their influence, the following day Gol-kar's deputy chair, who had attended the editors' meeting, announced that legislators were inclined to delay passage "until the new House convenes."[48] Two days later, however, all four parliamentary factions voted to pass the bill.

CONFRONTATION

On September 23, 1999, a day before its term ended, the outgoing legislature passed the state security bill by unanimous "acclaim."[49] In a report on the vote, one newspaper highlighted "a widely-held perception that the new legislation was approved under pressure from the [Habibie] government, and the military in particu-lar."[50] Ironically, while the government, backed by the military, pushed through this legislation that would have empowered it to ban public demonstrations, it was mass protest magnified by media coverage that blocked the final step in the bill's passage.

Before the bill could become law, President Habibie needed to sign it. On Sep-tember 24, observers still expected him to do so. At this point, however, students who had been massing since the day of the vote stepped up their rallies. As dem-onstrations intensified, thousands of protesters, joined by city residents, converged outside the parliamentary complex.[51] Similar rallies sprang up in other cities, and by that evening there were reports of demonstrators throwing stones and detonating fuel bombs, soldiers beating protesters, and police firing tear gas and rubber bullets into the crowds.[52] Seven people died, including a fourteen-year-old and a university student shot in the head by a sniper while sitting with friends on a curb.[53]

The protesters' key demand was that legislators rescind their approval of the bill. Military officers responded by challenging the authenticity of the protests, claiming they were instigated by provocateurs employing ruffians to disturb public order.[54] Others, particularly General Wiranto, argued that the public simply lacked sufficient understanding of the bill.[55]

The crackdowns ignited a fierce public backlash. On September 25, twenty-nine student groups and civic organizations issued a statement condemning Habibie and Wiranto for the deaths. The statement demanded both revocation of the security bill and Wiranto's resignation. Significantly, it also "called on Indonesians not to support Habibie's bid for another term as president."[56]

While outgoing legislators had ignored the mounting opposition, pressure on Habibie was more direct. At the height of the protests, he tried to defuse tensions by announcing that he would delay signing the bill. A military spokesperson explained, "The delay is to allow the dissemination of information on the bill so that people will be able to understand and accept this bill." State Secretary Muladi [one name] explained that the delay would last only seven to ten days, long enough for the gov-ernment to "socialize" the law.[57] By the next afternoon, September 26, Habibie went further, stating that he was ready to give up the presidency, though only through con-stitutional means, and was "willing to accept criticism through demonstrations and other public protests."[58]

This announcement was arguably one of the most critical moments in Indonesia's break from authoritarian rule. In any democratic transition, there is one paramount question: Will the ruling party give up power? Until that moment when Habibie expressed willingness to concede the presidency it was not clear, with the military preparing for a state of emergency, that the new legislature would ever get the chance to vote him out of office. In short, Habibie's announcement marked the first real indication that Golkar would accept defeat in an electoral contest and relinquish its long control of the executive. It signaled, moreover, a real restraint on the ruling party's capacity for maneuver—a counterforce created by a more independent media, a vocal public, and empowered elements in opposition parties.

HABIBIE'S FINAL BID

None of these events eliminated President Habibie from the race, much less assured an opposition party's win. Megawati and her cadres still lacked the will and the skills to build coalitions with other parties, and without such support, neither PDIP nor any other party would be able to form a government.[59] This situation left the door open for rivals, including Golkar, to strengthen their own positions via coalition building.

Once the new parliament convened to elect Indonesia's next president on October 1, just four days after Habibie's announcement, other parties started horse-trading, and PDIP's vulnerability soon became clear. Within days, Megawati's party lost two top posts in a deal between Golkar and the Central Axis coalition of Muslim parties. While Golkar threw its support behind the leader of the Central Axis, Amien Rais (head of the National Mandate Party), winning him the powerful position of chair of the parliament, his followers, in turn, helped Golkar's Akbar Tanjung become Speaker of the DPR.[60]

With these two damaging defeats showing PDIP's weak position, Habibie, despite all that had come before, remained the front-runner. But on October 14, before his long-anticipated accountability speech to the MPR, much of the new assembly stayed seated when he entered the hall, and some even booed—shows of disrespect inconceivable in Suharto's time.[61] The speech that followed failed to win the assembly over. "As expected," David Jenkins wrote, "speaker after speaker rose to assail the President, zeroing in on the Suharto, East Timor and Bank Bali issues."[62]

Simultaneously, public pressure on delegates—from media coverage and the cell-phone-toting protesters who were following events via live broadcasts—was also far more direct than any previous session. At least four times during the president's speech, Wimar Witoelar recounted, "Parliament members interrupted the proceedings saying that they [had] just received cell phone calls that students were being clobbered and Pak [Mr.] Wiranto can you please tell your guys to lay off."[63]

While the country followed the deliberations on television and radio, delegates found it hard to ignore the expectations that were building. "For the first time," *FEER* correspondents said, "national television [was] broadcast[ing] party factions' sharp criticism of a sitting president, as the cameras watched Habibie's face for reaction." One Golkar legislator close to Habibie added, "It was shocking . . . but I think this is really good for democracy."[64]

As it grew clearer that Megawati might not get the presidency, Witoelar recalled, "a lot of people . . . questioned how backroom politics could alienate the politics of the streets." This disconnect "wouldn't have been on the public's mind if the media were not there to follow every step of the debates in the MPR." He compared the immediacy of this feedback to the insulated MPR session the previous November "when people were actually getting killed, and it was only Wiranto who I knew was talking on his handphone to his snipers up in the Hilton apartments." During the "Black Friday" crackdown that had followed, the MPR session had been "totally secluded from the outside." In this 1999 general session, by contrast, the two "melted" together. "The catalyst" for this change, said Witoelar, "is again [broadcast] media."[65]

The National Democratic Institute noted another development critical to the new accountability and public engagement the media introduced into these debates. In contrast to previous parliamentary sessions, "the general public was much more attentive to this General Session because, unlike in the past, its outcome had not been scripted in advance."[66] *Asiaweek*'s Jose Manuel Tesoro noted, "Nor were delegates beholden to a single party, the long-ruling Golkar, as they were when the MPR met again last November."[67] In short, events created a better chance for an open-ended contest.

Despite the barrage of criticism, Habibie's bid for the presidency was still viable. "In addition to Golkar's 120 elected seats," one journalist explained, Habibie was believed "to have bargained for the loyalty of 50 regional delegates."[68] With his advantage in the Islamic anti-Megawati block, plus the thirty-eight TNI votes Golkar hoped to win by adding Wiranto to its ticket, Habibie still held a winning margin. "Habibie is actually politically dead," an insider commented. "But Indonesian politics seem to be very much lacking an ethical and moral [dimension]."[69]

Once again, however, public opinion, now openly displayed, had created new checks on what MPR members could do. Even those in elected posts, emboldened by a popular mandate, could not ignore signs that the country was unlikely to accept another Habibie presidency. *Kompas*, providing one of these signs, conducted a poll finding that an overwhelming 70 percent of respondents "rejected" Habibie's speech outright, faulting his performance in almost every area.[70]

Louder still was the message from more than ten thousand protesters who gathered outside parliament as Habibie delivered his speech—a message punctuated by Molotov cocktails and violent clashes with police.[71] Simultaneously, at the Hotel Indonesia traffic circle, thousands of Megawati's supporters threatened unrest, even "revolution," if she did not win the presidency. And at the Jakarta Stock Exchange, one thousand people from the business community staged an anti-Habibie protest.[72] That same day, the military faction tipped the scales against Habibie when Wiranto decided not to join his ticket.

By the time that Habibie had finished his speech, the public display of opposition overwhelmed plans to keep him in the presidency for another term. On October 19, the day before the presidential vote, MPR delegates formally rejected Habibie's speech, an act tantamount to a no-confidence motion. Later that day, Habibie bowed out of the race.

In the end, stacking the parliamentary vote in Golkar's favor turned out to be easier than controlling a liberated media and the response of a galvanized civil society. As one Golkar analyst explained, "[I]t is not such a difficult thing to get the numbers for Habibie in the MPR." It would have been "quite another thing," however, "to get public acceptance for a five-year Habibie presidency."[73]

ELECTION MINUS HABIBIE

Habibie's exit ended—for the time being—the shift toward democratic reversal, clearing a path for the chief opposition candidate, Megawati Sukarnoputri, to capture the presidency. Even before the MPR rejected Habibie's speech, observers were predicting that a Megawati victory was "the most likely . . . outcome."[74] After Habibie's exit, moreover, and a failed attempt to field Akbar Tanjung that prompted one legislator to pull a gun, Golkar was struggling to find a viable presidential candidate.[75]

At this point, the election was, by most accounts, Megawati's to lose. But both she and her party, PDIP, were still reluctant to forge alliances. Going into the MPR vote, PDIP's largest ally was the National Awakening Party (Partai Kebangkitan Bangsa, PKB), controlling fifty-one seats and led by Muslim cleric Abdurrahman Wahid. Golkar, by contrast, had formed a coalition with the Muslim parties of the Central Axis group, who together controlled 150 seats and were determined to keep Megawati out of the presidency. On the eve of the ballot, as delegates bustled around making deals, the 695 members of the MPR remained roughly divided between the these two opposing alliances, with the thirty-eight representatives from the military sitting on the fence.

With Habibie out and Megawati stalemated, the only remaining viable candidate was Wahid himself. But few viewed the near-blind, outspoken cleric as a serious contender. His PKB had won only 10 percent of the 462 DPR seats, or 7 percent of the wider 695-member plenary parliament (MPR). Even if Wahid garnered additional support for his own candidacy, insiders still expected him to end up throwing his votes behind Megawati.[76]

PDIP's delegates seemed confident of victory. According to one correspondent, their "earlier secret deals with [Akbar Tanjung's] wing of Golkar, and their firm belief that Mr. Wahid [would] back down," led PDIP leaders to believe they had well over the 348 votes needed to win the presidency. They retired for the night on October 19, apparently unconcerned by the ongoing negotiations among the other parties.[77]

When PDIP's delegates arrived at the MPR complex for the scheduled presidential vote the next morning, the situation took them—and nearly everyone else—by surprise. During the night, Wahid had formed an alliance with the head of the National Mandate Party, Amien Rais, and other Central Axis leaders. Fifteen minutes before the vote, he struck a bargain with the dominant Golkar faction, gaining "at least 150 votes in return for [his] support for their vice-presidential candidate." In exchange, he reportedly promised Golkar "10 seats in his 35-member cabinet."[78] With this final burst of lobbying, and some last-minute politicking with the minor Bulan Bintang party, Wahid won the presidency by a comfortable margin of sixty votes.

Megawati accepted her former ally's surprising win without complaint. Outside, however, the news set off a fresh wave of protests as thousands of her supporters stormed through the streets surrounding parliament, burning tires and stoning security forces.[79] After losing the MPR chair to the National Mandate Party, the position of DPR Speaker to Golkar, and now the presidency to Wahid, PDIP—although the winner of the popular vote—was almost completely marginalized in the new government. The situation had troubling implications for both the credibility of the 1999 elections and the legitimacy of Wahid's new administration.

The MPR's next vote would decide the vice presidency, already promised by Wahid to Golkar. Once again, however, concern over the reaction of the demonstrators outside their windows—and the public they represented—limited legislators' freedom to maneuver. After twenty-four hours of debate, they decided, with Wahid's backing, to make Megawati the new vice president. Celebrations broke out among her supporters. The oath-taking ceremony was a triumph for *reformasi*, as the MPR, now chaired by the opposition leader Amien Rais, swore in two of the other main leaders in the opposition movement that ousted Suharto—Abdurrahman Wahid and Megawati Sukarnoputri. After a quarter-century in power and months of skillful maneuvering, Golkar had lost its lock on executive power.

The contrast could not have been more striking between this presidential election and March 1998, when Suharto ran unopposed to win his seventh term in a unanimous vote by a Golkar-led legislature. In only eighteen months, the election of the Indonesian president had swung from a ceremonial exercise yielding predetermined outcomes to a highly competitive contest impossible to call right up to the moment of the vote.

At the same time, as Wahid settled into the presidency, one could argue that the bizarre frenzy of horse-trading that wrested the position from Megawati, a popular opposition leader and the daughter of a revered former president, was an even greater distortion of the voters' intent, as expressed in the June ballot, than a Habibie win would have been. Golkar had at least placed second, in a forty-eight-party contest, claiming 22 percent of the popular vote. Wahid's PKB had earned only 10 percent.

From a populist perspective, the victory of a small minority party in a series of backroom deals may seem a shallow triumph for Indonesia's *reformasi* movement. Yet whatever one might say about Wahid's closed-door maneuvering, the process that ended with his victory was not predetermined. If we return to Przeworski's uncertainty frame, this development becomes critical. More broadly, the substitution of Golkar's rigged outcomes with an open-ended parliamentary contest that led to the election of a long-shot opposition leader represented, on balance, significant progress in Indonesia's transition.

DYNAMICS OF SCANDAL

The key development that derailed Golkar's manipulation and made this outcome possible was public disclosure of the party's campaign finance fraud. Yet revelations of embezzlement alone were not what made the ensuing Baligate scandal significant. The country had already been alerted to widespread electoral malfeasance by *Tempo*'s June 1999 exposé of systematic fraud in Golkar's campaign on the island of Sulawesi.[80]

In both cases, through disclosure of fraud, the media were playing the watchdog role arguably central to their function in supporting democratization, imposing transparency on the electoral process and forcing accountability on the nation's leaders. *Tempo*'s report, for example, pressured the Central Election Supervising Committee (Panwaspus) to recommend legal action against Golkar.[81] But while some outlets reported this development, none conducted their own follow-up investigations.[82] Consequently, few reported the Sulawesi fraud, and little came of the case. In short, *Tempo*'s revelations, though authoritative, eye-opening, and damning, did not garner the widening attention necessary to produce a "scandal," a phenomenon that, by definition, involves "causing general public outrage."[83] By contrast, the Baligate revelations set in motion a media "feeding frenzy," that is, a sudden barrage of nonproprietary follow-up coverage whose sum was a *grande scandale d'État* that, in the end, brought down the president.

Explanation for the different trajectories of the stories lies in key distinctions between the potential of the two journalistic genres employed—the investigative report and the insider leak—to produce political scandal. Unlike *Tempo*'s well-researched probe into election fraud in Sulawesi, it was not investigative reporting that launched Baligate, but instead documents leaked to a financial analyst, Pradjoto, by an inside source—most likely Golkar's own deputy chair.[84]

As partial, partisan, and often speculative stories that raise more questions than they answer, leak-based reports, unlike well-researched investigations, generate narrative tension as rival outlets rush to fill these gaps with their own coverage. Even though this follow-up may not promote reform or correction, it still serves to keep the story alive and stoke public outrage, or at least interest. A key internal dynamic in Baligate (and later election scandals) was this building of narrative tension, especially acute as evidence of malfeasance emerged piece by piece through strategic leaks and the partisan pursuit of revenge.

Tempo's exposé of fraud in Sulawesi was, by contrast, a self-contained narrative. Even when the requisite inquiry by Panwaspus provided corroboration, the story still lacked tension, and thus momentum.[85] The narrative tension in Baligate, by contrast, seemed escalating and endless as mysteries unfolded, attention grew, and reporters cultivated new sources.

In sum, the Baligate revelations were in no way more spectacular than the findings of *Tempo's* exposé. But the peculiar journalistic genre that carried them, the insider leak, had embedded within it internal imperatives that drove news outlets to follow it doggedly to its denouement, regardless of political consequences.

When Indonesia's newly elected parliament met in October 1999, the 695 delegates, representing dozens of political parties, were deciding not only the outcome of the presidential election but also the country's political future. The advent of enduring democracy in Indonesia required, symbolically and substantially, that the Golkar party lose the presidency for the first time in three decades. If Golkar had retained the executive, the June elections would not have been the start of genuine democracy, but simply the seventh in a succession of rigged electoral rituals ending with Golkar back in power—legitimacy affirmed, collusive pacts renewed.

Through the confluence of new political laws and Golkar's skillful manipulation of the electoral process, the balance of parties in parliament left the country poised for just such a scenario. This manipulation and the broad complicity of other actors, including much of the media, had effectively perpetuated the engineered outcomes of the Suharto era.[86]

After a year of revolution and reform, Indonesia's political process seemed, on the surface, little changed. Thousands of demonstrators had filled the capital streets. A powerful autocrat had fallen from power. The country had held its first open elections in more than forty years. Yet Golkar was set to retain control of the presidency. Not even solid investigative reporting revealing major electoral fraud had slowed this trajectory. But just weeks before Habibie's expected triumph, the media-driven Baligate scandal broke the ruling party's hold on power. More critically, it began to unravel the fabric of collusion underlying Golkar's careful negotiations with other political parties who, as later revelations showed, had also reaped the rewards of embezzlement and electoral manipulation.[87]

The media's overall influence in this period was complex, even contradictory, reflecting this sector's dual character as both self-interested and civic-minded in checking the power of other players. Media outlets profited from sales and advertising revenues through sensational coverage, whether of intraelite backstabbing or serious political controversy. Even at the peak of media independence during the Bank Bali scandal, journalistic commentary on the push for a full investigation of the case was mixed. Nevertheless, at critical junctures, members of the media, individually and collectively, appeared to be self-consciously forcing accountability on officials and defending the transition. Equally central to the checking of reversal were the synergies between the media and civil society groups, still including thousands of students. These synergies and increased transparency, furthered to a surprising extent by baser forces, would become critical again in the future, each time helping to block a threatened reversal of democratization.

CHAPTER SEVEN

SCANDAL AND DEMOCRATIC CONSOLIDATION

Under democracy one party always devotes its chief energies to trying to prove that the other party is unfit to rule—and both commonly succeed, and are right.
—H. L. Mencken, *Minority Report*

After over four decades of dictatorship, the unexpected election of Abdurrahman Wahid to the presidency in October 1999 was a remarkable, albeit ambiguous, development. Wahid's win, if nothing else, allowed a new party to take control of the country's powerful executive. It did not, however, undo the compromised outcome of the June parliamentary elections. Compounding the symbolic damage to the democratic process, systemic fraud had helped the old regime's Golkar party capture enough legislative seats to slow, if not stop, political reform and secure impunity for leaders of the old regime.

In the face of this political paralysis, the mass media served as the most critical force for moving the transition forward. Although the Baligate scandal was a spectacular controversy that had mesmerized the nation and discredited Suharto's handpicked successor, the use of press scandal as political weapon was not a one-time phenomenon. Just as Baligate broke Golkar's lock on the presidency, so a succession of new scandals would tar all the major parties and unleash cycles of retribution through revelation.

These media clashes would pitch Indonesia into a maelstrom of factional infighting that, perhaps paradoxically, helped put the transition back on track. The media's role at this juncture affirmed the importance of sober analysis and carefully researched investigative journalism, but also demonstrated that media tendencies often faulted for degrading public debate in advanced democracies can play an emergent function in warding off the reversal of democratic transitions. The resulting confrontations began to shatter collusive arrangements that continued to compromise the country's electoral, judicial, and economic contests. As intraelite conflict intensified from 2000 to 2004, the media would become the main arena for its mediation, launching an era of politics by scandal that marked a turning point in Indonesia's transition and made the media central to the next phase of democratic consolidation.

WAHID'S PRESIDENCY

When President Wahid began his term in November 1999, little had changed in Indonesia's balance of political forces despite eighteen months of reform. Baligate had ended President Habibie's political career, but even without the executive, his Golkar party remained in a strong position. Thanks to its solid showing in the June elections and the skewed distribution of parliamentary seats, the former ruling party controlled a quarter of the DPR—more than double the seats won by the new president's own National Awakening Party (PKB). With thirty regional branches, moreover, Golkar's reach extended far beyond any other party. Most importantly, the powerful post of DPR Speaker now belonged to its chair, Akbar Tanjung.

Ironically, as head of the legislature, Tanjung also controlled access to the PricewaterhouseCoopers (PwC) audit that investigated Habibie's and Golkar's role in the Bank Bali scandal. A summary of the audit had been released, but the more revealing full report, documenting the transfer of Rp15 billion to the Golkar Election Committee, was being held back.[1] Though Tanjung was not implicated directly by the audit, he was still Golkar's chair and a key fundraiser, which gave him cause to avoid releasing the full report. On October 19, 1999, the day before the presidential election, the Supreme Court ordered that the document be handed over to parliament. But the court's decision did not mention any public right to access. In the following weeks, Tanjung was still refusing to disclose the full report—even to the joint DPR committee charged with investigating the affair.[2]

It was at this point that the executive turnover that brought a new party to power proved significant in Indonesia's democratic transition. It seems likely that, had Golkar maintained control of the presidency, the full PwC audit would have remained locked away, safe in the hands of the same party implicated by its findings. A Wahid presidency, however, led not by Golkar but by his PKB, shattered the decades-long partnership between the executive and legislature that allowed those in power to suppress damaging information.

Upon assuming office, Wahid began pushing for the release of the full PwC report. The IMF added to this pressure by continuing to withhold $4.7 billion in loans pending disclosure of the full four-hundred-page audit.[3] Members of the media, the public, and leaders of rival parties joined this chorus. In November 1999, Tanjung finally gave in, only weeks before the parliament's deadline for the Bank Bali committee to complete its investigation.

Subsequent legal proceedings, however, proved disappointing. Attempts to prosecute the principals led to acquittals or outright dismissals. After a year of investigation, the government failed to produce a single conviction in one of the most carefully documented scandals in the republic's history. While Baligate had been key in derailing Golkar's campaign to retain the executive, the judicial process responsible for its prosecution remained hostage to political manipulation.

Nonetheless, the Wahid government's initial demand for the PwC report's release was promising for the transition. Upon taking office, the new president told journalists to be tough on his administration, affirming his commitment to press freedom and democratic reform.[4] In November, Wahid went further, dissolving the once-feared Ministry of Information that had controlled the media for four decades. In mid-February 2000, Wahid skillfully pushed the former Indonesian National Army commander, General Wiranto, out of his cabinet, winning commendation from reform factions and political observers. Fikri Jufri of *Tempo* said the president was moving like "a knight in chess" and praised him for being "consistent in his inconsistency."[5] Likewise, the *Jakarta Post* said, "Indonesians would do best to get used to [Wahid's] peculiar style of leadership," and called Wiranto's peaceful removal "a great achievement and a giant step in the right direction for the country."[6]

Overall, Wahid's reform agenda, though widely applauded, did not go far enough for some and went too far for others. Thus his honeymoon with the media and the multiparty coalition that brought him to power was relatively brief. During his first six months he managed to alienate much of the new legislature, in part by repeatedly snubbing the two largest parties, Golkar and PDIP, in endless cabinet reshuffles. By January 2000, rumors about growing tensions between the new administration and military leaders prompted US officials to warn the military "not to try to seize power."[7]

By April, patience with Wahid's erratic ways ran out, even among reform forces, when he abruptly fired two prominent members of Golkar and PDIP from his coalition cabinet. When he refused to offer sufficient justification, legislators summoned him to a hearing, bringing the president into open conflict with the two largest parties in parliament.[8] Wahid's interference in the prosecution of three business tycoons who refused to repay state loans also generated widespread criticism.[9] Perhaps most disappointing for ordinary Indonesians, however, were the administration's failures in handling corruption cases against former president Suharto and his son Tommy.

Some legislators began proposing impeachment hearings. Representatives of the Crescent and Star Party were at the forefront, calling for an emergency parliamentary session to remove Wahid for trying to lift the government's thirty-four-year ban on Communism.[10] Critics complained about many other aspects of Wahid's presidency, from nepotism and overseas junkets to increasingly autocratic leadership.[11] But when his enemies finally moved to push him from power, they focused on two scandals that set off a new media feeding frenzy and implicated Wahid in the same corruption he had vowed to eradicate.

CONCATENATION OF SCANDAL

While the Bank Bali case was sputtering along in a string of acquittals, members of the media were "having a field day" over a new scandal involving Wahid and Bulog, the state's rice distribution agency.[12] The case centered on a $4.1 million loan that the foundation overseeing Bulog's pension fund had granted to Wahid's personal masseur, Alip Agung Suwondo. The story broke in May 2000, when the head of the nongovernmental organization Government Watch called a press conference to accuse Suwondo of channeling these funds to four private bank accounts.[13] The scandal then widened over revelations that Suwondo and others involved were shareholders in Wahid's airline, Awair, causing speculation that the missing Bulog funds were financing this new company.[14] Suwondo's disappearance overseas added to the drama.[15]

The flight of the masseur sparked immediate interest, but misuse of Bulog funds had been going on for so long and involved so many people that it was hard to imagine this incident could evolve into a major scandal. As observers pointed out, Suwondo had taken "lunch money" compared with the amounts involved in other scandals—Baligate, Suharto's accumulation of $45 billion, and countless abuses of Indonesia's other cash cow, the state oil company Pertamina.[16]

Disappointment over the government's handling of other cases also made observers cynical about the Bulog scandal's potential to escalate, particularly since it involved an incumbent administration. As the *Jakarta Post* explained, "The scandal is developing into an all too familiar pattern where a simple issue is made so complicated and hazy . . . that the guilty parties will eventually escape prosecution."[17] Similarly, *Tempo* concluded that its investigation "could ultimately just end in political horse trading."[18]

But the scandal, dubbed "Buloggate," did snowball, in part because its origin as a leak produced a natural press drama, replete with the narrative tension of an unfolding story that rival media could pursue.[19] As *Detikworld* said, "Jam-packed with all the twists and turns of a good thriller, the case just gets more interesting."[20] Above all, its pursuit served President Wahid's political opponents.

At the center of the scandal was Bulog, a much-abused vehicle for funding corruption, found that same May to have leaked Rp2.7 trillion (approximately $30 million) from its nonbudgetary funds over the previous five years.[21] Given the scale of the leakage and Golkar's long control over Bulog, it was surprising that Golkar would choose corruption involving the agency to attack Wahid. Yet Golkar leaders publicly lambasted Wahid as if their own party somehow held the high ground in managing Bulog's accounts. Leading the charge was the DPR Speaker and Golkar chair Akbar Tanjung, who had announced in May that the president must disclose all he knew, warning that any failure on Wahid's part to provide "a satisfactory explanation" would damage his credibility.[22]

Using Bulog to attack Wahid set in motion a cycle of reciprocal revelations that ultimately would escape Golkar's control. But for the present, the party's influence in parliament protected it from repercussions. In June 2000, Wahid's PKB retaliated, initiating a probe into the suspected Rp2.7 trillion leak from Bulog under Golkar's earlier administration. PKB targeted Tanjung directly, faulting him as state secretary under Habibie for allowing Bulog to keep these discretionary funds separate from its official budget, despite directives from the IMF to integrate the two.[23] In July, PKB demanded investigation into irregularities cited in an audit of Taperum, the Civil Servants Housing Savings program in operation during Tanjung's term as minister of public housing. When the media confronted him over "Taperumgate," Tanjung, according to an observer, "could not conceal his ire."[24]

On September 21, Indonesia Corruption Watch added its own evidence to the allegations mounting against the DPR Speaker.[25] As both scandals widened, in January 2001 PKB legislators renewed their demand for a probe into Taperum while lodging another complaint against Tanjung—this time, concerning financial leakage from an Inter-Parliamentary Union conference held the previous September.[26] A few days later, the National Ombudsman Commission recommended investigation into allegations from Tanjung's own nephew that he had forged documents in a 1995 land sale when serving as minister of public housing.[27]

On February 2, 2001, Wahid's party, PKB, announced that they had submitted three separate proposals, signed by 110 legislators, demanding inquiries into these and other scandals implicating Golkar, including a massive hemorrhaging of funds from the Central Bank's liquidity assistance scheme (Bantuan Likuiditas Bank Indonesia, BLBI) and additional losses from Bulog's nonbudgetary funds.[28] If these charges were accurate, the sums disappearing from Bulog's accounts were substantial by any standard, but the leakage from BLBI's accounts was staggering. A PKB leader noted that as much as "96 percent . . . of the Rp144 trillion BLBI funds have been embezzled, and none of the 157 persons [implicated] have been jailed."[29]

Yet even the BLBI revelations failed to generate anywhere near the attention given the scandals implicating Wahid. In the midst of his attacks on Tanjung, three magazines—*Gatra, Panji Masyarakat,* and *Forum Keadilan*—published cover stories alleging that Wahid had once had an illicit relationship and offered as evidence an incriminating photo.[30] It was only when Wahid's minister of defense, Mohammad Mahfud, began using the media to fight back that the president's party found the means to regain leverage against Golkar. That same February, Mahfud leaked information to the media indicating that Golkar had siphoned off Rp90 billion from Bulog's nonbudgetary funds to finance its 1999 election campaign.[31] Less than two weeks later, the PKB faction demanded a special DPR investigation into "Golkargate."[32]

Although these latest allegations seemed to promise a "Buloggate II," none of the accusations against Tanjung and his party produced official investigations. Nor did they take the heat off the president. Not long after Buloggate I broke, Wahid suffered another blow from revelations that he had accepted a $2 million donation from the sultan of Brunei, Hassanal Bolkiah. This new scandal quickly became "Bruneigate." Though he denied any wrongdoing in the Bulog case, Wahid did admit to taking money from Brunei but claimed to have donated it all to humanitarian causes.[33]

On August 28, 2000, a coalition of 237 legislators from six parties voted to establish a parliamentary committee to investigate the president's role in the two scandals, Buloggate and Bruneigate.[34] On October 28, police officially cleared the president of wrongdoing related to Bulog. But three months later, the investigating committee reported that Wahid had knowingly "avoided legal procedures" to raise funds for Indonesia's war-torn provinces, using Bulog funds and the sultan of Brunei's $2 million gift.[35]

Wahid refused to recognize the legality of the committee, viewing its probes as a ploy to push him from power. On February 1, 2001, the Golkar-dominated DPR passed a resolution to censure the new president. The following month, Wahid had his minister of justice read a fifteen-page speech to the DPR apologizing for "any possible unpleasant or unacceptable behaviour." Yet the president maintained his innocence, calling the charges against him "baseless" and challenging the legitimacy of the investigations.[36]

WAHID'S TURN AGAINST THE MEDIA

Throughout his two-year term, Wahid maintained an ambiguous relationship with the media that grew steadily worse in the period preceding his downfall. On National Press Day in February 2000, only months after taking office, the president gave journalists what *Kompas* called "a special present" in the form of a lengthy critique. He complained about both Indonesian and foreign reporting on East Timor and Aceh. But his main reproach was that domestic media reports magnified conflicts between him and other national leaders, particularly General Wiranto and Vice President Megawati. At the same time, he emphasized that his critique came out of a deep sense of camaraderie with the media, claiming to have long been a *wartawan tanpa surat kabar*, or a "journalist without a newspaper."[37]

In mid-April, Wahid's defense minister, Juwono Sudarsono, lambasted Indonesia's private television stations for inflaming provincial conflicts. He acknowledged the necessity of press freedom in a democracy but suggested that the cost was becoming too great. Comments on talk shows "have worsened . . . social conflicts," he said. "Politicians' rhetoric has incited their own supporters to attack each other."[38]

When the Indonesian media began pursuing Buloggate I, turning the story of Wahid's scheming masseur into a serial drama, Wahid's defenders began to see a darker agenda behind their coverage. In October 2000, the deputy secretary general of Wahid's party, Chotibul Umam Wiranu, accused the press of cooperating with "political forces . . . inside and outside the legislature" to overthrow his government. In a speech on October 6 before the Muslim association, Nahdlatul Ulama, he announced that "60 percent" of the nation's publications were part of this "print media conspiracy." He added, "In the near future, two electronic media will appear to join the anti-government strength."[39]

In November, Wahid attacked the international media for alleged misrepresentations, accusing "a foreign television station" of reporting that "millions" had attended a pro-independence rally in Aceh, when "[i]n fact, less than 100,000 people turned up."[40] In January 2001, members of Wahid's cabinet began calling the media "anti-government" and "over-critical" of government policies. One said, "freedom of the press is being 'overused' by most media." Further faulting their coverage of Aceh, the defense minister, Mahfud, said that the media "seem to enjoy gore, revealing exactly how rebels are killed and the gruesome details of local people killed in crossfires, ignoring mounting TNI and police dead."[41] The Ministry of Foreign Affairs then announced that foreign journalists were now required to obtain special permission to visit Indonesia's "hotspots"—notably, Maluku, West Papua, and Aceh.[42]

That same week in the province of Riau, the paramilitary wing of Nahdlatul Ulama, once headed by Wahid himself, and his supporters from the Cirebon City People's Forum in East Java forced their way into the offices of three newspapers to demand public apologies for publishing photographs of posters caricaturing the president. The caricature—the president's head affixed on a baby's body—had been on posters captioned "No Worries" waved by demonstrators outside the parliamentary complex in January. Nahdlatul Ulama's paramilitary "Banser" forces occupied one newspaper office and smashed furniture until editors agreed to print page-one apologies for several days running. Wahid did not respond directly, instead claiming that the media had been using events, such as bombings in Jakarta on Christmas Eve, "for their own interests."[43]

A meeting in mid-February with the managing director of the government-owned TVRI added a new dimension to the growing similarity between Suharto's and Wahid's tactics for handling negative reporting. According to *Tempo*, Wahid "urged TVRI to stop broadcasting any reports critical of the presidency." His logic, reminiscent of Suharto's standard justification for censorship, was that "such reporting could potentially trigger mob violence" among his supporters, particularly in East Java, where there was already unrest. Allegedly threatened with dismissal, the managing director, Chaerul Zen, ordered TVRI "to immediately brief news editors . . . to comply with [the president's] appeal." The editors were also instructed "to stop broadcasting reports" on calls for a special session of parliament.[44] On March 25, while twenty thousand "radical" Muslim students were shouting outside the palace demanding that the president resign, Wahid announced, "The media have been making slanderous accusations against me."[45]

At this point, Wahid said that he remained "reluctant to bring newspapers to court because it would create a depressing effect on press freedom."[46] In May 2001, however, he began threatening criminal prosecution against media outlets for "defamation," a violation still punishable under the criminal code by six years' imprisonment.[47] The same week, officials acknowledged that the government had established a "media monitoring team" with the aim, said Wimar Witoelar, who was by then a presidential spokesperson, of checking misleading information and preventing officials from making "careless statements [that] will cause unrest."[48]

As tensions rose, Wahid showed signs of desperation in the face of a looming showdown between his supporters and the forces preparing to unseat him. On May 28, 2001, he cited media irresponsibility to justify issuing an executive order granting emergency powers to his minister of security, later characterizing the directive as a step to prevent a "catastrophe."[49] The same day, Wahid's attorney general, Marzuki Darusman, announced that his office had found no evidence implicating the president in either Buloggate or Bruneigate.[50]

The next day, violent demonstrations in support of Wahid broke out in East Java but did not dissuade the MPR from voting for a special impeachment session. In response, four thousand Wahid supporters stormed the parliamentary compound. On June 1, the president dismissed his attorney general and security minister, to whom he had just granted emergency powers. Two days later, he suspended the chief of police for opposing a state of emergency. Several cabinet reshuffles followed, and on July 6, Wahid again threatened a state of emergency.[51]

On July 21, the MPR began impeachment proceedings by summoning the president to deliver an accountability speech. Wahid refused, appearing instead on national television to denounce the parliament's actions as illegal and argue that only a new round of elections could resolve the current crisis.[52] Two days later, Wahid issued a decree "freezing" both the entire parliament and the former ruling party, Golkar, and promising new elections within the year.[53] The decree also ordered the military to stop the impeachment proceedings, prompting the armed forces commander to announce the military's unified opposition to the president's directive. That same morning, Indonesia's Supreme Court ruled the president's decree illegal. Within hours, Wahid's vice president, Megawati Sukarnoputri, became Indonesia's fifth president.[54]

One could argue that Wahid's turn against the media, a precursor to proroguing parliament, reflected a development common in fragile democracies—a growing conviction among leaders that they must defer democracy to save it. Instead of exercising his "right of reply," Wahid justified his plan to impose emergency powers in part by asserting that controls on the media were necessary to head off destabilizing intergroup conflict.[55] At the same time, his turn against journalists, as one editorial noted, was "completely out of character."[56] Wahid was, after all, a leader who prided himself on advocating free speech and, despite fierce backlash, had fought to end the country's three-decade ban on Communist writings and ideas. His volte-face raised serious questions about the depth of the country's democratization and showed that the executive branch itself remained inclined, even under the progressive politics of a new president, toward restraints on public speech.

By this point in the transition, members of the media were prepared to resist executive pressure, but they were also trying to survive in a newly competitive environment that could give scandals, in a sense, a life of their own. Media ownership remained an important factor in decision-making. But even after publishing the alleged Wahid mistress story, editors of *Gatra*, owned by Suharto's crony Bob Hasan, confessed that a primary motive had been to boost circulation.[57] This competitive environment, as much as journalistic commitment to a watchdog role or even political bias, drove the coverage that helped bring Wahid down. In a media arena now dominated by market forces, once a news story gained momentum, particularly if triggered by a leak, narrative tension and the pressure of competition tended to push it forward, even if individual outlets wished to ignore a revelation damaging to the president or another public figure. Though an advocate of press freedom in opposition, Wahid developed an antagonistic, increasingly intolerant stance toward negative reporting as president, viewing critical coverage, whether negative or constructive, as essentially adversarial.

Buloggate II

Wahid's moves to rein in the media were a natural response to his fear of losing public support that ironically cost him the very allies he needed to fend off
impeachment. They were also a precursor to his eventual declaration of the state
of emergency that precipitated his fall. But events might well have gone the other
way, returning the country to autocratic rule. His successor, Megawati Sukarnoputri, was more cautious, though both her administration and the political parties
that put her in power were, from the outset, even more uncomfortable with the
country's noisy, meddlesome, and "irresponsible" media. Yet even as news outlets
navigated this continued hostility, they were becoming a primary, if not *the* primary,
mediator of the intraelite conflict that was now a defining feature of the country's
politics.

As Megawati began her term in July 2001, Golkar's second-place strategy in the
1999 elections appeared to have paid off. Under Wahid, the former ruling party had
seemed almost impervious to the corruption charges leveled against it by rival parties
and civil society groups. After Wahid's fall, Golkar had sufficient seats to continue
obstructing democratic reform and evade accountability for its 1999 electoral fraud. But
this influence began to fray when charges over Golkar's use of Bulog funds suddenly
resurfaced in October, putting Golkar on the defensive and transforming Mahfud's
press leak of the previous February into a full-blown scandal. Though this second
Buloggate did little to slow Wahid's steady slide toward impeachment, it nonetheless
changed the course of Indonesia's transition.

While the rest of parliament had ignored the PKB's demands to investigate Golkar's chair, Tanjung, for misuse of Bulog funds, Wahid had not. Just before he fell,
he had his attorney general open a probe and declare former Bulog chief Rahardi
Ramelan an official suspect. Ramelan left the country, and Megawati's new government did nothing, reportedly observing an agreement with leaders of several factions
"to avoid cross-party political aggression."[58]

A flaw in this agreement was its failure to include other key players set on ousting Tanjung from his Golkar leadership. These included Wahid's party, PKB, which
was "determined," said journalist John McBeth, "to exact revenge for Tanjung's role
in ousting Wahid in August."[59] Legislators representing the provinces of Irian Jaya,
Maluku, Sulawesi, and Kalimantan reportedly also began plotting to rid the party of
Tanjung in early October.[60] Most critically, as it turned out, leaders of the Indonesian
Association of Muslim Intellectuals, a think tank founded by the former president
Habibie, "recruited" Ramelan to their own mission to rid Golkar of Tanjung, convinc-
ing him to return to Indonesia for questioning.[61]

Ramelan's return revived the government's investigation. On October 9, during
an interview at the attorney general's office, he "spilled the beans," announcing that
in March 1999 he had given Rp40 billion from Bulog's nonbudgetary funds directly to
Tanjung.[62] During questioning, Ramelan explained that President Habibie and certain
members of his cabinet had allocated the money for use, under Tanjung's supervision,
as aid to people hurt by the economic crisis.[63] To make sure the revelation reached the
public, Ramelan repeated his explanation to reporters.

This revelation became the moment when the long-observed code of silence
in Golkar's ranks cracked. Even so, the state prosecutor's office, now controlled by
Megawati, did not act. But the revelation received wide media coverage, stirring the
public, particularly students, to turn on Tanjung. Then, on October 23, fifty legislators

from five factions submitted a petition to the DPR leadership demanding a parliamentary probe into the affair, proposing formation of "Special Committee Buloggate II."[64]

Golkar's leaders had already acted to counter such a move, demonstrating the power they still wielded. Tanjung's first response to Ramelan's disclosure was to admit the transaction but deny any impropriety. He insisted that he had not diverted any funds to Golkar's election coffers, but had channeled them directly to a charity for food distribution under the government's Social Safety Net program.[65] Next, the Golkar legislator Ferry Mursyidan Baldan spoke out, warning those contemplating a DPR investigation: "Don't push Akbar to play his trump card, it would affect many people, including the current government." Tanjung then approached Megawati's husband, Taufik Kiemas—who was himself vulnerable to Tanjung's "trump card" threat—to pressure Kiemas to help block the special investigation.[66]

Megawati was in a difficult position even without Tanjung's threat to her husband. She had already alienated her one-time ally, PKB, by backing Wahid's impeachment. Her administration relied on a fragile coalition with former enemies in Golkar and the same Muslim parties who had stridently opposed her candidacy back in 1999. Her own vice president, Hamzah Haz—leader of the largest Muslim party, the United Development Party—was now a vocal detractor and among those most eager to see her government fall. As one insider explained, "The hardline Muslim parties are now backing the investigation into [Tanjung] because they feel it will weaken Megawati's powerbase and make her easier to overthrow."[67]

Yet PDIP could not ignore mounting public pressure, led by student groups demanding Tanjung's punishment, for action on this latest Bulog fraud.[68] On October 16, 2000, the coalition of four civil society organizations that had filed suit against Golkar in June met with officials at the attorney general's office to demand a formal inquiry into Ramelan's allegations.[69] Tanjung responded by daring them to continue their pursuit, claiming that there was no evidence of his "misappropriating" Bulog funds.[70]

The state's poor record in prosecuting high-profile corruption cases helped explain Tanjung's confidence. In case after case, including the famous Bank Bali trials, defendants had received acquittals after prosecutors filed flimsy cases and neglected to present evidence that had already been gathered. Though the causes of this dysfunction were widely known, the media nevertheless leaked an external audit revealing that the attorney general's office was riddled with institutionalized corruption. Influenced by bribes or political pressure, prosecutors routinely distorted due process, most frequently by filing weak charges or burying evidence.[71]

At this sensitive juncture, the news media became a remedy for the problem this leaked report exposed, doing the job state prosecutors would not. As it turned out, the critical evidence that moved the case would come the following October from an exposé by the once-banned magazine *Tempo*. In its cover story of October 29, 2001, *Tempo* reported "the involvement of senior Golkar officials" in the diversion of Bulog funds—officials who were "apparently working hard to cover their tracks." Effectively foiling this cover-up, the magazine dissected Tanjung's story of forwarding Bulog funds to an unnamed foundation. According to this investigation, a Golkar insider had learned from Tanjung's lawyers that a "foundation that could be used as 'camouflage' had been found" with links to Golkar's deputy treasurer. The source added that Tanjung's lawyer had then "boasted that he had successfully lobbied senior officials of the 'Round Building' [the attorney general's office] to go along with this plot." The conspirators had finally settled on a third scheme that hinged on the assumption that

Bulog's former deputy financial chief under President Habibie, Achmad Ruskandar, would back their story by testifying that he had "witnessed the money being handed over directly to a charity called 'institution RJ.'" The source who had provided the confidential file said, "This is the final plot that Akbar is going to play" at the attorney general's office.[72]

When Tanjung finally talked to state prosecutors, his story matched this third scheme. After two weeks of escalating, if contradictory, pressures, President Megawati gave legal clearance for her attorney general, M.A. Rachman, to question Tanjung. On October 31, Tanjung obeyed a summons to the attorney general's office as a "witness" in the case. During questioning, he stuck to his story that the Rp40 billion had gone to a charity for food distribution, and finally produced a name—the Raudatul Jannah Islamic Foundation, the same "RJ" named in *Tempo*'s exposé.[73]

The scheme was proceeding as planned until the Bulog deputy Achmad Ruskandar unexpectedly deviated from script, giving damaging testimony on November 20. He not only failed to mention the involvement of a Raudatul Jannah foundation but also admitted placing three checks totaling Rp40 billion into Tanjung's hands, thus contradicting Tanjung's earlier claim that he had never received any money directly.[74]

Tempo also reported that Bulog officials had withdrawn ten checks totaling Rp40 billion from two banks, citing evidence that these had gone to two Golkar treasurers and "members of the Golkar General Election Victory Board," and were "intended for campaign needs in the regions." The most incriminating part of *Tempo*'s report, however, was documentation that Golkar's treasurers had issued receipts for half of the Rp40 billion. "Later," said *Tempo*, "Akbar took back the original receipt[s] for Rp20 billion, promising to replace [them] with a new one for the entire sum: Rp40 billion." The replacement never happened. "Fortunately," *Tempo* added, "a photocopy was safely kept in secret by a key player in the affair."[75] The key player later turned out to be Ruskandar, the very man who was turning state's evidence.

MEDIA'S ROLE

For the first time, Golkar's chair appeared cornered—"trapped," in *Tempo*'s assessment.[76] He also found himself on the wrong side of media publicity, just as President Wahid had. The print press, particularly the newsweeklies, had been pursuing Buloggate II doggedly since early October, when Rahardi Ramelan first made his sensational disclosure of paying Rp40 billion to Tanjung. Radio and television talk shows likewise filled the air with lively discussion of the case, giving instant celebrity to Tanjung's critics.

By late October, members of Tanjung's party were using the media to distance themselves from their chair. Golkar official Muchyar Yara, looking "for the entire world like someone preparing Tanjung for a ritual sacrifice," speculated on Metro-TV that Tanjung had probably "fudged the truth" in his story about the Raudatul Jannah foundation.[77] Others lobbied to remove Tanjung from party leadership.[78]

The media were now critical to the unfolding scandal in other ways. When Tanjung finally arrived at the attorney general's office for questioning, the foreign press reported that he went not to explain Ramelan's disclosure but to respond to "[domestic] media questions about what exactly he did with $4 million in government funds in 1999, on the eve of the last election."[79] On November 19, the state news agency, Antara, confronted Tanjung about "media reports" that he had issued the two receipts highlighted in *Tempo*'s exposé. Tanjung denied the charge, stating, "There were no such receipts."[80]

That same week, *Tempo* devoted its cover to a picture of Tanjung with a Pinocchio nose and his mouth papered shut by a check. The Pinocchio cover prompted "an angry visit by incensed Golkar officials to the magazine's office." *Tempo* responded "that Golkar had not cared less when the magazine dished out equally harsh coverage to ex-president Abdurrahman Wahid over the first so-called Buloggate scandal [that] eventually led to his downfall."[81]

Again, on December 1, Tanjung's friends in Golkar fought back, threatening, via the media, to establish a "rival" parliamentary committee to investigate the misuse of Bulog funds by other political parties.[82] A *Jakarta Post* editorial accused Golkar of "hold[ing] the entire nation hostage," arguing that "the Buloggate II inquiry should be started precisely because Golkar has resorted to blackmail [and] threats" to block it.[83]

Tanjung's—and Golkar's—credibility hinged on the claim that the Rp40 billion went to the Raudatul Jannah charity, and not, as *Tempo*'s exposé indicated, to Golkar's election activities. But the Indonesian media openly challenged Tanjung's story, reporting that the charity had been formed only recently and was, moreover, headed by Golkar executives.[84] Under this pressure, even the attorney general's office and Antara began probing the story's inconsistencies.

By early 2002, the tide appeared to have turned against Tanjung. On January 7, state prosecutors named the Golkar chair an official suspect, charging him with impropriety in authorizing as state secretary the disbursement of Rp40 billion from Bulog's nonbudgetary funds.[85] Though Tanjung's friends lobbied heavily to allow him "an honorable retreat," President Megawati herself rejected his request that the attorney general's investigation be dropped.[86]

Tanjung's image suffered further through ridicule in the press, with more withering caricatures and photo captions.[87] Following the Pinocchio edition, *Tempo*'s cover showed Tanjung cowered in a corner biting his thumb.[88] A few weeks later, he appeared in a bright yellow matador costume waving a symbol of his fabricated "RJ" foundation before an angry bull, the symbol of the ruling party, PDIP.[89]

Now embattled on all fronts, Tanjung lashed out at the media. He had steered clear of direct confrontation with *Tempo*, whose reports arguably had done him the most damage. But when the small daily *Rakyat Merdeka* published a caricature of him bare-chested and sweating as an official "suspect," he filed a libel suit.[90]

After Megawati refused Tanjung's request to drop the attorney general's investigation, Tanjung, according to Golkar insiders, had no choice but "to feed information" to the media that "would implicate other leading politicians in a variety of scandals" and thereby force a compromise.[91] The threat apparently had some impact. Though the attorney general's office seemed to be pursuing its investigation, observers believed that naming Tanjung a "suspect" was part of a cover-up to save him by avoiding a parliamentary inquiry. By the end of January, legislators from PDIP reported that they were being coerced into following the party's position on the case.[92]

Tanjung was exploiting two weak spots in PDIP's armor. The party's flurry of backpedaling, said the *Asia Times*, was "an about-face triggered by Akbar's [dual] threat to withdraw support for Megawati and make public alleged corruption by her husband." Moreover, it was widely believed by this time that all the major political parties, PDIP included, had accepted money from Bulog before the 1999 elections.[93] Since Golkar had control over Bulog's accounts during their diversion, this wide dispersal among major parties seemed clever foresight that protected Golkar from future fallout for this graft. Indeed, by March 2002 only PKB and the "Reform Faction" (Partai Amanat Nasional and Partai Keadilan) remained committed to a DPR investigation, but they held just ninety-two of the DPR's five hundred seats.[94] Some feared that a series of scandals implicating all the major parties in Bulog corruption would simply make voters cynical. "The real casualty," said the *Economist*, "may be democracy itself."[95]

By February 25, interest in Buloggate II had "waned," seeming to vindicate these concerns about a surfeit of scandal.[96] Nonetheless, Tanjung had already been convicted in the court of public opinion.[97] In March, pressure on Megawati's PDIP began to build again, made more acute by internal dissatisfaction and, perhaps most critically, threats from international donors to withhold billions in aid.[98] University students once again took to the streets, demanding a parliamentary probe into Buloggate II. "More student protests are expected to come," the *Asia Times* predicted, "which means Indonesia is facing yet another turbulent, uncertain year [that] could mark the beginning of the end to the leadership of Megawati."[99]

The other major parties were equally reluctant to anger the public by voting against the probe. Instead, as DPR leaders decided in early March to postpone the decision for a parliamentary investigation, the media again became the wild card, reporting PDIP leaders' paralysis and maintaining pressure for some resolution.[100]

In a turn of events that caught nearly everyone off guard, especially the DPR Speaker Akbar Tanjung, the attorney general had him arrested and placed him in detention. On the morning of March 7, 2002, Tanjung arrived at the attorney general's office for his third interview, "beaming" and shaking hands with reporters.[101] Seven hours later, he emerged, jumped in his black Land Cruiser, and sped toward the compound gate, nearly mowing down an official in his path and stopping only when blocked by a police truck and an armed barricade. "Under flash bulbs and cameras," *Tempo* wrote, "the famous figure stooped weakly. He was Akbar Tanjung, and his face looked glum and dejected."[102] The head of the party that had ruled Indonesia for more than three decades was under arrest.

This dramatic denouement was a strong indication that the cycle of media exposé and political scandal that had brought down President Habibie and his successor Wahid was a key driver in post-*reformasi* politics. But two days later, in a telenovela twist in this cycle of revenge, the attorney general's office suddenly disclosed that one of Tanjung's codefendants, a "contractor" named Winfried Simatupang, had just "returned" most of the Rp40 billion allegedly diverted from Bulog into Golkar's campaign coffers.[103] On March 12, Simatupang handed over the final Rp7.5 billion. He claimed he had simply been hiding the money "under his mattress" for the past three years, producing the clearest proof yet that had it not gone to any food distribution activities, but also supporting Tanjung's claim it had not gone to Golkar.[104]

Most significantly, the return of the money helped Tanjung deny that he had personally profited. Things starting looking up for the Golkar leader. When he now refused to relinquish his authority as party chair, calls quieted for an extraordinary conference to name a successor.[105] Consequently, on March 26 as his trial on graft charges got underway, the DPR voted to back Tanjung's continued tenure as Speaker.[106]

GOLKAR'S COMEBACK VIA SCANDAL

From the outset, political interests compromised the case against Tanjung, who remained, as DPR Speaker and Golkar head, the second most powerful person in Indonesia. On March 16, 2002, the *Jakarta Post* reported, "Efforts to salvage corruption suspect Akbar Tanjung became increasingly transparent when [the] Attorney General's Office investigators suddenly declared the Golkar chairman's dossier complete," taking only a few hours to study the files before handing them over to the court, a step that usually "takes at least two weeks."[107]

On March 25, Tanjung's trial began. The court charged him with "directly or indirectly causing financial or economic loss to the state."[108] Although a close relationship between the chief justice and another Golkar party boss reduced the trial's credibility, Tanjung's indictment was still unprecedented. No official at his level had ever faced such proceedings.[109]

But that same week, a group of Golkar legislators went back on the offensive, fighting scandal with scandal. Shifting attention from Tanjung's trial, they began lobbying to summon President Megawati to explain an extrabudgetary Rp30 billion donation made on February 25 to a military housing project, a scandal later called "Banpresgate."[110] Under such pressure to compromise with Golkar, on April 2 PDIP appeared to have resolved its internal debate over Buloggate II. In public statements clearing Golkar of connections to the diverted money, party leaders who had once been among the loudest in demanding a DPR probe now announced that the money had gone to "individuals" and "private institutions"—in other words, not to any political parties.[111]

Amid media charge and countercharge, Tanjung's trial was under way. The prosecution had a strong case, armed with fifteen cashed checks amounting to Rp40 billion and solid leads to trace the money to Golkar accounts.[112] But the public prosecutor, Fachmi [one name], seemed more intent on clearing Tanjung than indicting him; Fachmi directed most charges at Tanjung's hapless codefendants—Simatupang (who had returned the stolen money) and Dadang Sukandar (Raudatul Jannah's alleged founder). Both appeared willing to take the fall for the party's chair. At this critical juncture, however, the media, led by *Tempo*, openly challenged Fachmi to stop stalling. In its detailed coverage, *Tempo* revisited evidence already gathered, including documentation that Golkar treasurers had cashed two Bulog checks for Rp10 billion apiece.[113] But the attorney general's office dismissed this documentation because the magazine only had photocopies of the endorsed checks, not the originals.[114]

On April 6, the attorney general's office suddenly released Tanjung on the personal guarantee of his wife, who wanted him home to celebrate her birthday.[115] Despite strong evidence to support their case, prosecutors had already given Tanjung several gifts—notably, incompetence in the form of "vague" charges, and "careless" and "confusing" dossiers providing the defendant cause to demand dismissal.[116] Tanjung's prosecutors, moreover, aimed their case mainly at the Raudatul Jannah foundation, setting the stage for his codefendants to take the fall and thus clearing Tanjung and Golkar of any wrongdoing.[117] On the trial's first day, it seemed Tanjung's prosecution was heading for the same denouement as defendants in the Bank Bali scandal—exoneration on grounds of prosecutorial incompetence.[118]

A week later, however, Tanjung and his party were blindsided from another direction when the separate trial of former Bulog chief Rahardi Ramelan took an unexpected turn. On April 23, Ramelan's defense counsel, Trimoelja D. Soerjadi, uncovered details of a plot to conceal Tanjung's involvement in the diversion of Bulog funds. While questioning Tanjung as a witness in Ramelan's trial, Soerjadi revealed that at a meeting back in October 2001, Tanjung and his lawyer, Hotma Sitompul, "had attempted to persuade Ramelan to lie to investigators."[119] Significantly, the justice in

Ramelan's trial was Lalu Mariyun, famed for excusing the former president Suharto from standing trial and later for acquitting his son Tommy in a land scam case.[120]

In the middle of Soerjadi's unexpected line of questioning, Justice Mariyun abruptly announced an early lunch break. Soerjadi, however, preempted any such maneuver by using the media to make his revelations public, relating details of the scheme to reporters and producing sensational headlines, such as "Akbar Tried to Make Me Lie."[121] As the press kept up its coverage, *Tempo* was still leading, with a feature headlined "Buloggate II: Forty Billion Lies."[122] On June 4, hundreds of demonstrators from civic and student organizations renewed pressure on PDIP to support a parliamentary probe of Buloggate II, forcing party leaders to move a planned meeting to another location.[123]

Ongoing testimony against Tanjung in his own trial also continued to hurt his case, particularly Simatupang's confession on May 7, 2002, that his return of the Rp40 billion in March had only been a part of a "scenario" to clear Tanjung.[124] Then on May 20, former president Habibie inflicted further damage, sending written testimony with incriminating details from his home in Germany.[125]

On July 24, the Central Jakarta District Court convicted Tanjung for his part in Buloggate II. The prosecution asked for the minimum four-year jail term, but the court decided to be even more lenient, sentencing him to only three years. After filing an appeal, Tanjung remained at liberty and retained both his leadership positions.[126] Two years later, in February 2004, the Supreme Court ended the controversy by over-turning Tanjung's conviction, freeing him to run for president in future elections.

Throughout these cycles of media-driven scandals, Golkar's use of political black-mail to avoid investigation and threaten other parties, particularly PDIP, was a set-back for democratization. Tanjung's tenacity in holding on to his two political posts became a triumph for him and, in many ways, his party. Yet his ability to influence court proceedings was checked by the new transparency the media were imposing on the judicial process. With this transparency, even his ultimate success in the Supreme Court could not undo the damage to his political career. Before Buloggate II, Tanjung was a serious contender for the 2004 presidential election; by the time the election campaign got underway, in the aftermath of all this critical coverage, he could not even win his party's nomination. Golkar was also tarnished, faring poorly in the 2004 elections with its new candidate. Two years into the transition, powerful interests still wielded influence, but the political contests between elections, rocked by media scandals and revenge politics, became increasingly difficult to control.

Megawati and the Press

As the daughter of Indonesia's first authoritarian president and heir to the corporatist principles of his reign, President Megawati responded to media criticism with the reimposition of controls in the name of public order. The administration's record on democratic reform was, therefore, mixed—marked by a weak commitment to freedom of speech and an underlying hostility to the media that surfaced in various manifestations.

One of Megawati's first acts as president in 2001 was to reestablish the Ministry of Information, a key artifact of authoritarian rule abolished by her predecessor, renaming it the Ministry of Communications and Information. She appointed the Golkar leader Syamsul Mu'arif to head the revived agency but, to appease her critics, limited his power to the rank of "state minister." Mu'arif justified the ministry's reinstatement by arguing that "all citizens in remote places should have the opportunity to obtain information."[127]

The decision provoked a barrage of protest from journalists, artists, students, nongovernmental organizations, and professional media associations, including the government-sponsored Association of Indonesian Private Radio Stations.[128] Their main concern was that the Ministry of Information's return would lead to a revival of the New Order's heavy-handed controls. As subsequent events showed, this threat was real. While the media and parliamentary advocates would continue to contest these controls, scandal itself re-entered the arena almost as an independent force, damaging Megawati's chances to retain the presidency and undercutting her attempts at repression.

In December 2001, Megawati's new information ministry vindicated critics' fears by proposing to add thirty-seven articles to the 1999 Press Law, one of *reformasi's* signature reforms, to curb "excessive freedom of the press."[129] The proposed amendments would have empowered the courts and police to take action against media outlets and individual journalists who appeared to violate professional or ethical standards. Before the DPR Commission I, Mu'arif explained that his office was more focused on educating the media and public on existing provisions in the Press Law than pushing for major revisions. But he again stressed that the police would have the power to punish violators under the criminal code.[130]

This proposal to reinforce the police role in arbitrating disputes over media content marked a departure from the model developed during *reformasi* that instead had empowered the newly independent National Press Council to mediate. To mute criticism, Mu'arif announced that his "information campaign would be conducted in cooperation with the Ministry of Justice and Human Rights and the Press Council." But the National Press Council's executive director, Lukas Luwarso, expressed strong disapproval, stating, "I don't think it would be wise to use the Criminal Code to settle any dispute involving the press."[131]

This negative reaction to amending the Press Law forced Mu'arif to abandon his proposal.[132] But then on March 2002, the government denied a work permit renewal to Australian journalist Lindsay Murdoch. The denial set off new alarms that the government was returning to the capricious media controls that had characterized Suharto's New Order. Murdoch's articles had angered officials, particularly a report that nearly two hundred East Timorese children had been taken from their families in West Timor's refugee camps since 1999 and placed in orphanages and "privately owned dormitories."[133] Another article revealed that Indonesian soldiers, during a hunt for separatist leaders in Aceh, had poured boiling water over a four-month-old baby to elicit cooperation from his mother before going on "a killing, looting and burning spree through the village."[134]

The foreign ministry characterized the denial of Murdoch's visa extension as a technical matter. But the head of the Alliance of Independent Journalists, Solahuddin [one name], said, "this incident has signaled a journalist could be punished without any reason."[135] The *Wall Street Journal* editorialized that "if the authorities in Jakarta can now refuse to renew the visa of a foreign correspondent who was allegedly 'causing too much trouble,' then it will not be difficult . . . to move against . . . domestic journalists."[136]

As ominous as these statements sounded for journalists, President Megawati's hostility underscored the risks the new president herself faced, in a postauthoritarian context, as she worked out her relationship to the press. In stark contrast to the relaxed media relations of her predecessor, Wahid, and regular meetings with "ordinary people," Megawati, from the start, worked to avoid all direct contact with journalists and any situation involving unscripted public discussion.[137] One of her first acts was to eliminate the post of presidential spokesperson. Then in late January 2002, the palace issued a formal ban on "door-stop interviews" with their impromptu questioning of the president and vice president. Instead, journalists wishing to ask a question would now have to submit a formal request in advance.[138]

Commenting on the ban, communications professor Muhammad Budhyatna said, "If she thinks she does not need the press anymore, the media will not help her when she makes a wrong move that could be fatal. They will have a field day deriding her."[139] At a March seminar, former *Tempo* editor Goenawan Mohamad predicted, "I am afraid another attempt will be made to reduce press freedom." But the same media that had once scurried for safety "like a crab" under Suharto's rule had since undergone a fundamental transformation. If the government were to attempt a crackdown, Mohamad warned, "there is no alternative but to fight again, and we are ready."[140]

Instead of direct confrontation, the media pursued a succession of financial scandals that slowly transformed Megawati's public image from *reformasi* hero to grasping politician. In contrast to the high drama of Baligate and Buloggate II, which combined wholesale theft with electoral manipulation, Megawati's administration featured mid-range graft for personal gain.

Typical of these controversies was the Banpres scandal, or Banpresgate, which emerged in February 2001 when Megawati's rivals raised questions about a Rp30 billion "donation" to a military housing project. Djamal Doa of the opposition United Development Party, who served on the DPR's budget and finance commission, had been the first to raise questions, taking the matter directly to the press.[141] On March 26, Doa told the entire press corps of his plans to submit a summons request to DPR leaders.[142] The following day, however, after consulting with colleagues in his party, Doa spoke to the media to do damage control for Megawati in close collaboration with PDIP. The state secretary, Bambang Kesowo, explained that the Rp30 billion donation had come out of a "defunct" presidential assistance program called Banpres (Bantuan Presiden). With this explanation, Doa withdrew his summons request.[143] Nonetheless, questions reverberated in the media, tarnishing Megawati's reputation.

Two years of such coverage eroded Megawati's political capital. In the run-up to the July 2004 presidential election—the first direct election of a president in the country's history—one op-ed observed, "A day does not go by without [media attacks on the shortcomings] of Megawati's administration ranging from alleged corruption to treacherously neglecting the reform movement."[144] Consequently, in the April 2004 parliamentary elections, Golkar made a surprising comeback, taking the lead at nearly 22 percent of the vote, with Megawati's PDIP following at a close second at 18.5 percent. But with the switch to a direct presidential election, strong showings for individual parties no longer translated into a clear lead for a party's chosen candidate.

By the time of Indonesia's presidential election in July, a dark-horse candidate, Susilo Bambang Yudhoyono from the small party Partai Demokrat, President Wahid's former security minister, surged ahead of rivals, winning in a run-off race that October and delivering "a shocking defeat" for Megawati and her party.[145] For a fourth time during these first five years of transition, media exposure of scandal had played a central role in precipitating a major turnover in executive leadership—this time, defeating President Megawati, the former dictator's daughter who had reimposed restrictions on media freedom.

Looking back on the events of Indonesia's second year of democratic transition, Suharto's old party remained a powerful force in parliament even after losing the presidency. Despite strong evidence of its reliance on fraud, Golkar did not lose any parliamentary seats to compensate for unfair gains. Instead, the party gained control of more than a quarter of the DPR. It then used this dominance to obstruct investigation into scandals that damaged its reputation while pursuing those that furthered its interests. Other parties, also vying for position, joined Golkar in using these scandals to bring down the new president, Abdurrahman Wahid.

Behind these games of political survival lay a web of collusive arrangements as pervasive in post-Suharto Indonesia as they had been under Suharto. The prevalence of such arrangements—implicating all three post–New Order presidents, their families, and all but two of the forty-eight parties that contested the 1999 elections—threatened to stall, if not reverse, the democratic transition as Wahid's enemies collaborated to protect themselves and block reforms that threatened their interests.

The media also played a key role in Wahid's fall through both principled investigations of financial fraud and unprincipled insinuations of personal impropriety motivated by profit and political bias. Wahid's turn against news outlets was a logical reaction to attack by and through the media and a larger campaign to force him from power. Nevertheless, his attempted crackdown put the transition at risk as much as any comparable government repression in a struggling democracy—whether perpetrated by Ferdinand Marcos in the Philippines, Mohamed Morsi in Egypt, or most recently Recep Erdogan in Turkey.

Though orchestrated by partisans defending the old guard, Wahid's ouster reflected a pivotal change in the country's politics. For good or ill, the new president's fate demonstrated that, in post–New Order Indonesia, the executive no longer controlled the other branches of government. Of equal import was the media's new power, through negative coverage and National Press Council pressure, to block Wahid's plan to use emergency powers to control public speech.

On balance, however, the use of corruption scandals for political attack was the more significant development in Indonesia's democratic transition. During Suharto's long reign, as much as under Wahid's short-lived presidency, intraelite conflict had been a constant in the country's politics. Under Suharto, however, such infighting was resolved behind closed doors with outcomes fixed by executive fiat to avoid threatening the interests of the ruling regime. In the new era, conflicts now played out in public, adding a much higher degree of uncertainty to their resolution and their impact on the prevailing balance of power.

This increasingly public resolution of conflict reduced the viability of elite pacts, breaking down collusive arrangements that had earned Indonesia its status as the world's most corrupt economy.[146] Indeed, Golkar's ability to block a serious probe of the Buloggate II scandal by threatening to expose similar crimes by other parties demonstrated its continued influence. In the end, however, the party failed to negotiate a resolution that could protect Akbar Tanjung, its chair and, before this scandal, its best hope for winning the presidency in 2004. Nor could Golkar operatives find a way to remove Tanjung from the party to contain the ensuing damage. The country had changed from the days of Suharto's New Order, and there were now too many elements beyond Golkar's control.

Megawati confronted the same problem and found her attempts to rein in journalists blocked by both media and public backlash. In a parallel development that gains greater significance in the next chapter, before leaving office, Megawati also inadvertently helped create another vehicle for imposing accountability, the Corruption Eradication Commission, which further complicated the maintenance of collusive pacts.

The story of the commission's emergence provides another window into the odd synergies generated in the mix of pressure for reform, often magnified by the media, and the unpredictable unfolding of intraelite conflict. In it, civil-society mobilization and self-serving political maneuvering converge to impact events where either alone might have failed. More broadly, in the *reformasi* period, the media became players in the twists and turns of elite maneuvering that now unfolded in public, adding a much higher degree of uncertainty to competitions over power, patronage, and public opinion. And this uncertainty in the smaller political contests between elections helped ward off a return to the fixed outcomes of electoral contests under authoritarianism. In this struggle, the press and public would develop a growing alliance with the Corruption Eradication Commission that would not only inject recurring flux and competitiveness into electoral contests but also institutionalize the regular imposition of the transparency required for democracy's consolidation.

CHAPTER EIGHT

MEDIA AND CIVIL SOCIETY

> To live in freedom one must grow used to a life full of agitation, change and danger; to keep alert the whole time with a restless eye on everything around: that is the price of freedom.
>
> —Alexis de Tocqueville, *Journeys to England and Ireland*

By 2014 Indonesia was coming to the end of a twenty-year period of political change that offers insights into the precarious process of democratization. The country's successful postauthoritarian transition raises a key question: How does democracy—from the cultivation of norms to the maintenance of institutions—become self-perpetuating, or at least resilient, over the longer term? Societies aspiring to this stage of democratic consolidation face a near-universal challenge from democratization's inherent inclination toward reversal. As Indonesia's experience during the post-*reformasi* decade of 2004 to 2014 illustrates, a nation's media can play a significant role in breaking up the collusive intraelite pacts whose sum is often reversion to authoritarianism or a slide into pseudodemocracy.

During this transitional period in Indonesia, contending forces were arrayed, despite changes in composition over time, between two broad sectors. One was established elites who had accrued assets or systemic advantage during the long Suharto era and had much to gain from reversal. The other was a coalition of prodemocracy forces who drew institutional strength from reform-oriented government agencies and enjoyed periodic mass support, often mobilized by the still-independent actors in the media.

If democracy is, as the former US secretary of state Madeleine Albright argues, "among the most fragile" forms of government, then this fragility is even more pronounced in postauthoritarian nations where entrenched elites have ample resources to push for a restoration of the old order.[1] In Indonesia's protracted transition, we see constant pressure by reactionary elements, first, to discredit, dismantle, or co-opt the agencies promoting the integrity of the democratic process, and second, to enact legislation that would privilege and protect colluding elites.

As an established economic bloc, Suharto's family and cronies retained enormous wealth in cash and corporations that could readily fund lawsuits, legislative initiatives, and electoral campaigns to accelerate this tendency toward reversal. By contrast, prodemocracy forces were a mass movement taking crisis-driven action to defend progress already achieved. The nation's media played a mixed role, but overall furthered democratic consolidation by serving as not only vehicles of reform-oriented mobilization, but also purveyors of scandal and sites of heated, at times vituperative, contestation.

DYNAMICS OF INDONESIA'S DEMOCRATIZATION

While press freedom is commonly used as a barometer for democracy's health, Indonesia's experience demonstrates the need to understand how media outlets perform that freedom, facilitate its exercise for others, and thereby become key actors in sustaining democracy's robustness over time. This assertion raises two questions: How did Indonesia's media, in serving their own interests and those of others, impact the country's democratic transition? And how does Indonesia illuminate the possibilities of comparable change elsewhere around the globe?

Applying Adam Przeworski's concept of "uncertainty"—the inherent unpredictability of fair and open contestation—to the problem of democratic consolidation indicates that a free and competitive media can serve as a main vehicle in breaking up elite collusion. More specifically, the media's regular showcasing of scandal can be a key driver in promoting the transparency and the circulation of elites that are central to a functioning democracy. Focusing on this undertheorized role of the media provides insight into why some democratic transitions succeed, leading to consolidation, while others either fail or settle into a chronic state of pseudodemocracy.

During the first stage of Indonesia's transition, members of the mainstream and underground media facilitated a historic political opening and challenged the legitimacy of the Suharto regime. But it was in the immediate postauthoritarian period, from 1999 to 2014, that these actors made their most critical contribution through the more difficult process of consolidation. The Indonesian case thus sheds light on the media's centrality in furthering what Przeworski calls the institutionalization of uncertainty—that is, the process by which the unpredictability of democratic contestation comes to be tolerated and ultimately defended, functioning as both a force for consolidation and a key deterrent to reversal.[2]

Though Indonesia's transition began on a hopeful note after Suharto's forced resignation in 1998, its prospects for consolidation were tenuous from the outset, threatened by numerous factors that left the country vulnerable to reversal. Most of the conditions that had sustained authoritarianism under Suharto's thirty-two-year reign—judicial corruption, electoral fraud, and a politicized military—remained in place. Executive abuse of discretionary powers, moreover, persisted long after his fall, perpetuated via practices that helped players manipulate the outcomes of public contests.

If such practices persist in any transition, circumstances will be ripe for a return to authoritarian rule or, at best, the emergence of a hybrid regime akin to the scholar Larry Diamond's "pseudodemocracy," where formal democratic institutions, such as multiparty elections, mask "the reality of authoritarian domination."[3] Under Suharto, Indonesia had long cultivated its own "Pancasila democracy," since recognized as thinly veiled authoritarianism. The veil that allowed the regime to call the country democratic was its routine exercise of multiparty elections that ended predictably in victory for Suharto's Golkar party.[4]

With this history in mind, Indonesians pushed forward with electoral reform in 1998–99 to foster genuine competition among the new array of political parties. When the country held its first postauthoritarian elections in June 1999, the unprecedented win by an underdog opposition party, PDIP, appeared to be a significant achievement. But as subsequent events showed, elections—even those that bring new leadership—are not necessarily sufficient to consolidate democracy. Despite the fact that observers declared these parliamentary elections "free and fair," their results were as expertly engineered as any under Suharto, designed to give a symbolic victory to the opposition while keeping the old ruling party in power.

Critical media coverage might have restrained the ruling party's manipulation, but nearly all Indonesia's news outlets downplayed reports of electoral fraud. Despite the victory of an opposition party and the media's liberation, the 1999 elections produced a partial reversal in the country's democratic transition through a return to the manipulated outcomes and restrained journalism typical of Suharto's New Order. The electoral manipulations, the media's reticence in challenging them, and the failure of reform in other arenas made it difficult to see where democratization, particularly the institutionalization of uncertainty, had made significant headway.

The transition regained its foothold only after these elections were ratified in July 1999 and the media switched gears, exposing some of the fraud that had compromised the voting and thereby derailing the old guard's campaign to keep Suharto's hand-picked successor in office. It was at this sensitive point that the internal transformation of the media began to have a significant external impact. Another Habibie presidency, won via electoral subterfuge or collusive compromise, would have subverted both the spirit and the logic of democratic reform, regardless of any progress an opposition party's lead in the June elections might represent.

But the subsequent exposure of campaign finance fraud in the Bank Bali scandal, amplified by the media to become "Baligate," halted this slide toward reversal. The damage to Habibie's candidacy blew the presidential race wide open for the first time in over thirty years. The contest that then unfolded was anything but predictable, and its outcome anything but predetermined. It was, instead, taut with uncertainty right up to the final parliamentary tally that repudiated Habibie and selected a reformist opposition leader, Abdurrahman Wahid. In short, Baligate, and the media's relentless coverage of it, helped set the democratic transition back on course, not by invalidating the June ballot and forcing new elections but by injecting uncertainty at the next stage—the parliamentary selection of the president.

One could view the opposition's upset victory more skeptically, as a fluke producing a mixed victory for democratic forces. While Golkar's maneuvering to retain the executive failed, the final result—Wahid's win in the parliamentary vote for president—was still little more than a backroom deal among the major Muslim parties designed to keep both Habibie and the winner of the popular vote, Megawati Sukarnoputri, out of the presidency. But whatever the election's ultimate significance, the media's saturation coverage of Baligate was not an anomalous phenomenon yielding a one-time impact. This controversy that upset the balance of elite bargaining was, instead, the first in a long series of media-driven scandals, each of which rocked the country's political equilibrium and revealed deals and betrayals taking place in the highest corridors of power. From Baligate onward, these exposés launched an era of politics by scandal that made the media a lead player within intraelite conflict, unleashing cycles of revenge and making unpredictability a constant in Indonesian politics, while introducing new elements of transparency and circulation of leadership.

Over the next five years, from 2000 to 2004, there was a relentless cycle of attack and counterattack mediated, and sometimes instigated, by the media. Media controversy in itself was not new. Since the country's independence in 1949, the news media had often been used for political revenge. Indeed, Suharto's last minister of information, Alwi Dahlan, observed in 1999 that pitting people against each other is the nature of the news media. Under Suharto, Dahlan added, this tendency was overwhelmingly one-sided as the ruling regime used news outlets "to get" those in disfavor and mediate score settling not as a neutral conduit but as an adjunct of executive power.[5]

In the less centralized politics of the post-Suharto period, autonomous elite rivalries, shaped by media exposure and civil-society response, increasingly decided who would rise and fall. As mediators of intraelite conflict, the nation's media, now more detached from state power, acted both independently and as vehicles for rival political forces, adding a much higher degree of uncertainty to competitions over power, patronage, and public opinion.

This loss of executive control over the outcomes of intraelite conflict was most evident in the succession of scandals from Baligate to Banpresgate. The former ruling party, Golkar, used media-driven scandals to impeach Abdurrahman Wahid. Then difficulties in containing scandal and conflict began to impact the same actors who had helped orchestrate Wahid's fall, particularly Akbar Tanjung, Golkar's chair and best hope for retaking the presidency in 2004. Throughout these controversies, there was also ample evidence that major players from all the political parties were trying, as Tanjung had, to rig the system, colluding to cancel out their respective political sins and maintain their current positions. But collusion and cover-up became more difficult as the media, driven by market competition and partisan maneuvering, began to impose greater transparency.

As revelations set off cycles of revenge, scandals began fracturing elite pacts and taking on a life of their own in ways impossible under the New Order. Each time such arrangements broke down, Indonesian political life became more fluid and more open, moving democratization forward. Most critically, the media—now greatly expanded, more amorphous, and highly competitive—could no longer simply broker cynical deals for elite benefactors. As warring factions used the media to maneuver against each other and as news outlets weighed in independently, media exposés and contentious public discourse began to play a central yet unpredictable role in mediating these proliferating intraelite conflicts. It was the playing out of political conflict via the media, more than any other change associated with the transition, that allowed Indonesia to move away from authoritarian stasis and closer to the institutionalized uncertainty of democracy.

A DECADE OF CONSOLIDATION, 2004–2014

In the decade of democratic consolidation after 2004, the fitful struggle between a prodemocracy coalition comprising elements of civil society and certain members of the media, on the one hand, and an ad hoc alliance of actors favoring reversal, on the other, culminated in the 2014 presidential campaign, which became, in effect, a showdown between these contending forces. During the same decade, the overall trend toward transparency and open political contests continued, reinforced by constitutional amendments passed in the first years of *reformasi* that strengthened parliament, removed nonelective legislative seats, established new protections for civil liberties, and introduced direct elections for president and vice president. Through these changes, reformers revised Indonesia's constitution to invest citizens with the right to freedom of speech and a free media, and to draw clearer divisions among government institutions, imposing checks on their jurisdictions and powers.

Each of these developments also advanced democratic consolidation by making it more difficult to game the system and block the circulation of leadership. Contests for the executive became more transparent and competitive as direct elections and new mechanisms of accountability, particularly the introduction of "quick counts" on polling day, curtailed manipulation. Freed in 2006 from the threat of criminal penalties for insulting the president and vice president, the media became increasingly aggressive in pursuing stories that implicated incumbents, which in turn undermined the ability of ruling parties and their coalitions to maintain control of the executive.[6] As Indonesian democracy struggled toward a slow consolidation during this critical decade, the media became vehicles of proreform mobilization, as well as sites of partisan contestation and personal vendetta, together maintaining the transparency and uncertainty necessary for further democratization.

Despite these advances, the transition continued to face an unremitting pull toward reversal. Even as democratic attitudes and media practices took root and unpredictability became the norm, political actors continued to maneuver to insulate themselves from the uncertainty of fair and open contestation. This decade saw a notable increase in cross-party alliances among legislative candidates that led the country into a state of political development that Daniel Slater and Erica Simmons call "collusive democracy." Such a system, they argue, is marked by the effective merger of all major parties into a cartel, as actors try to reduce the uncertainty of genuine competition, entering into "promiscuous" power-sharing arrangements that make elected representatives virtually interchangeable. This collusion also forecloses the possibility of a viable political opposition, as legislators undermine democratic accountability by making themselves "collectively irremoveable through the ballot box."[7]

If democratization requires widespread acceptance of competitive contests and their uncertain outcomes, efforts by Indonesia's representatives to insulate themselves between elections were a serious setback. Through such power sharing and lack of transparency in legislative decision-making, parliament became, by 2009, largely unaccountable to voters.[8] Much of the country's judiciary also colluded to protect themselves (and their financial patrons) from exposure and accountability.[9] Even as media revelations of malfeasance and chains of reciprocal incrimination began to expose individual wrongdoing, institutional accountability remained minimal.

Members of the judiciary and the legislature also colluded in 2004–14 by using new and old laws to discourage the airing of criticism that could damage their reputations or threaten their incumbency. Among these regulations, the most chilling were the country's plaintiff-friendly defamation laws. Despite abolition of the New Order's notorious "hate-sowing articles," passage of the 1999 Press Law, and enactment of constitutional amendments protecting free expression, a maze of civil and criminal defamation statutes remained in place to allow litigation against reporters and ordinary citizens for speech nominally protected by these higher laws.[10]

Journalists charged with libel under the criminal code petitioned the courts to use the Press Law, which, they argued, should override legislation from the colonial and authoritarian eras. Accordingly, in 2006 the Supreme Court overturned the conviction of *Tempo*'s chief editor, Bambang Harymurti, for a report suggesting that the business magnate Tomy Winata had been responsible for a textile market fire in 2003. The court ruled unanimously that the defendant should have been tried under the Press Law, not the criminal code.[11] It stopped short, however, of issuing a blanket injunction barring the use of the criminal code against journalists in such cases. Since Indonesian higher court rulings do not serve as binding precedent for lower courts, this decision offered journalists little protection from future criminal convictions in similar cases.[12]

These defamation laws protected politicians who used them to avoid scrutiny. In 2008, parliamentarians went further, passing five new laws to silence critical speech. The Information and Electronic Transactions Law, for example, allows courts to imprison anyone accused of defamation via the internet or other digital media (such as cell phone texting) for up to six years.[13] With these laws readily available to aggrieved business owners and officials, corruption exposés, letters to the editor, customer service complaints, and even private emails have all provoked lawsuits that have landed people in prison.

In the post-Suharto era, the internet, the twenty-first century's primary driver of modernization, also came under increasing attack by Islamic conservatives who portrayed it as a hydra-headed threat to public morality. In their effort to impose religious controls over public expressions of sexuality, which they branded "pornography," such groups villainized the internet to reestablish moral standards. After three years of deliberation, a parliamentary committee released draft legislation in 2006 proposing bans on suggestive dancing, public kissing, wearing scanty apparel, and any other act that could "arouse desire."[14] The proposal set off protests among critics worried that its language, encouraging the public to "participate in the prevention of the production, dissemination, and use of materials of pornography," would empower groups such as the Islamic Defenders Front in their campaigns to police public morality. Such groups, for example, had already carried out attacks on nightclubs they regarded as "dens of sin."[15]

Shortly before its passage in October 2008, its sponsors claimed that an amended version of the antipornography bill "accommodated all interests in society." Even after revisions, however, many believed that the bill's prohibitions were untenably broad and vague, defining pornography as all "pictures, sketches, illustrations, photographs, articles, sounds, voices, moving pictures, animations, cartoons, conversations, body movements or other forms of messages . . . that contain obscenity or sexual exploitation."[16] Although over one hundred legislators walked out on the proceedings in protest, members of conservative Islamist parties held sway, and the legislation passed into law.[17]

Deeper Transformation

Even with the antipornography law's passage, conservative alarm over the nation's impending moral crisis continued, with rhetoric reaching beyond the nation to invoke a higher order. In retrospect, it seems that the country's relative stability since 2004 had fostered a resurgence of the corporatist values of integralism across a widening spectrum of Indonesian society. Not only did orthodox Islamic groups seek rigid controls over gender and a purge of heterodox Muslim believers, even journalists' associations, once strong advocates of civil rights, moved to exclude entire media genres, particularly "infotainment," from legal protections.[18] The continuing appeal of integralist ideology, reinforced by Muslim mass mobilization, provided a strong political foundation for future attacks on freedom of expression.

Mitigating these trends, however, a new logic transforming the country's political culture began competing with and even replacing New Order perceptions of normality and deviance. For a half century under both Sukarno and Suharto, the corporatist doctrine of integralism had assumed an underlying congruity in the interests of citizens and rulers that provided the rationale for the curtailment of civil rights. From this idea of essential harmony, Suharto's later enforcement of "positive interaction" among the media, state, and society helped his regime stigmatize the airing of conflict and justify closing off channels of dissent. In effect, this doctrine rejected the individualism and confrontational politics associated with Western democracy and encouraged an unquestioning faith in those in power. Following Suharto's ouster, *reformasi* advocates were generally successful in repudiating this doctrine, although its tenets retained sufficient appeal to fuel conservative attempts at rolling back media freedoms.[19]

Also mitigating retrogressive pressures, the transformative impact of the media's new role in Indonesia went beyond the expansion of public discourse, and even beyond the restoration of uncertainty to political contestation. In any transition, the media can help ward off reversal in part by reinforcing perceptions among those in power that a majority of the public, if not unambiguously supportive of democratic governance, at least would not favor a return to authoritarianism. In post-Suharto Indonesia, members of the media were often their own best advocates in reinforcing impressions of public support for media freedom. When asked how Indonesians would respond to a crackdown on speech in 1999, government figures responded that neither the media nor the "people" would allow it.[20] As the transition progressed, opinion polls periodically confirmed similar perceptions.[21]

A case that confirmed ordinary Indonesians' support for freedom of speech and their antipathy to laws protecting the powerful culminated in a digital cause célèbre. In May 2009, a nursing mother of two, Prita Mulyasari, was subjected to three weeks of pretrial detention after Omni International Hospital charged her with defamation. Her crime: she had sent an email a year earlier to about twenty friends, complaining that the hospital's doctors had badly misdiagnosed her symptoms and given her dengue fever shots when she actually had the mumps.[22]

While Prita was in jail awaiting almost certain conviction, an angered internet community launched an intensive online campaign in her defense, establishing a Facebook group that quickly gained several hundred thousand supporters. Politicians running for office, including former president Megawati, visited her in prison, and members of parliament pressured the hospital and the public prosecutor for a quick resolution.[23] When a court fined her nearly $22,000 and sentenced her to six months' incarceration, supporters formed the Help Prita Movement to collect coins in a dozen Indonesian cities.[24] Politicians, businesspeople, cab drivers, street vendors, grade-school children, and even scavengers were active in raising money. Through this unprecedented outpouring of public concern, the campaign collected nearly $90,000.[25] Finally, on December 29, 2009, the Tangerang High Court reversed Prita's conviction. After being tried, acquitted, retried, then acquitted again, she became an international celebrity who eventually brought Omni and its lawyers to their knees, lodging a countersuit against the hospital for $106 million.[26]

Prita's case resonated with widespread anger at a legal system that, in the words of one observer, "tends to side with the powerful and crush the weak into pieces."[27] Support for her provided a vehicle for holding the powerful to account—in this case, not only Omni but also the police, the courts, and parliamentarians complicit in maintaining this unbalanced system. Yet in the end, victory for Prita meant defeat in key ways for freedom of expression. Because of the Indonesian legal system's ambiguous sense of precedent, the case overturned Prita's conviction but spared the country's defamation laws. Ultimately, it did not empower her followers so much as drive home the lesson that freedoms brought by the transition remained tenuous, enforced or abrogated at the whim of the powerful and still demanding crisis-driven defense via mass mobilization.

This criminalization of criticism, fostered by collusion in all three branches of government, was a blow to democratic consolidation, giving the more powerful the means to punish both media and citizens for imposing accountability. Fear of repercussions, in turn, constrained efforts to reduce the country's pervasive corruption, recognized as a major impediment to economic development and an indicator that democratic transition was stagnating.

Despite setbacks for transparency and free speech, Indonesia's ranking on the Corruption Perceptions Index improved steadily over time, suggesting some long-term impact from reformists' efforts, particularly those of the Corruption Eradication Commission (Komisi Pemberantasan Korupsi, KPK), established six years earlier.[28] Somewhat surprisingly, not long after its inception in 2003, this body evolved into an effective institution—an anomaly among other government bodies and a notable break from a string of toothless predecessors.[29]

Though its origins lay in demands from *reformasi* activists, passage of the legislation that brought the KPK into being was influenced as much by intraelite conflict as any desire for reform. Back in 1998, when anti-Suharto momentum had been at its peak, pressure from students, journalists, international donors, and nongovernmental organizations had forced Indonesia's highest legislative body, the MPR, to pass a decree, "Clean Governance Free from Corruption, Collusion and Nepotism," that directed the DPR to fulfill its anticorruption mandate. Several initiatives resulted, but each failed from a lack of powers, funding, or both.[30]

Nonetheless, one such initiative created in 2000 under President Wahid, the Wealth Audit Board, began imposing limited transparency. When it started investigating wealth held by Megawati's family, the new president was quick to replace it with a body she believed she could control. In short, though Megawati gained credit for signing the 2002 bill that created the KPK, her motivations were both "political vengeance" and self-protection from the very scrutiny the KPK was designed to impose.[31] Yet armed with surprisingly strong powers, including surveillance, wiretapping, access to bank and tax information, the authority to arrest suspects, and an unprecedented requirement to pursue all cases to prosecution, the KPK ultimately became a powerful ally of independent media and civil society, and a thorn in Megawati's side.[32]

Through its ongoing investigations of official malfeasance, the KPK also mitigated the criminalization of critical speech by allowing journalists more leeway to report on official corruption cases and provide the commission with information gathered from their own investigations. Political rivalries and self-serving motives also facilitated the KPK's collection of evidence.

By July 2009, the KPK claimed a 100-percent conviction rate in eighty-six bribery and graft cases.[33] With these successes and an apparent commitment to protecting the public interest, the KPK won strong support among the Indonesian middle class, even though the total of eighty-six cases over a six-year period was hardly significant in a country ranked at the time among the most corrupt in the world.[34] As political observer Aristides Katoppo noted, "You know, with corruption in Indonesia, if you start operating on this patient, you will have nothing left on the body."[35]

The KPK's record nevertheless helped General Susilo Bambang Yudhoyono build his reform credentials after his election to the presidency in 2004, propelling him to reelection five years later. But like Megawati, President Yudhoyono was guilty of corruption, including campaign finance fraud, prompting the KPK to investigate him and his family. As the commission gained more enemies, Yudhoyono reportedly turned his back when it came under attack.[36]

The most dramatic instance of this backlash against the KPK came in early 2009, when several top police officials colluded to disgrace two of its key members. Starting just after Yudhoyono's reelection, when he had little incentive to defend the commission, the attack threatened to stall, if not reverse, the fight against corruption. The KPK's vulnerability without high-level support highlighted the continued fragility of democratic consolidation. Yet another crisis elicited mass mobilization, this time through a civil society campaign called Save the KPK.

The controversy arose over an apparent conspiracy by the chief of detectives, the attorney general's office, and the brother of a fugitive businessman to frame two KPK deputy chairmen, Chandra Hamzah and Bibit Samad Rianto. Acting on charges of extortion and bribery, police arrested the two in July 2009, igniting demonstrations in several Indonesian cities by protesters who took this as an effort to undermine the KPK. Using their wiretapping powers, however, KPK officers fought back by monitoring the conspirators' phones. After insiders leaked some of these tapes, the media became central actors by airing recorded conversations between senior police, prosecutors, and the brother of the fugitive businessman who had fled KPK prosecution in 2008. The tapes revealed an explicit conspiracy to save the fugitive's brother by accusing Chandra and Bibit of soliciting bribes from him. Adding to the drama, other taped conversations contained claims of Yudhoyono's involvement.[37]

Within weeks, the ensuing controversy, known as Cicak vs. Buaya (Gecko versus Crocodile), grew to Baligate proportions. Even media outlets compromised by business interests jumped into the fray, driven, as in Baligate, by a mix of competitive pressures and civic duty. Following patterns first evident in the alliance between media and civil society that had defeated the 1999 Security Bill and its martial law provisions, this new battle required a sustained public mobilization. Members of the media promoted this turnout, but the critical development that empowered citizens and the media was their new ability to use the internet to pressure officials.

As the new Constitutional Court opened its hearings on the case, television stations broadcast excerpts from the tapes and riveted the country with hours of live proceedings. But the most critical development came when Bibit and Chandra's supporters launched a Facebook campaign, similar to that in the Prita case, with a target of one million members.[38] An earlier statement by the police chief implicated in the case ("How dare a gecko [the KPK] challenge a crocodile [police and prosecutors]?") provided both the nickname and the visual icon of the fight, inspiring a flood of gecko-and-crocodile images on websites, magazine covers, T-shirts, and bumper stickers.[39] By early November, the Facebook campaign had passed its million-member target. On December 1, the attorney general's office dropped its charges against the KPK deputy commissioners, Bibit and Chandra.[40]

Their release likely saved the KPK itself, whose legislative mandate might not have been renewed by the president. The KPK continued to face near-constant siege, as those benefitting from corruption, in the words of one journalist, tried to "sabotage [its] reputation, tie its leaders up in bogus legal cases, cut its financing or legislate it out of existence."[41] Despite ongoing attacks, the KPK would survive as an institutionalized force for transparency, backed by sympathetic news outlets and public pressure.

THE 2014 PRESIDENTIAL ELECTION

Five years after the KPK's public exoneration, the contending forces of democratization and reversal were suddenly embodied in the two leading candidates in the 2014 presidential election: Joko Widodo (Jokowi), a small business owner who championed democratic reform, and Lieutenant General (Ret.) Prabowo Subianto, Suharto's former son-in-law, who advocated a return to a more authoritarian order.

After a succession of electoral victories that carried him from the mayoralty of Solo in 2005 to the governorship of Jakarta in 2012, Jokowi started the 2014 campaign with a strong lead.[42] His high popularity stemmed from his modest beginnings and his success in enacting populist reforms, expanding health care and education while reducing corruption through transparency.[43] Four months before the election, however, Jokowi began losing ground to Prabowo, who employed a militant nationalism while deriding Jokowi's moderation as weakness. Prabowo also capitalized on public frustration with corruption, blaming democracy while promising to abolish direct elections for regional heads and repeal post-Suharto constitutional amendments. Appealing to nostalgia for the country's authoritarian past, he appeared at campaign rallies on horseback surrounded by uniformed supporters, sporting Suharto-style dress and Sukarno-style rhetoric.[44]

In the midst of this campaigning, Prabowo's team began disseminating disinformation that Jokowi was Communist, Chinese-Singaporean, and secretly Christian. Aiding in this "black propaganda," Prabowo also enjoyed heavy promotion from media mogul Hary Tanoesoedibjo and Golkar head Aburizal Bakrie, who together controlled five major television channels.[45] Through these tactics and endorsements, Prabowo garnered growing support, primarily from the middle and upper classes.

Other media, particularly *Tempo*, began challenging smears against Jokowi and reporting on Prabowo's checkered past in a conscious attempt to break his momentum.[46] Then in June 2014, a month before the election, an anonymous source leaked a military investigation's findings that Prabowo, as commander of the Kopassus special forces back in 1998, had ordered the abduction and torture of student activists. As social media and news outlets seized upon the report, it quickly escalated into a national scandal. By reviving one of the most traumatic episodes of the 1998 transition, the source, believed to be a military general, used the media to damage Prabowo.[47] Pro-Jokowi media outlets, in turn, used the leak to increase audiences and counter the rise of a candidate potentially hostile to freedom of speech.[48]

While Prabowo's past left him vulnerable to such attacks, for some it also increased his strongman appeal, and his popularity continued to rise.[49] This development triggered alarm among human rights organizations and other observers, who saw it as an indication of the country's continued susceptibility to authoritarian reversal and mobilized to monitor electoral fraud.[50] On the day of the ballot, this monitoring showed Jokowi winning by over 6 percent. Prabowo nevertheless declared victory based on manipulated quick counts, and his allies in the media, particularly outlets owned by Tanoesoedibjo and Bakrie, reported this victory as fact. In response, a group called Guard the Elections (Kawal Pemilu) organized seven hundred volunteers via Facebook to allow the public to compare official vote tallies with original data from polling stations, an initiative crucial to discrediting Prabowo's declaration of triumph. Three days after Jokowi was sworn in as Indonesia's next president in October 2014, Prabowo finally conceded.

Despite the support for Prabowo from major news outlets owned by his allies, the election of Jokowi represented a hard-fought victory by the same alliance of reformist media actors and civil society that has been central to Indonesia's democratization struggle for the past twenty years. For many, this outcome served as confirmation of the country's successful consolidation.[51] Prodemocracy forces had come together to overcome the continued power of a reactionary, old-guard coalition and discredit resurgent authoritarian ideals. This win by an outsider who rose without personal wealth or elite connections also produced meaningful circulation of leadership. Corruption scandals—fueled by leaks, investigations, and partisan vendetta—facilitated this circulation of leadership, inflicting substantial damage on the ruling party, Partai Demokrat, and frustrating President Yudhoyono's dynastic ambitions.[52] Other "new-wave politicians" with clean reputations committed to fighting graft were also rising to high office at this time, notably Jakarta's new governor, Basuki "Ahok" Tjahaja Purnama and Bandung's governor, Ridwan Kamil.[53]

Only weeks after his inauguration, however, the new president's limitations became clear as legislators from Prabowo's campaign coalition, who controlled 60 percent of parliament, and others from Jokowi's own PDIP party began collaborating to undermine reform initiatives. Significantly, to avoid conflict, Jokowi did not defend the KPK during his first year in office.[54] Yet the agency continued its investigations, jailing or driving from office some of the most powerful in Indonesian politics, notably the DPR Speaker, Setya Novanto. Only three months after Donald Trump called him "a great man" at a campaign rally in New York, Novanto was forced to resign as Speaker in December 2015, following public protests and intense media coverage of his attempts to extort $4 billion from a mining company.[55] Commenting on the public pressure, Natalia Soebagjo, the executive director of the Center for the Study of Governance at University of Indonesia noted, "Corruption cases are spoken about openly in the media, and in social media, corruption issues often go viral."[56]

Comparing Novanto's fall to Watergate, observers viewed it as a "turning point" in Indonesia's fraught political history.[57] However, Novanto again earned his title, "Mr. Teflon," when Golkar elected him chair in 2016 and subsequently reappointed him Speaker of the DPR.[58]

The PDIP chair and former president, Megawati Sukarnoputri, also repeatedly put Jokowi in a difficult position with her own maneuvering, pushing cabinet appointments on him that were heavily criticized by his supporters. In early 2015, a KPK investigation revealed wrongdoing by Jokowi's nominee for police chief, Budi Gunawan. Public pressure, amplified by mainstream and social media, forced the president to withdraw the nomination, prompting retaliation from the police, who declared two KPK commissioners suspects on dubious charges. In March, an organization called the Indonesian Grassroot Society Movement, known for its crowds-for-hire intimidation, reported *Tempo* to the police for allegedly libelous coverage of Gunawan's bank accounts.[59] Then in July, an aspiring politician, Maruli Hendra Utama, filed suit against *Tempo* for defaming PDIP through its reporting on police actions against KPK commissioners.[60]

These actions, seen as "criminalizing" anti-corruption efforts, sparked a new public outcry, covered heavily by the media, that forced Jokowi to order his attorney general to drop both cases.[61] Finally, in 2016, seven out of ten parliamentary factions, led by PDIP, lobbied intensely to revise the 2002 law that had established the KPK by stripping the agency of key powers. But once again, sustained media attention and activist mobilization via social media generated sufficient public pressure to induce politicians to reverse course.[62]

Commentators who wrote on these attacks on the KPK tended to be pessimistic, seeing in them evidence of the agency's vulnerability to eventual co-optation or collapse. Yet each time, mainstream and social media mobilized civil society intervention, and the KPK survived as the institutionalization of *reformasi*'s original demands for transparency. Backed by the public's support, even protectiveness, KPK investigators persevered, angering targets and inviting more attacks. Yet in mid-2016, the agency announced plans to expand its jurisdiction to the private sector. In December 2016, President Jokowi finally declared his "full support" for strengthening the KPK at a national conference on eradicating corruption.[63] Nonetheless, parliament launched another of its attempts to curb the KPK with an inquiry into its purported overreach, sparking "public condemnation" so strong that even Prabowo's party was forced to withdraw its support for the investigation.[64]

Weathering lawsuits and other threats, news outlets also continued to report KPK findings supplemented by their own investigations, setting in motion scandals that exposed corruption and often led to policy change, resignations, or prison. By mid-2017, the KPK was again investigating Speaker Novanto, this time for his involvement in a $244-million identity card scam called eKTPgate.[65] After months of dramatic developments in the case, the Jakarta Corruption Court found Novanto guilty of complicity in the scam and sentenced him to fifteen years' imprisonment with a subsequent five-year ban on any political activity—a stinging rebuke for a man who personified the power and corruption that the Golkar party had acquired during the three decades of the Suharto dictatorship. The former DPR Speaker and Golkar chair now sits in prison in the Sukamiskin Penitentiary in Bandung.[66]

In the aftermath of the Speaker's spectacular downfall, members of the DPR approved a new bill (RUU KUHP) further curtailing the KPK's powers, the latest and perhaps the most strategic attempt to curb the autonomy of this independent investigative body.[67] Whatever fate might await the KPK, both the eKTP scandal and the attacks on the commission were manifestations of the "agitation, change, and danger" that are, as Alexis de Tocqueville once said, inescapable in maintaining democratic freedom.[68] The outcomes of such contests are ephemeral, but conflict itself is a constant.

THE PROCESS OF DEMOCRATIC CONSOLIDATION

Throughout Indonesia's twenty-year transition, synergies between public mobilization and self-serving political maneuvering helped ward off authoritarian reversal. Although each crisis seemed intensely individual in the historical moment, these recurring battles reveal an emerging pattern that lends them greater significance, represented in figure 1.

At the outset of each incident, media players, such as journalists and their respective news outlets, reported intraelite conflict and revelations of wrongdoing, sometimes triggering scandals, and then provided platforms for critical debate and political attack. In any transition, this sequence, even those elements that may seem detrimental to healthy public discourse, can perform numerous functions that facilitate continued democratic consolidation, or at a minimum, slow a slide into pseudodemocracy or electoral authoritarianism. By increasing information available to the public, the media can induce civil society mobilization. When citizens receive new information,

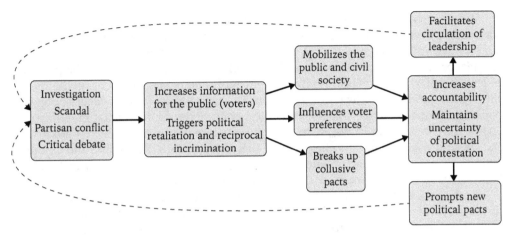

Figure 1. Political reporting in democratic consolidation

their voting preferences may change, which increases uncertainty over election outcomes. Revelations of malfeasance can also trigger partisan vendetta and reciprocal incrimination, further increasing transparency and breaking up collusive pacts. The sum of these functions can strengthen accountability and help maintain the flux of open political contestation, facilitating the circulation of leadership. The perennial instinct to avoid accountability and uncertainty may inspire players to form new collusive pacts. But the ensuing corruption is likely to fuel new media-driven scandals, creating conditions that can set the cycle in motion all over again.

During Indonesia's key years of democratic consolidation, 2004 to 2014, commentators periodically worried that media focus on scandal and partisan conflict would produce apathy, cynicism, or simple "politics fatigue," detrimental to the health of democracy. In 2013, however, a national survey revealed that, despite a widespread perception that corruption was rife in all levels of government and business, the vast majority of Indonesians still preferred democracy over authoritarianism. Indeed, 76 percent reported that if "parliamentary elections were held today," they would "definitely vote." Only 5 percent said they would not.[69]

Despite valid concerns about divisive politics as a key threat to democratic consolidation and stability, one could argue that in any democracy, the greater threat is not divisive politics or irresponsible journalism but collusion. When prevalent among those with electoral, judicial, or economic power, collusion reduces public influence over policy and paralyzes the competition necessary to democracy's functioning. The convergence in Indonesia among watchdog journalism, elite conflict (mediated by an imperfect yet competitive press), and an active civil society (newly empowered by social media) has helped break up the collusion endemic to the country's politics.

CROSS-NATIONAL COMPARISONS

Indonesia's comparatively successful transition has important implications for other emerging democracies worldwide. In the quarter century since the Cold War's end, the once heady overthrow of authoritarian regimes has subsided into a generally dismal mix of pseudodemocracies, dictatorships, and failing states—all indicating the central importance of the far less dramatic process of democratic consolidation.

Whether by sudden coup or slow accretion of collusive pacts, a democratic transition's reversal can occur at virtually any point after the fall of an authoritarian regime—immediately, with the reconstitution of an old guard coalition (military, cronies, or an alliance of both), or later, through a leader identified with the previous order who plays upon mass disappointment with democracy and sentimentality for the bygone era. Though the political response to such threats varies widely, successful opposition usually entails some combination of intraelite conflict, mass mobilization, and media exposé. Admittedly, such synergies operate in comparatively few countries. But these few also happen to be some of the world's more democratic and dynamic nations—whether in Asia (Indonesia, the Philippines, South Korea), Africa (Tunisia, South Africa), or Latin America (Brazil, Chile, Mexico).

Among these cases, three share notable similarities with Indonesia, particularly in the ways that major scandals and the media more broadly have influenced their trajectories toward democratization. After seven decades of one-party rule, Mexico experienced a recent democratic transition in which the media played a central role. In a detailed study of this volatile process, Chappell Lawson found that liberalization of the media was a powerful force. Of equal import, a series of government scandals that the media aired in a kind of "feeding frenzy" was critical to voters' turn against the entrenched regime.[70] Not only did the scandals of the 1990s damage the regime's legitimacy, but their "rapid succession," instead of producing voter fatigue or cynicism, appeared "to indict the system as a whole" and thereby generate demand for more fundamental change. Moreover, Lawson continues, "scandals signaled to political elites that the rules of the game had changed and that certain older practices would now be exposed to public scrutiny. More aggressive media coverage thus created a new context for political decision making."[71]

The rising political uncertainty and these media-driven scandals finally pushed the ruling Institutional Revolutionary Party from the presidency in 2000, breaking the seventy-one-year lock on power that had made Mexico a one-party autocracy. The democratic transition that followed suffered from many of the problems that Indonesia faced, particularly a steady pull toward reversal through corruption and skillful maneuvering by the old guard to retain power and position. The victorious opposition candidate, Vicente Fox, had campaigned on a promise to exterminate the "scorpions, vermin, and snakes" associated with the ruling party, but a continuing grip on state governorships preserved the nexus of patronage that had long been the foundation for its rule. After just twelve years out of power, the Institutional Revolutionary Party and its mediagenic candidate, Enrique Peña Nieto, built upon that local base to capture the presidency in 2012 and restore the party's systemic corruption.[72]

Reporting on this restoration in 2015, the economic analyst Rodrigo Aguilera presented a grim assessment of Mexico's prospects, using the term "the Mexican disease" to describe the factors that have impeded democratic consolidation, including barriers to social mobility, entrenched rent seeking, cultural acceptance of corruption, and symbiotic relationships between politicians and drug cartels.[73] Aguilero offered little hope, observing that Peña Nieto, the ruling party, and the rest of the power structure appeared impervious to pressure for change, even in the face of spectacular breaking scandals, including revelations that a crony favored with billions in government contracts had built a $4-million house for the first lady in the capital's most exclusive neighborhood.[74]

This assessment, however, appears to have been unduly pessimistic. In the face of this scandal and a succession of similar exposés, the president's approval ratings began to plummet, and his party suffered "stinging defeats" in the June 2016 state elections, losing six of the nine state governorships it had held some for decades.[75] The results were particularly significant in Mexico City, where the insurgent Morena party, led by reformist Andrés Manuel López Obrador, led in the balloting for the capital's constituent assembly.[76] In response to a mass citizens' campaign, in 2017 President Peña Nieto established a body akin to Indonesia's KPK, the National Anti-corruption System, and enshrined it in the constitution—a development observers called "a watershed moment."[77] When the president tried to hobble the anticorruption drive by appointing his party's campaign lawyer as attorney general, a media exposé of the nominee's use of a fake address to avoid taxes on his Ferrari blocked the move.[78] In 2018, after months of continued protests over corruption, Peña Nieto's party suffered a stunning defeat in the July presidential elections, bringing the opposition leader López Obrador to power.[79]

The most promising democratic transition of the Arab Spring, that of Tunisia, also shows the potential power of media-driven scandal, set in motion by a fusion of civic-minded journalism and partisan maneuvering, to fend off authoritarian reversal. Throughout its first half century as an independent state, Tunisia had an entrenched authoritarian apparatus, headed in 1957–87 by Habib Bourgiba and then, after a palace coup in 1987, by his prime minister, Zine al-Abidine Ben Ali, who took office promising democratic reforms. By 1994, however, this would-be reformer's rule had become marked by judicial corruption, torture, repression, and terror campaigns. By establishing an overseas newspaper and a presence in the French mainstream media, exiled oppositionists cultivated democratic values and circulated exposés of the regime's spreading corruption.[80] In the aftermath of the 2011 uprising that toppled Ben Ali, the new government embarked on reforms that included laws protecting freedom of speech and freedom of association. The democracy movement's success in establishing robust protections for the latter reflects serious attempts at reform after Ben Ali's harsh repression of unions and other civil society organizations.[81]

In the wave of change that accompanied this dictator's downfall, media law reform led to a decree containing eighty articles pertaining to freedom of speech and information that seemed to offer new protections for the media. But as in Indonesia, failure to eliminate older, contradictory articles in the penal code enabled the use of criminal libel laws to silence journalists and curb a watchdog media.[82] Nevertheless, Tunisia's ranking on the World Press Freedom Index climbed by thirty places in 2015–16 to rank at 96 out of 180 countries.[83] When scandals have broken, moreover, they have followed a similar trajectory to that seen in Indonesia and other comparable cases, serving to break up collusive pacts that can lead to reversal.

The most dramatic of these scandals began in December 2012, when the freelance journalist Olfa Riahi posted documents on her blog implicating the minister of foreign affairs from the Islamist Ennahda Party in embezzlement and an extramarital affair. The documents contained receipts showing the minister's use of both state coffers and a Chinese government slush fund to rent the Sheraton Hotel for his personal use. Although she obtained the documents from a partisan-motivated insider leak, Riahi spent six weeks verifying their contents by tracking the data back to original sources in China. While Salafist extremists sent her death threats and prosecutors filed criminal charges, observers debated whether the scandal signaled the "rise of investigative journalism" in Tunisia or was merely an example of political attack.[84]

The resonance of this "Sheratongate" scandal was heightened as Tunisia plunged into a serious political crisis marked by the assassinations of two liberal leaders and increasing opposition to perceived power grabs by the Islamist ruling party. In response to rising public pressure, the Ennahda Party was forced to leave power, and a caretaker government under the prime minister, Mehdi Jomaa, put the democratic transition back on track by presiding over the drafting of a new constitution that the US secretary of state, John Kerry, called a "model" for "the world."[85]

The firestorm that this scandal ignited followed a familiar pattern: a journalist airs documents obtained from a partisan-motivated source; through the dynamics of intraelite and intermedia competition, the story grows into a scandal sparking public outrage; and the denouement helps defend the country's democratic revolution from reversal, in this case, by aspiring Islamist authoritarianism. Without Riadhi, observed journalism professor Thomas Bass, Tunisia's transition "might have come to a dead end."[86]

While a freelance journalist used a blog to spark reform in Tunisia, in South Korea the mainstream media—both television and the establishment newspapers—became central to a concerted, collective effort in 2016 to address the nation's deepening corruption. For nearly thirty years since the end of authoritarian rule in 1988, scandal had already played a recurring role in disrupting collusion between the nation's powerful executive and equally powerful conglomerates, or *chaebol*. After liberation from the Japanese in 1946, South Korea developed as a state with a close, even collusive, alliance with the *chaebol* that would eventually control nearly 80 percent of the economy. Subsequent public pressure for democratization took two forms: violent uprisings against dictators in 1961 and 1987 and, since 1988, a combination of media-driven scandal and mass mobilization to check the corruption of legally elected presidents. Throughout the country's more recent quarter century of electoral democracy, these dynamics succeeded in periodically breaking up collusive pacts between the *chaebol* and the executive, allowing South Korea to develop a deeply rooted mass aspiration for greater political integrity.[87]

These trends culminated in the largest corruption scandal in the country's history, which began in 2016 and followed, to a significant degree, the political patterns seen in Indonesia and Tunisia. Given the structural collusion between the country's chief executive and the *chaebol* for nearly forty years, every South Korean administration has taken office with an inclination toward deepening corruption that, in retrospect, has only been checked by media exposé and mass protest. The presidency of Park Geun-hye, the daughter of the country's long-serving dictator, General Park Chung-hee, was no exception. From the time she took office in February 2013, her entourage set in motion a typically corrupt relationship with the *chaebol*, extracting $70 million over the next three years in personal bribes and donations to two foundations controlled by the president's "shaman" adviser, Choi Soon-sil, who gained her exceptional influence by purporting to speak with the ghost of the president's murdered mother.[88]

For nearly three years, presidential power quashed repeated media attempts to expose this increasingly sordid nexus of corruption. In 2014, the newspaper *Segye Ilbo* reported on documents that implicated Choi's family. But President Park turned on the paper, interrogating its journalists, threatening affiliated companies with an audit, and demanding the dismissal of its president. A police officer investigated as the source of the leak committed suicide after leaving a note saying, "Listen journalists! The people's right to know is what you live and exist for. Please do your job."[89] A year later, the conservative journal of record, *Chosun Ilbo*, published an exposé charging the senior presidential secretary with extracting "donations" from thirty conglomerates for the newly established Mir Foundation. Again the administration struck back, smearing the paper by charging that its chief correspondent had received free trips courtesy of the Daewoo shipping *chaebol*.[90]

A few months later, however, one of Choi's personal assistants, Ko Young-tae, began leaking video footage of Choi's undue influence over the president to *Chosun Ilbo*'s affiliate, TV Chosun.[91] Perhaps intimidated by pressure over the Daewoo revelations, the station suppressed the information for over a year.[92] Meanwhile, the opposition Justice Party began raising questions about $71.8 million in *chaebol* donations to Mir and another foundation, K-Sports, both believed to be controlled by Choi.[93]

Then on October 24, 2016, a rival cable channel, JTBC, aired a blockbuster story about a tablet allegedly owned by Choi showing that she had edited at least forty-four of the president's speeches. Within a day, TV Chosun began releasing Ko's videos, which showed Choi's autocratic manner of ordering presidential aides about—an indication of her extraordinary authority.[94] In the media free-for-all that followed, news outlets released a growing body of evidence of the corrupt relationship between the *chaebol* and Choi's foundations, Mir and K-Sports.

Investigations also produced evidence that the Park government was engaging in practices that threatened a return to the country's authoritarian past. One probe turned up a 2015 "black list" of more than nine thousand names, targeting prominent filmmakers, actors, artists, and writers in ways that a special prosecutor found "seriously undermined the freedom of thought and expression." Aides to President Park, including a former culture minister, engaged in systematic harassment of any prominent critic, "reviving a practice of past military dictators, like her father, Park Chung-hee."[95]

Public reaction to the emerging revelations was unprecedented. The largest mass demonstrations in the country's history filled Seoul's streets, while *chaebol* executives began appearing before parliament to confess their "donations" to the Mir and K-Sports foundations, which many believed were fronts for the president. Empowered by this potent combination of media-driven scandal and popular protest, in December 2016, South Korea's three opposition parties pushed through a motion that led the parliament to impeach the president and send her case to the country's constitutional court, forcing her to step aside.[96]

In a country where, as one journalist put it, political scandals "are a dime a dozen," and "most people tune out the news," observers began asking how this scandal could snowball so quickly.[97] A commonly cited factor was the realization, as one citizen said, that the president, "who we thought was . . . a mentally stable person, has been relying on a damn shaman cult her whole life."[98] Many were also troubled by the discovery that someone with no official position could be acting, behind the scenes, as the most powerful person in the country. There was a palpable "sense of betrayal" for Koreans who had seen Park as "a corruption-free version of her father."[99]

All these factors seemed at first to center on Park. If the scandal had played out like those in the past, her impeachment and removal from office in March 2017 would have satisfied the crowds, and she would have joined a procession of presidents disgraced at the ends of their terms, allowing politics to continue as usual. But ongoing revelations instead drew scrutiny to broader issues, particularly the pay-to-play relationships that had developed between the government and the *chaebol*. When investigation into Choi family privilege revealed that special admission had been granted to Choi's daughter by an otherwise highly competitive elite university, the anger was visceral.[100]

With each new development, outrage broadened, moving from an initial focus on influence peddling in the executive to anger at a larger system of patronage that left many feeling shut out, with few ways to advance. The national protests grew from calls for the president's removal to wider demands for structural change, producing a potentially important break from the past. Instead of focusing solely on the president, investigations culminated in the unprecedented arrest of Samsung's de facto leader, Lee Jae-yong, in February on charges of paying $36 million to the shaman adviser. "What we need is a great national cleanup," said Moon Jae-in, the opposition leader who succeeded Park as president in the May 2017 elections. "We must sternly punish politics-business collusion, a legacy of the dictatorial era, and take this as an opportunity to reform chaebol."[101]

DEMOCRATIC CONSOLIDATION IN GLOBAL CONTEXT

The cases from Indonesia, Mexico, Tunisia, and South Korea share a commonality relevant to the core problem of this study: democratization's inherent inclination toward reversal. Each country's transition seems chronically precarious, poised to slide back to authoritarianism or sink into a permanent state of pseudodemocracy. In each case, a nexus of collusion that facilitated corruption and protected leaders from accountability became a major factor slowing democratic consolidation. Each new spiral into deeper corruption and collusion, each layer of insulation protecting entrenched interests, further weakened the mechanisms of accountability and reduced opportunities to effect circulation of leadership. In three of these countries—Indonesia, Mexico, and South Korea—the danger posed by these trends was less reversion to authoritarianism than a potential slide into pseudodemocracy. At different moments, however, all four faced a risk of state capture by antidemocratic forces that threatened a point of no return—rising Islamists in Tunisia, moneyed drug cartels in Mexico, a budding autocrat in South Korea, and an aspiring strongman in Indonesia.

In all these countries, however, civic-minded actors—journalists, students, watchdog organizations, and human rights groups—made sustained attempts to impose accountability. The resulting revelations increased public awareness that corruption and malfeasance remained at untenable levels, despite democratization's promises of reform. Such awareness by itself was not necessarily progress. For years, media scholars have debated over the potential effect of "scandal fatigue," or "politics fatigue," on democratic publics. In their 2004 global survey of political scandal, Howard Tumber and Silvio Waisbord argue, as noted above, that "democracies are inherently prone to be regularly shaken by scandals," and the media, particularly in mature democracies, have "short-lived attention" that "makes scandals prone to have a brief existence," inducing a "a numb public opinion" and little substantive change.[102] The concern that too much news of scandal will alienate people from the political process and promote apathy calls into question this study's underlying premise that watchdog reporting is good for democracy.

However, findings from closer examination of this phenomenon, sometimes referred to as "media malaise," suggest that greater consumption of news in general, including negative stories, may foster increased civic engagement. Waisbord describes a fatigue reaction to heavy political scandal reporting in Latin American countries but also notes that public engagement tends to increase when scandals expose offenses directly affecting ordinary citizens.[103] In her own study testing the media malaise theory, Pippa Norris also presents evidence of this positive correlation between news consumption and civic engagement.[104]

A more comprehensive survey of findings on "watchdog journalism" in democratization by Sheila Coronel reveals a mixed picture indicating both the potential and limitations for all such journalism, including scandal reporting, in furthering democratization.[105] In a public lecture in 2008, Coronel argued that Philippine investigative journalists kept showing the public how bad corruption was, reporting scandal after scandal, but this awareness rarely went anywhere. People who were guilty were not thrown out of office because the constitutional mechanisms for rotation of officeholders were not well connected to public opinion. It was this disconnect, this lack of rotation, that produced "politics fatigue." As fatigue set in, she explained, the market for "critical" reporting would shrink, setting in motion a vicious cycle.[106]

Yet in all the cases examined above, a mixture of motives—cynical, self-serving, and civic-minded—converged to break up collusion and maintain the fluid political contestation essential to democracy. The periodic emergence of major scandals has overcome this disconnect between press exposé and political reform, showing the power of media attention to force a changing of the guard. Scandals that alter the course of history have a key distinction: Revelations issue from, and enter into, a volatile matrix of competing forces and actors, driven by varying and sometimes conflicting motives. It is the often unexpected combination of revelations and motivations that produces the *grande scandale d'État* that can arrest, even if only temporarily, authoritarian reversal.

In the ensuing political dramas, fueled by media competition, public outrage, civil society mobilization, partisan rivalries, and personal vendetta, intraelite conflicts spill out into the open. In the glare of publicity from traditional and social media, would-be conspirators turn on each other, and public figures move opportunistically to survive or even capitalize on the uproar. These chain reactions can break up collusive pacts and spur turnover in leadership as politicians and their parties gain or lose public favor.

In all four of these postauthoritarian countries, scandals contributed to a general flux in the balance of power, maintaining uncertainty in the contests between the contests—that is, the battles in courtrooms and the court of public opinion playing out on a daily basis between elections. The rise and fall of political fortunes between elections is also part of the necessary institutionalization of the regular, rule-bound rotation of leadership in democratic consolidation.

Clearly the watchdog role of the media, including scandal reporting that demands resolution, has its limits as an extrainstitutional force for change, even if aided by mobilized publics and independent anticorruption agencies, such as Indonesia's Corruption Eradication Commission. But in democratizing nations beset by a recurring pull toward reversal, such journalism remains a vehicle for consistently loosening collusive pacts and reintroducing uncertainty into democratic contestation.

Such reporting, moreover, is arguably integral to consolidation of the conditions that make democracy self-perpetuating—fostering what Pippa Norris calls "a virtuous circle," which in turn furthers a process that Samuel Valenzuela refers to as "virtuous institutionalization."[107] The media contribute to such developments by imposing transparency that makes the recapture of the state by antidemocratic forces more difficult and by helping create an informed citizenry able to express preferences not just in periodic and carefully controlled elections but on a regular basis via multiple venues open to public interaction, input, and influence. Reporting practices focused on scandal and partisan conflict, though often divisive, can also deepen democracy's hold simply by normalizing its perpetual state of contestation. At a minimum, constant exposure to the idea of politics as a contest helps reinforce the values associated with open contests—most critically, the necessity of unfixed outcomes and fair play. But over time, contest frames and the regular showcasing of scandal can also accomplish a more fundamental change by making rigged contestation seem unnatural, a violation of peoples' individual values and, ideally, the values of a broader national culture.

In Indonesia, the media's embrace of a watchdog role and shift to the regular airing of political conflict were changes essentially incompatible with, even subversive of, the integralist doctrine of relations between state and society that it replaced. More broadly, in any emerging democracy, the media's reinforcement of public demand for open contestation and transparency not only helps ward off reversal but is, at many levels, antithetical to the return of authoritarianism.

In the relentless interplay between democracy and collusion, between transparency and stasis, scandals and the alliances between media and the public that amplify them are possibly a weak tool. But in systems compromised by endemic collusion and intractable corruption, they remain one of the only tools available. If the inherent inclination of democratization is toward reversal, then the tendency of the media, and democracy itself, to pit people against each other may be the best defense. As the Indonesian case indicates, by serving as both a public watchdog and, perhaps counterintuitively, a platform for intraelite conflict, partisan vendetta and political scandal, the news media can serve as a country's front line and, possibly, last defense against democratic reversal. The airing of scandals and a larger watchdog role may not be a cure-all, but media failure to play this role, and thereby impose transparency, can facilitate the return of authoritarian rule.

Once democratic procedures consolidate, however, all parties in the process can play more conventional roles. The routinization of democracy, its rituals and rules, tends over time to reduce the need for heroic interventions by all players, including the media, thus obviating the more positive role of political scandal. More conventional scandal emerges almost endlessly from its eternal sources of sex and money. But *grande scandale d'État* should slowly disappear, arising only when forces of reversal threaten radical change that will effectively rig the system and block the circulation of contending parties. At such moments, scandal once again can serve a critical function.

The media's centrality in the process of consolidation makes them vulnerable to attack by atavistic forces. Conversely, overt attacks on the media can become a potent symbol for resistance to the return of autocratic rule, inspiring public protests to discourage further abuses or force an autocratic leader out of power. Defense of free speech can become powerfully symbolic for antiauthoritarian forces, inspiring further struggles for democratic consolidation.[108] Actions to control or intimidate the Indonesian media have, since Suharto's fall, provoked backlash—often sparked by a flood of condemnation from news outlets themselves.

From the perspective of journalism itself, the lingering idealism of an antiauthoritarian struggle, particularly when shared by working journalists, also promotes the ideal of a critical distance from power holders. Much of Indonesia's media community, like many Philippine reporters during the post-Marcos period, cut their teeth on the political drama of overthrowing an autocratic regime while immersed in prodemocracy rhetoric. Within this community, watchdog journalism, and the investigative reporting associated with it, are valued for more than their profit potential. Journalists who have fought to rid a country of a corrupt dictatorship are less likely to let the logic of commercial profit be the sole arbiter of value. And even when commercial news outlets stop funding investigative journalism, societies emerging from authoritarianism tend to have dedicated individuals who establish nonprofit programs, funded by both domestic and international donors, to help the country maintain high-quality journalism—organizations like the Philippine Center for Investigative Journalism, or in Jakarta, the Institute for the Studies on Free Flow of Information.

Even after a decade of postauthoritarian publishing success, *Tempo*'s chief editor, Bambang Harymurti, was critical of readers who placed too much faith in a commercial model of journalism to ensure their continued access to independent reporting. Since such journalism is not, he said, free, as Americans assume water should be, both strong sales and support from nonprofit organizations, including watchdog groups, are critical in a news outlet's adherence to high professional standards. But he also emphasized the importance of *Tempo*'s economic independence, in contrast to the compromises necessary for outlets owned by major conglomerates.[109]

The central role of the media is necessitated by another unstated aspect of democratic transitions: leaders in emerging democracies almost inevitably disappoint. Indonesia has so far weathered profound disillusion with all five post-Suharto presidencies. But beneath that visible failing, the system of checks and balances changed, quite fundamentally, with the country's rejection of Pancasila democracy and its embrace of a liberal democracy, including a free media, with all its flaws and contentiousness. As *Tempo* founder Goenawan Mohamad once suggested, this better democracy we all keep hoping for may not exist.[110] In reality, perhaps the best we can hope for is a rule-based game that does not promise good governance but facilitates the circulation of leaders who aspire to good governance and are held accountable by a mix of the best and the worst in human nature.

Comparisons among the democratic transitions in Indonesia and nations in Asia, Africa, and Latin America return us to the question raised at the outset: How does democratic consolidation, or democracy itself, become self-perpetuating? For democracy advocates, the findings from this study are likely to be both discouraging and heartening.

One point these cases highlight is that consolidation does not proceed solely from the good intentions of political actors, whether journalists, politicians, business leaders, or foreign powers. In an ideal world, the media would perform their watchdog functions as an objective tribune of the fourth estate, identifying problems for solution by responsible elected leaders and informing civil society groups. These groups would, in turn, pressure leaders to fulfill their obligations to the democratic process, thereby allowing the free flow of political contestation.

In reality, media organizations are owned by actors with conflicts of interest, journalists face competing pressures, and politicians are frequently compromised or corrupt. Yet in Indonesia and the comparable transitions discussed above, civic-minded journalists made use of self-serving sources often pursuing un-civic-minded agendas, including partisan maneuvering, political ambition, and personal vendetta. In each context, moreover, intraelite conflict and intermedia competition were critical forces in compelling news outlets to air information damaging to those in power, overcoming caution and efforts at suppression.

In any democracy, the recurring pull of collusion can, if unchecked, move toward oligarchy, autocracy, even authoritarianism. Among societies transitioning from authoritarian rule, these tendencies are manifest in the pressures for a return to the old order and continued control sought by oligarchs over material resources and political power.[111] In the absence of countervailing forces, such pressures would likely lead to a reconstitution of the collusion and corruption of the original regimes. For both established and emerging democracies, there often needs to be some force, apart from the formalities of court and constitution, to check these trends and strengthen transparency and open contestation. In most cases, effective checks come from some combination of intraelite competition, civil society mobilization, and media investigation.

Amid an untidy spectacle of electoral fraud, political compromise, or parliamentary paralysis, members of the media, whether intentionally or inadvertently, can play a pivotal role in breaking up collusive pacts and restoring the fluidity of uncertain outcomes so fundamental to democratic contestation. In Indonesia, oligarchic elites continue to dominate the nation's economy. Following this trend, media ownership has grown increasingly concentrated in the post-Suharto era, a development accelerated by digitalization.[112] Within this new landscape, oligarchs, taking advantage of the media's freedom, have only grown more powerful. But ownership is still not monolithic.[113] Independent players wield influence, and oligarchs use the media not only to protect their interests but also to compete with rivals, thereby opening up political space that allows democratic consolidation to continue. As they pursue multiple agendas within this space, the media remind us once again that democracy is not a fixed and final product but rather a process of endless contestation. The system may seem volatile, the media spectacles dispiriting, and the future perpetually uncertain. But this ungainly combination can check collusion and promote the circulation of leadership, the essential attribute of any democracy.

Without discounting the importance of economic and judicial reforms, the most complex and contradictory aspect of change in Indonesia, from the perspective of this analysis, has been in the political arena, with a succession of corruption scandals that have exposed endemic graft among the nation's highest officials. By airing these scandals and imposing transparency on intraelite conflict, the media have played a central role in dissolving the authoritarian stasis fortified for over forty years by corruption and collusive pacts. Played out in the public sphere in these decades of transition, such contestation has rejuvenated the pluralist competition that is the core of democratization in Indonesia and, arguably, elsewhere around the globe.

Appendixes

Note on the Collection of Headlines

In selecting sample headlines to show the changing tenor of press content covering the years 1985 (appendix 1) and 1990 (appendix 2) from holdings at University of Wisconsin–Madison's Memorial Library, I avoided months with a single, dominant news event. During my own fieldwork in 1998–99 (appendix 3), I made parallel collection efforts from Jakarta street vendors, following the pattern of the earlier effort. As publications closed from insolvency or repression and new ones opened, changes in the print market over the fourteen-year span of these three tables made it impossible to sample the same set of publications for each year. Despite the idiosyncrasies of collection, these three "ordinary" months are reasonably representative of their respective eras' news tabloid and magazine street vendor fare.

Appendix 1

Tabloid and news magazine headlines, Jakarta, September 1985

Headline	Source	Date
"Chris Kanter: 'Small Is Beautiful'" *"Chris Kanter: "'Kecil Itu Indah'"*	*Eksekutif*	Sept. 1985
"Market and Business Opportunities Search for Open Niche" *"Pasar dan Peluang Bisnis Mencari Segmen Terbuka"*	*Promosi Ekonomi*	Sept. 1985
"Excess Liquidity: Who's at Fault?" *"Ekses Likuiditas . . . Salah Siapa?"*	*Infobank*	Sept. 1985
"Will Economic Recession Spread Again?" *"Resesi Ekonomi Akan Berjangkit Kembali?"*	*Keuangan*	Sept. 1985
"Moerdiono: To China No Recommendation Needed" *"Moerdiono: Ke Cina Tak Perlu Rekomendasi"*	*SWA Sembada*	Sept. 1985
"Fire: Able to Be Controlled?" *"Kebakaran: Mampukah Diatasi?"*	*Topik*	Sept. 4, 1985
"Shifting Palapa [satellite], Oh, Shifting Palapa" *"Palapa Bergeser, Oh, Palapa Bergeser"*	*Tempo*	Sept. 7, 1985
"Who Needs Indonesia's Products?" *"Siapa Butuh Buatan RI?"*	*Wahyu*	Sept. 10–24, 1985

(continued)

(Continued)

Headline	Source	Date
"Poverty in the Islamic World" *"Kemiskinan di Dunia Islam"*	*Panji Masyarakat*	Sept. 11, 1985
"How to Choose a Governor? A Story from Riau" *"Bagaimana Memilih Gubernur? Sebuah Cerita dari Riau"*	*Tempo*	Sept. 14, 1985
"National Games Week XI: United, Accomplished, Profligate" *"PON XI: Bersatu, Berprestasi, Berhura-hura"*	*Panji Masyarakat*	Sept. 21, 1985
"Where Will They Go after PHK [layoffs]?" *"Ke Mana Mereka Setelah PHK?"*	*Tempo*	Sept. 21, 1985
"Nurcholis Madjid: Concept of Islamic Community Weak" *"Nurcholis Madjid: Wawasan Umat Islam Lembek"*	*Wahyu*	Sept. 25–Oct. 10, 1985
"Seizing the SE-Asia Medal" [image of Bob Hasan on cover] *"Berebut Medali SE-Asia"*	*Tempo*	Sept. 28, 1985

APPENDIX 2

Tabloid and news magazine headlines, Jakarta, May 1990

Headline	Source	Date
"Critiquing the Capital Market" *"Menggugat Pasar Modal"*	*Forum Keadilan*	May 1990
"Idul Fitri and the Populist Spirit" *"Idulfitri dan Semangat Kerakyatan"*	*Media Dakwah*	May 1990
"Air Base Safeguards" *"Pengaman Pangkalan Udara"*	*TSM: Teknologi & Strategi Militer*	May 1990
"Struggle for Lots: Thamrin-Sudirman-Kuningan" *"Rebutan Kapling: Thamrin-Sudirman-Kuningan"*	*SWA Sembada*	May 1990
"Clerics, Politicians, Officials, Artists Analyze Idul Fitri" *"Ulama, Politisi, Pejabat, Artis Mengurai Idul Fitri"*	*Panji Masyarakat*	May 1–10, 1990
"[Japanese prime minister] Kaifu Comes Carrying Money?" *"Kaifu Datang Bawa Uang?"*	*Tempo*	May 5, 1990
"Who Do Followers of Islam Support?" *"Umat Islam Dukung Siapa?"*	*Panji Masyarakat*	May 11–20, 1900
"Housing Credit Fever" *"Deman Rumah Kredit"*	*Editor*	May 12, 1990
"Cleansing Oneself from PKI" *"Bersih Diri tentang PKI"*	*Tempo*	May 12, 1990

Headline	Source	Date
"Look Out! Mafia [rising from the] Ground" *"Awas! Mafia Tanah!"*	*Jakarta-Jakarta*	May 12–18, 1990
"Women Slayer in Your Midst" *"Perempuan Pembunuh di Sekitar Anda"*	*Editor*	May 17, 1990
"Flood of Boat Refugees" *"Banjir Manusia Perahu"*	*Tempo*	May 19, 1990
"Women Clerics in Australia" *"Ustadzah Kita di Australia"*	*Panji Masyarakat*	May 21–30, 1990
"'Total Support' Debate" [illustrated with a crowd holding Suharto's picture] *"Debat Kebulatan Tekad"*	*Tempo*	May 26, 1990
"Presidential Candidate, ABRI, and Islam: 'Total Support'" *"Calon Presiden, ABRI, dan Islam: Kebulatan Tekad"*	*Editor*	May 26, 1990

APPENDIX 3

Tabloid and news magazine headlines, Jakarta, February 1999

Headline	Source	Date
"Debtor's Tricks of the Elephant Class" *"Trik Pengutang Kelas Gajah"*	*SWA Sembada*	Jan. 28–Feb. 10, 1999
"Beware of the Provocateur" [illustrated with a photograph of Yorries Raweyai] *"Awas Provokator"*	*D&R*	Feb. 1–6, 1999
"East Timor: 'Thank You, Good Bye'" *"Timor Timur: 'Thank You, Good Bye'"*	*Forum Keadilan*	Feb. 8, 1999
"East Timor Time Bomb" *"Bom Waktu Timor Timur"*	*D&R*	Feb. 8–13, 1999
"Suharto in the Election" *"Soeharto di Pemilu"*	*Tempo*	Feb. 9–15, 1999
"Executive Turnover as Top Crumbles" *"Giliran Eksekutif Puncak Tumbang"*	*SWA Sembada*	Feb. 11–24, 1999
"Political Choice of Ethnic Chinese" *"Pilihan Politik Keturunan Cina"*	*Tempo*	Feb. 14–22, 1999
"Pounding Hearts [in] Chinese Community" *"Dag Dig Dug Masyarakat Cina"*	*D&R*	Feb. 15–20, 1999
"Shoot on Sight BANG!!!" *"Tembak di Tempat DOR!!!"*	*Sumber*	Feb. 16–22, 1999
"Watching Wiranto" *"Cermati Wiranto"*	*DëTAK*	Feb. 16–22, 1999
"Cendana Family Fractured" *"Keluarga Cendana Pecah"*	*Sinar Reformasi*	Feb. 17–23, 1999
"8 People to Be Charged by Suharto" *"8 Orang Bakal Dituntut Soeharto"*	*Berita Keadilan*	Feb. 17–23, 1999

(continued)

(Continued)

Headline	Source	Date
"Pertamina [oil company] Dissolved" *Pertamina Dibubarkan*	*Perspektif*	Feb. 18, 1999
"Controversy over $200 Million Flight Overseas" *"Kontroversi Exodus US$200 Miliar ke Luar Negeri"*	*Realitas*	Feb. 18–24, 1999
"Enjoying BDN's Free Credit" *"Nikmatnya Kredit Gratis BDN"*	*Kontan*	Feb. 19, 1999
"120 Prabowo Loyalist Officers Soon to Be Replaced" *"120 Perwira 'Orang2' Prabowo Segera Diganti"*	*Aksi*	Feb. 19–25, 1999
"Riady-Habibie New Duet Sweeps Away Suharto-Uncle Liem" *"Riady-Habibie Duet Baru Gusur Soeharto-Om Liem"*	*Siaga*	Feb. 19–25, 1999
"Freedom [now] or Later" [illustrated with an image of Xanana Gusmão] *"Merdeka atau Nanti"*	*Tempo*	Feb. 28, 1999
"Habibie Crushed" *"Habibie Hancur"*	*Megapos*	Feb. 21–27, 1999
"PRD Comeback" *"PRD Comeback"*	*Tokoh*	Feb. 22–28, 1999
"The Prabowo Problem: Habibie Takes Up Challenge" *"Soal Prabowo: Habibie Menantang"*	*Sinar*	Feb. 22–28, 1999
"Suharto Threatens Amien Rais—Hunt Down the Wiretapper" *"Soeharto Ancam Amien Rais Memburu Penyadap Telepon"*	*Gugat*	Feb. 22–28, 1999
"Habibie [back-]Stabbed by People Close to Him" *"Habibie Ditikam Orang-Orang Dekatnya"*	*DëTAK*	Feb. 22–28, 1999
"Where Did the Cassette Come from?" *"Dari Mana Datangnya Kaset"*	*Tekad*	Feb. 22–28, 1999
"The Politics behind Habibie & Prabowo" *"Politik di Balik Habibie & Prabowo"*	*D&R*	Feb. 22–28, 1999
"[Suharto's] Repentance Not Enough" *"Ndak Cukup dengan Tobat"*	*Ummat*	Feb. 15, 1999
"Elder Brother Nun: Soeharto Is the Key" *"Cak Nun: Soeharto Faktor Kunci"*	*Garda*	Feb. 15–28, 1999
"Rain of Gunfire in One's Own Land" *"Hujan DOR di Negeri Sendiri"*	*Panji Masyarakat*	Feb. 17, 1999
"Investigation: The Hartarto Family Rice Business" *"Investigasi: Bisnis Beras Keluarga Hartarto"*	*Panji Masyarakat*	Feb. 17, 1999
"Feisal Tanjung Speaks: From Prabowo to Wiranto" *"Feisal Tanjung Bicara: Dari Prabowo Sampai Wiranto"*	*Tajuk*	Feb. 15–Mar. 3, 1999
"Intel: Puppet Master or Instigator" *"Intel: Dalang atau Pecundang"*	*Gatra*	Feb. 20, 1999
"Muladi and Andi M. Ghalib Bribery Case" *"Kasus 'Upeti' Muladi dan Andi M. Ghalib"*	*Forum Keadilan*	Feb. 22, 1999

Headline	Source	Date
"'Don't Worry, Father Harto [Suharto] Will Not Return'—Exclusive Interview with Tutut" *"'Jangan Takut, Pak Harto Tidak Akan Kembali'— Wanwancara Khusus dengan Tutut"*	*Forum Keadilan*	Feb. 22, 1999
"Whoa, Close Call" [illustrated with an image of Habibie and Ghalib on a telephone-cord tightrope] *"Aduh, Keserimpet"*	*Tempo*	Feb. 23–Mar. 1, 1999

NOTES

SOURCE ABBREVIATIONS

ABRI	Angkatan Bersenjata Republik Indonesia
AFP	Agence France Presse
AJI	Aliansi Jurnalis Independen
AP	Associated Press
AT	*Asia Times*
AWSJ	*Asian Wall Street Journal*
CPJ	Committee to Protect Journalists
DJ	Dow Jones
FEER	*Far Eastern Economic Review*
ICJ	International Commission of Jurists
IHT	*International Herald Tribune*
IO	*Indonesian Observer*
IPS	International Press Service
ISAI	Institut Studi Arus Informasi
JG	*Jakarta Globe*
JOMC	Joint Operations Media Center (General Election Commission)
JP	*Jakarta Post*
LAT	*Los Angeles Times*
LSPP	Lembaga Studi Pers & Pembangunan
MI	*Media Indonesia*
NYT	*New York Times*
SCMP	*South China Morning Post*
SMH	*Sydney Morning Herald*
SP	*Suara Pembaruan*
ST	*Straits Times*
TN	*The Nation* (New York)
WP	*Washington Post*
WSJ	*Wall Street Journal*

INTRODUCTION

1. Susanto Pujomartono, "Pers Indonesia Pasca Soeharto," in *Reformasi Media Massa*, ed. Ery Sutrisno (Jakarta: AJI, 1998), 36–38. Unless otherwise noted, all translations are my own.

2. Lukas Luwarso, "Wajah Media Massa Kita," in Sutrisno, *Reformasi Media Massa*, 26.

3. Ibid., 29.

4. Ibid., 30–31.

5. Louise Williams, "Poor Little Rich Kids," *SMH*, October 24, 1998.

6. Samuel P. Huntington, *The Third Wave: Democratization in the Late Twentieth Century* (Norman: University of Oklahoma Press, 1991), 266–67.

7. Huntington, *Third Wave*; Scott Mainwaring, Guillermo O'Donnell, and J. Samuel Valenzuela, introduction to *Issues in Democratic Consolidation: The New South American Democracies in Comparative Perspective*, ed. Scott Mainwaring, Guillermo O'Donnell, and J. Samuel Valenzuela (Notre Dame, IN: University of Notre Dame Press, 1992), 4.

8. Huntington, *Third Wave*, 15, 209–79; Robert A. Dahl, *Polyarchy: Participation and Observation* (New Haven, CT: Yale University Press, 1971), 203.

9. Juan J. Linz, introduction to *The Breakdown of Democratic Regimes*, ed. Juan J. Linz and Alfred Stepan (Baltimore: Johns Hopkins University Press, 1978), 3.

10. Scott Shane, *Dismantling Utopia: How Information Ended the Soviet Union* (Chicago: Ivan R. Dee, 1994); Kuldip R. Rampal, "Press and Political Liberalization in Taiwan," *Journalism Quarterly* 71, no. 3 (1994): 637–51; Gladys Ganley, *Unglued Empire: The Soviet Experience with Communications Technologies* (Norwood, NJ: Ablex, 1996); Gary D. Rawnsley and Ming-yeh T. Rawnsley, "Regime Transition and the Media in Taiwan," in *Democratization and the Media*, ed. Vicky Randall, 106–24 (London: Frank Cass, 1998).

11. Mainwaring, O'Donnell, and Valenzuela, introduction, 4.

12. See Krishna Sen and David T. Hill, eds., *Politics and the Media in Twenty-First Century Indonesia: Decade of Democracy* (Abingdon, UK: Routledge, 2011); Mercy Ette, "Agent of Change or Stability? The Nigerian Press Undermines Democracy," *Harvard International Journal of Press/Politics* 5, no. 3 (2001): 67–86; Richard Gunther, Jose Ramon Montero, and Jose Ignacio Wert, "The Media and Politics in Spain: From Dictatorship to Democracy," in *Democracy and the Media: A Comparative Perspective*, ed. Richard Gunther and Anthony Mughan, 28–84 (Cambridge: Cambridge University Press, 2000); Karl Jakubowicz, "Media in Transition: The Case of Poland," in *Media Reform: Democratizing the Media, Democratizing the State*, ed. Monroe E. Price, Beata Rozumilowicz, and Stefaan G. Verhulst, 203–31 (London: Routledge, 2002); G. Hyden and M. Leslie, "Communications and Democratization in Africa," in *Media and Democracy in Africa*, ed. G. Hyden, M. Leslie, and F. Ogundimu, 1–28 (New Brunswick, NJ: Transaction, 2002); E. O. Ojo, "The Mass Media and the Sustainable Democratic Values in Nigeria: Possibilities and Limitations," *Media, Culture & Society* 25, no. 6 (2003): 821–40; Matthew Loveless, "Media Dependency: Mass Media as Sources of Information in the Democratizing Countries of Central and Eastern Europe," *Democratization* 15, no. 1 (2008): 162–83; Aje-Ori Anna Agbese, *The Role of the Press and Communication Technology in Democratization: The Nigerian Story* (New York: Routledge, 2007); Marta Dyczok, "Do the Media Matter? Focus on Ukraine," in *Media, Freedom and Democracy: The Post-Communist Experience*, ed. Marta Dyczok and Oxana Gaman-Golutvina, 17–41 (Bern: Peter Lang, 2009); Zola Maddison, "Information's Role in Emerging Democratic Societies—the Case of Indonesia," *Information for Social Change* 25 (Summer 2007): 26–32; Robert B. Horwitz, *Communication and Democratic Reform in South Africa* (Cambridge: Cambridge University Press, 2006); Katrin Voltmer, *The Media in Transitional Democracies* (Cambridge: Polity, 2013); Philip N. Howard and Muzammil M. Hussain, *Democracy's Fourth Wave? Digital Media and the Arab Spring* (Oxford: Oxford University Press, 2012); Krishna Sen and Terence Lee, eds., *Political Regimes and the Media in Asia* (New York: Routledge, 2008); Angela Romano, *Politics and the Press in Indonesia: Understanding an Evolving Political Culture* (New York: Routledge, 2003).

13. Adam Przeworski, *Democracy and the Market: Political and Economic Reforms in Eastern Europe and Latin America* (Cambridge: Cambridge University Press, 1991), 14.

14. Andreas Schedler, *The Politics of Uncertainty: Sustaining and Subverting Electoral Authoritarianism* (New York: Oxford University Press, 2013), 1.

15. Adam Przeworski, "Some Problems in the Study of Transition to Democracy," in *Transitions from Authoritarian Rule*, ed. Guillermo O'Donnell, Philippe C. Schmitter, and Laurence Whitehead (Baltimore: Johns Hopkins University Press, 1986), 58.

16. Ibid., 57.

17. Huntington, *Third Wave*.

18. Silvio R. Waisbord, *Watchdog Journalism in South America: News, Accountability, and Democracy* (New York: Columbia University Press, 2000), 243.

19. Vicky Randall, introduction to *Democratization and the Media*, 5; Sheila S. Coronel, "The Role of the Media in Deepening Democracy," United Nations Public Administration Network, 2003, http://unpan1.un.org/intradoc/groups/public/documents/un/unpan010194.pdf.

20. Przeworski, *Democracy and the Market*, 26.

21. Przeworski, "Some Problems."

22. Randall, introduction, 3.

23. Merlyna Lim, "The Internet, Social Networks, and Reform in Indonesia," in *Asia Encounters the Internet*, ed. K. C. Ho, R. Kluver, and K. Yang (London: Routledge, 2003), 113–28; Jeffrey Winters, "The Political Impact of New Information Sources and Technologies in Indonesia," *Gazette: The International Journal for Communication Studies* 64, no. 2 (2002): 109–19.

24. Przeworski, *Democracy and the Market*, 13.

25. See Andie Tucher and Dan Bischoff, "Scorned in an Era of Triumphant Democracy," *Media Studies Journal* 9, no. 3 (1995): 160.

26. See T. E. Patterson, "Of Polls, Mountains: U.S. Journalists and Their Use of Election Surveys," *Public Opinion Quarterly* 69, no. 5 (2005): 716–24; Jay Rosen, "Brainless: The Media and Horse Race Journalism," *Pacific Free Press*, January 20, 2008.

27. See James M. Fallows, *Breaking the News: How the Media Undermine American Democracy* (New York: Vintage Books, 1997), 53.

28. Lanny Davis, *Scandal: How "Gotcha" Politics Is Destroying America* (Basingstoke, UK: Palgrave Macmillan, 2006), 5–6.

29. Quoted in Vicky Randall, "The Media and Democratization in the Third World," *Third World Quarterly* 14, no. 3 (1993): 640.

30. Quoted in Hervin Saputra, "If Internet and Media Compete for Ripping Up Privacy," trans. Rosmi Julitasari, *VHR Media.com*, accessed August 7, 2010, http://www.vhrmedia.com/If-Internet-and-Media-Compete-for-Ripping-Up-Privacy-focus4621.html.

31. Howard Tumber and Silvio R. Waisbord, "Introduction: Political Scandals and Media across Democracies, Volume I," *American Behavioral Scientist* 47, no. 8 (2004): 1031–32, 1035.

32. Alastair Bellany, *The Politics of Court Scandal in Early Modern England: News Culture and the Overbury Affair, 1603–1660* (Cambridge: Cambridge University Press, 2002), 74–135, 261–78.

33. Sarah Maza, *Private Lives and Public Affairs: The Causes Célèbres of Prerevolutionary France* (Berkeley: University of California Press, 1993), 38.

34. Marcus Daniel, *Scandal and Civility: Journalism and the Birth of American Democracy* (New York: Oxford University Press, 2009).

35. Alex Hall, *Scandal, Sensation and Social Democracy: The SPD Press and Wilhelmine Germany 1890–1914* (Cambridge: Cambridge University Press, 1977).

36. Chappell H. Lawson, *Building the Fourth Estate: Democratization and the Rise of a Free Press in Mexico* (Berkeley: University of California Press, 2002), 9.

37. Miklós Sükösd, "Democratic Transformation and the Mass Media in Hungary: From Stalinism to Democratic Consolidation," in Gunther and Mughan, *Democracy and the Media*, 146–47.

38. See Lim, "Internet, Social Networks, and Reform," 113–28.

39. Pippa Norris, *A Virtuous Circle: Political Communications in Post-industrial Democracies* (Cambridge: Cambridge University Press, 2000).

40. Larry Diamond, *Developing Democracy: Toward Consolidation* (Baltimore: Johns Hopkins Press, 1999), 162.

41. Benedict Anderson, *Imagined Communities: Reflections on the Origin and Spread of Nationalism* (London: Verso, 1991), 35n63.

42. Sharif Abdel Kouddous, "After Mubarak, Fighting for Press Freedom in Egypt," *TN*, June 20, 2011.

43. See Daniel Lynch, *After the Propaganda State: Media, Politics, and "Thought Work" in Reformed China* (Stanford, CA: Stanford University Press, 1999).

1. ORIGINS OF MEDIA CONTROLS

1. Saafroedin Bahar, Ananda B. Kusuma, and Nannie Hudawati, eds., *Risalah Sidang Badan Penyelidik Usaha-Usaha Persiapan Kemerdekaan Indonesia (BPUPKI), Panitia Persiapan Kemerdekaan Indonesia (PPKI) 28 Mei 1945—22 Agustus 1945* (Jakarta: Sekretariat Negara Republik Indonesia, 1995).

2. Quoted ibid., 71.

3. Quoted ibid., 258, 79.

4. Peter Burns, *The Leiden Legacy: Concepts of Law in Indonesia* (Leiden: KITLV, 2004), 244–46.

5. Ibid.

6. See David Reeve, "The Corporatist State: The Case of Golkar," in *State and Civil Society in Indonesia*, ed. Arief Budiman, 151–76 (Melbourne: Centre for Southeast Asian Studies,

Monash University, 1990); David Bourchier, "Totalitarianism and the 'National Personality,'" in *Imagining Indonesia: Cultural Politics & Political Culture*, ed. Jim Schiller and Barbara Martin-Schiller, 157–85 (Athens: Ohio University Center for International Studies, 1997).

7. Bahar, Kusuma, and Hudawati, *Risalah*, 260–61.

8. Quoted ibid., 35.

9. Ibid., 36–37, 17.

10. Website of the Embassy of the Republic of Indonesia, Washington, DC, accessed November 21, 2017, http://www.embassyofindonesia.org/index.php/national-symbols/.

11. Adam Schwarz, *A Nation in Waiting: Indonesia's Search for Stability*, 2nd ed. (Boulder, CO: Westview, 1999), 10, 41.

12. Quoted in Bahar, Kusuma, and Hudawati, *Risalah*, 260–63, 299.

13. Ignatius Haryanto, *Pembredelan Pers di Indonesia: Kasus Koran Indonesia Raya* (Jakarta: LSPP, 1995), 41.

14. ICJ, *Indonesia and the Rule of Law: Twenty Years of "New Order" Government* (London: Pinter, 1991), 86.

15. Haryanto, *Pembredelan Pers*, 42.

16. Togi Simanjuntak, ed., *Wartawan Terpasung: Intervensi Negara di Tubuh PWI* (Jakarta: ISAI, 1998), 25–27.

17. Haryanto, *Pembredelan Pers*, 43–44.

18. The declaration occurred a few months before the government's official announcement of a state of emergency and martial law in March 1957.

19. Schwarz, *Nation in Waiting*, 16.

20. Robert Cribb and Colin Brown, *Modern Indonesia: A History Since 1945* (London: Longman, 1995), 82–83.

21. Sukarno, "Saving the Republic of the Proclamation (1957)," in *Indonesian Political Thinking: 1945–65*, ed. Herbert Feith and Lance Castles (Ithaca, NY: Cornell University Press, 1970), 86.

22. Reeve, "Corporatist State"; Bourchier, "Totalitarianism and the 'National Personality.'"

23. Simanjuntak, *Wartawan Terpasung*, 39, 34; Oey Hong Lee, *Indonesian Government and Press during Guided Democracy*, Hull Monographs on Southeast Asia 4 (Zug, Switzerland: Inter Documentation, 1971).

24. Lee, *Indonesian Government*.

25. Penetapan Presiden No. 6/1963 tentang Pembinaan Pers.

26. Simanjuntak, *Wartawan Terpasung*, 26, 53–61.

27. Quoted in Schwarz, *Nation in Waiting*, 6, 11.

28. Cribb and Brown, *Modern Indonesia*, 51.

29. Herbert Feith, *The Decline of Constitutional Democracy in Indonesia* (Ithaca, NY: Cornell University Press, 1962), 556–608.

30. For example, Daniel Lev has characterized the 1950–57 period of democracy in Indonesia as "much condemned but extraordinarily successful." Speech before the Indonesia Forum, Jakarta, November 19, 1998.

31. Schwarz, *Nation in Waiting*, 6, 42.

32. Ibid., 18; Cribb and Brown, *Modern Indonesia*, 83.

33. Quoted in Schwarz, *Nation in Waiting*, 19–20.

34. Ibid., 22.

35. David Hill, *The Press in New Order Indonesia* (Nedlands: University of Western Australia Press, 1994), 34.

36. Act No. 11/1966 on the Basic Provisions on the Press, as amended by Act No. 4/1967, in L. M. Gandhi, *Undang-undang Pokok Pers: Proses Pembentukan dan Penjelasannya* (Jakarta: Rajawali Pers, 1985), 4–36.

37. Hill, *Press in New Order Indonesia*, 37.

38. Schwarz, *Nation in Waiting*, 32.

39. Daniel Dhakidae, "The State, the Rise of Capital and the Fall of Political Journalism: Political Economy of the Indonesian News Industry" (Ph.D. diss., Cornell University, 1991), 179.

40. Peter McCawley, "Some Consequences of the Pertamina Crisis in Indonesia," *Journal of Southeast Asian Studies* 9, no. 1 (March 1978): 6.

41. Dhakidae, "The State, the Rise of Capital," 172–75.

42. Ibid., 168–89.

43. John Bresnan, *Managing Indonesia: The Modern Political Economy* (New York: Columbia University Press, 1993), 172–75.

44. Ibid., 165.

45. Quoted in Dhakidae, "The State, the Rise of Capital," 183–84.

46. Ibid., 207–8.

47. Schwarz, *Nation in Waiting*, 28–31.

48. Ibid., 32.

49. ICJ, *Indonesia and the Rule of Law*, 104.

50. Quoted in Schwarz, *Nation in Waiting*, 32.

51. Haryanto, *Pembredelan Pers*, 138.

52. Dhakidae, "The State, the Rise of Capital," 214.

53. Bresnan, *Managing Indonesia*, 135–39.

54. Dhakidae, "The State, the Rise of Capital," 85.

55. Hill, *Press in New Order Indonesia*, 37.

56. Schwarz, *Nation in Waiting*, 33–35.

57. Bresnan, *Managing Indonesia*, 163.

58. Cribb and Brown, *Modern Indonesia*, 131.

59. A.S. Hikam, *Politik Kewarganegaraan: Landasan Redemokratisasi di Indonesia* (Jakarta: Per-nerbit Erlangga, 1999), 76.

60. ICJ, *Indonesia and the Rule of Law*, 104.

61. Quoted in Dhakidae, "The State, the Rise of Capital," 177.

62. Ibid.

63. Ibid., 309, 310.

64. Hill, *Press in New Order Indonesia*, 39.

65. Dhakidae, "The State, the Rise of Capital," 317, 319.

66. Heri Akhmadi, *Breaking the Chains of Oppression of the Indonesian People: Defense Statement at His Trial on Charges of Insulting the Head of State* (Ithaca, NY: Southeast Asia Program, Cornell University, 1981), 78.

67. Quoted in Dhakidae, "The State, the Rise of Capital," 323.

68. Ibid., 320–23.

69. Act No. 21/1982 on Amendments to Act No. 11/1966 on the Basic Provisions on the Press, as amended by Act No. 4/1967, in Bambang Sadono, *Penyelesaian Delik Pers Secara Politis* (Jakarta: Pustakan Sinar Harapan, 1993), appendix 6, 158–65.

70. Quoted in ICJ, *Indonesia and the Rule of Law*, 102.

71. Quoted in Todung Mulya Lubis, *In Search of Human Rights: Legal-Political Dilemmas of Indonesia's New Order, 1966–1990* (Jakarta: Gramedia), 288.

72. Schwarz, *Nation in Waiting*, 39.

73. Keputusan Dewan Pers No.79/XIV/1974 tentang Pedoman Pembinaan Idiil Pers.

74. Quoted in Dhakidae, "The State, the Rise of Capital," 459.

75. Yasuo Hanazaki, *Pers Terjebak* (Jakarta: ISAI, 1998), 47–48.

76. Reinforcing this impression, the anthropologist Clifford Geertz stated, "With the Java-nese, you don't see the violence coming until it happens. Once the politeness and deference and controlled demeanor collapse, then all hell will break loose." Quoted in Philip Shenon, "Of the Turmoil in Indonesia and Its Roots," *NYT*, May 9, 1998.

77. Dhakidae, "The State, the Rise of Capital," 168–88.

78. Quoted in Hanazaki, *Pers Terjebak*, 47–48.

79. "Somehow, at one time, the notion was born that politics is dirty." Pramoedya Ananta Toer, "Literature, Censorship and the State: How Dangerous Are Stories?," an essay written for acceptance of the 1995 Ramon Magsaysay Award for Journalism, Literature and Creative Com-munication, trans. Marianne Katoppo, published in *Suara Independen*, no. 04/I, September 1995.

80. ICJ, *Indonesia and the Rule of Law*, 111.

81. Susanto Pujomartono, "Pers Indonesia Pasca Soeharto," in *Reformasi Media Massa*, ed. Ery Sutrisno (Jakarta: AJI, 1998), 10.

82. Dhakidae, "The State, the Rise of Capital," 459.

83. Hanazaki, *Pers Terjebak*, 47–48.

84. Vatikiotis, *Indonesian Politics under Suharto*, 104.

85. Ketetapan Majelis Permusyawaratan Rakyat Republik Indonesia No.II/MPR/1978 ten-tang Pedoman Penghayatan dan Pengamalan Pancasila (P4) dan Penegasan Pancasila Dasar Negara.

86. Cribb and Brown, *Modern Indonesia*, 136.

87. INDOC, *Indonesian Workers and Their Right to Organize: March 1984 Update* (Leiden: INDOC, 1984), 13–15.

88. Thomas Fuller, "Indonesia Acts to Reform Language," *IHT*, December 22, 1999.

89. Pietra Widiadi, "Politik Bahasa dalam Pemberitaan," paper presented at Workshop Wartawan Multikulturalisme, Hotel Fortuna, Surabaya, February 25–29, 1999.

90. In 1999, the *Jakarta Post* provided definitions for over six hundred acronyms in common use in Indonesia at the time. *JP*, May 4, 1999.

91. Hill, *Press in New Order Indonesia*, 47.

92. Hanazaki, *Pers Terjebak*, 82.

93. Lubis, *In Search of Human Rights*, 288.

94. The periods covered were January 9–14 and March 14–18, 1995. The papers surveyed were *Kompas, Suara Pembaruan, Media Indonesia, Jakarta Post*, and *Republika*. Hanazaki, *Pers Terjebak*, 81.

95. For example, quoting an army commander on November 14, *Kompas* reported, "Disturbance in Dili Is Regretted and Will Be Examined until Complete." Quoting a government minister on November 16, the paper used the passive voice in the headline, "A Special Investigative Team Will Be Formed"; and again when quoting President Suharto on November 18, "Handling Is to Be Done with Care and Coordinated as Well as Possible." On November 16, a *Kompas* headline read, "Foreign Minister Ali Alatas: An Investigatory Team to Be formed in East Timor."

96. *Kompas*, November 14, 16, and 18, 1991.

97. Quoted in Pujomartono, "Pers Indonesia Pasca Soeharto," 11–12.

98. In making these remarks, the authors of this history were referring to the work of the sociologist Richard V. Ericson. Simanjuntak, *Wartawan Terpasung*, 96.

99. Jalaluddin Rakhmat, "Revolusi Komunikasi," in *Mencuri Kejernihan dari Kerancuan: Kumpulan Transkrip Wawancara Perspektif Baru Bersama Wimar Witoelar* (Jakarta: Gramedia Pustaka Utama, 1998), 401–9.

100. Quoted in Hill, *Press in New Order Indonesia*, 47.

101. Goenawan Mohamad, personal communication, Jakarta, August 23, 1996.

102. Damien Kingsbury, *The Politics of Indonesia* (Melbourne: Oxford University Press, 1998), 111.

103. Hill, *Press in New Order Indonesia*, 46–47.

104. Quoted ibid., 47.

105. Ibid., 35; Susumu Awanohara, "Jakarta's Journalists Engage in a Guerilla War against Tight Guidelines: The Media Freedom Fighters," *FEER*, March 1, 1984.

106. Simanjuntak, *Wartawan Terpasung*, 78–110.

107. Haryanto, *Pembredelan Pers*, 54, 55–56.

108. Quoted in Simanjuntak, *Wartawan Terpasung*, 86.

109. Ibid., 86–87.

110. For example, SK Menteri Penerangan RI No. 47/1975, based on recommendations from the National Press Council.

111. Simanjuntak, *Wartawan Terpasung*, 100.

112. Hill, *Press in New Order Indonesia*, 69.

113. Interview with Atmakusumah Astraatmadja, in Simanjuntak, *Wartawan Terpasung*, 115–16.

114. Ibid., 100–101.

115. For theoretical analysis of the context of this legacy in the emergence and consolidation of an elite oligarchy in Indonesia, see Jeffrey A. Winters, *Oligarchy* (Cambridge: Cambridge University Press, 2011); Richard Robison and Vedi R. Hadiz, *Reorganising Power in Indonesia: The Politics of Oligarchy in an Age of Markets* (London: Routledge, 2004); Michele Ford and Thomas B. Pepinsky, eds., *Beyond Oligarchy: Wealth, Power, and Contemporary Indonesian Politics* (Ithaca, NY: Cornell University Press, 2014); Ross Tapsell, "The Political Economy of Digital Media," in *Digital Indonesia: Connectivity and Divergence*, ed. Ross Tapsell and Edwin Jurriëns, 56–74 (Singapore: ISEAS, 2017).

116. Andrew Nette, "Hunt for Suharto's Wealth a Political, Legal Maze," IPS, October 28, 1998.

117. "Indonesian Govt: 159 Pertamina Partners Linked to Cronyism," DJ, October 9, 1998.

118. Dan Murphy, "Things Fall Apart," *FEER*, May 13, 1999.

119. "Indonesia Spells Out Steps Taken to Eradicate Suharto-Era Corruption," AFP, September 1, 1998.

120. "MPR Asked to Rule on Soeharto," *JP*, October 22, 1998.

121. Masyarakat Transparansi Indonesia, *Penelitian Keputusan Presiden Yang Menyimpang 1993–1998: Laporan Akhir Tim Kerja Bidang Hukum* (Jakarta: Masyarakat Transparansi Indonesia, 1999).

2. DELEGITIMATING AUTHORITARIANISM

1. Tim Wartawan, *Buku Putih "Tempo": Pembredelan Itu* (Jakarta: Alumni Majalah TEMPO, 1994), 17–25.

2. Ayu Utami, "A Letter from a Reporter," in *Banning 1994*, ed. AJI (Jakarta: AJI, 1994), 9.

3. Marsillam Simanjuntak, "Unsur Hegelian dalam Pandangan Negara Integralistik" (MA diss., University of Indonesia, 1989).

4. Articulated more fully in his later book, Marsillam Simanjuntak, *Pandangan Negara Integralistik* (Jakarta: Grafiti Pers, 1994), 254.

5. David Bourchier, "Totalitarianism and the 'National Personality,'" in *Imagining Indonesia: Cultural Politics & Political Culture*, ed. Jim Schiller and Barbara Martin-Schiller (Athens: Ohio University Center for International Studies, 1997), 221–22.

6. Marsillam Simanjuntak, "Bicaralah dan Nyatakan!," *Tempo*, September 15, 1993, 33, cited in *Indonesian Politics and Society: A Reader*, ed. David Bourchier and Vedi Hadiz (London: Routledge, 2014), 218.

7. Robert W. Hefner, *Civil Islam: Muslims and Democratization in Indonesia* (Princeton, NJ: Princeton University Press, 2011), 162.

8. Bourchier, "Totalitarianism and the 'National Personality,'" 227–28.

9. Goenawan Mohamad, *Sidelines: Thought Pieces from "Tempo" Magazine*, trans. Jennifer Lindsay (Jakarta: Lontar, 1994), 69.

10. Ibid., 9–10.

11. Ibid., 47–48.

12. Ibid., 67–68.

13. Ibid., 73.

14. Ibid., 75–76.

15. Goenawan Mohamad, *Conversations with a Difference: Essays from "Tempo" Magazine*, trans. Jennifer Lindsay (Jakarta: PT Tempo Inti, 2002), vii–viii.

16. Mohamad, *Conversations with a Difference*, vii.

17. Mohamad, *Sidelines*, 65.

18. Ibid., 47, 13.

19. Y. B. Mangunwijaya, "The *Indonesia Raya* Dream and Its Impact on the Concept of Democracy," in *Democracy in Indonesia: 1950s and 1990s*, ed. David Bourchier and John Legge, 56–74 (Clayton, Victoria: Monash Papers, 1994), quoted in Angela Romano, *Politics and the Press in Indonesia: Understanding an Evolving Political Culture* (New York: Routledge, 2003), 2.

20. Soeharto, *Pikiran, Ucapan, dan Tindakan Saya: Otobiografi, Seperti Dipaparkan kepada G. Dwipayana dan Ramadhan K. H.* (Jakarta: Citra Lamtoro Gung Persada, 1989), 549, translated by Stefan Eklöf in *Power and Political Culture in Suharto's Indonesia* (Copenhagen: NIAS Press, 2003), 113.

21. Mohamad, *Sidelines*, 75–76.

22. On Tempo's provocative role, see Janet Steele, "Representations of 'The Nation' in *Tempo* Magazine," *Indonesia* 76 (Oct. 2003): 143.

23. Philip Kitley, *Television, Nation, and Culture in Indonesia* (Athens: Ohio University Press, 2000), 245.

24. Ibid., 180–186; personal observations of TVRI's evening news program, *Berita Nasional*, three times weekly from June 15 to August 16, 1996.

25. Kitley, *Television, Nation, and Culture*, 18.

26. Ibid., 150, 169, 307.

27. Sumita Tobing, "Development Journalism in Indonesia: Content Analysis of Government Television News" (PhD diss., Ohio University, 1991), 4.

28. Kitley, *Television, Nation, and Culture*, 176.

29. Respectively, RCTI, TPI (Cipta Televisi Pendidikan Indonesia), Indosiar (Indosiar Visual Mandiri), ANteve (Cakrawala Andalas Televisi), and SCTV (Surya Citra Televisi).

30. Kitley, *Television, Nation, and Culture*, 239.

31. Ibid., 262.

32. Krishna Sen, "Media Politics in Indonesia," *Pacific Review* 16, no. 4 (2003): 573–89.

33. Wimar Witoelar, "Prakata," in *Perspektif Bersama Wimar Witoelar* (Jakarta: Yayasan Obor Indonesia, 1995), xi.

34. Wimar Witoelar, interview with author, Jakarta, April 23, 1999.

35. Wimar Witoelar, "Bertanya, Mewakili Audience," in *Mencuri Kejernihan dari Kerancuan: Suatu Eksperimen dalam Komunikasi* (Jakarta: PT Gramedia Pustaka Utama and InterMatrix Bina Indonesia, 1998), 15.

36. Bernard M. Timberg, *Talk: A History of the TV Talk Show* (Austin: University of Texas Press, 2002), 164.

37. Witoelar, "Prakata," xii.

38. Witoelar, "Bertanya," 7–8.

39. Ibid., 10.

40. Edwin Jurriëns, *From Monologue to Dialogue: Radio and Reform in Indonesia* (Leiden: Brill, 2009), 52.

41. Witoelar, "Bertanya," 5; Witoelar, "Tidak Mencerdaskan Orang," in *Mencuri Kejernihan dari Kerancuan*, x; Witoelar, "Bertanya," 10.

42. Wimar Witoelar, "Expresi Melalui Cerpen," in *Perspektif Bersama Wimar Witoelar*, 599–611.

43. Ibid.

44. Ibid.

45. Ibid.

46. Ibid.

47. Witoelar, "Tidak Mencerdaskan Orang," xxviii.

48. "Dari *DëTIK* ke *Time*," *Panji Masyarakat*, July 1–10, 1994.

49. "Stop the Press," *Newsweek*, July 4, 1994. The tabloid's circulation reached 450,000 after only fifteen months in press.

50. "Laporan Utama: Habibie dan Kapal Itu," *Tempo*, June 11, 1994.

51. Duncan McCargo, "Killing the Messenger: The 1994 Press Bannings and the Demise of Indonesia's New Order," *Harvard International Journal of Press/Politics* 4, no. 1 (Winter 1999): 37.

52. Wartawan, *Buku Putih*, 19.

53. Quoted in Ahmad Taufik, *Semangat Sirnagalih: 20 Tahun Aliansi Jurnalis Independen* (Jakarta: AJI, 1994), 50.

54. Wartawan, *Buku Putih*, 103.

55. PP Menpen No.01/Per/Menpen/1984 tentang Surat Izin Usaha Penerbitan Pers (SIUPP).

56. Wartawan, *Buku Putih*, 100–101.

57. Mahanizar, "Janganlah Mematikan Nafkah," in *Mengapa Kami Menggugat*, ed. Bambang Bujono, Putu Setia, and Toriq Hadad (Jakarta: Yayasan Alumni TEMPO, 1995), 44.

58. Rachlan Nashidik, "Change Comes from Resistance," in AJI, *Banning 1994*, 92.

59. Quoted in Wartawan, *Buku Putih*, 46.

60. Ibid., 48.

61. "Messages of Sympathy Flow in to the Closed Magazines," *JP*, June 23, 1994.

62. Wartawan, *Buku Putih*, 66–67.

63. Quoted ibid., 98. RCTI, however, did not air this interview.

64. Article 19, *Muted Voices: Censorship and the Broadcast Media in Indonesia* (London: Article 19, 1996), 10.

65. Quoted in Wartawan, *Buku Putih*, 109.

66. Arbi Sanit, "Pembredelan di Era Keterbukaan: Selamat Tinggal *Tempo*, *Editor* dan *DëTIK*," *Panji Masyarakat*, July 1–10, 1994.

67. Wartawan, *Buku Putih*, 34.

68. Utami, "Letter from a Reporter," 8.

69. Stanley [Yoseph Adi Prasetyo], "Shattering the Myth of the Press Industry," in AJI, *Banning 1994*, 18.

70. Goenawan Mohamad, "Pengantar," in Wartawan, *Buku Putih*, vii.

71. Ibid.

72. Wartawan, *Buku Putih*, 70–71.

73. Quoted ibid., 86, 38, 45.

74. Onghokham, "The New Order Returns to Zero," in AJI, *Banning 1994*, 47.

75. Arief Budiman, "The Press's Fears, Our Fears," in AJI, *Banning 1994*, 26.

76. For an account of the first offer to "save" *Tempo* by Suharto's son-in-law, Prabowo Subianto, see Janet Steele, *Wars Within: The Story of "Tempo," an Independent Magazine in Soeharto's Indonesia* (Singapore: Equinox, 2005), 146.

77. David Hill, *The Press in New Order Indonesia* (Nedlands: University of Western Australia Press, 1994).

78. Wartawan, *Buku Putih*, 103–4.

79. Aristides Katoppo, interview with author, Jakarta, April 20, 1999; Wartawan, *Buku Putih*, 104.

80. Margot Cohen, "Journalistic License? Press Freedom May Have Received a Shot in the Arm—but the Shadow of Control Lingers," *FEER*, November 11, 1999; Steele, *Wars Within*, 146.

81. "*Tempo*'s 'Successor' Must Have Editorial Independence," *JP*, July 18, 1994.

82. Stanley, "Shattering the Myth," 19.

83. Wartawan, *Buku Putih*, 22.

84. "Life Goes On, amid Bitterness for Former *Tempo* Staff," *JP*, June 18, 1995.

85. "PPP Suggests Dialog to End Media Ban Crisis," *JP*, July 4, 1994.

86. "21 Tahun Pembredelan *Tempo*: Memicu PHK, Pemerintah Panik," *Tempo.co*, June 21, 2015, https://nasional.tempo.co/read/676973/21-tahun-pembredelan-tempo-memicu-phk-pemerintah-panik.

87. Quoted in Atmakusumah, foreword to Hill, *Press in New Order Indonesia*, n.p.

88. Santoso, Ayu Utami, and Tony Hasyim, "SIUPP Dibatalkan, SIUPP Diharapkan," *Forum Keadilan*, July 21, 1994.

89. Yasuo Hanazaki, "The Indonesian Press in an Era of Kerterbukaan: A Force for Democratisation?" (PhD diss., Monash University, 1996), 22.

90. Wartawan, *Buku Putih*, 130–31. The new magazine was first called *Opini*, then *Berita*.

91. Hill, *Press in New Order Indonesia*, 97. This short-lived publication was called *Simponi*.

92. Hanazaki, "Indonesian Press," 108.

93. "Statement of Indonesian Journalists," July 5, 1994, provided to the author by AJI officer Heru Hendratmoko and later cited in Taufik, *Semangat Sirnagalih*, 67–68.

94. Hendrik Dikson Sirait, *Melawan Tirani Orde Baru* (Jakarta: AJI, 1999), 73.

95. "They Won't Lie Down," *Economist*, September 17, 1994.

96. Quoted in Atmakusumah, foreword, n.p. Of those who met, 58 signed the declaration.

97. Wartawan, *Buku Putih*, 108.

98. Ibid.

99. Human Rights Watch/Asia, "Press Closures in Indonesia One Year Later," *Human Rights Watch/Asia* 7, no. 9 (July 1995), https://www.hrw.org/report/1995/07/01/press-closures-indonesia-one-year-later.

100. John McBeth, "Troublesome Types: Jakarta Tightens Screws on Local Journalists," *FEER*, April 6, 1995. *Independen* published twelve issues before being banned.

101 Article 19, *Pengadilan Pers di Indonesia: Kasus Aji dan Pijar* (London: International Center Against Censorship, 1995), 9–10.

102. Human Rights Watch/Asia, "Press Closures," 1–3.

103. Heru Hendratkmoko, personal communication, Jakarta, February 26, 1999.

104. Toriq Hadad and Bambang Bujono, "Pendahuluan: Tonggak Sejarah dari Pokok Halim," in Bujono, Setia, and Hadad, *Mengapa*, 9.

105. Ibid., 12–13.

106. Atmakusumah, foreword, n.p.

107. Statement by Nurhasyim Ilyas, in Bujono, Setia, and Hadad, *Mengapa*, 70.

108. Bambang Bujono, Putu Setia, and Toriq Hadad, "Dari Gugatan sampai Duplik," in *Mengapa*, 94, 98.

109. Ahmad Taufik, "Menegakkan Benteng Terakhir Demokrasi," in Bujono, Setia, and Hadad, *Mengapa*, 22.

110. Rully Kesuma, "Jangan Main Hompimpah," in Bujono, Setia, and Hadad, *Mengapa*, 48.

111. Ahmed Kurnia Soeriawidjaja, "Hanya Sebagian dari Perlawanan," in Bujono, Setia, and Hadad, *Mengapa*, 23.

112. Hidayat Surya Gautama, "Rasa Sesak Karena Teraniaya," in Bujono, Setia, and Hadad, *Mengapa*, 39.

113. Ivan Haris, "Semut Aje Bales Ngegigit," in Bujono, Setia, and Hadad, *Mengapa*, 41–42.

114. Ibid., 14, 5.

115. "Court Rules in *Tempo*'s Favor," *JP*, May 4, 1995

116. See Bujono, Setia, and Hadad, *Mengapa*, 259–60, for the testimony of Sjamsul Basri, a member of the Press Council who confirmed that the Ministry of Information did not consult the Press Council before canceling the license.

117. Mohamad, "Pengantar," 2–7.

118. Ibid.

119. John McBeth, "Up Tempo," *FEER*, May 18, 1995.

120. Siam Alamsjah, "Respons Itu Masih Terbatas," in Bujono, Setia, and Hadad, *Mengapa*, 219–20.

121. "Mengabulkan Kasasi Menpen," *Kompas*, June 14, 1996.

122. "Wawancara Box Forum Khusus dengan Goenawan Mohamad: Putusan Kasus *Tempo*," *Kompas*, June 13, 1996.

123. "Hakim Benyamin Decegah Ditampilkan di TV," *Media Indonesia Minggu*, May 21, 1995.

124. Human Rights Watch/Asia, "Press Closures," 2–3; "Poetry-Meeting Banned," *TAPOL Bulletin* 125, October 1994, 6–9; "Dasar Hukum Keharusan Izin Dipertanyakan," *Kompas*, September 10, 1994; "Yang Terpuruk di Perizinan," *Media Indonesia Minggu*, June 18, 1995.

125. Amnesty International, *Indonesia: Arrests, Torture and Intimidation: The Government's Response to Its Critics*, November 27, 1996, AI Index no. ASA 21/70/96, https://www.amnesty.org/download/Documents/168000/asa210701996en.pdf.

126. Anne Heaton, "Ordeal in Indonesia," *TAPOL Bulletin* 125, October 1994, 24.

127. Mohamad, "Pengantar," vii.

128. Online sources included *Kabar dari Pijar* (http://www.pijar.net/kdpnet/index.html), SiaR (http://apchr.murdoch.edu.au/minihub/siarlist/maillist.html), *Xpos* (ekspos@hotmail.com), and *Tempo Interaktif* (http://www.tempo.co.id). See also David T. Hill, "Media Alternatif," *Forum Keadilan*, September 23, 1996; and Gerry van Klinken, "Indonesia on the Net," *Inside Indonesia* 51 (July–September 1997), http://web.archive.org/web/20080722064139/http://www.insideindonesia.org/content/view/860/29.

129. Krishna Sen and David T. Hill, *Media, Culture and Politics in Indonesia* (London: Equinox, 2006), 98–100.

130. Later, Witoelar likened the shows to cockroaches, popping up as quickly as the government could squash them. Wimar Witoelar, interview with author, Jakarta, July 10, 2009.

131. Stanley, "Shattering the Myth," 21–22.

132. Wartawan, *Buku Putih*, 30.

133. See, for example, Aristides Katoppo, quoted in Wartawan, *Buku Putih*, 53.

134. Mochtar Pabottingi, "Limits of the New Order, Limits of the Nation," in AJI, *Banning 1994*, 86.

135. Onghokham, "New Order Returns," 47.

136. Julia Suryakusuma, "The Ironies of Openness," in AJI, *Banning 1994*, 45.

137. McCargo, "Killing the Messenger," 29.

138. Goenawan Mohamad, personal communication, Jakarta, August 23, 1996.

139. Vince Boudreau, "Currency Crisis and Fragmented Mobilization in New Order Indonesia," in *Indonesia's Interregnum: A Torturous Transition to Democratic Development*, ed. Eduardo C. Tadem (Quezon City: University of the Philippines, Center for Integrative and Development Studies, 2000), 103.

140. Heru Hendratmoko, personal communication, Jakarta, January 28, 1999; Nicholas Kristof, "Two Forces That Tug at Indonesia," *NYT*, May 22, 1998.

3. SUHARTO'S FALL

1. Edward Aspinall, *Opposing Suharto: Compromise, Resistance, and Regime Change in Indonesia* (Stanford, CA: Stanford University Press: 2005), 121.

2. US Department of State, *Indonesia Report on Human Rights Practices for 1997* (Bureau of Democracy, Human Rights, and Labor, US Department of State, January 30, 1998), section 2, Respect for Civil Liberties, including (a) Freedom of Speech and Press.

3. Ibid.

4. Human Rights Watch, "Torture, Disappearances, and Arrests of Indonesian Activists," press release, April 1, 1998.

5. Goenawan Mohamad, "Pengantar," in *Buku Putih "Tempo": Pembredelan Itu* (Jakarta: Alumni Majalah TEMPO, 1994), viii–ix.

6. Webb Keane, "Freedom and Blasphemy: On Indonesian Press Bans and Danish Cartoons," *Public Culture* 12, no. 1 (December 2009): 47–76.

7. Ahmad Taufik, "Menegakkan Benteng Terakhir Demokrasi," in *Mengapa Kami Menggugat*, ed. Bambang Bujono, Putu Setia, and Toriq Hadad (Jakarta: Yayasan Alumni TEMPO, 1995), 22; Ahmad Taufik, personal communication, Jakarta, March 9, 1999.

8. Ging Ginanjar, personal communication, Jakarta, August 31, 2010.

9. AJI, ed., *Banning 1994* (Jakarta: AJI, 1994); Bujono, Setia, and Hadad, *Mengapa*.

10. Daniel Dhakidae, "The State, the Rise of Capital and the Fall of Political Journalism: Political Economy of the Indonesian News Industry" (Ph.D. diss., Cornell University, 1991), 62–63.

11. Wartawan, *Buku Putih*, 84–85.

12. Quoted in Bujono, Setia, and Hadad, *Mengapa*, 8.

13. For this second incarnation, however, AJI took the precaution of publishing the newsletter from Australia. Heru Hendratmoko, personal communication, Jakarta, February 9, 1999. The underground newsletters *Xpos* and *Bergerak* also appeared in hard copy and online. Other organizations that put out critical newsletters included Pijar, whose bulletin *Kabar Dari Pijar* provoked office raids and arrests in 1995. Angela Romano, "The Open Wound: Keterbukaan and Press Freedom in Indonesia," *Australian Journal of International Affairs* 50, no. 2 (July 1996): 157–69. See also David T. Hill, "Media Alternatif," *Forum Keadilan*, September 23, 1996.

14. Andreas Harsono, "Indonesia: From Mainstream to Alternative Media," *First Monday* 1, no. 3 (September 1996), http://ojphi.org/ojs/index.php/fm/article/view/480/401.

15. Romano, "Open Wound."

16. Harsono, "Indonesia."

17. Marcus W. Brauchli, "Magazine Long Critical of Suharto Finds Itself Looking for a New Role," *WSJ*, June 3, 1998.

18. Quoted in Seth Mydans, "Activists Thrust Agendas into Post-Suharto Void," *NYT*, June 28, 1999.

19. Janet Steele, *Wars Within: The Story of "Tempo," an Independent Magazine in Soeharto's Indonesia* (Singapore: Equinox, 2005), 259–68.

20. Quoted ibid., 268.

21. Andrew Nette, "Hunt for Suharto's Wealth a Political, Legal Maze," IPS, October 28, 1998.

22. George J. Aditjondro, "Chopping the Global Tentacles of the Suharto Oligarchy," keynote address at the conference "Towards Democracy in Indonesia: Seize New Zealand Suharto Assets," Auckland University, March 23, 2000.

23. Masyarakat Transparansi Indonesia, *Penelitian Keputusan Presiden Yang Menyimpang 1993–1998: Laporan Akhir Tim Kerja Bidang Hukum* (Jakarta: Masyarakat Transparansi Indonesia, 1999).

24. "Indonesia's State Oil Firm 'Lost 6.1 Billion Dollars to Inefficiency,'" AFP, July 14, 1999.

25. "Suharto Family 'Has US$15b Fortune,'" *ST*, May 17, 1999.

26. "Indonesian Govt: 159 Pertamina Partners Linked to Cronyism," DJ, October 9, 1998.

27. Dan Murphy, "Things Fall Apart," *FEER*, May 13, 1999.

28. George J. Aditjondro, *Dari Soeharto ke Habibie: Guru Kencing Berdiri, Murid Kencing Berlari: Kedua Puncak Korupsi, Kolusi, dan Nepotisme Rezim Order Baru* (Jakarta: Pijar Indonesia & Masyarakat Indonesia untuk Kemanusiaan, 1998).

29. John Colmey and David Liebhold, "Suharto, Inc.: All in the Family," *Time Asia*, May 24, 1999.

30. Louise Williams, "Poor Little Rich Kids," *SMH*, October 24, 1998.

31. "More Land Holdings of the Former First Family Have Been Uncovered," *ST*, December 2, 1998.

32. Grainne McCarthy, "Asia Econ Growth Doesn't Merit Rate Hikes—Deutsche Bank," *WSJ*, March 23, 2000.

33. Michael Spencer, quoted ibid.

34. "The Rot in Indonesia," editorial, *NYT*, March 6, 1998.

35. Heru Hendratmoko, "Keroposnya Sebuah Mitos: Pers Indonesia," in *Masyarakat dan Negara, Kado untuk Prof Soetandyo Wignjosoebroto MPA*, ed. Basis Susulio, 161–70 (Surabaya: Airlangga University Press, 1997).

36. A reading of the media coverage for the last three months of 1997 indicates that English-language newspapers, such as the *Jakarta Post* and the *Indonesian Observer*, carried the most critical coverage.

37. Seth Mydans, "Indonesian Students Keep Protests Well Within the Pale," *NYT*, March 29, 1998.

38. Kristof, "'People Power' Unrest of Indonesian Campuses," *NYT*, April 29, 1998.

39. Quoted in Mydans, "Indonesian Students."

40. Allan Nairn, "Indonesia's 'Disappeared,'" *TN*, June 8, 1998.

41. John Roosa, "Reappearance of the Disappeared," email report, April 23, 1998.

42. Allan Nairn, "Indonesia's Killers," *TN*, March 30, 1998.

43. Roosa, "Reappearance."

44. Aspinall, *Opposing Suharto*, 203.

45. Quoted in Kristof, "People Power."

46. Nairn, "Indonesia's Killers."

47. Quoted in Mydans, "Indonesian Students."

48. Roosa, "Reappearance."

49. Harsono, "Indonesia."

50. "Presiden di Tengah Krisis," *D&R*, March 7, 1998.

51. Budiman S. Hartoyo, interview with author, Jakarta, March 31, 1999.

52. Quoted in Lukas Luwarso and Dadang Rhs, "AJI Condemn Soeharto Statement," press release from AJI, April 18, 1998, https://peace.home.xs4all.nl/pubeng/pdm/ajics.html.

53. The original Indonesian reads, "Harga kejujuran lebih mahal dari harga sembako." Reuters photo, published in Seth Mydans, "At Pivotal Time, Suharto Gets 7th Term,"*NYT*, March 11, 1998.

54. Nairn, "Indonesia's 'Disappeared.'"

55. Roosa, "Reappearance."

56. Gerry van Klinken, "Indonesia on the Net," *Inside Indonesia* 51 (July–September 1997), http://web.archive.org/web/20080722064139/http://www.insideindonesia.org/content/view/860/29.

57. "Chronology of Indonesian Crisis," Reuters, October 18, 1999.

58. Kukuh Sanyoto, interview with author, tape recording, Jakarta, May 19, 1999.

59. Kukuh Sanyoto, "Indonesian Television and the Dynamics of Transition," in *Media Fortunes, Changing Times: ASEAN States in Transition*, ed. Russell H. K. Heng (Singapore: Institute for Southeast Asian Studies, 2002), 95.

60. Quoted in Mark Landler, "Riots Break Out in Jakarta after Shooting of Students," *NYT*, May 14, 1998.

61. Ibid.

62. Richard Stevenson, "8 World Leaders Urge Suharto Show Restraint in Handling Indonesian Turmoil," *NYT*, May 16, 1998.

63. Philip Shenon, "U.S. to Appeal to Indonesia Military to Stop Crackdown," *NYT*, April 14, 1998.

64. Mark Landler, "Indonesian Capital Engulfed by Rioting," *NYT*, May 15, 1998.

65. Tim Gabungan Pencari Fakta, *Laporan Akhir Tim Gabungan Pencari Fakta Peristiwa Tanggal 13–15 Mei 1998* (Jakarta: Tim Gabungan Pencari Fakta, October 23, 1998).

66. An oft-cited and, as it turns out, misleading statistic in circulation at the time was that Chinese Indonesians, though only 3 percent of the population, controlled 70 percent of the economy. See George Aditjondro, "The Myth of Chinese Dominance in Indonesia," *JP*, August 14, 1998.

67. Mark Landler, "The Target of Violence in a Time of Wrath," *NYT*, May 15, 1998.

68. See, for example, Martin R. Jenkins, "Nation Basks in Self-Deception," *JP*, May 13, 2000; Tim Gabungan Pencari Fakta, *Laporan Akhir*.

69. Wimar Witoelar, "The Role of the Media and the Recent Changes in Indonesian Politics," University of Wisconsin–Madison, Center for Southeast Asian Studies Friday Forum Lecture Series, October 22, 1999.

70. Ariel Heryanto, "Flaws of Riot Media Coverage," *JP*, July 15, 1998.

71. Landler, "Riots Break Out."

72. Quoted in Seth Mydans, "2 Top Figures in Indonesia Clash on Seeking Suharto's Resignation," *NYT*, May 19, 1998.

73. Dewi Loveard, "Diary: A Depressing Journey through Central Java," *Asiaweek*, September 25, 1998.

74. Mydans, "2 Top Figures."

75. Mark Landler, "In Indonesia, the Grab for Power May Hinge on the Rivalry of 2 Generals," *NYT*, May 18, 1998.

76. Nicholas Kristof, "High Stakes for Suharto: No Graceful Way Out?," *NYT*, May 19, 1998.

77. Mydans, "2 Top Figures."

78. Seth Mydans, "In a Suharto Fief, 'Hang Suharto!'" *NYT*, May 19, 1998.

79. Kristof, "High Stakes."

80. Nicholas Kristof, "A Toothless Tiger? Army's Will Is Doubted," *NYT*, May 21, 1998.

81. Mydans, "2 Top Figures."

82. Nicholas Kristof, "Filling Power Vacuum: Will Army Rule?" *NYT*, May 21, 1998.

83. Mark Landler, "Joyfully, Indonesian Students Thumb Noses at Authority," *NYT*, May 20, 1998.

84. Seth Mydans, "Army Out in Force to Halt Protests Aimed at Suharto," *NYT*, May 20, 1998.

85. Seth Mydans, "Suharto Steps Down after 32 Years in Power," *NYT*, May 21, 1998.

86. Philip Shenon, "U.S. Steps Up Pressure on Suharto," *NYT*, May 21, 1998.

87. Seth Mydans, "Top General Strengthens His Grasp on Power," *NYT*, May 23, 1998.

88. Mydans, "Suharto Steps Down."

89. Endy M. Bayuni, "Indonesia's Journalists Will Preserve Their New Freedom," *WSJ*, August 12, 1998.

90. Aspinall, *Opposing Suharto*, 254.

91. Bayuni, "Indonesia's Journalists."

92. Aspinall, *Opposing Suharto*, 252.

93. For further analysis, see Duncan McCargo, "Killing the Messenger: The 1994 Press Bannings and the Demise of Indonesia's New Order," *Harvard International Journal of Press/Politics* 4, no. 1 (1999): 29–47.

94. Aspinall, *Opposing Suharto*, 129.

4. *Reformasi*

1. Jeffrey Winters, "Leadership in Indonesian Politics," keynote address at the conference "Indonesia Next," Jakarta, May 2001.

2. Quoted in Tim Healy and Jose Manuel Tesoro, "Judging Habibie," *Asiaweek*, September 4, 1998.

3. "Two out of Three Indonesians Will Fall below Poverty Line: ILO," AFP, August 31, 1998.

4. David Lamb, "Clouds Haven't Lifted in Post-Suharto Indonesia," *LAT*, October 1, 1998.

5. Louise Williams, "Rubber Bullets Warning as Prices Rocket," *SMH*, September 1, 1998.

6. "Indonesia on the Brink," *Singapore Business Times*, September 11, 1998; Dewi Loveard, "Indonesia's Mean Streets," *Asiaweek*, September 25, 1998; Lamb, "Clouds Haven't Lifted."

7. Lamb, "Clouds Haven't Lifted."

8. Neil Weinberg, "What Devaluation Hath Wrought," *Forbes*, October 5, 1998.

9. Williams, "Poor Little Rich Kids"; David Jenkins, "Habibie's Challenge," *SMH*, October 26, 1998; Weinberg, "What Devaluation Hath Wrought."

10. Quoted in Jenkins, "Habibie's Challenge."

11. "Bid to License Journalists Rapped," *ST*, July 17, 1998.

12. "Press Gets New Freedom," *JP*, editorial, July 31, 1999.

13. Seth Mydans, "Suharto Steps Down after 32 Years in Power," *NYT*, May 21, 1998.

14. Gerry van Klinken, "Round Two: Suharto's Comeback?," *Inside Indonesia*, June 22, 1998; Jeremy Wagstaff, "Habibie's Speech Fails to Sway Skeptics: Ability to Deliver 'Civil Society' in Doubt," *WSJ*, August 17, 1998; Seth Mydans, "New Leader Vows Early Elections for Indonesians," *NYT*, May 26, 1998.

15. Marcus W. Brauchli, "Magazine Long Critical of Suharto Finds Itself Looking for a New Role," *WSJ*, June 3, 1998.

16. Eyewitnesses claimed to have seen Yosfiah pull the trigger. See "UN Links Ex-Jakarta Minister to Timor Murders—Paper," Reuters, February 3, 2001.

17. Mohammad Yunus Yosfiah, interview with author, Jakarta, June 10, 1999; Mohammad Yunus Yosfiah, *Forum Aspirasi*, TVRI, March 15, 1999, quoting Thomas Jefferson, letter to Colonel Edward Carrington, January 16, 1787.

18. Peraturan Menteri Penerangan Republik Indonesia No. 01/PER/MENPEN/1998 tentang Ketentuan-Ketentuan Surat Izin Usaha Penerbitan Pers. The form required a signature from a Ministry of Information official (usually the director general of press, printing and graphics), but from my observations at the ministry in 1999, approval appeared to be automatic. If the office was not busy, one could complete the entire process in a matter of minutes. By contrast, in the early 1990s, *Jakarta-Jakarta* spent close to Rp300 million (around $130,000) just to secure a new SIUPP when the ministry forced it to become an entertainment magazine after it published a controversial report on the 1991 army-perpetrated massacre in Dili, East Timor. Yosep Adi Prasetnyo, "Kepemilikan Modal di Media Massa dan Implikasinya bagi Kebebasan Pers: Mencari Format Organisasi Kewartawan yang Ideal, Notelensi Diskusi II," in *Reformasi Media Massa*, ed. Ery Sutrisno (Jakarta: AJI, 1998), 112.

19. Surat Keputusan Menteri Penerangan Republik Indonesia No. 133/SK/MENPEN/1998.

20. Surat Keputusan Menteri Penerangan Republik Indonesia No. 134/SK/MENPEN/1998.

21. S. Leo Batubara, speech delivered at "Demokrasi, Kebebasan Pers, dan Hukum Seminar," Universitas Atma Jaya, Jakarta, April 7, 1999.

22. This stipulation applied to publications that had ceased operations for six months or more. R. H. Siregar, speech delivered at "Demokrasi, Kebebasan Pers, dan Hukum Seminar," Universitas Atma Jaya, Jakarta, April 7, 1999.

23. AJI, "Aturan Baru Menteri Penerangan: Reformasi Setengah Hati," AJI statement, apakabar@clark.net, June 6, 1998. The relevant regulations were Permenpen No. 1/1998, SK Menpen No. 133/1998, and SK Menpen No. 134/1998.

24. A total of 289 licenses were granted under Suharto. Jose Manuel Tesoro, "Indonesia: Learning the Ropes of Press Freedom," *UNESCO Courier* 2 (February 2000): 43–45; Sheila Coronel, "Media-Indonesia: After the Euphoria, Press under Attack," IPS, June 2, 2000.

25. The changing tone and topics of Indonesia's print coverage are evident in appendixes 1, 2, and 3, which comprise sample headlines from Jakarta's leading news magazines and tabloids in 1985, 1990, and 1999.

26. Reported in Seth Mydans, "With Suharto Empire under Fire, 2 Kinsmen Are Ousted from Jobs," *NYT*, May 30, 1998; Seth Mydans, "Reeling Indonesia Gets Fiscal Break," *NYT*, May 31, 1998.

27. Mydans, "New Leader Vows."

28. "Pelanggaran HAM di Aceh," TPI, August 22, 1998; "Pelucutan Senjata di Tim-Tim," TPI, March 14, 1999.

29. David T. Hill, *The Press in New Order Indonesia* (Nedlands: University of Western Australia Press, 1994), 88.

30. A. Lin Neumann, "Radio Reformasi: Climate of Political Openness Frees Jakarta's Airwaves," *FEER*, September 17, 1998.

31. "'Talk-Show' Menjadi Unggulan TV Swasta," *Kompas*, June 25, 1998.

32. A good example was a debate on April 1, 1999, between Sri Bingtang Pamungkas, a former political prisoner and chairman of the Indonesian Democratic Union Party, and Ryaas Rasyid, the outspoken director general of the Ministry of Home Affairs. Throughout the discussion, Rasyid and Pamungkas got so caught up in their debate they began interrupting each other and generally ignored the host's attempts to moderate. *Pro dan Kontra*, TPI, April 1, 1999.

33. Melinda Quintos de Jesus, "'Coming of Age': Media and Society," *Manila Times*, November 12, 1998.

34. For example, in his State of the Nation address on August 15, 1999. See Kafil Yamin, "Habibie's Piecemeal Approach Riles Critics," IPS, August 24, 1998; "Indonesian Student Protests Should Be Allowed: Minister," AFP, October 25, 1998; "Indonesian Press Appeals to Govt Officials for Openness," AP, October 27, 1998.

35. "Bid to License Journalists"; Yamin, "Habibie's Piecemeal Approach."

36. "Indonesia: Military Intervention in Labour Disputes," *Asian Food Worker*, September 1998.

37. Hikmahanto Juwana, "Special Report Assessing Indonesia's Human Rights Practice in the Post-Soeharto Era: 1998–2003," *Singapore Journal of International & Comparative Law* 7 (2003): 646.

38. Jenny Grant, "Actress Summonsed over 'Insult,'" *SCMP*, September 19, 1998; Ratna Sarumpaet, personal communication, Jakarta, March 4, 1999.

39. Suzanne Charl, "Indonesia's Students Traditionally Speak Out for the Voiceless," *TN*, October 5, 1998.

40. That which does not offend, she points out, requires no protection. Jean Goodwin, lecture, "Communication Studies C30: Contemporary Problems in Freedom of Speech," Northwestern University, Evanston, IL, January 16, 1998.

41. Quoted in Subhatra Bhumiprabhas, "Media: Pressing for Their Freedom," *TN*, May 22, 2008.

42. "Pemerkosaan di Bulan Mei 1998: Cerita & Fakta," *Tempo*, October 6–12, 1998.

43. "Jejak Cendana di Banyuwangi." Witnesses described the perpetrators as groups of men, dressed in black coats and masked in the style of Japanese ninja assassins, who displayed unusual physical prowess and then vanished into thin air. Yusi A. Pareanom, Ardi Bramantyo, Andari Karina, and Zed Abidien, "Pembunuhan Berantai di Bumi Osing," *Tempo*, October 19, 1998; "Kisah Mateha yang Tak Mati-Mati," *Tajuk*, October 15, 1998. See also "Murders May Be Organized: Kontras," *JP*, October 10, 1998; Nicholas D. Kristoff, "Fears of Sorcerers Spur Killings in Java," *NYT*, October 20, 1998; Kees van Dijk, "Mysterious Killings," in *A Country in Despair: Indonesia between 1997 and 2000* (Leiden: KITLV Press, 2001), 359–77; S. Saiful Rahim, *Merah Darah Santet di Banyuwangi* (Jakarta: Metro Pos, 1998). The earliest victims in July 1998 had been identified as "sorcerers" (*dukun santet*), killed in what many assumed to be local acts of vengeance related to the alleged practice of black magic. In August, however, the body count jumped to nearly fifty; it doubled again in September, when the profile of victims suddenly expanded to include Muslim clerics, many of them members of Nahdlatul Ulama. By mid-December, the number had reached 248, featuring ever more grisly displays, including chopped up body parts thrown into nearby mosques or hung from trees in bags. Jason Brown, "The Banyuwangi Murders: Why Did over a Hundred Black Magic Practitioners Die in East Java Late in 1998?" *Inside Indonesia*, April–June 2000; "Mystery Murder Spree Takes New Twist in Indonesia," Reuters, October 2, 1998; Derwin Pereira, "Special Report: Java's Ninja Terror," *ST*, October 30, 1998.

44. Kafil Yamin, "Killings of Islamic Teachers Spread Fear," IPS, November 2, 1998.

45. Bhimo Widadi, Augustono, and Dwi Ani, "Kuantar ke Gerbang Kehancuran," *DëTAK*, November 3–9, 1998.

46. See Yamin, "Killings of Islamic Teachers."

47. SiaR, for example, reported that their sources questioned the suspicious circumstances of the killings. One source said the killers were clearly professionals. "Before acting, they cut the electricity throughout the village. Who [else] could do such a thing?" "Satuan ABRI Diduga di Belakang Pembantaian Banyuwangi," SiaR email list, October 7, 1998, http://apchr.murdoch.edu.au/minihub/siarlist. See also "Ninja Operation, Intelligence Operation," *Gatra*, October 31, 1998; "Kasus Dukun Santet di Banyuwangi: Pelaku Pembantaian Dibayar Rp250.000," *SP*, October 7, 1998; "Security Involvement in Anti-religious 'Ninja' Killings," *Kedaulatan Rakyat* October 30, 1998. Findings of investigating teams from NU, Partai Keadilan, and Kontras also suggested military or government involvement. Assailants, for instance, were seen arriving in vehicles bearing nonlocal license plates, using maps of the area that allowed them easy escape, and assisted by electricity blackouts that preceded several attacks. "Murders May Be Organized." Partai Keadilan also found it suspicious that police, who were normally slow to respond, would appear, unsummoned, within minutes when locals captured a suspected "ninja." "Conclusions of the Fact-Finding Team of Partai Keadilan of East Java," cited in S. Saiful Rahim, *Merah Darah Santet di Banyuwangi* (Jakarta: Metro Pos, 1998).

48. "Jejak Cendana di Banyuwangi: Pengakuan desertir Kopassus," November 3–9, 1998; "Pengakuan Desertir Kopassus: Target Kelompok Cikarang Gagalkan Kongres PDI," *DëTAK*, November 3–9, 1998.

49. "Pengakuan Desertir Kopassus."

50. "Nggak Ada Desertir Kopassus," interview with Major General Syamsul Ma'arif (Kapuspen ABRI), *DëTAK*, November 3–9, 1998.

51. See John Sidel, *Riots, Pogroms, Jihad: Religious Violence in Indonesia* (Ithaca, NY: Cornell University Press, 2006), 138–39.

52. Tim Gabungan Pencari Fakta, "Laporan Akhir Tim Gabungan Pencari Fakta Peristiwa Tanggal 13–15 Mei 1998," executive summary, Jakarta, October 23, 1998 (released to the public on November 3, 1998).

53. See George Junus Aditjondro, "Guns, Pamphlets and Handie-Talkies: How the Military Exploited Local Ethno-religious Tensions in Maluku to Preserve Their Political and Economic Privileges," in *Violence in Indonesia*, ed. Ingrid Wessel and Georgia Wimhoefer, 228–53 (Hamburg: Abera, 2001).

54. Charl, "Indonesia's Students."

55. Chapter VI, Ketetapan Majelis Permusyawaratan Rakyat Republik Indonesia, No. XVII/MPR/1998 Tentang Hak Asasi Manusia, Bab 5, Pasal 19.

56. Video montage of the 1998 parliamentary special session, *Anteve Gema Senayan*, ANteve, November 13, 1998.

57. The main stations providing live coverage were Ramako-FM, Trijaya-FM, RRI's Produa-FM, Sonora, and Elshinta. For a detailed report on the role of radio in 1998 in covering these events, see "Mendengar Radio Dengan Back Sound Desingan Peluru," *Republika*, November 24, 1998.

58. Lukas Luwarso, "Protes Atas Kekerasan Aparat terhadap Wartawan," AJI statement, Jakarta, November 13, 1998.

59. Ibid. ANteve also reported this complaint. *Gema Senayan*, ANteve, November 11, 1998.

60. *Cakrawala*, ANteve, November 12, 1998.

61. Figures on the number killed vary in reports on the incident, even within the same sources, numbering anywhere from five to nineteen. In a later and more definitive report, the *Jakarta Post* confirmed sixteen deaths, including six university students, but noted that the head of the nongovernmental organization Kontras put the number at nineteen, adding that at least six students remained missing. "Parents of Dead Students Seek Justice," *JP*, December 2, 1998.

62. 7 p.m. report, TVRI, November 14, 1998.

63. For a more detailed analysis, see chapter 5; Wimar Witoelar, "Black Friday Due to Impudence," *JP*, November 21, 1998.

64. Ketetapan Majelis Permusyawaratan Rakyat Republik Indonesia, No. XVII/MPR/1998 Tentang Hak Asasi Manusia, Bab 5, Pasal 19.

65. This impression is based on conversations with journalists and editors in November and December of 1998. The fragility of the press's position was also a main theme of a discussion on media freedom led by Atmakusumah Astraatmadja (then director of the Dr. Soetomo Press Institute) and held in Jakarta on November 16. See "Expert Warns against Moves to Gag Freedom of the Media," *JP*, November 19, 1998.

66. *Tajuk* faced a suit from the Greater Jakarta Regional Military Command (Kodam Jaya) over a report published on September 3, 1998, "Saksi-saksi Setelah 100 Hari," that implicated the regiment, and Major General Sjafrie Sjamsuddin in particular, in orchestrating the May 1998 riots. See "Buruk Muka, Pers Digugat," *Xpos*, September 12–18, 1998, http://apchr.murdoch.edu.au/minihub/xp. Similarly, the governor of South Sulawesi, Zainal Basri Palaguna, charged *D&R* with libel after the magazine published a report in June 1998 exposing his involvement in corruption. The papers *DëTAK* and *Merdeka* also found themselves in trouble with the minister of internal affairs after reporting on his role in a 1996 PDI congress that led to the party's split. *DëTAK* had to fend off a lawsuit by a former Kopassus commander, Colonel Chairawan K. Nusyirwan, who had been discharged over the magazine's reports on the Banyuwangi murder sprees. Ezki Suyanto, interview with author, Jakarta, March 10, 1999.

67. Heru Hendratmoko, email communication, Jakarta, February 9, 1999.

68. Ibid.

69. The group also began drafting a broadcasting law to go with the print media law, and later changed its name to the Indonesian Press and Broadcasting Society (Masyarakat Pers dan Penyiaran Indonesia).

70. Mohammad Yunus Yosfiah on "Dialog Khusus," hosted by Yunuk Parwati, TVRI, September 29, 1998.

71. "Kasus *Panji Masyarakat* Batu Ujian untuk Kebebasan Pers," editorial, *Kompas*, February 24, 1999; "Sebuah Ujian untuk Integritas Wartawan," *Berita Buana*, February 20, 1999; "Wakil Pemimpin Umum *Panji Masyarakat* Beri Kesaksian," *Republika*, February 20, 1999.

72. The exact number of media outlets that obtained copies of the original cassette is difficult to confirm since most later stories on its contents simply referenced the transcript from *Panji*'s report. (*Panji Masyarakat* received its copy of the cassette in mid-February. Uni Zulfiani Lubis, interview with author, Jakarta, April 30, 1999.) However, insiders at *Kompas*, *Tempo*, and *DëTAK* acknowledged privately that their publications had each received a copy. The small tabloid *Berita Keadilan* also at least had access to a copy, used for its January report on the conversation (which went largely unnoticed), cited below. Eventually, several television and radio stations aired the conversation using their own copies.

73. The passage in Indonesian reads, ". . . kalau cuma dua jam juga nanti orang, wah, sandiwara apa lagi *nih*." Quoted in "Beredarnya Rekaman Ghalib-Habibie: Halo, Ghalib dan Habibie di Sini," *Panji Masyarakat*, February 24, 1999. The Indonesian word *sandiwara* could also be translated as "farce," but more generally refers to any staged drama or play-acting.

74. Translated from the transcript in "Beredarnya Rekaman Ghalib-Habibie."

75. "The Tale from the Tape," *JP*, February 20, 1999; "Sulit Hindari Kesan Intervensi Kekuasaan atas Kasus Hukum," *Kompas*, February 22, 1999. See also the comments of the Indonesian Legal Aid and Human Rights Association lawyer Hendardi [one name], in "Isi Rekaman Mengejutkan," *SP*, February 20, 1999.

76. "Percakapan Rahasia Habibie-Ghalib Soal Soeharto," *Berita Keadilan*, January 6–12, 1999.

77. "Beredarnya Rekaman Ghalib-Habibie."

78. "Isi Rekaman Mengejutkan"; "Berharap Selamat dari Kata 'Mirip,'" *Berlian*, February 22–28, 1999.

79. In Jakarta and Surabaya, over a dozen street hawkers and newsstand owners I spoke with in late March said that after the story, most increased their orders of the magazine. Even with this added stock, in the first weeks after the story, some said they would still run out of copies by midmorning.

80. "Rekaman Diteliti, Asli atau Rekayasa," *SP*, February 19, 1999; Trimoelja D. Soerjadi, interview with author, Surabaya, February 28, 1999.

81. "ABRI to Probe Phone Tap Scandal," *JP*, February 20, 1999.

82. Uni Zulfiani Lubis, interview with author, Jakarta, April 30, 1999.

83. Ibid.

84. An exception was Sonora-FM, whose chief editor was one of the fourteen summoned even though the station had not aired the cassette. This mistake was a source of amusement to the staff at Ramako-FM, who *had* broadcast the cassette but were not called in. Deddy Rachmat, personal communication, Jakarta, March 17, 1999.

85. ANteve news director Azkarmin Zaini, quoted in "Polisi Bingung," *Surya*, February 24, 1999.

86. Uni Zulfiani Lubis, interview with author, Jakarta, April 30, 1999.

87. Ibid.

88. Ridlo Aryanto, "Roy Suryo, Pioneer in Multimedia Documentation," *JP*, February 4, 2001.

89. "Bergaya Mafia," *DëTAK*, March 23–29, 1999. Suryo mentioned this concern shortly after arriving in Jakarta. Roy Suryo, personal communication, Jakarta, March 17, 1999. BIA's involvement in the disappearances, as well as in the torture during interrogation later reported by those who escaped, was well-documented in investigations by both nongovernmental organizations and the US State Department. See Allan Nairn, "Indonesia's 'Disappeared,'" *TN*, June 8, 1998.

90. Roy Suryo, personal communication, Jakarta, March 17, 1999. Regardless, the story of Suryo's encounter with BIA further fueled rumors that military intelligence was behind the leak. Deddy Rachmat, personal communication, Jakarta, March 17, 1999.

91. "Penyadapan," *Jurnal 30*, Ramako-FM, March 17, 1999.

92. *Panji Masyarakat* advertising department, personal communication, Jakarta, April 30, 1999.

93. M.S. Zulkarnaen, interview with author, Jakarta, April 30, 1999.

94. Budiman S. Hartoyo, interview with author, Jakarta, March 31, 1999.

95. Ezki Suyanto, interview with author, Jakarta, March 10, 1999.

96. Uni Zulfiani Lubis, interview with author, Jakarta, April 30, 1999.

97. Ezki Suyanto, interview with author, Jakarta, March 10, 1999.

98. Ibid.

99. Print coverage of the case moved away from the contents of the recorded conversation almost immediately. In their initial reports, Jakarta's main dailies focused overwhelmingly on national security questions and officials' search for the source of the wiretap. See, for example, "Presiden Soal Pembicaraan dengan Jaksa Agung: Selidiki Yang Bocorkan," *Kompas*, February 19, 1999; "Skandal Penyadapan Telpon: Ada Orang Berbahaya Dekat Habibie," *Berita Buana*, February 19, 1999; "Teroris Hadir di Mana Saja," *Lensa*, February 27–March 5, 1999; "Kemungkinan Orang Dalam Terlibat," *MI*, February 20, 1999; "ABRI to Probe Phone Tap Scandal and Officials Say Palace Phone System Safe," *JP*, February 20, 1999; "DPR Minta Pangab Beri Penjelasan: 'Itu Kejahatan Spionase Terencana,'" *Republika*, February 20, 1999; "Kasum: Mungkin ABRI Lakukan Konspirasi," *Republika*, February 20, 1999. Several broadcasters, beginning with ANteve, did keep attention on Habibie and Ghalib's alleged conversation by airing the actual recording, allowing audiences to judge the tape's authenticity for themselves, and later print coverage in this vein included calls for impeachment proceedings and demands for Ghalib's resignation. See, for example, "Mathori: Habibie Harus Di-Impeach, PKB Desak Presiden Copot Jaksa Agung," *Jawa Pos*, February 25, 1999; "Habibie Harus Ubah Kebijakan," *Kompas*, February 25, 1999; "FPP Cari Dukungan Impeachment," *Jawa Pos*, February 27, 1999. Ultimately, however, the shift in attention to security served Habibie by taking the focus off the "charade" investigation of Suharto, allowing defenders to rail instead against the unknown traitor who was trying to "bring down the government." "'Itu Kejahatan Espionase Terencana,'" *Republika*, February 20, 1999.

100. For more on this consensus, see Mary E. McCoy, "The Media in Democratic Transitions: Institutionalizing Uncertainty in Post-Suharto Indonesia" (PhD diss., Northwestern University, 2005).

101. Tarman Azzam, quoted in "PWI Siap Bantu Majalah *Panji Masyarakat*," *SP*, February 22, 1999.

102. Act No. 11/1966 on the Basic Provisions on the Press, as amended by Act No. 4/1967 and later amended by Act No. 21/1982.

103. Specifically, the elucidation of the amendment states, "the Right of Refusal . . . does not apply in matters involving especially the order and security of the State." Elucidation on Chapter V, Article 15, sections (6) and (7) of Act No. 21 of 1982, amending Act No. 11/1966 on the Basic Provisions on the Press, as amended by Act No. 4/1967.

104. Ketetapan Majelis Permusyawaratan Rakyat Republik Indonesia, No. XVII/MPR/1998 Tentang Hak Asasi Manusia, Bab 5.

105. One such law mentioned repeatedly was Telecommunications Law No. 5/1964, which states in Article 22, "Whoever reports news, or disseminates news, that was obtained without permission, or is not in the public interest, can be sentenced to a year in prison and a fine of Rp100,000." "*Panji* Tak Langgar Kode Etik," *Kompas*, February 20, 1999. Article 15 of this same law reads, "Whoever disseminates news that is unconfirmed, exaggerated, or incomplete, and that can provoke a public disturbance . . . can be sentenced to up to two years in jail." "Polri Bentuk Tim, Wiranto Gerak, Pemimpim Majalah *Panji* Dijemput Paksa," *Jawa Pos*, February 20, 1999. In addition, both the wiretapper and the media outlets who aired the transcript could have been charged with violating Article 322 of the criminal code, which carried prison penalties for airing state secrets. See Indriyanto Seno Adji, "Pembocoran Berita dan Delik Pers," *Kompas*, February 23, 1999.

106. Quoted in "Soal Telpon, Habibie Marah Besar," *Jawa Pos*, February 24, 1999.

107. Adji, "Pembocoran Berita dan Delik Pers."

108. "Soal Telpon."

109. Conclusions from AJI discussion of the *Panji* case, Hotel Fortuna, Surabaya, February 25, 1999.

110. See "Hentikan Pemanggilan Wartawan," *Suara Merdeka*, February 24, 1999; Ichlasul Amal, "Interview: Jadi Sasaran Tembak," *Jawa Pos*, February 24, 1999.

111. "Anti-graft Body Has Ammo to Fight Further," *SCMP*, July 22, 1999; "ICW Distrusts Government's Stance on Ghalib Case," *JP*, July 22, 1999.

112. Janet Steele, "The Making of the 1999 Indonesian Press Law," *Indonesia* 94, no. 2 (October 2012): 1–22. The law, for example, guarantees press freedom as a basic civil right, codifies the right to protect sources and to access and disseminate information, and outlaws press censorship, banning, or attempts to block radio or television broadcasts. Law No. 40/1999.

113. Karin Deutsch Karlekar, *License to Censor: The Use of Media to Restrict Press Freedom* (Washington, DC: Freedom House, September 2011), 31, https://freedomhouse.org/sites/default/files/inline_images/License%20to%20Censor%20-%20Media%20Regulation%20Report.

114. "Pemerkosaan di Bulan Mei 1998"; "Jejak Cendana di Banyuwangi: Pengakuan Desertir Kopassus," *DëTAK*, November 3–9, 1998.

115. "Golkar Unveils Four Names for 1999/2004 Presidency," *JP*, February 17, 1999; "Golkar Tests Waters on Habibie: Analysts," *IO*, February 22, 1999; "Gerakan Gembosisasi Itu Telah Dimulai," *Jawa Pos*, February 24, 1999.

116. See, for example, Sheila S. Coronel, "The Role of the Media in Deepening Democracy," United Nations Public Administration Network, 2003, http://unpan1.un.org/intradoc/groups/public/documents/un/unpan010194.pdf; Silvio R. Waisbord, *Watchdog Journalism in South America: News, Accountability, and Democracy* (New York: Columbia University Press, 2000).

117. See, for example, "Pencalonan Habibie Sebagai Presiden: Sembilan Bulan Saja Habibie Tidak Mampu . . ." *Merdeka*, February 20, 1999; "Soal Penyadapan Telpon: Berdampak terhadap Pencalonan Habibie," *Kompas*, February 21, 1999; "Skandal Telepon, Kunci Karier Politik Habibie," *Suara Merdeka*, February 24, 1999; "Mungkin Sesaat Lagi Habibie Habis," *Demokrat*, February 1999; "Tesis: Ngotot Pun Habibie Akan Sulit," *Oposisi*, February 4–March 2, 1999; Dede N. P., Dahlan, and Junianto Setyadi, "Di Sana Clinton, di Sini Habibie," *Bangkit*, March 1–7, 1999.

118. Adam Przeworski, "Some Problems in the Study of Transition to Democracy," in *Transitions from Authoritarian Rule*, ed. Guillermo O'Donnell, Philippe C. Schmitter, and Laurence Whitehead (Baltimore: Johns Hopkins University Press, 1986), 58.

5. Media in Retreat

1. Personal observation, Aryaduta Hotel, Jakarta, June 22, 1999.

2. See, for example, the Team Seven member Ryaas Rasyid's interview in *Gatra*, September 22, 1998.

3. John McBeth, "Dawn of a New Age," *FEER*, September 17, 1998.

4. "Political Bills Offer No Guarantee of Fair Polls," *JP*, November 12, 1998.

5. See Michael Richardson, "Indonesia Braces for Vote on Reforms, *NYT*, November 9, 1998.

6. An exception was the United Development Party.

7. Jenny Grant, "Media Show Anger at Military Muscle," *SCMP*, November 13, 1998.

8. "Habibie Pledges to Stay until the End of 1999," *JP*, November 13, 1998.

9. "Political Bills Offer No Guarantee."

10. For example, Diah Purnomowati, Arif A. K., and Wenseslaus Manggut, "Mahasiswa Menuntut Parlemen Menentukan?" *Tempo*, November 9, 1998.

11. "Empat Tokoh Reformis Akhirnya Bertemu," *Kompas*, November 11, 1998; "'SI Tandingan' di Ciganjur," *MI*, November 11, 1998.

12. *Cakrawala* and *Gema Senayan*, ANteve, November 11, 1998; *Liputan 6 Petang*, SCTV, November 11, 1998; Syamsul Ma'arif, interview, SCTV, November 11, 1998; *Sekilas Info* and *Seputar Indonesia*, RCTI, November 11, 1998; *Berita Nasional* and *Dunia Dalam Berita*, TVRI, November 11, 1998.

13. *Liputan 6 Petang*, SCTV, November 12, 1998.

14. *Bulletin Malam*, RCTI, November 12, 1998.

15. MPR Resolution No. 11 (No. XI/MPR/1998) included an explicit directive to prosecute Suharto in Article 4.

16. Harmoko, speech before the MPR, November 13, 1998, broadcast on *Liputan Sidang Istimewa MPR—Rapat Paripurna IV*, TVRI, November 13, 1998.

17. Jakarta-based journalists, personal communication, November 13, 1998. See also Louise Williams, "Students Bay for Blood as Politicians Jostle for Position," *SMH*, November 14, 1998.

18. W. Kukuh Sanyoto, interview with author, Jakarta, May 19, 1999.

19. *Berita Nasional*, TVRI, November 13, 1998.

20. B. J. Habibie, televised address, *Berita Nasional*, TVRI, November 14, 1998.

21. On November 13, Indosiar announced that "out of control security forces" had beaten up several citizens described as "powerless," and explained that city bus drivers did not mind

carrying students to demonstrations "precisely because they support the students." *Fokus*, Indosiar, November 13, 1998.

22. *Aktualitas*, ANteve, November 13, 1998.

23. *Cakrawala*, ANteve, November 13, 1998; *Liputan 6 Petang*, SCTV, November 13, 1998.

24. *Berita Nasional*, TVRI, November 12, 1998.

25. 7:00 p.m. report, TVRI, November 13, 1998.

26. Amien Rais, interview, *Seputar Indonesia*, RCTI, November 13, 1998.

27. Ibid.

28. The station did balance this perspective by interviewing Mar'ie Muhammad, a former finance minister but identified as a "former student activist," who demanded an explanation from the military and that those involved be put on trial. *Seputar Indonesia*, RCTI, November 13, 1998.

29. With the exception of two interviews with Abdurrahman Wahid, on *Seputar Indonesia*, RCTI, November 11, 1998, and *Cakrawala*, ANteve, November 14, 1998.

30. *Liputan 6 Petang*, SCTV, November 14, 1998.

31. See, for example, statements by MUI representatives (*Berita Nasional*, TVRI, November 13, 1998), Amien Rais (*Berita Nasional*, TVRI, November 13, 1998), and Agung Laksono (*Liputan 6 Petang*, SCTV, November 14, 1998).

32. Harmoko, statement broadcast on *Liputan Sidang Istimewa MPR—Rapat Paripurna IV*, TVRI, November 13, 1998.

33. *Dunia Dalam Berita*, TVRI, November 13, 1998.

34. *Fokus*, Indosiar, November 14, 1998.

35. B. J. Habibie, *Aktualitas*, ANteve, November 14, 1998.

36. "Calls Mount for Habibie and Wiranto to Step Down," *JP*, November 16, 1998; "Pressure on Habibie, Wiranto to Resign," AFP, November 14, 1998; *Berita Nasional*, TVRI, November 14, 1998; *Persepsi*, TVRI, November 14, 1998. Indosiar aired demands that Wiranto resign. *Fokus*, Indosiar, November 14, 1998. But coverage on the other private stations focused almost solely on the theme of unseen forces manipulating the students. *Cakrawala*, ANteve, November 14, 1998; *Liputan 6 Petang*, SCTV, November 14, 1998; *Seputar Indonesia*, RCTI, November 14, 1998.

37. Wimar Witoelar, "Black Friday Due to Impudence," *JP*, November 21, 1998.

38. Achmad Tirto Sudiro, *Berita Nasional*, TVRI, November 14, 1998.

39. *Dunia Dalam Berita*, TVRI, November 14, 1998.

40. Indosiar's coverage was an exception. See *Fokus*, Indosiar, November 14, 1998.

41. Alih Saham, "Rongrongan Gaya Orde Baru," *WartaEkonomi*, December 1, 1998.

42. Greg Earl, "Habibie Supporters Move to Control TV Networks," *Australian Financial Review*, November 24, 1998.

43. Imam Wahjoe L., "Tarik-Ulur Pasal Status Quo," *D&R*, January 25–30, 1999.

44. "Experts Discount Social Revolution but Urge Caution," *JP*, December 28, 1998. See also John McBeth, "Dawn of a New Age," *FEER*, September 17, 1998.

45. Djufri Asmoredjo, quoted in Karaniya Dharmasaputra and Edy Budyarso, "Tukar Guling dan Jurus Pelampung," *Tempo*, January 25, 1999.

46. Sander Thoenes, "Path for Free Elections Cleared," *FT*, January 28, 1999.

47. "Dinamika Pemilu Daerah," *Kompas*, May 7, 1999.

48. See, for example, "LDP [Liberal Democratic Party] Denies Pledge to Aid Golkar Scheme," *JP*, March 26, 1999; "Netralitas Pemilu Masih Terancam," *Berita Buana*, March 26, 1999; "PRD Akan Boikot Pemilu," *Inti Jaya*, March 26, 1999; "KIPP Protes Terhadap Parpol Diskriminasi," *Inti Jaya*, March 26, 1999; "Keterlaluan, Minta Gaji Rp 10 Juta," *Merdeka*, March 25, 1999; "Lho, Itu Kan Gaji Presiden," *Merdeka*, March 25, 1999; "Andi Mallarangeng Dimaafkan," *Merdeka*, March 25, 1999; "Mobil Anggota KPU Dibagikan," *Merdeka*, March 25, 1999; "ABRI Sedang Pilih-Pilih Partai," *Merdeka*, March 24, 1999; "Parpol Dilarang Terima Bantuan Asing," *MI*, March 24, 1999; "Parpol Tidak Boleh Terima Bantuan dari Negara Asing," *MI*, March 22, 1999; "Masih Sulit Hilangkan Kebiasaan Lama Golkar," *Kompas*, March 23, 1999; "Saksi Mata 'Money Politcs' di MPR: Diberi Jas dan Diajak Main Golf," *Merdeka*, March 22, 1999; "Tokoh-tokoh Barnas: Hanya Golkar Yang Mampu Sogok Anggota MPR Rp1 10 M," *Merdeka*, March 22, 1999. On KPU corruption, see "Tatkala Anggota KPU Bermobil Baru," *MI*, March 27, 1999; "Analysts Express Doubts about KPU's Credibility," *JP*, March 26, 1999; "Netralitas Pemilu Masih Terancam."

49. This observation is based on a survey of evening news on five television stations and print coverage in six national newspapers from January to May 1999.

50. This figure is based on an estimate of 112 million votes cast. Seth Mydans, "Delays Mount in Indonesia Vote Count," *NYT*, June 27, 1999. The number of registered voters (127.6 million) is based on KPU figures. "KIPP Records 19,504 Violations," *JP*, July 10, 1999.

51. Carter was quoted in a number of articles at the time. "Carter Group Sees 'Festival of Democracy' in Indonesia," Kyodo News Service, June 9, 1999; Indira Lakshmanan, "Carter Gives a Good Grade to Indonesian Free Election," *Boston Globe*, June 9, 1999; "Japan Hails Indonesian Polls as Free and Fair," AFP, June 9, 1999; "Indonesia Poll Free and Fair: Japan's Top Monitor," Jiji Press Ticker Service, June 9, 1999; "Indon Election Free, Fair and a Triumph, Downer Declares," AAP Newsfeed, June 8, 1999; "Observers, Officials Say Indonesian Elections Free, Fair," Xinhua News Agency, June 8, 1999; "A Big Step for Indonesia," *LAT*, June 9, 1999.

52. "Asian Observers Say Indonesian Polls Free Except in East Timor, Aceh," AFP, June 10, 1999.

53. These figures exclude violations in Aceh and East Timor. Atika Shubert, "Indonesia Tally Delayed Again amid Charges of Voter Fraud," *JP/IHT*, June 10, 1999. The number of polling stations is taken from "Komisi Pemilihan Umum," in the International Press Information Kit distributed at the JOMC, Aryaduta Hotel, Jakarta, May 18, 1999.

54. "Some Areas Demand that Polls Be Repeated," *JP*, June 10, 1999.

55. Ibid.

56. "Delays Plague Provincial Ballot Counts," *JP*, June 29, 1999.

57. "Observations on the Elections," anonymous submission to Joyo News Service, June 14, 1999, http//:www.asia-pacific solidarity.net/southeastasia/indonesia/netnews/1999/and24_v3.htm#More%20reports%20on%20poll%20violations%20flow%20in.

58. "How They Share the 462 DPR seats," *JP*, July 16, 1999; "Vote Gained by Top Five Parties for DPR," press release, JOMC, 6:02 p.m.–8:17 p.m., July 14, 1999.

59. "Some Areas Demand."

60. "Money Politics," editorial, *JP*, May 12, 1999. Further evidence of misappropriation came out in later scandals, such as Buloggate II. Bill Guerin, "Indonesia Prepares Black Sheep for Sacrifice," *AT*, October 26, 2001.

61. John McBeth, "Unpopular Decision: Election Overseers Allow Party Leaders to Decide Who Wins," *FEER*, May 6, 1999.

62. Reports from the General Election Commission's Joint Operations Media Center reinforced this impression. For example, its report on June 15 projected that PDIP, with 35.5 percent of the popular vote, would win 139 seats, while Golkar, with only 20.7 percent, would capture just 99 seats. "Indonesian Election: PDI-P Ahead with 58% Votes Counted," press release, JOMC, June 15, 1999.

63. The Golkar-dominated Irian Jaya received thirteen seats for its population of two million, while the opposition-party stronghold of Jakarta was allocated only eighteen seats for its population of ten million—meaning there was one seat for every 282,000 registered voters in Jakarta versus one seat for every 77,000 in Irian Jaya. "How They Share." See also "Vote Gained by Top Five Parties for DPR," press release, JOMC, 6:02 p.m.–8:17 p.m., June 14, 1999.

64. See, for example, Robert Caro's description of how Lyndon Johnson won the 1948 US Senate race by holding back his tallies in the machine-controlled Rio Grande Valley until he knew his opponent's total and then trumping him with late reports. Robert A. Caro, *The Years of Lyndon Johnson: Means of Ascent* (London: Bodley Head, 1990), 181–91, 264–67, 307–17.

65. "Vote Gained by Top Five Parties for DPR," press release, JOMC, 7:20 a.m.–4:18 p.m., June 10, 1999.

66. Ibid.

67. "Vote Gained by Top Five Parties for DPR," press release, JOMC, 6:02 p.m.–8:17 p.m., June 14, 1999.

68. Based on the 1999 election law (UU No. 3/1999) and detailed in a National Election Commission decree (Surat Keputusan KPU No. 40/1999), the imbalanced electoral system gave each province one seat for every 450,000 residents and automatically granted an additional seat to all Level II voting districts in each province (*kabupaten* and *kotamadya*, or "regencies" and "townships"), regardless of population. Thus, dozens of regencies and townships in the less populous outer islands, versus almost none in Java and Bali, gained added value per vote. This electoral logic, as veteran observer Aristides Katoppo later affirmed, allowed pro-Golkar forces

to delay release of final tallies from these secure outer island provinces until the count indicated the number of seats they would need to form a government. Aristides Katoppo, personal communication, Jakarta, June 9, 1999.

69. Data on the 1997 elections is from David Jenkins, "The New Indonesia: Soeharto's Legacy," *SMH*, October 27, 1998.

70. "Hidup PDI Perjuangan, Hidup Amien Rais," *Tempo*, May 24–30, 1999.

71. Tanjung predicted that Golkar would win at least 102 of the 462 seats contested, compared to his estimate of 137 for PDIP. Shoeb Kagda, "Habibie Will Get Enough Votes: Golkar," *Business Times* (Singapore), July 3, 1999.

72. Gerry van Klinken, "Indonesia's Politics Enters a New Ball Game," opinion, *JP*, August 11, 1999.

73. Together the Islamic parties—United Development Party (PPP), Justice Party (PK), the Crescent Star Party (PBB), and several smaller ones—stood to win up to 12 percent of available seats. Kafil Yamin, "Presidential Aspirant Walks Political Minefield," IPS, July 1, 1999.

74. Kagda, "Habibie Will Get Enough."

75. "How They Share." Although the original number of MPR representatives that would select the next president had been set at seven hundred, the five provincial delegates from East Timor could not be chosen in September, given conditions there following the August 30 referendum, reducing total MPR membership to 695.

76. Three months later, *Kompas* estimated that the number of votes for a Habibie presidency, through coalition building, could be as high as 295 if one added Golkar's 120 to the United Development Party's possible 40 to 70 votes from representatives of provinces Golkar had won in the parliamentary elections and 65 from the sectoral representatives. Votes for Megawati, the paper predicted, would likely reach a maximum of 233. C. P. F. Luhulima, "Hitung-hitungan Presiden RI Medatang," *Kompas*, October 8, 1999.

77. For one exception, see Derwin Pereira, "Golkar Expecting Fewer Votes than PDIP," *ST*, June 10, 1999.

78. "Ballot Counting Runs at a Snail's Pace," *JP*, June 9, 1999; "Delays Plague Provincial Ballot Counts"; Seth Mydans, "Delays in Vote Count Have Indonesians Worried about Cheating," *NYT*, June 10, 1999. Though more balanced, the *Financial Times* also quoted KPU statements uncritically. Sander Thoenes, "Fret over Slow Result," *FT*, June 10, 1999. See also Grainne McCarthy, "Indonesian Market Euphoria Turns Sour as Vote Count Drags," DJ, June 10, 1999; John McBeth, "Counter-Productive: Frustrations Grow as Poll Count Drags On," *FEER*, July 7, 1999; "Political Bickering Clouds Indonesian Vote Count a Month after Polls," AFP, July 7, 1999.

79. Primadi's words were "Ada keganjilan . . . ," which he translated for me at the time as "There is something fishy. . . ." Riza Primadi, personal communication, Aryaduta Hotel, Jakarta, June 9, 1999.

80. Riza Primadi, personal communication, Aryaduta Hotel, Jakarta, June 10, 1999. I later asked why his station was paying so little attention to the reports of cheating that arrived each day from the various independent monitoring groups. He explained that there were too many; if SCTV began reporting some, they would have to report them all, and that would be "too much for one screen." Riza Primadi, personal communication, Aryaduta Hotel, Jakarta, June 12, 1999.

81. Hans (*Pro-Kontra*), Rio (*Sehat*), Ansel Deri (*Rajawali*), and Djoko Murnantyo (*Penabur*), personal communication, Jakarta, June 12, 1999.

82. Raymond Kaya, personal communication, Jakarta, June 12, 1999.

83. Even the *Jakarta Post*, one of the most critical voices in the Indonesian press, gave credibility to this explanation in extensive quotes from the KPU. "Ballot Counting Runs"; "KPU Agrees to Restart Selection of Interest Groups," *JP*, August 10, 1999. See also "Buyung Vows to Investigate Alleged KPU Corruption," *JP*, June 28, 1999; "Corruption out of Hand in Padang," *JP*, June 28, 1999.

84. Personal observation, Aryaduta Hotel, Jakarta, June 22, 1999.

85. "Pemilu 1999," *Kompas.com*, accessed July 27, 2014, http://indonesiasatu.kompas.com/pemilumasa.

86. While *Tempo* was the most aggressive of the mainstream newsweeklies in its coverage of election fraud, several others also produced cover-story exposés, including "Membonkar Kolusi di KPU," *Tajuk*, June 24, 1999, and "Pemilu Bagi-bagi Uang: Baramuli Digugat Utang Jutaan Dolar," *Gamma*, July 25, 1999.

87. Ahmad Taufik and Verrianto Madjowa, "Sebar Uang, Pemilu Diulang," *Tempo*, June 21–27, 1999. *Tempo*'s follow-up stories on Baramuli included "Baramuli, Sang Operator," *Tempo*, August 30–September 5, 1999," and "Faktor Baramuli Itu," *Tempo*, September 20–26, 1999.

88. "Pemilu 1999: Kesempurnaan Yang Retak," *Tempo*, June 28–July 4, 1999.

89. After its own investigation, Indonesia's Central Election Supervising Committee (Panwaspus) corroborated the *Tempo* reports and recommended legal action against Baramuli, who responded by threatening to sue *Tempo* for libel. "Election Watchdog Wants Baramuli Tried," *IO*, July 22, 1999.

90. Reluctance to promote competitors can also reduce follow-up reporting. For example, see Duncan McCargo, *Politics and the Press in Thailand* (London: Routledge, 2000), 168.

91. A conversation in May 2001 with Frans Seda, who served as finance minister to Suharto and economic advisor to Habibie, confirmed this reading and also explained why his party, PDIP, made little protest in response to Golkar's manipulation of the electoral process. Seda said that not only was PDIP disorganized at that time but also, after so many years of getting only a very small percentage of the vote in the elections of the New Order, party members were barely able to believe that the 1999 elections had been fair enough to allow their party to be in the lead at all. Personal communication, Madison, WI, May 19, 2001.

92. "10 Parties 'Shared Rp 109b from Bulog,'" *JP*, March 16, 2002; Marianne Kearney, "Media 'Also Received Bulog Funds,'" *ST*, June 20, 2002.

93. Wahid reportedly asked Wiranto for "assurances that the military would stay neutral right up to the presidential election." Derwin Pereira, "Gus Dur's Hush-Hush Talks with Wiranto," *ST*, June 10, 1999.

94. Personal observation, Jakarta, July 1999.

95. Keith B. Richburg, "Election Protest Sparks Violence in Indonesia," *IHT/WP*, July 2, 1999.

96. Personal observations at the scene of the shooting. *Forum Keadilan* published a close-up photo of the violence on its cover on July 11, 1999.

97. Desi Anwar, "Indonesian Politics a Far Cry from Democracy," *JP*, July 22, 1999.

98. John Aglionby, "Indonesia in Turmoil over Poll Dispute," *Guardian*, July 26, 1999. The dissenting parties together won 6.38 percent of the approximately 117 million votes cast. The seventeen parties who did sign off won 93 percent. Four parties did not show up. Jeremy Wagstaff and Puspa Madani, "Several Indonesian Parties Refuse to Ratify Election, Delaying Results," *WSJ*, July 27, 1999; Anwar, "Indonesian Politics"; "Political Bickering." See also Nicole Gaouette, "Sour Grapes Spoil Indonesia Election Result," *Christian Science Monitor*, July 28, 1999.

99. "KPU Agrees to Restart."

100. Jusuf Wanandi, "The Next Move in Indonesian Politics," opinion, *JP*, July 28, 1999.

101. Ibid. Both alternatives—that is, allowing the winning party in each region to take all five seats for that region and the KPU's preference to assign the five seats per region to reflect the votes won by all parties—would add to Golkar's lead.

102. "KPU Agrees to Restart."

103. Ibid.

104. Lukas Luwarso, personal communication, July 24, 1999; Haris Jauhari, email correspondence, August 11, 1999.

105. Haris Jauhari, email correspondence, August 16, 1999.

106. Haris Jauhari, personal communication, Jakarta, July 28, 1999.

107. Haris Jauhari, personal communication, Jakarta, July 27, 1999.

108. Ibid.

109. Lukas Luwarso, email correspondence, August 13, 1999.

110. Haris Jauhari, email correspondence, August 11, 1999.

111. Luwarso, email correspondence, August 13, 1999; Jauhari, email correspondence, August 16, 1999.

112. Letter to the head of the General Election Commission, "Pernyataan sikap 20 organisasi wartawan menolak keberadaan utusan golongan wartawan di MPR," Jakarta, August 11, 1999. The letter was signed by Lukas Luwarso (Alliance of Indonesian Journalists), Haris Jauhari (Indonesian Television Journalists Association), Budiman S. Hartoyo (Indonesian Journalist Association-Reformasi), Arbain Rambey (Indonesian Photojournalists Association), Ichsan Loulembah (Indonesian Alliance of Radio Journalists), and M.A. Nasution, representing the Indonesian Press Society, a group consisting of fifteen journalists' organizations.

113. Haris Jauhari, email correspondence, August 20, 1999.

114. Letter to the head of the General Election Commission.

115. Jauhari, email correspondence, August 20, 1999.

116. With the elimination of East Timor's five provincial seats, the minimum number of MPR votes Habibie would need to secure the presidency was 348 (out of 695). Eleven days before the October 20 election, *Kompas* predicted that Habibie was likely to win at least 333 votes, including 70 from the provincial candidates of the 14 provinces Golkar had won, and "as many as 65" from the sectoral groups whose representatives "for the most part," *Kompas* said, "had been chosen by B.J. Habibie." By contrast, PDIP's candidate, Megawati, would likely win only 233 votes: 153 from her own party, 55 from provincial delegates, 15 now expected from the National Awakening Party (Wahid's party), and up to 10 from two of the smaller parties—the Justice and Unity Party and the Love the Nation Democratic Party. The paper predicted the military's 38 representatives would not support her. Luhulima, "Hitung-hitungan Presiden RI Mendatang."

117. Notable exceptions included *Tempo*, whose June investigative reports are discussed above, and the *Jakarta Post*, which did not play up accounts of irregularities, but did publish regular reports as they came in.

6. BALIGATE AND ALL THE GATES

1. Quoted in David Jenkins, "The Awful Choice," *Age*, October 19, 1999, https://www.newspapers.com/newspage/123512452/.

2. "60,000 Troops to Secure MPR Session," *JP*, September 25, 1999.

3. Adam Przeworski, "Some Problems in the Study of Transition to Democracy," in *Transitions from Authoritarian Rule*, ed. Guillermo O'Donnell, Philippe C. Schmitter, and Laurence Whitehead (Baltimore: Johns Hopkins University Press, 1986), 58.

4. J. Samuel Valenzuela, "Democratic Consolidation in Post-transitional Settings: Notion, Process and Facilitating Conditions," in *Issues in Democratic Consolidation: The New South American Democracies in Comparative Perspective*, ed. Scott Mainwaring, Guillermo O'Donnell, and J. Samuel Valenzuela (Notre Dame, IN: University of Notre Dame Press, 1992), 9.

5. Ibid., 9–10.

6. Ahmad Taufik and Verrianto Madjowa, "Sebar Uang, Pemilu Diulang," *Tempo*, June 21–27, 1999.

7. "Bank Bali Dibobol Habibie," SiaR email list, July 30, 1999.

8. "Bank Bali Believed to Be Involved in 'Money Politics,'" *Kompas*, July 31, 1999.

9. "Indonesia: Golkar Executive Denies Party Got Money from Bank Bali," Antara, August 3, 1999. That evening, SCTV forced Bank Indonesia's governor, Sjahril Sabirin, to comment. "Sjahril Vows Probe into IBRA Scandal," *JP*, August 4, 1999.

10. "Baligate: The Political Fallout," *ST*, August 15, 1999.

11. "The People's Money," *JP*, August 11, 1999.

12. Sanjoto Sastromihardjo, "Skandal Bank Bali 'Dipindah-rel-kan'?," *Business News*, August 10, 1999, reprinted in *Reformasi dalam Perspektif Sanjoto* (Jakarta: Yayasan Orbor Indonesia, 1999), 248–50; Jay Solomon, "In Indonesia, Crisis and Corruption Are Creating Financial Vigilantes," *WSJ*, September 21, 1999.

13. "Prominent Figures Responsible for Bank Bali Scam: Analyst," *Asia Pulse*, August 10, 1999.

14. Solomon, "In Indonesia, Crisis and Corruption."

15. "Golkar Terancam Diskualifikasi," SiaR email list, August 4, 1999.

16. "Tim Habibie Bobol Bank Bali," *Xpos* no. 27/II, August 8–14, 1999.

17. "IBRA Says Bank Bali US$80 Mln Commission May Be Cancelled," AFP, August 9, 1999.

18. "Delapan Pejabat BPPN Diperiksa," *SP*, August 13, 1999.

19. Kevin O'Rourke, *Reformasi: The Struggle for Power in Post-Soeharto Indonesia* (Crows Nest, Australia: Allen & Unwin, 2003), 247.

20. O'Rourke, *Reformasi*, 248. Baramuli was also the main figure in *Tempo*'s June Sulawesi election fraud exposé.

21. "Beredarnya Rekaman Ghalib-Habibie: Halo, Ghalib dan Habibie di Sini," *Panji Masyarakat*, February 24, 1999.

22. "The 10 Suspects," *ST*, August 15, 1999. See also Reiner Simanjuntak, "Frustration Escalates as Bank Bali Scandal Drags On," *JP*, September 20, 1999.

23. "The People's Money."

24. "Parliament's Special Team Should Not Disappoint Traders," *Kompas*, September 23, 1999.

25. Solomon, "In Indonesia, Crisis and Corruption."

26. "Pertarungan Golkar 'Hitam' dan 'Putih,'" *Suara Merdeka*, August 11, 1999; "Baligate: The Political Fallout," *ST*, August 15, 1999.

27. "Activist Says Marzuki Leaked Bank Bali Story," *JP*, August 13, 1999.

28. Wimar Witoelar, "The Role of the Media and the Recent Changes in Indonesian Politics," University of Wisconsin–Madison, Center for Southeast Asian Studies Friday Forum Lecture Series, October 22, 1999.

29. Solomon, "In Indonesia, Crisis and Corruption"; "Yudono Defends Keeping Full PwC Audit under Wrap," *JP*, September 30, 1999.

30. Witoelar, "Role of the Media."

31. National Democratic Institute, *The 1999 Presidential Election and Post-election Developments in Indonesia* (Washington, DC: National Democratic Institute, November 28, 1999), https://ndi.org/sites/default/files/1079_id_preselect_5.pdf.

32. "Rudy Says Journal Exists, Keeps Mum on Contracts," *JP*, September 10, 1999; Simanjuntak, "Frustration Escalates."

33. "House Team Says Baramuli Is Involved in Bank Bali Scandal," *JP*, September 18, 1999.

34. "Yudono Defends."

35. Quoted in Simanjuntak, "Frustration Escalates."

36. Sander Thoenes, "Military's Power Undimmed by Humiliations," *FT*, September 21, 1999.

37. Ibid.

38. "Menanti Runtuhnya Rupiah," *Kontan*, September 20, 1999; "Bocoran Pricewaterhouse dan Jejak Sang Menteri," *Tempo*, September 13, 1999. "Baramuli off the Hook—Intervention, Cover-Ups Mar Baligate Revelation," *IO*, September 23, 1999; "Ronde Pamungkas Bank Bali," *Tempo*, September 27, 1999.

39. Interview with Tony A. Prasetyantono, "All the President's Men Simply Buy Time," *JP*, September 24, 1999.

40. "Parliament's Special Team."

41. Law No. 40/1999.

42. "TNI" replaced "ABRI" (Angkatan Bersenjata Republik Indonesia, or Armed Forces of the Republic of Indonesia) as the name for Indonesia's military in April 1999, reflecting a new separation from the national police.

43. Thoenes, "Military's Power Undimmed."

44. "State Security Bill Faces Tough Protest," *JP*, September 15, 1999.

45. "Indonesian Students Return to Parliament to Protest," AFP, September 17, 1999.

46. Ted Bardacke, "Indonesian Students Killed in Protest against New Law," *FT*, September 24, 1999.

47. "More Antisecurity Bill Protests Hit Jakarta," *JP*, September 16, 1999; "PAN and PKB Reject State Security Bill," *JP*, September 17, 1999.

48. "Parties Rethink State Security Bill," *JP*, September 20, 1999.

49. "Indonesian Parliament Approved Army-Backed Bill on State Security," AFP, September 23, 1999.

50. "A Dubious Accomplishment," *JP*, September 24, 1999.

51. J. Wagstaff and M. Puspa, "Thousands of Indonesians Protest Security Bill Passed by Parliament," *WSJ*, September 24, 1999.

52. "Warning Shots, Teargas Fired to Disperse Indonesian Protests," AFP, September 23, 1999.

53. "University to Probe Death of Student in Jakarta Military Shooting," AFP, September 25, 1999.

54. "Akhirnya, Pemerintah Tunda RUU PKB," *Kompas*, September 25, 1999.

55. "Deliberation of State Emergency Bill to End," *JP*, September 22, 1999; "Indonesian President Delays Approval of the New Security Bill," AFP, September 24, 1999.

56. "Groups Lash Out at President, Military Chief over Protest Violence," AFP, September 25, 1999. For this statement and a list of the groups that issued it, see Yayasan Selendang Lila,

"Pernyataan Solidaritas untuk Demokrasi Indonesia," *Jaringan Pendidikan Lingkungan* (blog), September 26, 1999, https://groups.yahoo.com/neo/groups/jpl/conversations/messages/383.

57. "Indonesian President Delays Approval"; "Akhirnya, Pemerintah Tunda RUU PKB."

58. Juwono Sudarsono, quoted in "Habibie Ready to Give Up Power, Juwono Says," *JP*, September 27, 1999.

59. Mustofa, "Menimbang Kemungkinan Megawati," *Kompas*, October 15, 1999.

60. Jeremy Wagstaff, "Dark before Dawn: How Elite Made a Deal before Indonesia Woke Up," *WSJ*, November 2, 1999.

61. Jose Manuel Tesoro, "All Bets Are Off: In the Race for the Presidency, New Power Balances Are Surfacing," *Asiaweek*, October 15, 1999.

62. Jenkins, "Awful Choice."

63. Witoelar, "Role of the Media."

64. Quoted in John McBeth and Margot Cohen, "Unlikely Victor," *FEER*, October 28, 1999.

65. Witoelar, "Role of the Media."

66. National Democratic Institute, "1999 Presidential Election," 16.

67. Tesoro, "All Bets Are Off."

68. Nisid Hajari, "Taking It Right Down to the Wire," *Time*, October 25, 1999.

69. A "former political party leader" quoted in Jenkins, "Awful Choice."

70. "Press Freedom, Elections Are Habibie's Only Good Points: Poll," AFP, October 17, 1999.

71. Hajari, "Taking It Right Down."

72. David Lamb, "On Election Eve, Who Will Head Indonesia Is in Doubt," *LAT*, October 19, 1999.

73. Quoted in Jenkins, "Awful Choice."

74. Ibid.

75. Wagstaff, "Dark before Dawn." For more on backroom maneuvering during these two days, see "What Went On behind the Scenes," *Business Times* (Singapore), October 22, 1999.

76. Ron Moreau, "Duel of the Shadow Puppets: Don't Trust Appearances in This Week's Presidential Contest," *Newsweek International*, October 25, 1999.

77. Wagstaff, "Dark before Dawn."

78. Ibid.

79. "Megawati Party Accepts Defeat with Grace, Angry Followers Go on Rampage," AFP, October 20, 1999.

80. Ahmad Taufik and Verrianto Madjowa, "Sebar Uang, Pemilu Diulang," *Tempo*, June 21–27, 1999; *Tempo* staff, "Pemilu 1999: Kesempurnaan Yang Retak," *Tempo*, June 28–July 4, 1999.

81. "Election Watchdog Wants Baramuli Tried," *IO*, July 2, 1999.

82. "Panwas: 'Tindak Baramuli!' Diduga Lakukan Money Politics," *Suara Merdeka*, July 2, 1999.

83. *The New Oxford American Dictionary*, 3rd ed. (2010), s.v. "scandal."

84. "Baligate: The Political Fallout," *ST*, August 15, 1999.

85. "Election Watchdog."

86. "10 Parties 'Shared Rp 109b from Bulog,'" *JP*, March 16, 2002. On the diversion of funds to over two dozen media outlets and numerous religious organizations, see Marianne Kearney, "Media 'Also Received Bulog Funds,'" *ST*, June 20, 2002.

87. "10 Parties."

7. Scandal and Democratic Consolidation

1. "DPR Receives PwC's Full Audit Report," *JP*, October 20, 1999.

2. The joint committee formed from DPR Commissions II and IX.

3. "DPR Receives PwC's Full Audit Report."

4. "Indonesian President Urges Media to Be Tough with New Government," AFP, October 27, 1999.

5. Quoted in "Wahid's Strategy," AFP, February 14, 2000.

6. "Wiranto's Exit," editorial, *JP*, February 15, 2000.

7. "House Won't Oust Wahid: Speaker," *IO*, January 27, 2000. See also "Lower House to Summon Commander over US Envoy's Coup Rumour," *Rakyat Merdeka*, January 19, 2000.

8. "Wahid Says Sorry as Former Suharto Party Flexes Its Muscles," AFP, July 21, 2000.

9. George J. Aditjondro, "Focusing on Bulog, Brunei Scams," *JP*, January 10, 2001.

10. "PBB Seeks to Impeach Gus Dur over Communism Issue," *JP*, April 15, 2000.

11. See "Progress Will Require a Change of Attitude from Gus Dur," *IO*, June 28, 2000. For more corruption under Wahid, see George J. Aditjondro, "Post-Suharto Multi-party Corruption in Indonesia: The Absence of Control Mechanisms," paper presented at CAPSTRANS conference, University of Wollongong, NSW, Australia, December 4–6, 2000.

12. Achmad Sukarsono, "Outgoing Presidential Aide Warns of Indonesia Plot," Reuters, May 30, 2000.

13. "Bulogate," *JP*, May 30, 2000.

14. Johan Budi et al., "Return of the Masseur," *Tempo*, October 16–22, 2000.

15. Nuruddin Lazuardi, "Marathon Questioning for 'Abducted' Bulog Thief," *Dëtikworld*, May 26, 2000.

16. Marianne Kearney, "Weapons against Corruption (Indonesia), Where Have All the Rupiah Gone?" *ST*, May 20, 2001.

17. "Bulogate."

18. Budi et al., "Return of the Masseur."

19. Early uses of the term used the spelling "Bulogate." By the time the second major Bulog scandal broke, the most common spelling for both used the double *g*.

20. Lukamnul Hakim et al., "The Plot Thickens in the Case of Bulog's Missing Millions," *Detikworld*, May 25, 2000.

21. Devi Asmarani, "Lawmakers Launch New Probe into Bulog," *ST*, June 10, 2000.

22. "Gus Dur Told to Explain Bulogate," *JP*, May 31, 2000.

23. Asmarani, "Lawmakers Launch New Probe."

24. "House Speaker Akbar Hit by Graft Allegations," *JP*, July 10, 2000.

25. "ICW Urges Probe on Corruption Allegedly Involving House Chief," *IO*, September 22, 2000.

26. "Akbar Dismisses Call for Probe into Alleged Scams," *JP*, January 18, 2001.

27. "President's OK Needed to Question Akbar," *JP*, February 20, 2001.

28. "PDI-P, PKB Propose Probe into Other Scandals, Bombings," *JP*, February 3, 2001. See also D. Sangga Buana, Rin Hindrayati, and Lyndal Meehan, "Bank Liquidity Assistance Scandal: 16 Banks Tamper with Evidence," *Detikworld*, June 12, 2000.

29. Quoted in "PDI-P, PKB Propose Probe."

30. "Heboh Foto Intim Gus Dur-Aryanti," *Gatra*, August 28, 2000; "Aryanti Boru Sitepu: Gus Dur Bohongi Saya," *Panji Masyarakat*, September 6, 2000; "Aryanti Sengaja Menghina Presiden?," *Forum Keadilan*, September 10, 2000. See also Richard Lloyd Parry, "Clerical President Denies Sex Scandal," *Independent* (UK), August 30, 2000, https://www.independent.ie/world-news/clerical-president-denies-sex-scandal-26112725.html.

31. "Mahfud Clarifies Allegation of Golkar's Misuse of Funds," *JP*, February 14, 2001. Mahfud later acknowledged his source as the coordinating minister for the economy and former Bulog chief, Rizal Ramli.

32. "Rais Backs Investigation into Golkargate," *IO*, February 22, 2001.

33. Calvin Sims, "Indonesian President Goes on TV to Deny Corruption Allegations," *NYT*, January 31, 2001.

34. Jay Solomon and Puspa Madani, "Probe Targets Money Scandals Tied to Indonesia's Wahid," *AWSJ*, August 28, 2000.

35. Tom Wright and I. Made Sentana, "Exclusive: Indonesian Lawmakers Say Wahid Broke Law," *DJ*, January 31, 2001.

36. Dini Djalal, "Wahid Keeps a Nation Guessing as to His Fate," *Bangkok Post*, May 30, 2001; Lindsay Murdoch, "Wahid Apology Fails to Satisfy MPs," *SMH*, March 29, 2001.

37. Quoted in "Hadiah Istimewa Gus Dur untuk Wartawan: Kritik," *Kompas*, February 18, 2000.

38. Quoted in "Juwono Lashes Out at Private Television Stations," *JP*, April 17, 2000.

39. Quoted in "There Is a Print Media Conspiracy to Unseat Gus Dur: PKB," *JP*, October 6, 2000.

40. Quoted in "President Abdurrahman Says Some Media Get Paid to Spread Lies," *JP*, November 19, 2000.

41. Quoted in "Mahfud Blasts Media for Being Anti-government," *IO*, January 22, 2001.

42. "Indonesia Bars Foreign Journalists from Hotspots," Reuters, January 26, 2001.

43. Quoted in "Banser Para-military Preparing to Come to the Aid of 'No Worries' Wahid," *Laksamana.Net*, January 22, 2001, http://joyonews.org/JoyoNews.php?link=31170.

44. "President Orders 'Self-Censorship' of State Television Network," *Tempo*, March 26, 2001.

45. Quoted in "Wahid a Victim of Prejudiced Press," *Bangkok Post*, March 25, 2001.

46. Quoted ibid.

47. "Gus Dur Plans to Sue Media for Spreading Lies," *JP*, May 10, 2001.

48. Quoted in "Govt Establishes Media Watchdog," *IO*, May 11, 2001.

49. "Order Issued to Restore Security," *JP*, May 29, 2001; "Character Assassination and Criticism in the Indonesian Media," editorial, *Laksamana.Net*, June 25, 2001, http://joyonews.org/JoyoNews.php?link=39495.

50. "A Chronology of Wahid's 21 Months in Power," AFP, July 24, 2001.

51. Ibid.

52. Richard Lloyd Parry, "Embattled Wahid Says He Will Not Stand Down," *Independent* (UK), July 23, 2001.

53. "Gus Dur Suspends MPR, DPR," *JP*, July 23, 2001.

54. "Indonesian Military Opposed to Wahid's Decree," AFP, July 23, 2001.

55. "Character Assassination and Criticism."

56. "Press Censorship," editorial, *JP*, January 29, 2001.

57. "Serambi Redaksi," *Gatra*, September 11, 2000. For an extended interpretation of the possible motives behind press coverage of Wahid's alleged affair, see Nicole Andres, "Media-Elite Interactions in Post-authoritarian Indonesia" (PhD diss., Murdoch University, 2016), 164–76.

58. Laksamana Sukardi, "Will Mega Survive?," *Laksamana.Net*, October 22, 2001, http://joyonews.org/JoyoNews.php?link=45856.

59. John McBeth, "Indonesia's Golkar Party Faces Another Scandal," *FEER*, December 13, 2001.

60. Bill Guerin, "Indonesia Prepares Black Sheep for Sacrifice," *AT*, October 26, 2001.

61. Sukardi, "Will Mega Survive?"

62. Guerin, "Indonesia Prepares Black Sheep."

63. "AG to Summon Akbar, Wiranto," *JP*, October 11, 2001.

64. "Under Mega's Wing?," *Tempo*, October 30–November 5, 2001.

65. "Bulog Funds Were Spent on Food Assistance: Akbar," *JP*, October 11, 2001.

66. Guerin, "Indonesia Prepares Black Sheep."

67. "The Fall of Tanjung and Folly of Mega?," opinion, *Laksamana.Net*, October 25, 2001, http://joyonews.org/JoyoNews.php?link=46106.

68. "PDI Perjuangan Indecisive on Akbar Corruption Case," *JP*, October 31, 2001.

69. "AG to Summon Akbar, Wiranto."

70. "Akbar Denies Golkar's Involvement in Reported Bulog Fund," *JP*, October 17, 2001.

71. "Audit Exposes Graft in Attorney General's Office," *Laksamana.Net*, December 3, 2001, http://joyonews.org/JoyoNews.php?link=48043.

72. Quoted in D. Karaniya et al., "Sepuluh Lembar Cek di Tiga Skenario," *Tempo*, October 29–November 4, 2001.

73. Tertiani Z. B. Simanjuntak, "Akbar, Wiranto Grilled over Alleged Graft," *JP*, November 1, 2001. The foundation's name had many spellings in subsequent reports, but "Raudatul Jannah" appears to be the "correct" spelling insofar as the foundation existed to begin with.

74. Tiarma Siboro, "Damaging Revelations for Akbar," *JP*, November 20, 2001.

75. Karaniya et al., "Sepuluh Lembar Cek."

76. "Under Mega's Wing?"

77. Guerin, "Indonesia Prepares Black Sheep."

78. "Akbar Urged to Relinquish His Posts," *JP*, October 26, 2001.

79. Warren Caragata, "Sticky Money," *Asiaweek*, November 9, 2001.

80. Quoted in "Akbar Denies Issuing Receipts in Bulog Funds Disbursement," *JP*, November 19, 2001.

81. "The Elite Pact's Pinocchio Problem," *Laksamana.Net*, November 21, 2001.

82. "Golkar to Set Up 'Rival' Special Committee on Bulog Scandal," *JP*, December 1, 2001.

83. "Calling Golkar's Bluff," editorial, *JP*, December 5, 2001.

84. See the discussion of "local media" reporting in "Court Postpones Verdict on Case vs. Indonesia Ctrl Bk Head," AP, December 5, 2001.

85. "Corruption in Indonesia: The Wheel Turns," *Economist*, January 10, 2002.

86. "Mega Won't Help Tanjung," *Laksamana.Net*, January 10, 2002, http://joyonews.org/JoyoNews.php?link=49490.

87. See, for example, *Forum Keadilan*'s cover image showing Tanjung on the verge of tears. "Akhir Perjalanan Bung Akbar," *Forum Keadilan*, March 17, 2002. See also coverage by *Tajuk*, *Panji Masyarakat*, and *DëTAK* during this period.

88. "Akbar Terpojok, Siapa Senang," *Tempo*, November 26–December 2, 2001.

89. Yellow (the color of Tanjung's matador costume) is Golkar's color, and green (the color of the cape) is the color associated with Islam in Indonesia (Raudatul Jannah is an Islamic foundation, albeit most likely a fictional one). "Jurus Matador Akbar," *Tempo*, January 21–27, 2002.

90. "Mega Won't Help Tanjung."

91. Ibid.

92. Richel Langit, "Indonesia: See No Evil, Speaker No Evil," *AT*, January 31, 2002.

93. Ibid.

94. "Tanjung Inquiry Still Unlikely," *Laksamana.Net*, March 5, 2002, http://joyonews.org/JoyoNews.php?link=52201.

95. "Corruption in Indonesia."

96. "Former Indonesian President Quizzed over Graft," Reuters, February 25, 2002.

97. D. Karaniya, Adi Prasetya, and Levi Silalahi, "Endgame for Akbar," *Tempo*, March 12–18, 2002.

98. Vaudine England, "Akbar Detention Sign of New Reformist Zeal," *SCMP*, March 9, 2002.

99. Langit, "Indonesia: See No Evil."

100. See, for example, "Sikap Golkar Tergantung PDIP," *Tempo*, March 9, 2002; "Sekjen PDI P: Sikap Kami Tak Berubah," *Gatra*, March 17, 2002.

101. Gendur Sudarsono, Andari Karina Anom, and Rian Suryalibrata, "Akbar First, Golkar Next?," *Tempo*, March 12–18, 2002.

102. Karaniya, Prasetya, and Silalahi, "Endgame for Akbar."

103. Marianne Kearney, "Returned Bulog Funds 'a Bid to Get Akbar Off,'" *ST*, March 11, 2002.

104. Yogita Tahilramani, "Akbar Defiant as His Graft Trial Kicks Off," *JP*, March 26, 2002.

105. Edy Budiyarso and Syarief Amir, "He Is No Mandela," *Tempo*, March 12–18, 2002.

106. Kurniawan Hari, "House Leaders Rule Akbar Will Retain Speakership," *JP*, March 27, 2002.

107. Muninggar Sri Saraswati and Yogita Tahilramani, "Foul Play Apparent in Akbar's Case," *JP*, March 16, 2002.

108. "Rahardi Ramelan's Uphill Battle," *Tempo*, March 26–April 1, 2002.

109. Marianne Kearney, "Five Graft Cases in Recent Days: Jakarta Shows It Means Business," *ST*, March 20, 2002.

110. Kurniawan Hari, "Legislators Move to Summon Mega," *JP*, March 27, 2002.

111. Annastashya Emmanuelle, "Bulog Funds Went to Individuals: PDI Perjuangan," *JP*, April 3, 2002.

112. Tahilramani, "Akbar Defiant."

113. Ahmad Taufik, Hadriani Pudjiarti, and Ardi Bramantyo, "Justice for Akbar?," *Tempo*, March 26–April 1, 2002.

114. Sudarsono, Anom, and Suryalibrata, "Akbar First, Golkar Next?"

115. "'Lame-Duck Akbar' Back on Stage," editorial, *Laksamana.Net*, April 6, 2002, http://joyonews.org/JoyoNews.php?link=53760.

116. Tahilramani, "Akbar Defiant."

117. Taufik, Pudjiarti, and Bramantyo, "Justice for Akbar?"

118. Andrew Marshall, "Trial of Scandal-Hit Indonesia Bankers Ended," Reuters, December 1, 1999.

119. Muninggar Sri Saraswati, "'Akbar Tried to Make Me Lie,'" *JP*, April 24, 2002.

120. Tertiani Z. B. Simanjuntak, "Rahardi Handed Light Sentence for Graft," *JP*, December 26, 2002.

121. Saraswati, "'Akbar Tried to Make Me Lie.'"

122. Wens Manggut, Levianer Silalahi, and Ecep S. Yasa, "Buloggate II: Forty Billion Lies," *Tempo*, May 14–20, 2002.

123. Annastashya Emmanuelle, "Ruling Party Hesitant to Investigate Akbar," *JP*, June 5, 2002.

124. Muninggar Sri Saraswati, "Witness Admits Telling Lies to Save Akbar," *JP*, May 8, 2002.

125. Tertiani Z. B. Simanjuntak, "Habibie's Testimony Damaging for Akbar," *JP*, May 21, 2002.

126. Nafik and Fabiola Desy Unidjaja, "'How Can House Be Led by a Convicted Criminal?,'" *JP*, September 6, 2002.

127. Andreas Harsono, "Indonesian Journalists Troubled by Return of Ministry of Information," *Freedom Forum*, August 22, 2001.

128. Ibid.

129. "Indonesia's Media: Freedom or Professionalism?," *Laksamana.Net*, December 10, 2001, http://joyonews.org/JoyoNews.php?link=48361.

130. Kurniawan Hari, "Govt Moves to Rein In Press," *JP*, December 7, 2001.

131. Kurniawan Hari, "Press Council Asks to Handle Disputes," *JP*, December 8, 2001.

132. Article 19, "Freedom of Expression and the Media in Indonesia," *Article 19* (London and Jakarta: AJI, 2005), 44.

133. Lindsay Murdoch, "Timor's Lost Children," *Age* (Melbourne), June 18, 2001.

134. Lindsay Murdoch, "The Horror of Aceh: The Day the Soldiers Came," *Age* (Melbourne), May 14, 2001.

135. Quoted in "Media 'Ready to Fight' for Freedoms," *Laksamana.Net*, March 26, 2002, http://joyonews.org/JoyoNews.php?link=53230.

136. "A Chill Wind in Jakarta," editorial, *WSJ*, April 2, 2002.

137. "New Ministers Commend Role of Public Criticism," *JP*, November 4, 1999.

138. Achmad Sukarsono, "Indonesia's Megawati Puts Up More Barriers against Media," Reuters, January 29, 2002.

139. Quoted ibid.

140. Quoted in "Media 'Ready to Fight.'"

141. "Source of Presidential Donation Questioned," *JP*, March 19, 2002.

142. Kurniawan Hari, "House Leaders Rule Akbar Will Retain Speakership," *JP*, March 27, 2002.

143. "Megawati's Military Donation Explained," *Laksamana.Net*, March 28, 2002, http://joyonews.org/JoyoNews.php?link=53346.

144. Ray Anthony Gerungan, "Why Megawati Deserves Another Term," *JP*, October 15, 2003.

145. Andreas Ufen, "Political Parties in Post-Suharto Indonesia: Between *Politik Aliran* and 'Philippinisation,'" *South East Asia Research* 16 (2008): 1.

146. In late 1999, Transparency International's annual "demand-side corruption index" gave Indonesia a rating of only 1.7, tied for last place with Azerbaijan out of the 99 Asian-Pacific countries included. Eduardo Lachica, "Exporters' Bribery Habits Are Scrutinized in Asia," *AWSJ*, October 26, 1999.

8. Media and Civil Society

1. Madeleine Albright, speech delivered at the conference "Towards a Community of Democracies," Warsaw, June 26, 2000, quoted in Jane Perlez, "Vast Rally for Democracy Opens in a Polish Castle," *NYT*, December 26, 2000.

2. Adam Przeworski, *Democracy and the Market: Political and Economic Reforms in Eastern Europe and Latin America* (Cambridge: Cambridge University Press, 1991), 12.

3. Larry Diamond, Juan J. Linz, and Seymour Lipset, *Democracy in Developing Countries: Latin America* (Boulder, CO: Lynne Reiner, 1989), 8; Larry Diamond, "Elections without Democracy: Thinking about Hybrid Regimes," *Journal of Democracy* 13 (April 2002): 21–25.

4. This exercise characterizes what theorists have termed "electoral authoritarianism." See, for example, Andreas Schedler, *The Politics of Uncertainty: Sustaining and Subverting Electoral Authoritarianism* (New York: Oxford University Press, 2013).

5. Alwi M. Dahlan, interview with author, Jakarta, July 29, 1999.

6. For stories on scandals undermining President Yudhoyono's attempts at dynasty building and his party's hopes of retaining power, see Peter Alford, "SBY's Son Edhie Baskoro Quits as Scandal Rages," *Australian*, February 15, 2013; Rendi A. Witular, "House of Yudhoyono/Wibowo in the Making," *JP*, November 15, 2010.

7. Dan Slater and Erica Simmons, "Coping by Colluding: Political Uncertainty and Promiscuous Powersharing in Indonesia and Bolivia," *Comparative Political Studies* 30 (2012): 2–3.

8. Patrick Ziegenhain, "The Indonesian Legislature's Impact on Democratic Consolidation," in *Democratization in Post-Suharto Indonesia*, ed. Marco Bünte and Andreas Ufen (London: Routledge, 2009), 46.

9. Aristo Pangaribuan, "Court 'Brokers' Need to Be Broken," *JG*, December 2, 2009.

10. In 2009, Leo Batubara, former deputy chair of the National Press Council, cited thirty-seven articles in the criminal code alone that could send journalists to jail, and said that a pending bill to revise the code contained sixty-one articles that carried similar criminal sanctions. Interview with author, Jakarta, July 9, 2009.

11. Article 19, "Article 19 Applauds the Decision of the Indonesian Supreme Court to Overturn the Criminal Libel Conviction of Bambang Harymurti," *Article 19*, March 2, 2006.

12. "Indonesian Dispute Resolution 2015," *Conventus Law*, January 29, 2016; Human Rights Watch, *Turning Critics into Criminals: The Human Rights Consequences of Criminal Defamation Law* (New York: Human Rights Watch, 2010), https://www.hrw.org/report/2010/05/03/turning-critics-criminals/human-rights-consequences-criminal-defamation-law.

13. Other 2008 laws adding dozens of new provisions to silence the press included the Access to Public Information Law, the Pornography Law, and the State Secrecy Bill.

14. Julia Suryakusuma, "A Singer's Gyrating Rattles Indonesia," *IHT*, May 14, 2003; "One Step Forward . . . Two Steps Back," *Tempo*, October 1–6, 2008.

15. "One Step Forward"; Devi Asmarani, "Will Jakarta's Anti-porn Bill Protect or Repress?," *ST*, January 2, 2007.

16. I. Wayan Juniartha, "Activists Resume Opposition to Pornography Bill," *JP*, March 26, 2010.

17. Tini Tran, "Indonesian Provinces Plan to Ignore Anti-porn Law," AP, March 26, 2010.

18. See Arlina Arshad, "Indonesia to Crack Down on Porn over Ramadan," AFP, August 10, 2010; Kinanti Pinta Karana, "Indonesian Infotainment 'King,' Gossip Show Host Attempts to Defend Industry," *JG*, July 23, 2010.

19. See Bagus B. T. Saragih, "Cleric: Sharia Higher than National Law," *JP*, March 26, 2010.

20. H. Usamah Hisyam, member of parliament, United Development Party, personal communication, Jakarta, July 22, 1999; Muhammad Yunus Yosfiah, information minister, personal communication, Jakarta, June 10, 1999.

21. See, for example, "74,5% Warga Indonesia Setuju Demokrasi, 5,8% Ingin Diktator," *Sinar Indonesian Baru*, August 11, 2014, citing the survey, *Kinerja Demokrasi dan Pilpres 2014: Evaluasi Pemilih Nasional, Temuan Survei, 21–26 Juli, 2014* (Jakarta: SMRC, 2014).

22. Presi Mandari, "Indonesian Facebook Mum Wins Hospital Defamation Case," *SMH*, December 29, 2009.

23. Elske Schouten, "Facebook Group Thwarts Libel Case in Indonesia," *NRC Handelsblad*, December 31, 2009.

24. "Pennies for Prita Campaign Pulls in Rp 500 Million," *JG*, December 9, 2009.

25. Schouten, "Facebook Group Thwarts Libel"; Mong Palatino, "Justice in Jakarta," *Relativity Online*, February 1, 2010, www.relativityonline.com/home/justice-in-jakarta/.

26. Dessy Sagita, "Prita Takes a Firm Stand with Omni over Suit," *JG*, December 14, 2009.

27. Thamrin Amal Tomagola, quoted in Tifa Asrianti, "Putting in Their Two Cents," *JP*, December 13, 2009.

28. The country climbed from 114 of 177 in 2013, to 88 of 168 in 2015. Transparency International Corruption Perceptions Index, accessed September 25, 2016, https://www.transparency.org/cpi2014/in_detail.

29. Norimitsu Onishi, "Corruption Fighters Rouse Resistance in Indonesia," *NYT*, July 25, 2009.

30. Aleksius Jemadu, "Transnational Activism in Indonesia," in *Transnational Activism in Asia: Problems of Power and Democracy*, ed. Nicola Piper and Anders Uhlin (London: Routledge, 2004), 157; Sofie Arjon Schütte, "Government Policies and Civil Society Initiatives against Corruption," in Bünte and Ufen, *Democratization in Post-Suharto Indonesia*, 86–90.

31. Jeremy Mulholland, "Indonesia's Anti-corruption Drive," *New Mandala*, July 24, 2016.

32. Emil Bolongaita, "An Exception to the Rule? Why Indonesia's Anti-corruption Commission Succeeds Where Others Don't—a Comparison with the Philippines's Ombudsman," *U4 Issue* 4 (August 2010): 14, https://www.u4.no/publications/an-exception-to-the-rule-why-indonesia-s-anti-corruption-commission-succeeds-where-others-don-t-a-comparison-with-the-philippines-ombudsman.

33. Onishi, "Corruption Fighters Rouse Resistance."

34. "Indonesia, Thailand: Asia's Most Corrupt," *Bangkok Post*, April 9, 2009.

35. Aristides Katoppo, interview with author, Jakarta, July 11, 2009.

36. Christian von Luebke, "The Politics of Reform: Political Scandals, Elite Resistance, and Presidential Leadership in Indonesia," *Journal of Current Southeast Asian Affairs* 2, no. 1 (2010): 90.

37. Salim Osman, "KPK Plot Wiretap Played to Nation," *ST*, November 4, 2009; Tom Wright and Yayu Yuniar, "Tapes of Alleged High-Level Conspiracy Electrify Indonesia," *WSJ*, November 4, 2009.

38. "Gerakan 1.000.000 Facebookers Dukung Chandra Hamzah & Bibit Samad Riyanto," accessed September 25, 2016, https://www.facebook.com/group.php?gid=169178211590, cited in von Luebke, "Politics of Reform."

39. Tom Allard, "Bank Claims Smudge Yudhoyono's Clean Image," *Age*, November 21, 2009; Anissa S. Febrina, "The Animal Kingdom Rules," *JP*, November 18, 2009.

40. "A Groundbreaking Move?," *JP*, December 2, 2009.

41. Carl Giacomo, "Indonesia's Corruption Fighters in the Fight of Their Lives," *NYT*, February 20, 2015.

42. David Adam Stott, "Indonesia's Elections of 2014: Democratic Consolidation or Reversal?" *Asia-Pacific Journal* 12, no. 10 (March 2014), https://apjjf.org/2014/12/10/David-Adam-Stott/4087/article.html.

43. Yenni Kwok, "The 'Jokowi Effect' Could Be the Most Important Thing in Indonesia's Elections," *Time*, April 9, 2014.

44. Marcus Mietzner, "Indonesia's 2014 Elections: How Jokowi Won and Democracy Survived," *Journal of Democracy* 25, no. 3 (October 2014): 120.

45. "Garbage In, Garbage Out," *Tempo*, July 7–13, 2104.

46. "Obor Rakyat Sebarkan Berita Jokowi Pro Kristen," *Tempo.Co*, June 4, 2014, https://pemilu.tempo.co/read/news/2014/06/04/269582378/Obor-Rakyat-Sebarkan-Berita-Jokowi-Pro-Kristen.

47. "Manuver Para Jenderal di Balik Bocornya Surat DKP Prabowo," *TV One*, June 12, 2014.

48. MetroTV is owned by the National Democrat party chair, Surya Paloh. See Edward Aspinall, "Indonesia on the Knife's Edge," *Inside Story* 17 (June 2014), http://insidestory.org.au/indonesia-on-the-knifes-edge/.

49. Ben Bland, "Indonesia Strongman Prabowo Closes Gap on Rival Ahead of Poll," *FT*, June 24, 2014.

50. See, for example, Ken Miichi, "Democratization and the Changing Role of Civil Society in Indonesia," *Middle East Institute*, October 13, 2015, http://www.mei.edu/content/map/democratization-and-changing-role-civil-society-indonesia; Edward Aspinall, "Indonesian Democracy Stronger, but Not Yet out of the Danger Zone," *East Asia Forum*, July 13, 2014.

51. Aspinall, "Indonesian Democracy Stronger."

52. Yoes C. Kenawas and Fitriani, "Indonesia's Next Parliament: Celebrities, Incumbents and Dynastic Members?," *East Asia Forum*, May 31, 2013.

53. Nithin Coca, "Indonesia's Anti-corruption Fight," *Diplomat*, February 8, 2016.

54. Ibid.

55. Quoted ibid.

56. Quoted ibid.

57. Joe Cochrane, "A Corruption Scandal with a Silver Lining," *NYT*, December 18, 2015.

58. Joe Cochrane, "Top Indonesian Official, Long Seen as Untouchable, Gets Prison for Graft," *NYT*, April 24, 2018; John McBeth, "Indonesia's Mr Teflon Goes Free Again," *AT*, October 5, 2015, http://www.atimes.com/article/indonesias-mr-teflon-goes-free/.

59. "Shady Organization Targets *Tempo*," *JP*, March 12, 2015.

60. US Department of State, *Country Reports on Human Rights Practices for 2015: Indonesia* (Bureau of Democracy, Human Rights, and Labor, US Department of State, April 13, 2016), https://www.state.gov/documents/organization/252977.pdf.

61. "Jokowi Perintahkan Polri Hentikan Kriminalisasi terhadap KPK dan Pendukung-nya," *Kompas.com*, March 5, 2015, https://nasional.kompas.com/read/2015/03/05/21095941/Jokowi.Perintahkan.Polri.Hentikan.Kriminalisasi.terhadap.KPK.dan.Pendukungnya.

62. Haeril Halim, "KPK Law Amendment Delayed," *JP*, February 23, 2016.

63. "Jokowi Dukung Penguatan KPK, Reformasi Kejaksaan dan Polri," *Kompas.com*, December 1, 2016, https://nasional.kompas.com/read/2016/12/01/12502261/jokowi.dukung.penguatan.kpk.reformasi.kejaksaan.dan.polri.

64. John McBeth, "All Eyes on Indonesia's Identity Card Scam," *AT*, August 2, 2017.

65. "KPK Tells Setya Novanto to Get Over Rejected Pretrial Motion," *Tempo.co*, December 15, 2017, https://en.tempo.co/read/news/2017/12/15/055914130/KPK-Tells-Setya-Novanto-to-Get-Over-Rejected-Pretrial-Motion; "President Warns Police against Criminalizing KPK Leaders," *JP*, November 10, 2017.

66. Dony Indra Ramadhan, "Apa Kabar Setya Novanto di Lapas Sukamiskin?" *detikNews*, May 8, 2018, https://news.detik.com/berita/d-4010811/apa-kabar-setya-novanto-di-lapas-sukamiskin.

67. "KPK Khawatir RUU KUHP Ditunggangi & Lemahkan Pemberantasan Korupsi," *Merdeka.com*, May 30, 2018, https://www.merdeka.com/peristiwa/kpk-khawatir-ruu-kuhp-ditunggangi-lemahkan-pemberantasan-korupsi.html.

68. Alexis de Tocqueville, "Liberty. Trade. Dublin (7th July)," in *Journeys to England and Ireland*, ed. J. P. Mayer, trans. George Lawrence and K. P. Mayer (New Brunswick, NJ: Transaction, 1988), 116.

69. "Survey of Indonesian Public Opinion," International Republican Institute, June 19–27, 2013, http://www.iri.org/sites/default/files/2013%20September%2017%20Survey%20of%20Indonesian%20Public%20Opinion%2C%20June%2019-27%2C%202013.pdf.

70. Chappell H. Lawson, *Building the Fourth Estate: Democratization and the Rise of a Free Press in Mexico* (Berkeley: University of California Press, 2002), 139.

71. Ibid., 151.

72. Rodrigo Aguilera, "Democracy and the Mexican Disease," *Huffington Post*, January 22, 2015, https://www.huffingtonpost.com/rodrigo-aguilera/democracy-and-the-mexican_b_6525626.html.

73. Ibid.

74. Elisabeth Malkin, "Purchase by Mexican President Is under Scrutiny," *NYT*, February 3, 2015; Paulina Villegas and Frances Robles, "Deals Flow to Contractor Tied to Mexican President," *NYT*, July 30, 2015.

75. Lev Garcia and Mark Stevenson, "Ruling Party Sees Stinging Defeats in Mexican Elections," *AP*, June 6, 2016.

76. Danielle Cuddington and Richard Wile, "Declining Ratings for Mexico's Peña Nieto," *Pew Research Center: Global Attitudes and Trends*, August 27, 2015.

77. Azam Ahmed, "'A Bad Joke': Corruption Battle Stalls in Mexico, Watchdog Says," *NYT*, December 2, 2017.

78. Elisabeth Malkin, "Mexico's Attorney General Resigns under Pressure," *NYT*, October 16, 2017.

79. "The Victory of Andrés Manuel López Obrador Starts a New Era in Mexico," *Economist*, July 2, 2018, https://www.economist.com/the-americas/2018/07/02/the-victory-of-andres-manuel-lopez-obrador-starts-a-new-era-in-mexico.

80. Lise Garon, *Dangerous Alliances: Civil Society, the Media & Democratic Transition in North Africa* (London: Zed Books, 2003), 1, 154–67.

81. Shelley Deane, *Transforming Tunisia: The Role of Civil Society in Tunisia's Transition* (London: International Alert, 2013), https://www.international-alert.org/sites/default/files/publications/Tunisia2013EN.pdf.

82. Safa Ben Said, "In Tunisia, Press Freedom Erodes amid Security Fears," CPJ, October 27, 2015.

83. "2016 Press Freedom Index," Reporters without Borders, April 20, 2016, https://rsf.org/en/ranking/2016.

84. Mischa Benoit-Lavelle, "'Sheratongate' Shakes Tunisian Ruling Party," *Al-Monitor*, January 13, 2013.

85. Quoted in Thomas Bass, "A Woman Blogger's Scoop Helped Save Tunisia from Islamists," *Daily Beast*, April 6, 2014, https://www.thedailybeast.com/a-woman-bloggers-scoop-helped-save-tunisia-from-islamists.

86. Quoted ibid.

87. "History of Corruption: Different Generations of Chaebol Implicated in Scandals," *Hankyoreh*, December 6, 2016.

88. "Donations to Mir, K-Sports Need Scrutiny," *Korea Times*, September 23, 2016; Elizabeth Shim, "South Korea Leader's Friend Had Access to Secrets, Relayed 'Messages' from Late Mom," UPI, October 26, 2016.

89. Quoted in Choe Sang-hun and Motoko Rich, "How South Korea Ended Up on the Brink of Ousting a President," *NYT*, January 3, 2017.

90. Yoonjung Seo, "The South Korean Political Scandal Started with a Card Game in Macau," *WP*, November 6, 2016.

91. Chung Hyun-chae, "Scandal Unveils Choi Soon-sil's 'Boy Toy,'" *Korea Times*, October 30, 2016.

92. Choe Sang-hun, "Key Figure in Scandal's Latest Twist Is a Puppy," *NYT*, December 10, 2016.

93. "Donations to Mir."

94. Jung Min-ho, "How the Choi Soon-sil Scandal Unfolded," *Korea Times*, January 8, 2016.

95. Choe Sang-hun, "South Korea's Blacklist of Artists Adds to Outrage over a Scandal," *NYT*, January 13, 2017.

96. Choe Sang-hun, "Korea Vote Puts Nation in Limbo," *NYT*, December 10, 2016; Choe and Rich, "How South Korea Ended Up."

97. Se-Woong Koo, "The Choi Soon-sil Gate: The Saddest Political Drama Ever Told," *Korea Exposé*, November 1, 2016.

98. James Seo, "James Seo's Answer to Why Are South Koreans So Angry with Their President That 1 Million Protesters Took to the Street," *Quora.com*, December 8, 2016, https://www.quora.com/Why-are-South-Koreans-so-angry-with-their-President-that-1-million-protesters-took-to-the-street.

99. "Restoring Trust in South Korea," editorial, *NYT*, December 10, 2016.

100. Anna Fifield, "Here Is Everything You Need to Know about South Korea's Extraordinary Presidential Scandal," *WP*, November 3, 2016.

101. Quoted in Choe and Rich, "How South Korea Ended Up."

102. Howard Tumber and Silvio R. Waisbord, "Introduction: Political Scandals and Media Across Democracies, Volume I," *American Behavioral Scientist* 47, no. 8 (2004): 1031–32, 1035.

103. Silvio Waisbord, "Scandals, Media and Citizenship in Contemporary Argentina," *American Behavioral Scientist* 25, no. 3 (2004): 1072–98.

104. Pippa Norris, *A Virtuous Circle: Political Communications in Post-industrial Democracies* (Cambridge: Cambridge University Press, 2000), 19.

105. Sheila Coronel, "Corruption and the Watchdog Role of the News Media," in *Public Sentinel: News Media & Governance Reform*, ed. Pippa Norris, 111–36 (Washington, DC: World Bank, 2010).

106. Sheila Coronel, "People Power Fatigue: Democracy and Disillusionment in the Philippines," Friday Forum lecture, Center for Southeast Asian Studies, University of Wisconsin–Madison, April 18, 2008.

107. Norris, *Virtuous Circle*; J. Samuel Valenzuela, "Democratic Consolidation in Post-transitional Settings: Notion, Process, and Facilitating Conditions," in *Issues in Democratic Consolidation: The New South American Democracies in Comparative Perspective*, ed. Scott Mainwaring, Guillermo O'Donnell, and J. Samuel Valenzuela (Notre Dame, IN: Notre Dame Press: 1992), 62.

108. In Ukraine, the brutal murder of a journalist critical of the regime, Georgy Gongadze, in 2000 became a potent symbol to mobilize the democratic opposition. C. J. Chivers, "Yushchenko Steps Out Presidentially; Rival Grumbles," *NYT*, December 30, 2004; Tom Warner, "Ukraine Journalists Tell Government of Fear on the Job," *WSJ Europe*, September 28, 2000; Charles Clover, "Ukraine's President 'Linked to Missing Journalist,' MPs Told," *FT*, December 13, 2000.

109. Bambang Harymurti, interview with author, Jakarta, July 4, 2009.

110. Goenawan Mohamad, *Sidelines: Thought Pieces from "Tempo" Magazine*, trans. Jennifer Lindsay (Jakarta: Lontar, 1994), 73.

111. See Jeffrey A. Winters, *Oligarchy* (Cambridge: Cambridge University Press, 2011).

112. Ross Tapsell, *Media Power in Indonesia: Oligarchs, Citizens and the Digital Revolution* (London: Rowman & Littlefield, 2017); Ariel Heryanto and Stanley Yoseph Adi, "The Industrialization of the Media in Democratizing Indonesia," *Contemporary Southeast Asia* 23, no. 2 (2001): 327–55.

113. One observer noted that Indonesia's news media might best be described as a "multi-oligarchic free press." Anonymous reviewer, Cornell University Press, July 25, 2017.

INDEX

Page numbers in italics indicate illustrations; those with a *t* indicate tables.

CPSIA information can be obtained
at www.ICGtesting.com
Printed in the USA
FFHW020720090219
50452735-55660FF